Footprint Australasia

New Zealand

Darroch Donald

Listings

Introducing the island

About the region

Auckland, Northland & Coromandel Peninsula

Central North Island

Wellington & around

Marlborough & Nelson

Canterbury & the West Coast

Otago & Southland

Practicalities

Contents

About the author

Author and Scot, Darroch Donald, has three major passions in life: travel, photography and wildlife. After gaining a diploma in Wildlife Illustration in Wales in 1986, Darroch returned to Scotland and took up the position of assistant manager at the country's only purpose-built wildlife rehabilitation centre in Fife. This unusual work took him to many far-flung places including Saudi Arabia during the Gulf Eco-disaster in 1991 and eventually to New Zealand where he emigrated in 1992. There he acted as a wildlife consultant to the New Zealand government before bureaucracy and disillusionment forced him to explore other more creative avenues. In 1996 he published his first book 'Creatures', an account of his encounters with wildlife utilising all three disciplines of writing, photography and art. Darroch has since expanded his work to include travel. He is a veteran Footprint author and photographer having been responsible for the New Zealand guide since its inception in 2001. He is also the author of the East Coast Australia guide, wrote the Sydney Pocket Guide and co-authored the Australia Handbook. Darroch currently resides in Sorrento near Melbourne, Australia. To view Darroch's Australasian imagery and for travel photography tips log on to darrochdonald.com.

Rebecca Robinson served as co-photographer for the New Zealand colour guide. Since gaining a zoology degree at Melbourne University in 1999 she has worked a freelance natural science illustrator and nature/travel photographer in Australasia. In conjunction with a range of artistic projects she regularly collaborates with her partner and fellow photographer/travel writer Darroch Donald. To view Rebecca's Australasian imagery log on to rebeccarobinson.com.au.

Acknowledgements

Thanks once again to all the staff and representatives of the many regional visitor information centres, regional tourism offices and at Tourism New Zealand who provided invaluable advice and assistance for this guide. Also a mention for Ngahi Bidois for the use of his portrait on page 33.

Thanks too to all the team at Footprint, Felicity Laughton and Alan Murphy in particular. Combined we are perhaps proof that despite blowing each other's wigs off on occasion through frustration there is always a way to replace them, laugh and look almost marvellous.

Gratitude stupendicus (as ever), to my partner Rebecca, Tony, Brigitte and Grace for their stalwart support and understanding. No thanks whatsoever (as ever) goes to the 'Great Travel Karma Gods' for van registrations and breakdowns, laptop deaths, tent leaks, thefts and that strange 'Awe, you very hairy man' incident in a Rotorua hot pool. In summary, all the usual nonsense that makes travel writing and research the wonderful and woefully challenging enigma that it is.

About the book

The guide is divided into four sections: **Introducing the region**; **About the region**; **Around the region** and **Practicalities**.

Introducing the region comprises: At a glance (which explains how the region fits together); Best of New Zealand (top 20 highlights); Month by month (a guide to pros and cons of visiting at certain times of year); and Screen & page (a list of suggested books and films).

About the region comprises: History; New Zealand today (which presents different aspects of life in the country today); Culture & heritage; Nature & environment; Festivals & events; Sleeping (an overview of accommodation options); Eating & drinking (an overview of the country's cuisine, as well as advice on eating out); Entertainment (an overview of the country's cultural credentials, explaining what entertainment is on offer); and Activities & tours (which includes a 'Best photo locations' section).

Around the region is then broken down into six areas, each with its own chapter. Here you'll find all the main sights and at the end of each chapter is a listings section with all the best sleeping, eating & drinking, entertainment, shopping and activities & tours options plus a brief overview of public transport.

Picture credits

Contents

The Champagne Pool, Waiotapu Thermal Reserve, Rotorua.

Introducing the region

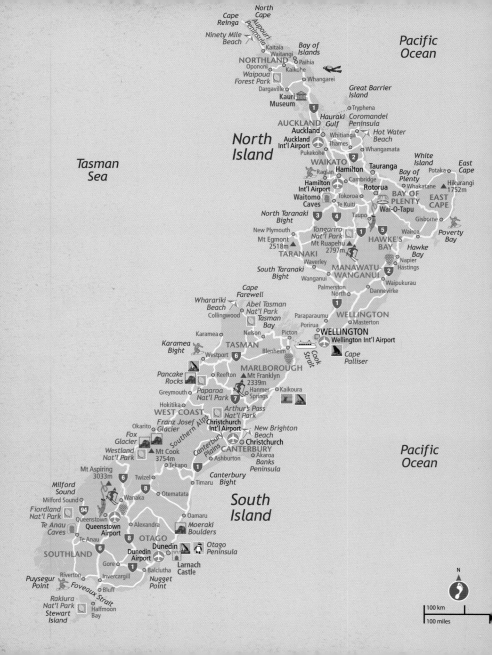

Introduction

Put Charles Darwin, Claude Monet and JRR Tolkien in a room and, combined, they still could not come close to the concept of New Zealand. This small yet incredibly diverse country is made up of two main islands, North and South, both of which are quite different. North is less mountainous and home to more than two-thirds of New Zealanders, or 'Kiwis'. For the tourist, North Island holds less aesthetic appeal than South, but few would miss, or indeed forget, the expansive views across Auckland from its hypodermic Sky Tower, or the colourful thermal features in and around Rotorua.

South Island offers, for many, the true essence of New Zealand. To travel through it is like a fun-filled lesson in geography and guarantees to have the digital camera running on overload: vast empty beaches; endless mountain ranges and rainforest; pristine lakes, waterfalls and fiords; giant glaciers; huge limestone caves and arches; natural springs and fizzing hot pools. When it comes to wildlife, your encounters will be as remarkable as they are varied and memorable, from the iconic kiwi to soporific sea lions. Activities? Well, where do you start? From the infamous bungee jumping to zorbing, some of the best tramping (walking) tracks in the world, or lazing around in hot pools, it's one mighty 'let's do it' menu.

Whatever your intention and with whatever time you can afford, visiting New Zealand is like making an appointment with Doctor Nature and Nurse Adrenalin. Simply put: it's time to 'take the cure'.

Maori designs on fence posts, Rotorua.

At a glance
A whistle-stop tour of New Zealand

Auckland, Northland & The Coromandel

Home to over a quarter of the New Zealand population, for the average visitor Auckland is about aesthetics as opposed to substance and is somewhat lacking in soul. Known as the 'City of Sails' there's no prize for guessing what features most in the congenial lifestyle this sprawling Pacific metropolis offers. Starting with the magnificent view from its iconic Sky tower it has much to see and do, but should not detract from the real New Zealand – the 'nature made', as opposed to the 'man'.

Heading against the tourist tide, a few days in Northland and The Bay of Islands offers a fine introduction to the country's beautiful coastal inventory and at Waitangi one can gain insight in to Maori culture and early colonial heritage.

During the high season the Coromandel Peninsula to the south and east of Auckland, serves as the principal holiday escape for stressed city residents, offering all that the classic Kiwi beach holiday can, from fishing to golf, surfing to bush walking. At other times it is less frenetic and you can find solitude amid some superb coastal scenery.

The lowdown

Money matters

For international visitors exchange rates are usually in their favour with the euro (2.02), UK£ (2.26) and US$ (1.36) to the New Zealand Dollar NZ$. All the major credit cards are widely accepted. Most hotels, shops and petrol stations use EFTPOS (Electronic Funds Transfer at Point of Sale), meaning you don't have to carry lots of cash with you. For safety, traveller's cheques are strongly recommended.

For a couple travelling in a campervan, self-catering and eating out occasionally and with an organized mid-range $ activity every third day you will need a minimum of NZ$300 a day. Petrol is not too expensive at around NZ$1.60 per litre (NZ$6 per gallon). It is possible to survive on NZ$80 per person at motor parks with your own jalopy. But that is with no eating out, or activity costs.

Insurance

Comprehensive insurance is highly recommended (including medical) with expensive items like laptops and cameras covered specifically. Like many travel destinations, tourists are a prime target for opportunist thieves in New Zealand.

Opening hours & holidays

Opening times are similar to Europe and the US. In the high season (November to March) shops generally remain open seven days a week (0900-1700 or 1730; tourist-oriented outlets often remain open in the evening), banks and post offices open at least Monday to Friday, and 24-hour food stores are common in the main centres.

Tourist information

The official New Zealand Visitor Information Network is made up of around 100 accredited visitor information centres, nationally known as I-SITES. They provide a general information booking service usually seven days a week and there is also a huge amount of free material. Some also have adjunct travel centres or handle regional and national travel bookings.

Useful websites

For general information start with purenz.com, the official website of the New Zealand Tourism Board. Others include destination-nz.com, searchnz.co.nz and tourism.net.nz. The Department of Conservation website doc.govt.nz provides detailed information on national parks and tramping tracks. For weather, refer to metservice.co.nz and the forecast charts metvuw.com. For New Zealand imagery refer to the authors website darrochdonaldnz.com.

Central North Island

The Central Plateau dominates the Central North Island and is part of an area that in geological terms is called the Taupo Volcanic Zone. Even the name sounds alluring. Geology rarely features much in the everyday or travelling psyche, but here it certainly does and has moulded tourism for centuries. Throughout the region volcanic features and thermal activity are never far away and dominate the scene from the North Island's highest peak Ruapehu, to Lake Taupo, the country's largest. Taupo and Rotorua both make the most of their earthly assets with hot pools, bubbly mud and geysers thrilling the crowds. Tauranga to the north is the Bay of Plenty's largest town and one of the countries fastest growing. Along with its neighbour Whakatane, it serves as base for dolphin-watching/swimming adventures and trips to White Island – the country's most active volcano. East is the remote East Cape and Gisborne, laid-back and proud to be (in human terms) the first place on earth to see the dawn. Further south in Hawke's Bay, the regional centres of Napier and Hastings are world renowned for their art deco architecture and thanks to a warm and sunny climate, a rash of world-class vineyards.

Introducing the region

The rich agricultural farmlands of the Waikato cover its greatest attraction like a green duvet. Beneath it a system of myriad subterranean limestone caves offer unique adventures. Then south of that the west coast is dominated by the classic cone-shaped Mount Taranaki that subtly oversees life in the pleasant coastal town of New Plymouth.

Like a thread cast upon pebbles, SH94 – the road to Milford Sound – in the heart of the park, is a New Zealand scenic classic with its terminus the great fiord and the mesmerizing icon of Mitre Peak

Wellington & around

The country's official capital is cast somewhat in the shadows of Auckland and Christchurch, but it seems perfectly happy with its muted profile and as the gateway to the South Island. Hemmed in by the surrounding hills and valleys it has a pleasant, intriguing, aesthetic and a large town – as opposed to a city feel. Wellington has many great attractions, principal of which is the state-of-the-art national museum Te Papa, a must-see for every visitor.

To the north of Wellington the university town of Palmerston North is often overlooked, yet worth a visit, as is the Kapiti Coast and in particular Kapiti Island, a nature reserve rich in birdlife and an astonishing demonstration of what the New Zealand environment used to be like.

East of Wellington, guarded by the Tararua Ranges is the Wairarapa Region, the rural escape for many Wellingtonians looking for relaxation and tasting tours of its boutique vineyards. Beyond that, yet still easily within range of the city, is the remote Palliser coast where the quirky fishing village of Ngawi and colonies of slumbersome fur seals reminder us that these days life is far too fast paced.

Marlborough & Nelson

Often referred to as New Zealand's 'little Norway' the myriad coves and bays of the Marlborough Sounds offer a fitting first impression of the diverse landscapes of the South Island. With a reputed 1500 km of coastline it is an aquatic maze ideally suited to a wide range of activities from kayaking and tramping (walking) to mountain biking, or simply getting off the beaten track.
To the south the fairly unremarkable town of Blenheim is surrounded by scores of vineyards all vying to produce the next best of the region's famed Sauvignon Blanc.

Nelson is considered the arts capital of the country and one of the most desirable places to live. It offers a fine climate and no less than five national parks within easy reach, including Abel Tasman with its picture-postcard beaches. Further west is Golden Bay a delightful region to spend a few days exploring Farewell Spit, or to feel a tad guilty leaving footprints on Wharariki Beach, arguably the country's most beautiful.

Canterbury & the West Coast

Canterbury is a large and geographically diverse region that encompasses the seemingly vast Canterbury Plains, the bare hills and glacial lakes of the McKenzie Country and, of course, the iconic snow-capped mountain ranges crowned by Mount Cook, the country's highest peak. On the coast, the now-flooded volcanic vents of the Banks Peninsula are in stark contrast to the flat plains that surround them.

In the shadow of the Banks Peninsula sits Christchurch, the largest city in the South Island. Dubbed 'the garden city' it retains much of its English heritage and also serves as the gateway to the Antarctic. North of the city the natural hot pools at Hanmer are a great attraction, as are the mighty leviathans that inhabit the coast off Kaikoura.

The West Coast has seen its gold boom come and go and now relies – between rainfalls – on its unparalleled beauty to lure tourists down its length from Westport, through Hokitika, Frans Josef and Fox glaciers to Haast. It is a magical

A typical landscape of the Otago Peninsula near Dunedin.

journey through a clean and green landscape of mountain, glacier, bush and beach, where nature dictates completely.

Otago & Southland

Perhaps more than any other region in New Zealand it is Otago that has something for everyone. In Dunedin it can boast a historic, attractive and congenial city, the size of which seems just right. Nearby, the beautiful Otago Peninsula is like a resplendent backyard, renowned for its rare and intriguing wildlife including the world's most accessible colony of albatross.

Elsewhere, literally Remarkable mountain ranges and those *Lord of The Rings* landscapes abound. Amidst it all of course is Queenstown, an 'Ooh I want to live here' kind of place if ever there

was one, and with more than 150 activities to choose from it is deservingly dubbed the activity capital of the country, reputedly even the world.

In stark contrast Southland is far quieter than Otago, but no less spectacular. Swathes of rich agricultural farmland give way to the vast wilderness that is Fiordland National Park. Little changed since Cook first sighted its dramatic coastline in 1770 it is now afforded World Heritage status. Like a thread cast upon pebbles, SH94 – the road to Milford Sound – in the heart of the park, is a New Zealand scenic classic with its terminus the great fiord and the mesmerizing icon of Mitre Peak.

Invercargill, the country's southernmost city, offers its own muted attractions and acts as a staging post to Stewart Island, or the understated beauty of the Catlins coast.

Best of
New Zealand

Top 20 things to see & do

8 Tongariro Crossing with Mount Ngauruhoe background.

❶ Cheeky keas

You might think kiwis are the celebrities of the New Zealand wildlife A-list, but it's debatable. What the kiwi is to avian weirdness, the kea is to character and delinquency. An intelligent, native alpine parrot encountered in only a few high altitude spots such as SH94 (The road to Milford, see below) they have turned the act of 'find the sandwich' into a best comedy Oscar winner. Page 38.

❷ Auckland's Sky Tower

'Hypodermic', a little bit 'space age', Auckland's iconic and seemingly omnipresent Sky Tower has been called many things since its completion in 1997. Call it what you like, at 328 m and on a clear day, the views from its lofty observation deck are stunning. Page 69.

❸ Island escapes

New Zealand's superb island escapes are not of the coconut and bikini variety. Here, it usually involves raw nature and a fascinating insight into what it was like before humans 'poisoned the paradise'. With the plague of introduced predators removed, island nature reserves like Tiritiri Matangi (page 79) or Kapiti (page 167) abound with native plant and birdlife, much of which is now rarely found on the mainland. Other islands well worth visiting include White Island – an active volcano (page 132) – or Waiheke with is world-class vineyards (page 79).

❹ Waitangi National Reserve

Described as the place where New Zealand's modern history began, this is where the controversial 'Treaty of Waitangi' between the native Maori and colonial 'Pakeha' (British) was signed in 1840. Beyond the city museums, Waitangi offers perhaps the most authentic and certainly one of the most memorable introductions to Maori culture, or more specifically, the 'culture clash'. Page 83.

❺ Beautiful beaches

Eclipsed by irresistible images of sun and surf from across the Tasman sea, New Zealand's beaches are not particularly well known, yet it can boast some of

6 The Luge, Rotorua.

the most beautiful in the world. Almost every region could stake a claim, be it Cathedral Cove in the Coromandel (page 95), The Abel Tasman National Park near Nelson (page 96), or the utterly wonderful Wharariki near Golden Bay (page 202).

❻ The Luge, Rotorua

Here's one that is guaranteed to turn a family of two adults and two kids in to, well, four kids! Think toboggan run, but with no ice. Think teatray with handles and a set of 'I just can't get used to them' brakes. Think a fetching red helmet and the facial expression of an unfortunate who has just discovered electricity by connecting themselves to the National Grid. Get the picture? Page 113.

❼ Champagne at Waiotapu?

Waiotapu, near Rotorua, is arguably the best – and certainly the most colourful – of New Zealand's thermal reserves. All the usual suspects are present, including some mesmerizingly melodic mud pools, steamy craters and the obligatory geyser. But without doubt the highlight is the orange-rimmed and gently fizzing flooded vent, aptly

Introducing the region

10 **The Art Deco National Tobacco Building, Napier.**

named the Champagne Pool – just turn left past The Devil's Home! Page 115.

⑧ Tongariro Crossing

The Tongariro Crossing is often touted as 'the best day walk in New Zealand', which in this country is an audacious claim. The challenging 17-km, nine-hour hike takes in much of the Central Plateau's varied and colourful volcanic features, including the symmetrical Ngauruhoe' and the Emerald Lakes, two small bodies of water that can put food colouring to shame. So, is it the best day walk? In good weather it certainly can be, in bad weather it's hellish, but these days don't expect much solitude. Page 125.

⑨ Waitomo & 'The Lost World'

Although only the geologically trained eye would suspect it, below the green and rolling hills of Waitomo there is a vast network of eroded limestone caves. This is karst country, a subterranean wonderworld, where you can take the dry option with a guided cave tour, or the active and the wet, by crawling, abseiling or simply floating through others. The ultimate is 'The Lost World Adventure' involving a 100-m abseil and a five-hour journey underground. Page 128.

⑩ Napier

Of all New Zealand's provincial centres it is perhaps Napier that has the most colourful and intriguing history. Almost completely levelled by an earthquake in 1931 much of the rebuilding was done in the classic art deco style. Today the pleasant seaside town is internationally recognized as having some of the finest examples in the world. Here, even the McDonalds is art deco. Page 136.

⑪ Classic Wine Trail

New Zealand produces some of the finest wines in the world and has several distinct regions that are a tasting utopia for either expert or layperson. The Classic Wine Trail from Hawke's Bay in the North Island to Marlborough in the South Island is described as 'a deliciously indulgent road journey that puts pleasure first'. Indeed. Page 139 or 188.

⑫ Te Papa Museum of New Zealand

Faithfully representing the nation's heritage since 1998, over twice the population of the nation itself (9.3 million) have passed through Te Papa's doors. As expected, there is a heavy emphasis on Maori heritage, *taonga* (treasures) and biculturalism, mixed with the inevitable early settler material and contemporary displays of all things Kiwi. Page 162.

⑬ Fly the Pitts Special

Bar the ubiquitous bungee, for any single activity in New Zealand to reach top billing is saying something, but when it comes to the ride of your life, this is fun to the extreme. The highly personable U-Fly-Extreme company based in Motueka offer the unforgettable – and perfectly safe – opportunity to fly (yes, you actually take the controls) of a Pitts Special aerobatic biplane over the Abel Tasman National Park. No 'ifs', no 'buts', just do it! Page 211.

⑭ Hanmer Springs

New Zealand is famous for its hot pools, a most welcome natural asset derived from its pervasive and restless volcanic activity. Rotorua and Taupo are the best-known venues, but the complex at

Hanmer Springs north of Christchurch is arguably the country's best. Page 227.

⑮ The Ocean's Who's Who at Kaikoura
In the coastal town of Kaikoura on the South Island's east coast it's not a guide book you need, but an 'Ocean's Who's Who'. Here it is all about flippers, flukes and feathers, with whale watching, or dolphin, seal and albatross encounters.   Page 228.

⑯ Mount Cook
The Maori call it 'Aoraki' (meaning 'Cloud Piercer') and from both sides of the Southern Alpine Range (depending on just how much piercing is happening) the country's highest peak is indeed spectacular. A flight around the mountain and over its associate glaciers on a clear day is rightly considered a New Zealand classic. Page 232.

⑰ Otago Peninsula
Renowned for its wildlife and coastal scenery, the Otago Peninsula acts like Dunedin's very own back garden. But this is more like something out of a fantasy novel than a lifestyle magazine. Here you have a real castle, colonies of penguins, soporific sea lions and albatrosses. Page 261.

⑱ The Road to Milford
The drive along State Highway 94 from Te Anau to Milford Sound is one of the most spectacular scenic road journeys in the world. Taking in the valleys of the vast World Heritage Fiordland National Park, as well as the Homer Tunnel and one of the country's most abiding icons, Mitre Peak, it is equally dramatic in fair weather or foul. Page 274.

⑲ Catlins Coast
The Catlins Coast owes its low-key reputation to its location. Set in a corner of the South Island, many visitors who have already been spoiled for choice elsewhere never make it here. The Catlins has some of the prettiest and most variant coastal scenery in the country, including Nugget Point. Page 280.

⑳ 1, 2, 3... Bungee
It's is not so much a matter of exultation and persuasion. You know what it is and that 'wee devil' within you is just beside himself at the very prospect. Yes, it's a rip-off financially, but it's perfectly safe, old age pensioners do it and besides it would be rude not to. Oh, and since you are going to do it, you might as well do it properly! Page 290.

17 Yellow-Eyed Penguin, Otago Peninsula.

Month by month

A year in New Zealand

Autumn creates a blaze of colour in the orchards of Otago.

September to November

September sees the beginning of spring and the tourist 'shoulder' season. International visitor numbers increase and skis are swapped for walking boots. Besides the echo of the European-like landscapes across Otago and in Christchurch, New Zealand's largely evergreen botanical inventory offers a muted response to nature turning the heating back on and bar a slightly brighter shade of green, aesthetically you would hardly notice.

Spring is generally wetter than autumn, especially in the North Island, but again don't bet on it. Overall spring it is a popular time to visit when the balance between price and availability verses overcrowding can be just right.

December to February

Come November the tourist season is once again in full swing and prior to the domestic holiday season over Christmas and New Year it is perhaps the best month to visit. The weather is generally warm and settled though not as dry or as reliable as January, February and March.

At a time when woolly sweaters, and frosty the snowman are an integral part of both life and season in the Northern Hemisphere, it can be quite disconcerting to venture south, where in effect, everything is the opposite. Of course it is the reason why many visit at this time, and why not. Mid-winter is replaced with mid-summer, black ice with ice cream and so on.

This is in effect the nation's annual holiday season and for much of January you will find that most of New Zealand has 'gone fishing', to the beach, or both. So it is all 'high season', high prices and all that goes with it. Many international visitors enjoy the buzz at this time. It is a great opportunity to meet 'Kiwis' away from the daily grind and every region has a busy events calendar. You will need to book all types of accommodation ahead of time and in the main centres up to four days in advance. Note this is not a good time to venture on the main tramping tracks or national parks like the Abel Tasman. They are chaotic and experiencing them at this time can tarnish the very essence of wilderness for which the country is famous.

One other word of advice: thanks to ozone depletion, the sun in New Zealand is dangerously strong so always wear a hat and strong sun block.

March is often the driest month. Being the shoulder season it is also good time to visit and there is a pleasant balance between the relatively settled weather and finding solitude when you want it. As a general rule, at this time of year expect fair weather conducive to any outdoor activity about 50% of the time.

There are still plenty of events staged throughout the country in March and April and you can be more relaxed and flexible with accommodation bookings. Note that early March sees the start of the grape harvests – always a fine time to visit the vineyards.

March to May

May sees the golden hues of autumn in the lower half of the South Island, particularly Otago. It is generally the only region where introduced, deciduous trees have thrived, though other exceptions include the 'Anglicized' gardens and parks of Christchurch (dubbed the 'garden city'). So, for those who love a European autumn, or indeed are unaccustomed to it, it is a nice time to be in the South Island. Elsewhere autumn comes and goes with less aesthetic drama and indeed all one would notice are more rainy days, colder temperatures and less daylight hours. But thankfully this is not like the UK or other parts of Europe where in winter you can go days without seeing the sun. Even in winter, if it rains the sun is never too far way.

June to August

Any time from late May through June the first snows arrive in the south and the ski season begins in earnest. The best venues are around Queenstown and Wanaka in the South Island and a little later in the season around National Park in the Central North Island. By July winter is in full swing. Inclement weather and shorter daylight hours affect all but snow-based activities. Despite that, very few tourism operators close altogether. Generally speaking all you might notice are a reduction in opening hours at restaurants or operating hours thanks to reduced daylight hours. In the ski resort towns like Queenstown and Wanaka in the South Island (and especially at weekends) there is nothing 'off' about the 'off-season' and prices remain high and bookings need to be made in advance. Elsewhere there is no need to pre-book and prices drop especially at motor parks. Keep your eye out for advertised bargains and if it is not advertised (unlike some countries) take it that it would be inappropriate to ask.

Obviously with the exception of the ski resorts, everything is far quieter and, for many, this holds much appeal.

Screen & page
New Zealand in film & literature

Films

The Piano
Jane Campion, 1993
This classic stars Holly Hunter, Sam Neill and Harvey Keitel, and tells the story of a Scottish immigrant and her daughter who are brought to New Zealand in an arranged marriage to a colonial landowner.

Once Were Warriors
Lee Tamahori, 1994
An adaptation of Kiwi writer Alan Duff's portrayal of a highly dysfunctional urban Maori family.

Lord of the Rings
Peter Jackson, 1999-2000
At a cost of more than $300 million, the trilogy was a far cry from Jackson's other projects, which included Heavenly Creatures, an intriguing tale of two troubled teenage girls. In 2010 the New Zealand location filming continues on The Hobbit.

The Last Samurai
Edward Zwick, 2004
Starring Tom Cruise and filmed in the shadow of Mount Taranaki on the North Island's west coast.

The World's Fastest Indian
Roger Donaldson, 2006
Starring Anthony Hopkins and based on the story of New Zealander Burt Munro, who built a motorcycle with which he set the land-speed world record in 1967.

Books

Fiction
Once Were Warriors
Alan Duff, 1990
A much-acclaimed disturbing and powerful insight into Maori domestic life.

To the Island, The Envoy from Mirror City and An Angel at my Table
Janet Frame, 1982, 1984
Known for her dramatic personal history of mental illness as well as her writing, Frame authored three volumes of autobiography as well as 11 novels, four collections of short stories and a book of poetry.

Going West
Maurice Gee, 1992
A story of unravelling relationships amidst the backdrop of Auckland and Wellington.

Bulibasha
Witi Ihimaera, 1994
An affectionate look at Maori sheep-shearing gangs in Eastland.

The Bone People
Keri Hulme, 1984
Winner of the Booker Prize.

The Haunting and The Changeover
Margaret Mahy, 1982, 1984
Children's writer and two-times winner of the Carnegie Medal.

Lord of the Rings locations

Tongariro National Park
Scenes depicting Mordor were filmed here with Mount Tongariro as Mount Doom. The Whakapapa ski area on Mount Ruapehu was where the battle of the Last Alliance was filmed. See page 122.

Wellington City
The base for the film production and many of the sets were created here. Mount Victoria was used for the scene where the Hobbits race to the ferry with the Nazgul in hot pursuit. See page 158.

West of Christchurch
Mount Sunday and Mount Potts were used for the set of Edoras and Meduseld. Rocky outcrops at the Poolburn Reservoir near Alexandra provided the backdrop for Rohan. Tours are available. See page 230.

Queenstown
Skippers Canyon was used for the Ford of Bruinen with Arwen fleeing the Nazgul. Deer Park Heights was used for the scene of the refugees escaping Rohan. The Remarkables ski field was used as Dimrill Dale. Twelve Mile Delta became the Ighilien Camp. Tours are available. See page 268.

Arrowtown & Glenorchy
Kawarau River and Chard Farm became Anduin and the site of the Pillars of the Kings. The Arrow River became the Ford of Bruinen where Arwen and Frodo escaped from the charging Nazgul. See page 270.

The Lord of the Rings Location Guidebook by Ian Brodie, ($50), provides details of the locations and how to get there. Go to harpercollins.co.nz.

The Collected Stories
Katherine Mansfield, 1945, 1974
The best-known collection of short stories from this internationally celebrated writer.

Season of the Jew
Maurice Shadbolt, 1987
A story about dispossessed Maori identifying with the Jews of ancient Israel.

Pictorial books
The best-known photographers of New Zealand's stunning scenery are Craig Potton and Andris Apse; their books are of a very high quality and contain some exquisite imagery.

History, politics & culture
History of New Zealand
Keith Sinclair, 1959
A dated but celebrated historical work, starting from before the arrival of Europeans.

The New Zealand Historical Atlas:
KoPapatuanuku e Takoto Nei
M McKinnon, editor, 1997
An overall insight, highly visual, easy to read and generally recommended.

Contents

About the region

A carpet of wild flowers in a paddock near Wanaka, Otago.

History

The first footprints

Due to its geographic isolation New Zealand was one of the last 'viable' lands to be settled by humans and therefore has a relatively young human history.

Though much debated and a simplification, Maori trace their ancestry to the homelands of 'Hawaiki' and the great Polynesian navigator Kupe, who is said to have made landfall in Northland, around AD 800. Finding the new land viable for settlement, Kupe named it Aotearoa – The Land of the Long White Cloud. Leaving his crew to colonize, Kupe then returned to Hawaiki to encourage further emigration. A century later the first fleet of waka (canoes) arrived in Aotearoa to settle permanently. It was the crew of these canoes that formed the first iwi (tribes) of a new race of people called the Maori.

The ancestral land called Hawaiki is thought to be Tahiti and the Society Islands, but exactly when and how these early Polynesians arrived and how they lived is in doubt. What is known is that they arrived sporadically in canoes and initially though struggling with the colder climate of New Zealand particularly in the South island, they persevered.

By the time the first European explorers arrived the Maori had developed their own culture, based on the tight-knit family unit and a tribal system not dissimilar to the Celts and Scots. In a desire to protect family, food resources and land the Maori, like the Scots, saw their fair share of brutal inter-tribal conflict. The Maori developed a highly effective community and defence system built within fortified villages or pa and cannibalism was also common. By the 16th century they had developed into a successful, fairly healthy, robust race. This period is known as the Classic Period. But despite the Maori successes in colonization, the subsequent environmental damage was dire and irreversible. A classic dynamic of cause and effect was set in place that would compromise the land forever. The Maori and the animals they brought with them (particularly dogs and rats) proved the nemesis of the unspoiled and isolated biodiversity of the land. Now, with the sails of European ships appearing above the horizon it was the Maori themselves who were facing the threat of annihilation.

European exploration

Although rumoured that the French or Spanish were actually the first Europeans to sight New Zealand, the first documented discovery was made in 1642 by Dutch explorer Abel Tasman. Tasman was sent to confirm or otherwise the existence of the hotly rumoured Great Southern Continent (Terra Australis Incognita) and if discovered, to investigate its viability for trade. Tasman's first encounter with the Maori proved hostile and without setting foot on land he fled to Tonga and Fiji. He christened the new land 'Staten Landt' which was later renamed 'Nieuw Zeeland'. It was Tasman's first and last encounter with the new land, but his visit led to New Zealand being put on the world map.

The next recorded European visit occurred with the arrival of the ubiquitous British explorer Captain Cook on board the Endeavour in 1769. It would be the first of three voyages to New Zealand. Cook's first landing, on 7 October in

Poverty Bay (North Island) was eventful to say the least, with what proved to be a classic culture clash with the resident Maori. Ignorance and fear on both sides led to a mutual loss of life, but unlike Tasman, Cook persevered and after further encounters managed to establish a 'friendly' relationship with the new people he called *tangata Maori* (the 'ordinary people').

European settlement & the clash of cultures

After news spread of the Cook voyages it did not take long for European sealers and whalers to reach New Zealand and rape the rich marine resources. By the 1820s the New Zealand fur seal and numerous species of whale had been brought to the verge of extinction. As the industries subsequently declined they were quickly joined or replaced by timber and flax traders. Others including adventurers, ex-convicts from Australia and some very determined (and some would say, much needed) missionaries joined the steady influx. Samuel Marsden gave the first Anglican sermon in the Bay of Islands on Christmas Day, 1814.

Inevitably, perhaps, an uneasy and fractious integration occurred between the Maori and the new settlers (or Pakeha as they were called) and, in tune with the familiar stories of colonized peoples the world over, the consequences for the native people were disastrous. Western diseases quickly ravaged over 25% of the Maori population and the trade of food, land or even preserved heads for the vastly more powerful and deadly European weapons resulted in the Maori Musket Wars 1820-1835. It proved a swift and almost genocidal era of inter-tribal warfare.

With such a melting pot of divergent cultures, greed and religion simmering on a fire of lawlessness and stateless disorganization, New Zealand was initially an awful place to be. Crime and corruption was rife. The Maori were conned into ridiculously unfavourable land-for-weapons deals and, along with the spread of Christianity and disease, their culture and tribal way of life was gradually being undermined. Such were the realities of early settlement that Kororareka (now known as Russell) in the Bay of Islands, which was the largest European settlement in the 1830s, earned itself the name and reputation as the 'Hellhole of the Pacific'. Amidst all the chaos the settlers began to appeal to their governments for protection.

The Treaty of Waitangi

By 1838 there were about 2000 British subjects in New Zealand and by this time the country was under the nominal jurisdiction of New South Wales in Australia. In 1833 James Busby was sent to Waitangi in the Bay of Islands as the official 'British Resident'. He was given the responsibility of law and order, but without the means to enforce it. Chaos reigned and finally, exacerbated by a rumour that the French were threatening to pre-empt any British attempt to claim sovereignty of New Zealand, Britain appointed Captain William Hobson as Lieutenant Governor to replace Busby. His remit was to effect the transfer of sovereignty over the land from the Maori chiefs to the British Crown. With the help of Busby who was now familiar with the ways and desires of the Maori, Hobson created what was to become the most important and controversial document in New Zealand history, the Treaty of Waitangi.

In the hastily compiled document there were three main provisions. The first was the complete cession of sovereignty by the Maori to the Queen of England. The second was the promise of full rights and possession of Maori lands and resources (but with the right to sell, of course). The third, and perhaps the greatest, attraction, given the chaotic environment, was the full rights and protection of Maori as British citizens. After two days of discussions, a few amendments and amidst much pomp and ceremony, over 40 Maori chiefs eventually signed the Treaty on 5 February 1840. With these first few signatures from the predominantly Northland tribes, Hobson went on a tour of the country to secure others.

To this day the Treaty of Waitangi remains a very contentious document. From its very inception it was inevitably going to be a fragile bridge between two very different cultures. Given the many differences in communication, translation and meaning, at best it was spurious or vague but worse still could, as a result, be easily manipulated in both actual meaning and subsequent enactment.

By the September of 1840 Hobson had gathered over 500 signatures, all in the North Island. Feeling this was enough to claim sovereignty over New Zealand he did so, and declaring the right of discovery over the South Island, made New Zealand a Crown Colony, independent of New South Wales and Australia. But the refusal and subsequent omission of several key (and powerful) Maori chiefs paved the way for regional disharmony and eventually war.

Maori (Land) Wars

In 1840 Hobson established Kororareka as the first capital of New Zealand, but given its reputation and history, he moved the seat of government to Auckland. With the increased influx of settlers, all greedy for land and resources, human nature very quickly superseded the legal niceties and undermined the fragile bridge of the new bicultural colony. In a frenzy of very dubious land deals between Maori and Pakeha (white settlers), as well as misunderstandings in methods of land use and ownership, resentment between the two was rife. This, plus the heavy taxes that were being demanded by the new and financially strapped government, strained the bridge to breaking point. The Maori were beginning to feel disenfranchised and began to rebel against British authority.

Legendary and belligerent chiefs like Hone Heke and Te Kooti (who for a time became the most wanted man in the land) put up a determined and courageous fight. But with far superior weaponry and organization the British quickly subdued the rebels. In return for their disobedience, and despite the treaty, they confiscated huge tracts of land. This land was then sold to new or already established settlers. By 1900 over 90% of the land was outside Maori ownership or control. They were a defeated people and, with little or no power and with continued integration, their culture was rapidly crumbling.

Natural resources, consolidation & social reform

Although development suffered as a result of the conflicts, timber, agriculture and gold came to the rescue. With the first discoveries made in the 1850s much of the economic focus shifted to the South Island and the seat of a new central (as opposed to provincial) government was moved to Wellington, which became the capital in 1876. The gold boom saw the Pakeha population grow dramatically and although it lasted only a decade, the infrastructures that it set in place paved the way for agricultural, timber and coal industries to quickly take over. In the agriculture sector alone, especially through sheep and dairy cattle, New Zealand was becoming an internationally significant export nation and prosperity continued. Towards the end of the 19th century the country also went through a dramatic and sweeping phase of social reforms. Well ahead most other Western nations, women secured the vote and pioneering legislation was enacted, introducing old-age pensions, minimum wage structures and arbitration courts.

But again, while the Pakeha prospered the Maori continued to suffer. Despite the Native Lands Act of 1865 that was established to investigate Maori land ownership and distribute land titles, by 1900 the Maori population had decreased to less than 50,000 and with the integration of Maori and Pakeha, pure Maori were becoming even more of a minority.

Prosperity & the world wars

By 1907 New Zealand progressed to the title of 'Dominion' of Britain rather than merely a 'colony' and by the 1920s was in control of most of its own affairs. By virtue of its close links with Britain, New Zealand and the newly formed (trans-Tasman) Australia and New Zealand Army Corps (ANZACs) became heavily embroiled in the Boer War of

The legend of Maui

According to Maori legend the great Polynesian demigod 'Maui-Tikitiki-a Taranga' who hailed from the original Polynesian homeland of Hawaiki created New Zealand. Maui was blessed with many god-like powers, with which to confront the world around him. Once, while out fishing with his five brothers, Maui used a piece of magic jawbone as a fishhook and his own blood as bait. Before long he caught an almighty fish and struggling to pull it to the surface placed a spell upon it to subdue it forever. This great fish became Te-Ika-a-Maui (the Fish of Maui) and in essence the North Island of New Zealand. The shape of the North Island is said to resemble the body of the fish, while the mountains and valleys were created when Maui's jealous brothers hacked hungrily at the fish with their greenstone mere (clubs). The South Island is 'Te-Waka-a-Maui' (the Waka of Maui) and Stewart Island 'Te-Punga-o-te-Waka-a-Maui' (the anchor).

1899-1902 and again in the First World War, at Gallipoli and the Western Front. Although noted for their steadfast loyalty, courage and bravery, the ANZACs suffered huge losses. Over 17,000 never returned with one in every three men aged between 20 and 40 being killed or wounded. Their First World War casualties remain the greatest of any combat nation.

After the First World War New Zealand joined the Western world in the Great Depression of the 1920s, but it recovered steadily and independently progressed in an increasing atmosphere of optimism. Again from a solid base of agricultural production it prospered and immigration, particularly from Britain, grew steadily. The population had now passed one million and it was enjoying one of the highest standards of living in the world.

Progress ceased temporarily with the outbreak of the Second World War and once again, the loyal ANZACs answered the call. With the spread of the conflict across the Pacific, it proved a nervous time for the nation, but with the dropping of the atomic bomb in Japan the threat ceased and the war was over.

New Zealand today

Te Apiti Wind farm, Tararua Ranges.

Post 1945

In 1947 New Zealand was declared an independent nation but maintained close defence and trade links with the Great Britain, the USA and Australia. In 1945 it became one of the original member states of the United Nations (UN) and later joined the ANZUS Defence Pact with the USA and Australia. Domestically, the country again prospered but the nagging problems of race relations, land and resource disputes between Maori and Pakeha still had to be addressed.

In 1975 significant progress was made with the formation of the Waitangi Tribunal, which was established to legally and officially hear Maori claims against the Crown. This method of addressing the problems continues to this day, but as ever, the misinterpretations of the treaty and its translation remain a major stumbling block.

New Zealand joined most of the developed world in the economic slump of the 1970s and 80s. In response to the economic decline, the government deregulated the country's economy, paving the way for free trade and New Zealand, like Australia, was beginning to see itself playing a far more significant role in the Asian markets as opposed to the traditional European ones.

One of the most important landmark decisions made on foreign policy in the 1980s was New Zealand's staunch anti-nuclear stand. In 1984 it refused entry to any foreign nuclear-powered ships in its coastal waters. This soured its relationship with the US who reacted by suspending defence obligations to New Zealand made under the ANZUS pact in the 1950s. This anti-nuclear stance is still maintained with considerable pride and is one that was only strengthened when the French Secret Service bombed the Greenpeace vessel *Rainbow Warrior* in 1985, causing national and international outrage. Relations with France were further soured in 1995 with the rather arrogant and insensitive testing of nuclear weapons in French Polynesia.

Throughout the 1990s the National Party continued successfully to nurture the free market economic policies first initiated by Labour. In 1999 the Labour Party were re-elected under the leadership of Helen Clarke. Her success as Prime Minister was to prove unprecedented, remaining in power until 2008 when Labour were ousted from government by the National Party under the leadership of new PM John Key.

The new millennium

Given its size and isolation New Zealand enjoyed considerable yet brief worldwide attention when on 1 January 2000 it was the first country to see the dawn of the new millennium. However, less appreciative attention was to follow after the infamous terrorist attacks of 11 September 2001 and the subsequent US-led military interventions in Afghanistan and Iraq. Unlike the Howard government of Australia, the New Zealand government led by Helen Clarke did not to align itself with that US policy and in a way repeated the fracas over the anti-nuclear stance of the 1980s. Most kiwis were very proud of Helen Clark's intelligent and (some say) truly democratic leadership at the time, despite the ramifications in current world affairs. The majority did not want to join the campaign in Iraq and its government rightfully and steadfastly exercised that voice. Kiwis are proud of their country and are more concerned about community and the environment than misguided patriotism, power and politics.

So returning to the shadows (bar the substantial hype surrounding the filming of Lord of the Rings) New Zealand remains a 'low-key' nation largely left to its own devices, blessed by an outstanding natural environment, healthy independence and the huge asset of a low and cosmopolitan population. It is not alone in its current economic struggles of course and a poor exchange rate and the ups and downs of free trade agreements may continue to cause problems as it did before the global financial meltdown. Its biggest social challenge is the continued and

The America's Cup

A significant event outside politics in 1995 was New Zealand's win in the coveted America's Cup yachting race. It was the first time the cup had been won by any nation other than the US and it was the cause of national celebration and pride. More than 300,000 people lined Queen Street in Auckland to congratulate the yachties' return. With the successful defence of the cup again in 2000 it seemed yachting would join rugby as the nation's world-dominating sport. After considerable amounts of money was spent to transform Auckland's waterfront into a state-of-the-art sailing arena, the Kiwi populace prepared themselves for what would surely be another convincing win in 2002/2003. But it was a dream that turned into a nightmare as amidst tactical errors, design faults and a snapped mast, former Kiwi team member Russell Coutts led a far superior outfit in the form of the Swiss Alinghi team to a 5-0 whitewash. In the 2007 campaign, Team New Zealand fought to reach the final but, despite valiant efforts, they lost to Alinghi for a second time and once again all hopes went out with the tide.

difficult journey down the road of biculturalism as well perhaps as some sensible long-term decisions pertaining to future levels of immigration and eco-tourism. It also has its abiding and mutually respectful yet sometimes fractious relationship with Australia to deal with. But perhaps New Zealand's greatest challenge lies in the conservation and protection of its environment, for which it is most famous and much loved. Indeed, with a world facing the specter of rapid and human induced climate change perhaps it can – like Sweden – set an example for the rest of the world to follow. Dubbed the 'Clean Green Land' it certainly has a reputation to fulfill and an innate respect for environment is certainly there, but it remains to be seen whether its government and people can truly embrace the reality that its relatively healthy ecological condition is in fact probably due to its lack of population, as opposed to the common and traditional human attitudes that have proved to be so ruinous elsewhere.

Culture
& heritage

A typical Maori carving depicting the face of a warrior, Rotorua.

Despite its relatively infant history, New Zealand provides a fascinating cultural mêlée. Before the early European explorers paved the way for widespread colonial immigration, the native Maori had developed their own highly individual way of life. Despite the fact that, like any other displaced people, they have struggled to maintain this identity and culture, thankfully 'Maoritanga' (Maoridom) is enjoying something of a renaissance in modern-day New Zealand. Maori issues are now taken very seriously within government and in legal circles, especially when it comes to land rights and the harvesting of natural resources. When it comes to tourism, however, the presentation of that native culture can be overly commercial.

If you can penetrate beneath the colourful yet rather plastic veneer you will be exposed to a different world. Whether it is through a stay on a *marae*, a cultural performance, a *hangi* (feast), or simple friendship, learning about the traditional Maori lifestyle will enhance your visit and a provide a sense of hope that biculturalism has an optimistic future. You will also find that through the solid roots of Maoridom and colonialism a unique Kiwi culture and identity is growing strong and steadfast.

Customs & traditions

The Iwi

The Maori are essentially a tribal race consisting of the *whanau* (family unit), extending to the *iwi* (tribe). Together they are referred to as the *tangata whenua*, which directly translated means 'people of the land'. The Maori relationship with their *tipuna* (ancestors) is considered to exist through their genetic inheritance, and an individual's own *whakapapa* (genealogy) can be traced right back to the gods via one of the original *waka* (migratory canoes). There are more than 40 in New Zealand with the largest being the Ngapuhi (descendants of Puhi) in Northland.

Mauri & Mana

In Maori culture all things whether living or otherwise possess *mauri*, *wairau* (spirit) and *mana*. To the Maori everything has a *mauri*; an essence that gives everything its special character and everything is viewed as a living entity. As such, the concept of *mauri* leads to a sense of unity between humans and nature. It infuses everything: things living and non-living, earth and sky. Sometimes it has no tangible presence at all, but always the mauri must be cared for and respected. When *kia moana* (seafood) is taken from the sea, a tree is felled, or any other thing is harvested, a *karakia* should be said beforehand and thanks given afterwards.

The meaning of mana goes well beyond words, but in essence means prestige, standing, integrity or respectability.

Tapu

Traditional Maori life is bounded by the customs, concepts or conducts of *tapu* (meaning taboo, or sacred) and *noa* (meaning mundane, or the opposite of *tapu*). If something is *tapu* – whether an object, place, action or person – it must be given the accordant respect. To do otherwise can result in ostracism, bad luck or sickness. A good example would be a burial place that is forever tapu or a food resource that is given seasonal *tapu* to encourage sustainability.

Of course in the modern day your average 'Maori Joe' cannot just place a tapu on anything he chooses – his beer for example – if this were the case there would be social mayhem! Placing a *tapu* is a matter that requires deliberation by the *iwi* and enactment by the elders after a meeting or *hui*.

The Marae

The marae is essentially the sacred 'place of meeting', or of simply 'being', that exists around a *wharae tupuna* (or ancestral meetinghouse). It is traditionally used as a communal centre, meeting place or sometimes a retreat. Strict customs and *kawa* (protocols) surround the *marae* and for any tourist who wishes to visit or stay it is important to be aware of these customs and the protocols.

The hangi

Pronounced 'hungi', this is the traditional Maori and Pacific Island feast or method of cooking. To the uninitiated, the concept of cooking your dinner in the ground may seem a bit odd, but it is actually incredibly efficient and produces a certain taste and texture in the food that is extraordinarily good. Hangis were designed for the masses and were as much a social occasion as anything else. Traditionally the men would light a large fire and place river stones in the embers. While the stones are heating a pit is dug in the earth. Then the stones are placed in the pit and sacking placed upon them (before sacking it was suitably fashioned plant material). Then, presumably, the boys went off for a beer while the good ladies of the tribe prepared the meat. Nowadays this includes chicken, wild pig and lamb, but was formerly moa, pigeon and seafood. Vegetables are added too, particularly the traditional sweet potato, kumara. Once cleaned and plucked the smaller items are wrapped in leaves (now foil) and the whole lot placed in a basket (traditionally woven leaves from the flax plant, now wire-mesh) and then the whole affair is covered with earth. Once covered the steam slowly cooks the food and the flavours are sealed in. Then a couple of hours later it is all dug up et voilá– it's time to feast. The succulence and smoked flavours of the food are gorgeous.

Although due to modern-day health and safety requirements it is not really possible to sample a proper *hangi* the commercial offerings by the Maori tourist concerns can still be very tasty and well worth the experience. Rotorua is the principal venue (see page 112). If you ever have the opportunity of a real one, do not pass it up.

The hongi

The *hongi* – the touching (not rubbing) of noses as opposed to the shaking of hands in Western Society – is unique to the Maori. That said the *hongi* is an action, which is equivalent to a hug or a kiss, and is often accompanied with a handshake.

Arts & crafts

The artistic styles used by the Maori were already well developed on their arrival in New Zealand and influenced by Polynesian tradition. In the absence of clay for pottery and metals with which to fashion rock or wood, they developed a unique style.

Wood or greenstone (*pounamu*) carving was the commonest form of craft either for functional purposes (like *waka*) or for decoration, on panels, pou (equivalent to Native American totem poles) or adorning *whare whakairo* (meeting houses). Kauri or totara were the commonest native wood types and it was fashioned into highly distinctive patterns using *pounamu* (greenstone), shells or sharp stones. Other forms of carving were the creation of pendants or *tiki*, which were made predominantly from whalebone or *pounamu*. These pendants often depict spiritual ancestors – or hei tiki – as well as legendary or sacred animals. Weapons like *taiaha pouwhenua* (long clubs) and *patu* (short clubs) were fashioned from wood, while *mere* (short, close-combat clubs) were traditionally fashioned from greenstone.

One of the best places to see traditional and contemporary Maori arts and crafts in creation is at the Maori Arts and Crafts Institute, at the Whakarewarewa Thermal Reserve in Rotorua (page 114).

Moko

The unique Maori facial tattoo (or *moko*) was traditionally applied using bone chisels, a mallet and blue pigment. The *moko* was predominantly the decoration of the higher classes with men covering their entire face (and sometimes their buttocks) while the women were decorated on the chin. To get the best idea of its design and permanence (let alone to imagine the pain), take a look at the superb realist paintings of the Maori elders done in the late 1800s by renowned New Zealand painters Gottfried Lindauer and Charles F Goldie. Examples are on display in major art galleries throughout the country, with the Auckland Art Gallery being especially good (page 71).

The international speaker Naghi Bidois.

Greenstone (Pounamu)

Greenstone, or jade, as it is better known, is *taonga* (precious) to the Maori and has been revered for centuries. The Maori called it *pounamu*. In New Zealand greenstone is found in the South Island, predominantly in Westland. The Maori called the South Island Te Wahi Pounamu (The Place of Greenstone) and they went to great lengths to find and transport the precious stone, before carving it into a range of items, both practical and ornamental. Foremost among these was the *mere* (a flat hand-held weapon), which were highly treasured and in the hands of a warrior was lethal. *Heitiki* (pendants), were also painstakingly carved, often in the form of mythical spirits and monsters. These *tiki* were passed on from generation to generation and in doing so, increased in *mana* (prestige or spiritual power). In the modern day, greenstone is mainly used to create ornaments and *tiki* for the tourist market. Hokitika, on the west coast of the South Island is the best place to buy it and see it being made (page 238).

The haka

The *haka* is a traditional dance that can look decidedly threatening and has been made famous worldwide by the pre-match performance of the All Blacks rugby team. The tradition and meaning of the haka however goes far beyond mere sport. In essence this is a *wero* (challenge) made by individuals and warrior groups and is part of a complex cultural protocol. Do not return the gestures, unless you want to be considered uncouth, culturally ignorant or have the desire to get your head removed.

Modern Maoritanga (the Way of the Maori)

The Maori language (see page 310), lifestyle, social structure, customs, spirituality, legends, arts and crafts are all enjoying something of a revival in modern-day New Zealand. The unique Maori culture and history are all very well represented in museums throughout the country, with both Auckland Museum (page 71) and the state-of-the-art Te Papa Museum of New Zealand in Wellington, in particular (page 162), offering a fascinating insight. Although there are thought to be no 'true' full-blooded Maori left in New Zealand, the majority of those of undisputed Maori descent remain staunchly and rightly proud of their ancestry and cultural identity. It is a sad fact that their cultural journey in the face of what many would call a 'European invasion' has been, and continues to be, a difficult and troubled one. To that end it is important for the visitor to be aware of the basics and to realize that New Zealand culture, in total, goes a lot deeper than the practice or development of a cosmopolitan mix of cultures imported from elsewhere. In a country that essentially has a very short human history and one that some critics declare as 'historically wanting', Maoritanga is, in essence, as old as it gets.

Nature & environment

New Zealand is a compact, diverse and ancient land that has been so isolated from any other land mass for so long that its biodiversity is described by some scientists as the closest one can get to studying life on another planet. Thanks to its long isolation, much of New Zealand's biodiversity is not only ancient, but endemic, with around 90% of its insects, 80% of its trees, ferns and flowering plants and 25% of its bird species, all 60 reptiles, four remaining frogs and two species of bat (the only native mammals) all found nowhere else on earth.

The 'Shaky Isles'

Given the fact New Zealand is located at the meeting point of the Pacific and Indo-Australian Plates, it is also a distinctly 'shaky' land of frequent earthquakes and constant volcanic activity. The Taupo Volcanic Zone in central North Island is one of the most active in the world. A string of volcanoes stretches from the currently active White Island in the Bay of Plenty, to the moody Mount Ruapehu in the heart of North Island. The area also has numerous thermal features including geysers, mineral springs, blowholes and mud

Vital statistics

New Zealand consists of three main islands – North Island, South Island and Stewart Island – with a handful of other small far-flung subtropical and sub-Antarctic islands. The total land area is 268,704 sq km (slightly larger than the UK).

New Zealand's boundaries extend from 33° to 53° south latitude and from 162° east longitude, to 173° west longitude, which results in a broad climatic range from north to south. It is bounded north and east by the South Pacific Ocean, on the west by the Tasman Sea and on the south by the great Southern Ocean. The nearest mainland is Australia, 1600 km west, which is roughly the same distance as New Zealand is in length. The country's highest mountain is Mount Cook (3753 m) and the longest river is the Waikato, which stretches 425 km from Lake Taupo to the Tasman Sea. The most northerly point of the North Island is Cape Reinga in Northland, while the most southerly point on the South at Slope Point. Slope Point is (surprisingly perhaps) 4831 km from Antarctica.

The banks of Emerald Lake, Tongariro.

pools, most of which can be found around Rotorua and Taupo. One of the largest volcanic eruptions in human history occurred in New Zealand in AD 186, the remnants of which is the country's largest lake – Lake Taupo. The most recent eruption occurred in 1995 (and again in 1996), when Mount Ruapehu – North Island's highest peak – had a moderate stomach upset. The country's most dramatic earthquake in recent history occurred in Napier on North Island's east coast in 1931 with the loss of over 250 lives.

As a result of this volcanic activity, its associated geological uplift and the 'sculpturing' that has occurred gradually over the millennia, New Zealand's landscape is rich and varied. In the South Island glaciers, braided rivers, lakes, fiords (flooded glacial valleys) and sounds (flooded riverbeds) abound, while from Stewart Island in the South to Cape Reinga in the north there are alluvial plains, wetlands, large natural coastal harbours and a rash of offshore islands. Due to the 'uplift' created by the clash of the two tectonic plates, the South

Island has many more mountain ranges than the North Island and boasts the country's highest peak, Mount Cook. Aoraki ('cloud piercer') as the Maori call it, stands less than 40 km from the west coast at a height of 3753 m. The country's longest river is the Waikato, which stretches 425 km from Lake Taupo to the Tasman Sea.

It's a fact...

New Zealand's most recent major earthquake was in July 2009 when a 7.8 struck in Fiordland, South Island. Due to the remote location it caused no structural damage or human injury. Scientists say as a result of the quake the country is now a few centimetres closer to Australia. Ask the average kiwi how they feel about that – it's entertaining!

The native pigeon or keruru is common throughout the country.

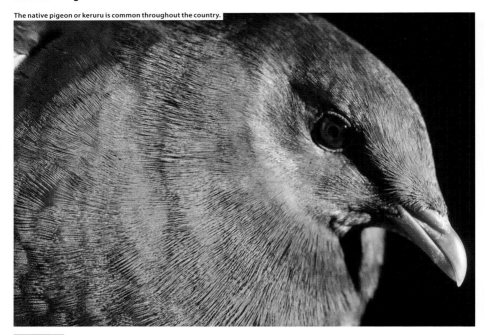

Wildlife

Although a mere echo of its former glory and ravaged by non-native (introduced) flora and fauna, modern-day New Zealand is still home to many endemic species. Your encounters will be many and memorable: from enchanting penguins to graceful albatrosses; cheeky keas to manic fantails, and rotund sea lions to breaching whales. Given the focus and fragility of its species, New Zealand is on the cutting edge of both conservation and ecotourism. As a visitor you will be able to experience both, working separately or in unison, and whether you love wildlife or are indifferent, you will be given a stark insight into our effect on the world and our place within it.

The following is just a mere sample of what you may encounter…

Birds

New Zealand does not have a huge bird list but what it does have is very special indeed. Of course, many species like the blackbird have been introduced, while others like the magpie paid a visit from across the Tasman and never left. But what truly belongs here is usually flightless, probably made Darwin over-excited and is certainly found nowhere else on the planet. Of course the great icon, the kiwi is a prime example. But before trying to summarize a creature of such delightful nonconformity, one should first consider the moa.

Moa were up to 3 m tall (the tallest avian ever) and looked a bit like an ostrich. There were around 11 species and they were very common. But sadly brains did not match the brawn. They had very little fear of anything and were flightless, so once the Maori arrived they were quickly hunted to extinction.

Of course though most have never heard of the moa, everyone has heard of a kiwi. They are to the avian world what the platypus is to the mammalian and the epitome of birdie weird. Flightless of course, they have no wings and their feathers are more like hairs. They are nocturnal and live in burrows. They have long whiskers almost like those of a cat, which, along with an acute sense of hearing and smell, are its ammunition in the hunt for food. It is the only bird with nostrils at the end of its beak and its egg-to-body weight ratio is legendary. The egg of a kiwi averages 15% of the female's body weight, compared to 2% for the ostrich. That's like giving birth to a prize pumpkin. Females tend to be larger than males and when it comes to the brown kiwi, the male tends to do most of the incubating. Now, how's that for weird? They mate for life, sleep for almost 20 hours a day (not weird at all) and live as long as 30 years. There are four living species, the brown kiwi, the little spotted, great spotted and the tokoeka. The brown is the most common species and the one you are most likely to see in captivity. The best and only chance the vast majority of visitors get to observe these quirky characters in one of the many darkened 'kiwi houses' scattered around the country. Some of the best are to be found at Kiwi Encounter in Rotorua (page 117), the DoC Wildlife Centre at Mount Bruce (page 172) and Willowbank Wildlife Reserve in Christchurch (page 223). The tokoeka of Stewart Island are the only wild kiwi that can be seen during the day, which creates something of a tourist pilgrimage to try to see them (see page 280).

Of course the coast is never far away in New Zealand and it is home to some of the nation's avian royalty. The world's only mainland colony of royal albatross is a major attraction on the Otago Peninsula, as are the twilight comings and goings of the yellow-eyed penguin, regarded as the rarest penguin species in the world. New Zealand is also known as the seabird capital of the world and a remarkable 70% of its total avian 'who's who' is pelagic (the global average is 3%). The list is long and includes mollymawks (which are similar to albatrosses), shearwaters and petrels.

Other notable seabird attractions include the colonies of gannets at Cape Kidnappers (near Napier, in Hawke's Bay) and on Farewell Spit, off the northern tip of the South Island.

Thousands of offshore islands are proving crucial to the conservation of the country's native wildlife. Many combine to form an invaluable flotilla of 'arks'; ultimately the only hope for many species. Once the Department of Conservation has eradicated formerly introduced predators like rats and possums, the remaining small pockets of resident birds, plants and animals are encouraged to re-colonize, and captive endemic breeds can be re-released. Some of the species that are now reliant on the 'arks' include birds like the kakapo (an ancient flightless parrot of which only 62 named individual remain), the kokako and takahe. To visit one of these vital reserves is to at least get a taste of the New Zealand of old and to experience the paradise lost. On one of these islands you enter a world of unique and ancient wildlife that shows little fear of humans, creating a near bombardment of the senses. The islands of Tiritiri Matangi (see page 79) and Kapiti Island off the Wellington coast (see page 167) are just two examples.

Tragically, like so much of the planet, New Zealand has now lost the vast majority of its natural forest cover. The impact on the whole ecosystem has been immense; most of the native forest that remains is confined to inaccessible areas and mountain slopes, with almost a quarter of that being in South Island's west coast region alone. The keruru (native pigeon), stitchbird, bellbird and the tui are all found in the lowland and forest habitats. The tui is quite common and you are bound to see, and certainly hear them. They boast a remarkable and entertaining range of whistles, grunts and knocks.

Of all the smaller birds encountered most folk's favourite is the enchanting little fantail. These charming little birds are a bit like butterflies on speed and your visit to New Zealand will more than once be enhanced by their inquisitive nature.

The kaka is one of New Zealand's three native parrot species. Once common throughout the

Birds of play

Ah yes, the notorious kea – possibly the most wonderful creature with wings. This highly intelligent, utterly entertaining avian delinquent lives high above the tree line, where it nests amongst rocks and feeds on just about anything edible. They are the only alpine parrot in the world. Forget about you finding them; if they are around they will find you. Nicknamed the 'cheeky kea' – thanks to their inherently inquisitive nature and extrovert behaviour – they are particularly fascinated by cars, rucksacks and shoelaces, or indeed anything that can be dismantled, demolished or eaten. To have a flock descend in the middle of your lunch break is a bit like an encounter with a class of unsupervised infants with severe behavioural disorders in a sweetie shop – out of control. I say children because that is truly how they behave and it certainly relates best to your subsequent reaction. They are so appalling, carefree and fun-loving that it is almost impossible not to just let them get on with it.

Along with the kea another notable bird of remote mountainous areas is the flightless takahe. They look like some congenial, prehistoric, purple chicken. Another ancient species once thought to be extinct; they were dramatically rediscovered in Fiordland in 1948. There is now an intensive breeding programme to attempt to secure their conservation, with only about 100 birds remaining in the wild and about the same again kept in captivity or on predator-free islands. The best place to see them is Tiritiri Matangi Island near Auckland (page 79), where several families (about 20 birds) are allowed to roam free.

country they are now confined mainly to old-growth forests. Although unmistakable in both call and plumage the average visitor would be lucky to see one in the wild, making your best bet the zoos or DoC wildlife centre at Mount Bruce in the Wairarapa (see page 172).

Even tamer than the kaka but sharing its love for a free lunch is the weka, a flightless member of the rail family, often encountered at campgrounds and car parks and very often amid mass hysteria mistaken for kiwi.

Mammals

It is remarkable to think that New Zealand played host to only one mammal before we arrived, a small bat, of which two species (the long-tailed bat and the short-tailed bat) evolved. The vast majority of its biodiversity has wings, or lost the need for them through evolution and the lack of predatory, terrestrial mammals. Why the lack of terrestrial mammals? Well, around 23 million years ago New Zealand was mostly underwater. To what extent exactly is pure speculation, but estimates range from about 18% to the full 'Jacques Cousteau'. But this considerable dunking does explain why so much of what did become established or evolve did so as or from air or sea-borne immigrants – which of course eventually included us.

Sea mammals feature heavily. The tiny and endemic Hector's dolphin (again, one of the rarest in the world) joins many other species of dolphin and some fur seals, particularly around Kaikoura, which of course is also a top spot for whale watching.

In New Zealand today, besides the bat, there is now a thoroughly cosmopolitan and unsavoury list of terrestrial mammalian guests. This extraordinary list of reprobates includes the Australian brush tailed possum (an estimated 70 million – 20 to every person), stoats, weasels, hedgehogs, rabbits, hares, wallabies, ferrets, rats, mice, pigs, cats, horses, deer, goats and the entire cast of 'Big Brother' New Zealand. Combined we (and they) have become to New Zealand's native wildlife, what 'land-ahoy' did for the dodo.

Insects

New Zealand has an impressive range of creepy-crawlies, ranging from the noisy and the colourful to the downright bloodthirsty. There is even one the size of a mouse! But don't cancel your flight ticket just yet. By far the noisiest insect in the country is the cicada, which in summer and en masse can create an ear-splitting din in almost any area of bush or forest throughout the country. There are many species in New Zealand with one of the most common being the aptly named clapping cicada, though sometimes you wish a locust would pop by and tell them that the show's over.

But perhaps the most remarkable native insect in New Zealand is the weta, an ancient creature that has been around for millions of years. A number of species are found in gardens, forests caves and rock crevices throughout the country ranging from the common tree weta to the cave weta. But without doubt the most impressive is the giant weta. At up to 9 cm in length and weighing up to 80 g they are about the size of a mouse (Whooooah) and the largest insect in the world. Imagine one of those under the toilet seat (it's ok they don't do toilet seats!).

Of course, if you go anywhere near the west coast of the South Island you will become very intimate with the infamous New Zealand sandfly. What these wee creatures will do to source a feed of blood is the very epitome of motivation, tenacity and the combined tactical repertoire of both the RAF and Luftwaffe during the Second World War.

Reptiles & amphibians

To describe the noble and endemic tuatara as the most ancient reptile on earth is impressive enough, but when you consider that these living fossils are even older than the landscape itself, it seems truly remarkable that they exist at all. They belong to a very singular order of reptiles known as beakheads that once roamed the earth (be it very slowly) over 225 million years ago. Sounds very much like the House of Lords in the UK. Once common throughout the country, but subject to predation and a widespread loss of habitat, the tuatara, has

sadly joined the long list of New Zealand creatures in decline and now exists on only on offshore islands. Given their status and natural habitat, your best chance of seeing a tuatara is in one of the country's zoos or museums. The Southland Museum in Invercargill is without doubt the most famous venue, having the most successful breeding and research programme in the world (see page 179). It also boasts perhaps the most famous tuatara in the land – 'Henry'. Henry is at least 110 years old – and guess what? After years of abstinence he has recently decided to once again take up that most desirable of pastimes – sex!

New Zealand's native frogs are also very old and very unusual. Called pepeketua they have hardly changed in 70 million years and have several distinctive features including no tadpole stage (young hatch from eggs almost fully formed and are then looked after by their parents) and they do not croak. There are also three introduced species of frog in New Zealand. One wonders if the natives go green with envy when they croak?

Flora

Like the country's animal life, much of New Zealand's plant life is beautiful, ancient and unique. Over 80% of the country's flowering plants are not endemic to any other land. But like the fauna, much of the country's plant life is in a worrying state of decline and tragically only about 15% of the New Zealand's original forest remains. The following are some of the most notable species that you are likely to see.

Alongside the iconic kiwi, the ponga or silver fern is New Zealand's other great national emblem and just one of a vast array of over 80 fern species. Depicted on everything from the national rugby jersey to the side of America's Cup yachts, the silver fern is a common sight in both the natural and commercial world. It is found throughout the mainly subtropical bush landscape, forming stands of almost prehistoric-looking umbrellas. A lush green colour on top, it is the silver underside that has created their notoriety.

Without doubt the most celebrated, yet overly utilized of the 100-odd forest tree species is the kauri. Occurring predominantly in the north of the North Island it was once the dominant tree of the region. With vast trunks often over 15 m in diameter, and 30 m tall, the kauri was prized by both the Maori for canoe building and by the early Europeans for masts and other shipbuilding materials. Sadly, over 90% of the trees were harvested and only a few ancient individuals remain.

New Zealand's best-known flowering tree is the beautiful pohutukawa; a gnarled-looking coastal evergreen that bursts into bright crimson flower for three weeks in December, earning it the affectionate label as New Zealand's Christmas tree.

Paradise lost?

New Zealand is often described as a natural paradise and given the isolation it enjoyed for millions of years it was just that, but on the day that man arrived, a mere 1000 years ago, it was not only 'paradise found', but was to become 'paradise lost'. Tragically, the 'introduction' of ourselves and all the non-native animals and plants we brought with us has caused more devastation to this clean green land than anything else in 80 million years of evolution. To say that the 'Land of the Long White Cloud' has been cast in to an abiding shadow of its former self would be putting it mildly.

In New Zealand today it makes the heart cry to experience the deathly hush of forests once alive to the sound of birds. At times it really is like standing in an ancient church that has been sacked of all its contents and robbed of both congregation and choir. Instead of a heads held high in

celebration, the whispers of prayer and beautiful arias of worship, the pose is one of despair, the atmosphere one of remorseful reflection and the sound, one of eternal silence.

Although the country is often dubbed clean and green, many agree that it is far more a result of low population than attitude. As a result of our presence 32% of indigenous land and freshwater birds and 18% of seabirds are now extinct. Even the kiwi, the very emblem of the nation and its people is severely under threat and without more financing, it too is expected to be completely absent on mainland New Zealand within the next two decades. To lose the kiwi itself – the very bird after which its native humans are named – seems unimaginable.

Great efforts are being made in the war of conservation by the Department of Conservation, which as a funded governmental department is a rarity in itself. Independent organizations and eco-tourism also play a major role. Numerous captive breeding and predator eradication programmes have been initiated to stop, or at the very least slow down, the decline of so many species. Indeed, New Zealand is on the front line of the global conservation war and thankfully some battles are being won. But these battles all defy the shortsighted, financial and technologically driven society of the modern day. Since the very act of conservation is a drain on funds rather than a source, the DoC is always underfunded and until core values change it will be long and difficult climb towards salvation.

Festivals & events

Fireworks at the Christchurch Summerdaze Festival.

A huge range of events and festivals are held throughout the year, ranging from the bizarre World of Wearable Art Awards to the spectacular Opera in the Park in Auckland.

i-SITES have listings of events and the NZTB website, purenz.com, or nzlive.com, have detailed nationwide events listings.

January

World Buskers Festival (Christchurch)
worldbuskersfestival.com
Circus, street and comedic talent from around the world.

February

Waitangi Day (Waitangi and nationwide)
The nation recognizes Waitangi Day, 6 February, with a public holiday and by staging various national or regional events to commemorate the signing of The Treaty of Waitangi, New Zealand's founding document in 1840.

Art Deco Weekend (Napier)
artdeconapier.com
Napier gears up and dresses up for its biggest annual event celebrating its internationally recognized art deco heritage. Charleston anyone?

New Zealand International Festival of the Arts (Wellington)
nzfestival.co.nz
Biennial multi-arts festival held in the capital city and considered the nation's premier cultural event (next in 2010).

Wine Marlborough Festival
wine-marlborough-festival.co.nz
Annual three-day celebration of wine, food and fashion in New Zealand best-known wine region.

The Speight's Coast to Coast
coasttocoast.co.nz
A grueling multi-sport event with around 800 hardy souls traversing 243 km of the South Island's rugged terrain from Hokitika on the Tasman to Christchurch on the Pacific, with a combination of running, kayaking and cycling.

Wildfoods Festival (Hokitika)
wildfoods.co.nz
Attracting around 13,000 people annually, this is an extravaganza of gourmet bush tucker based on natural (or unusual) food resources from the land and sea. How about a little wasp larvae ice cream, or some vegan gonads perhaps? There's also a lot of beer on offer to wash it all down.

Pasifika Festival (Auckland)
aucklandcity.govt.nz
A colourful, one-day celebration of all of this Pacific Island, with contemporary arts and music, traditional food, crafts and cultural performances.

Ellerslie International Flower Show
(Christchurch)
ellerslieflowershow.co.nz
Formerly held in Ellerslie Auckland, this is now a five-day annual gardening and lifestyle show considered the best in the southern hemisphere.

April

National Jazz Festival (Tauranga)
jazz.org.nz
Founded in 1962 and held every Easter, this is oldest and the largest celebration of jazz in the country.

May

New Zealand International Comedy Festival
comedyfestival.co.nz
Held simultaneously over three weeks in Auckland and Wellington and featuring well-known and emerging domestic and international talent.

June

New Zealand Gold Guitar Awards (Gore)
goldguitars.co.nz
After 36 years this has become a small, yet internationally recognized, festival and competition attracting over 700 competitors.

July

Carrot Carnival (Ohakune)
ohakune.info
And why not!

Queenstown Winter Festival
winterfestival.co.nz
Dubbed New Zealand's biggest winter party, this is a 10-day celebration of the famous activity capital's culture and community, with street parties, fireworks, music and of course plenty of on-the-piste mountain mayhem.

August

Christchurch Arts Festival
artsfestival.co.nz
The South Islands largest, with 18 days of arts, culture and entertainment across the city. It is biennial staged rather unusually in winter and in 'odd' years.

September

World of Wearable Art Awards (Wellington)
worldofwearableart.com
First begun in 1987 in New Zealand's arts capital Nelson, this has grown to become one of New Zealand's most unusual and successful events, described as 'Mardis Gras meets Haute Couture'. A purpose-built museum exhibiting some of the most memorable and award-winning costumes is based near Nelson (page 180).

November

Oamaru Victorian Heritage Celebrations
Held annually in and around the elegant historical precinct of Oamaru in coastal Otago, this is a weekend event of theatre and costume, with many appropriate (and authentic) historical props, from penny-farthings to steaming traction engines.

Sleeping

The Chateau Hotel, Tongariro National Park.

New Zealand offers the full range of tourist accommodation from exclusive luxury lodges to basic campsites. Indeed, such is the sheer variety that the only limitation beyond the budget is your own imagination.

Given the compact nature of the country, its modern infrastructure and in no small part its awesome natural aesthetics, many choose the independent option and hire a motor home or a campervan, or if on a limited budget purchase a vehicle temporarily for the trip. Then, by staying predominantly at motor parks, flexibility and freedom can be maximised. This is by far the best and most popular option in New Zealand and the kiwi tourism industry is well geared up for it.

But whatever accommodation you choose you will find a huge range on offer with the local and regional visitor information centres (i-SITES) or internet being the best places to both source and to book. There are also many books available including the AA accommodation guides (aaguides.co.nz) as well as numerous motor parks, motels, campsites and backpacker guides.

In the high season (November to March) and particularly around Christmas and the first two weeks in January you are advised to book all types of accommodation at least three days in advance.

Hotels

Hotels in New Zealand can generally be listed under one of four categories: large luxury hotels; chain hotels; boutique hotels; and budget hotels.

There are plenty of luxurious (four- to five-star) hotels in the major cities and prices range from $250-1000 per night. As you would expect, all rooms are equipped with the latest technology. They also have restaurants and leisure facilities including swimming pools, spa pools and gyms.

Standard chain hotels are commonplace, vary in both age and quality and include names such as Quality Hotels, Novotel and Copthorne. Found in all major cities and the larger provincial towns, their standard prices range from $130-300 but they have regular weekend or off-season deals. Most have restaurants, pools and a gym.

Boutique hotels vary in size and price but tend to be modern and of a luxurious standard. The smaller, more intimate boutique hotels are overtaking the major chains in popularity. On average double rooms here can cost anything from $175-400.

Given the flourishing backpacker industry in New Zealand, budget hotels struggle to exist and most often you will find the generic title equates to exactly that.

Qualmark...

The Qualmark star grading system, which is the official tourist operator star grading system in New Zealand, can help you choose the type of accommodation you are looking for, in the style that suits you. It ranges from 1 star (Acceptable), through 5 stars (Exceptional), with an additional category 'Exclusive' (Outstanding). Look out for the black and yellow signs with silver fern logo.

Lodges & B&Bs

There are a growing number of luxury lodges throughout the country and most sell themselves on their location as much as their architecture, sumptuous rooms, facilities and cuisine. Prices tend to be high, ranging from $200 to a mind-bending $2600 per night (which equates to almost eight months in a well-equipped motor park). B&Bs are not as common in New Zealand as they are in Europe, but can still be found in most places. They vary greatly in style, size and quality and can be anything from a basic double room with shared bathroom and a couple of boiled eggs for breakfast to a luxurious ensuite or self-contained unit with the full cooked breakfast. Again prices vary, with the standard cost being as little as $75-100. Many lodges and B&Bs also offer evening meals. Again, the visitor information centres (i-SITES) are the best place to both source and book.

Home & farmstays

Generally speaking if an establishment advertises itself as a homestay it will deliberately lack the privacy of the standard B&B and you are encouraged to mix with your hosts. The idea is that you get an insight into Kiwi life, but it may or may not be for you depending on your preferences and personality.

Farmstays of course give you the added agricultural and rural edge, and are generally recommended. Accommodation can take many forms from being in-house with your hosts or fully self-contained, and breakfasts and evening meals

All a bit much for the West Coast backpackers.

are often optional. You may find yourself helping to round up sheep or milking a cow and if you have kids (farmstays usually welcome them) they will be wonderfully occupied for hours.

Both homestays and farmstays tend to charge the same, or slightly lower, rates as B&Bs. New Zealand Farm Holidays, T09-412 9649, nzfarmholidays.co.nz based near Auckland, produces a helpful free catalogue listing about 300 establishments.

Motels

Motels are still the preferred option of the average Kiwi holidaymaker and business traveller. They are everywhere and reproducing furtively. They vary greatly, from the awful, stained 1950s love shacks to the new and luxurious condos with bubbly spa pool. There is usually a range of rooms available and almost all have at least a shower, kitchen facilities and a TV – though whether it actually works and has Sky TV (or doubles as a plant pot) depends on the price. Most are clean, comfortable and well appointed, while in others you may find yourself trying to sleep next to the main road. Prices vary from studio units at about $75-85, one-bedroom units from $85-120 and suites

accommodating families and groups for an additional charge for each adult. Many of the bigger and better establishments have a restaurant and a swimming pool. Many also make the most of the country's thermal features and have spas, sometimes even in your room.

Hostels

New Zealand is well served with hostels and budget accommodation establishments. Naturally, they vary greatly in age, design, location and quality. Some enjoy a busy atmosphere in the centre of town while others provide a quiet haven in the country. They also have a range of types of bedrooms on offer, with many having separate double and single rooms as well as the traditional dormitory. Dorms are usually single sex but sometimes optionally mixed. Camping facilities within the grounds are also common. Generally, hostels are good places to meet other travellers, managers are usually very knowledgeable and helpful; pick-ups are often free. Bikes, kayaks or other activity gear can often be hired at low cost or are free to use. Wherever you stay you will have access to equipped kitchens, a laundry, games or TV room, plenty of local information and, of course, phones and the internet. Prices vary little for a dorm bed, from $20 depending on season. Single rooms and doubles tend to be around $55, or about $30 per adult. In the high season and especially over Christmas through to March you are advised to pre-book everywhere at least three days in advance.

There are several major backpacking membership organizations in New Zealand that provide hostel listings and discounts.

Budget Backpacker Hostels Ltd (BBH) T03-379 3014, bbh.co.nz, has around 350 member establishments that must meet certain minimum quality criteria. These are listed in its Blue Book (free from i-SITES) along with handy descriptions, contact details and location maps of each hostel.

The **YHA (Youth Hostel Association NZ)**, T0800-278299/T03-379 9970, yha.co.nz, is part of a worldwide organization and they have about 70 establishments throughout New Zealand; the vast majority are associates as opposed to YHA owned and operated. Being part of a large organization, most are on a par if not better than the independent backpacker hostels. They all offer very much the same in standard of accommodation and facilities. They are also to be congratulated on their intensive eco-friendly policies with recycling not only provided in most hostels, but actively and enthusiastically embraced.

YHAs are only open to members but you can join in your home country (if YHA exists) or in New Zealand for an annual fee of $40 ($30 for renewals). Non-members can also stay at hostels for an additional charge of $3 per night. YHA membership cards can also entitle you to a number of discounts, including up to 30% off air and bus travel. Pick up the YHA Accommodation and Hostel Guide at any major i-SITE visitor centre.

Motor parks camps & cabins

New Zealand's fairly compact size and quality road network lends itself to road touring and it is very well served with quality motor parks and campsites. In fact, it is hailed as one of the best in the world. Motor parks can be found almost everywhere and not necessarily just in towns. The quality and age does of course vary. Some are modern and well equipped while others are basic. Almost all motor parks have laundry facilities and a few will charge a small fee ($0.20-1) for hot showers. Prices are generally very reasonable and range from $10-15 per person (child half price) for non-powered sites. Powered sites are often the same price or a few dollars more.

Most motor parks have a range of cabins from dog kennels to well-appointed alpine-type huts. They vary in price starting with a standard cabin with little more than a bed and electric socket for a mere $35 to a cabin with better facilities for up to $60 per night (for two) with an additional charge of $12-15 per person after that.

The **Top Ten** chain of motor parks, which has almost 50 nationwide, though up to $3 more expensive per night, is generally highly recommended (top10.co.nz).

Wild camping

'Where can I camp?' 'Assume nothing – always ask a local' is the catch-cry of the authorities and rightly so – wild camping with no respect for property and environment is not tolerated. The best advice is to stick to designated sites and to source them ask at the local visitor information centre (i-SITE), or regional Department of Conservation (DoC) office (doc.govt.nz). The website camping.org.nz is also useful.

The DoC has more than 100 basic campsites all over the country with many being in prime locations. They tend to provide clean running water, toilet facilities and BBQ areas, but rarely allow open fires. The national parks in particular are all excellently facilitated with comfortable well-equipped huts. There is usually a nightly fee of $2-10. Fees for huts are anything from $5-40 per night depending on category and location. If you plan to use DoC campsites and huts you are advised to research their locations, fee structures, rules and regulations and book well in advance.

Eating
& drinking

Whale mural outside a café in Kaikoura.

Food

Budget permitting, you are in for a treat. The quality of food in New Zealand is superb. Although there are many types of traditional cuisine and restaurants in evidence, the principal style is Pacific Rim. It dips into the culinary heritage of many of the cultures of the Oceania region as well as further afield like Europe. For dishes that have a distinctly Kiwi edge look out for the lamb (arguably the best in the world), pork, venison and freshwater fish like salmon or trout – though note you cannot buy trout commercially.

As you might expect there is also a heavy emphasis on seafood. The choice is vast with many warm-water fish like snapper of particular note. Other seafood delights include crayfish (the South Pacific equivalent to the lobster), oysters (the best being from Bluff in the South Island), paua (abalone), scallops and the famous green-lipped mussels. There are also some treats in store from below the ground. The kumara (sweet potato) will shed a whole new light on the humble spud, while many of the international vegetables like asparagus and broccoli come cheap (especially while in season) and are always fresh. From the tree the fruit of choice is of course the succulent kiwi fruit, which although not exclusively grown in New Zealand is deservedly celebrated. A traditional dessert in New Zealand is the pavlova; a sort of mountainous cake made of meringue and whipped cream. For a real traditional treat try a Maori *hangi* or feast. Prepared properly and without ketchup you will be amazed at just how good and different fish, meat and vegetables can taste when cooked underground.

Eating out

There are eateries to suit every taste and budget from the ubiquitous fast-food joints to world-class seafood restaurants. Auckland and Wellington (the latter has more cafés and restaurants per capita than New York) are particularly rich in choice with a vast selection of cafés, café-bars, brasseries and specialist international restaurants giving added puff to the celebrated Pacific Rim.

Eating out in New Zealand is generally good value, especially given the usually favourable foreign exchange rates. The vast majority of eateries fall into the 'mid-range' bracket ($18-25 for a main). Most cafés open for breakfast between 0700 and 0900 and stay open until at least 1700, and often until late into the evening or the early hours. This usually applies seven days a week with special Sunday brunch hours provided. Most mid-range restaurants open their doors daily for lunch (often 1100-1400) and dinner (from 1800). The more exclusive establishments usually open for dinner from about 1800, with some (especially in winter) only opening some weekday evenings and at weekend

Vegetarians are generally well catered for in the main centres and provincial towns.

Self-catering

If you intend to do your own cooking, supermarkets offer a wide choice of fare and are often open until around 2200. The main chains include Big Fresh, Woolworths and New World, with Pac-n-Save and Countdown being marginally cheaper. For fresh fruit and vegetables, stick to the numerous roadside or wholesale fruit markets where the difference in price and quality can be astonishing. If touring via motor parks always check to see if they have camp kitchen facilities as standards vary.

Other than 'L&P' (a fairly unremarkable soft drink hailing from Paeroa in the Waikato, North Island) New Zealand lacks a national drink. If there is one, it is the highly sub-standard and over-rated beer called Lion Red or branded bottled beers like 'Steinlager'. Rest assured, however, that all the main internationally well-known bottled beers are available, as are some good foreign tap ales like Guinness.

Beer and lager is usually sold by the 'handle', the 'glass' (pint) or the 'jug' (up to three pints). Half-pints come in a 12-fl oz (350 ml) glass. Rarely is a pint a proper imperial pint, it's usually just under. Drinks generally cost $7-8 for a pint, about $5-6 for a jug of cheaper domestic beers and up to $8 for a double shot of spirit. Alcohol is much cheaper in rural pubs and RSAs (Retired Servicemen's Associations), where you can usually get yourself signed in. The minimum drinking age has just been reduced from 21 to 18. Liquor shops (off licenses) are everywhere and alcohol can generally (in most places) be bought seven days a week. There is also a thriving coffee culture almost everywhere in the main towns and cities, so you will not go without your daily caffeine fix.

New Zealand's diversity of climates and soil types has borne an equally rich array of wines and after over a century of development the country now boasts many internationally recognized labels. Hawke's Bay and Nelson/Marlborough areas are the principal wine-producing regions. New Zealand Sauvignon Blanc is rated throughout the world as one of the best, but there is growing recognition for its Chardonnay, Pinot Noir, Cabernet Sauvignon and Merlot. The choice is vast and whether a connoisseur or a novice you are advised to experiment. If you can, visit one of the many vineyards that offer tastings and cellar sales. For more information about New Zealand wines refer to nzwine.com or winesnewzealand.co.nz.

Entertainment

Goodness gracious…

Despite the diminishing and undeserved reputation as a cultural backwater, New Zealand's entertainment scene is fresh and exciting. The major centres all boast numerous contemporary and historical venues that vie for a host of first-class domestic and international concerts and shows. Theatre, orchestral concerts, ballet, dance, comedy, rock and jazz are all well represented and annual or biennial festivals often attract well-known international acts. On a smaller scale you will find a vibrant nightlife in New Zealand cities and major provincial towns. Although not necessarily world class, the nightclubs, cabarets, pubs and local rock concerts will certainly have you shaking your pants. There's even Country and Western and line dancing. New Zealand also boasts two large, modern, 24-hour casinos in Christchurch and Wellington. Ticketek are the national administrators for information and ticketing and a full listing of shows and events can be sourced from their website, ticketek. co.nz or nzlive.com. The local press and national newspapers also have comprehensive entertainment events listings particularly at weekends (nzherald.co.nz).

Pubs & bars

The pub scene has come on in leaps and bounds over the last decade with new establishments opening up almost everywhere and shaking off the basic tavern and hotel image. Before the 1990s the vast majority of pubs in New Zealand were the archetypal male bastions and the type of establishments where ashtrays were built into the tables, pictures of the local hairy rugby team adorned the walls and the average Saturday night consisted of a good argument about sport, a band playing Deep Purple's Smoke on the Water, followed by a fight, copious wall-to-wall vomiting and a failed attempt to get home. Of course such places still exist in some rural outposts, but generally speaking, pubs and bars are now a much more refined and classy affair, yet still retain that congenial and laid-back traditional pub atmosphere. New Zealand has also caught on to the pseudo Irish pub fad and although some are gimmicky, others are very good, offering fine surroundings and beer to match. Many drinking establishments are also now attached to restaurants and cafés with outdoor seating. In December 2004 it became illegal to smoke in all pubs, restaurants and cafés in New Zealand, though many still provide segregated (legal) areas outside. Pubs and bars are generally open from 1100-2230 with many having an extended license to 2400 and sometimes even 0300 at weekends.

Clubs

The cities and major towns all have their fair share of nightclubs that consistently pump up the volume to whatever is the latest international vibe. Some, particularly in Auckland, often attract touring international DJs.

The central business district obviously contains the most venues and a good idea for sourcing the best is to ask the staff at the largest backpacker establishments, or the barmen and women of the classiest bars. There is often a cover charge and dress is smart casual.

Gay & lesbian

Like their trans-Tasman counterparts, New Zealand cities have a welcome and thriving gay scene and the nightclubs and bars particularly around K'Road and Ponsonby in Auckland are a focus for it. Of course this only adds to both the atmosphere and the fun.

Each February Auckland hosts the popular 'Hero Festival' – the national gay event of the year. The festival involves a street parade and entertainment in the Ponsonby area (hero.org.nz). Although certainly not on the scale of the world-famous Sydney Mardi Gras, it is enjoyed by thousands, both gay and straight. How could one, for example, possibly resist 'Drag Aerobics with Buffy and Bimbo' (buffyandbimbo.com)?

There are a number of specialist publications and independent groups to source the latest news, events and information, including gaypages.co.nz, pinkpagesnet.com/newzealand, gaynewzealand.com and gaytravelnet.com/nz.

Publications to look out for in the main centres include the long-established *Gay Express* (gayexpress.co.nz).

Music concerts & festivals

Many international rock stars now include at least one gig in Auckland in their itinerary, often as an adjunct to Australian gigs and they are easily accommodated in the outdoor sports stadiums or purpose-built facilities like Auckland's new Vector Arena.

The country also has its fair share of city- and region-based music festivals, including the Big Day Out (Auckland, January, bigdayout.com) and The World of Music and Dance Festival WOMAD (Taranaki, July, womad.co.nz).

Activities & tours

Oh dear, the phrase 'where on earth do you start' springs to mind and here in New Zealand it's attached to a bungee rope only to repeat itself!

Well, one thing is for sure, you're in the right place. New Zealand (and Queenstown in particular) is considered the activity capital of the world. In the South Island's infamous resort town there are over 150 activities to choose from with everything from the ubiquitous bungee jump to frisbee golf. The following are just a sample of activities considered Kiwi classics. There are of course many more on offer from sinking an ice axe into a glacier, to a deft wedge toward a velveteen green. The choice is ultimately up to you and of course your budget.

Bungee jumping

The strange practice of attaching a rubber band to your ankles and diving off a bridge has now become synonymous with New Zealand. Kiwi A. J. Hackett, who jumped from the Eiffel Tower in 1986 and from the Sky Tower in Auckland in 2000, developed the concept. Jumps vary from 'tasters' of 40 m (from a crane) to the 134-m 'Nevis' near Queenstown. Most sites are located in or around Queenstown in the South Island, where you can do it from a bridge, high above a canyon, or even at night. Folk have jumped in tandem, in canoes, on bikes and, of course, butt naked. At $80-240, a jump is not cheap, but it's a once-in-a-lifetime experience!

North Island: Auckland Sky Tower (see page 69), Lake Taupo (see page 119); **South Island:** Queenstown (see page 269). See also: ajhackett.com.

Caving

The underground world of the Waitomo Caves is a renowned subterranean playground. There are over 360 mapped caves, the longest of which is 14 km. Most have rivers that have carved a wonderland of caverns, pools, waterfalls and rapids. These are negotiated with a headlamp, in a wetsuit, and attached to a rubber ring. Added to that, there's a 100-m abseil into the 'Lost World' as well as the spectacle of glow-worms. There is a huge range of activities; almost all involve getting wet. Prices range from a 45-minute cave tour at $38 to the seven-hour 'Lost World' trip at $395.

North Island: Waitomo Caves (see page 128). See also: http://tourism.waitomo.govt.nz, waitomo.com, waitomo.co.nz.

Fishing

New Zealand is fishing heaven, noted as one of the best and most unspoilt trout- fishing venues in the world. All levels of experience are well catered for with numerous boat charters and guides from the relatively affordable $75 an hour to the all-mod-cons trips at around $200 an hour. Fishing licenses cost $21 for 24 hours and $105 for a season and are available online from New Zealand Fish and Game (fishandgame.org.nz) and at most fishing tackle outlets. The Pacific waters offer superb sea and big-game fishing. Costs vary from the three-hour novice trip to the organized and affordable three-day trips to catch that prize marlin.

North Island: trout fishing in Lake Taupo, Tongariro River and Lake Rotorua (see page 109); big-game fishing in Bay of Islands (see page 83), Tutukaka Coast (see page 82), Whitianga (see page 93) and Tauranga (see page 131); **South Island:** trout fishing Otago and Southland. See also: fishandgame.org.nz

Flight-seeing & aerobatics

For a real insight into what flying is all about, not to mention the stunning views, a flight in a fixed-wing aircraft or a helicopter is highly recommended. There are endless locations throughout the country and for as little as $125 for a 10- to 15-minute flight in a helicopter or a 30-minute flight in a small fixed-wing, it's well worth it. If you can only afford one flight, make it the helicopter flight around the Franz Joseph or Fox glaciers and summit of Mt Cook. Most operate out of the glaciers. This 30-minute trip ($275) on a clear day is truly breathtaking.

If you fancy having a go yourself, it's possible to fly a Pitts Special accompanied and under close scrutiny, on a 20-minute flight, $285, (uflyextreme.co.nz). This is one of the most exhilarating experiences of a lifetime (arguably even better than bungee jumping and tandem skydiving).

For a more sedate ride you could consider a trip by hot-air balloon, which, although not so common and more expensive (around $285), is available in a number of locations.

Motueka (see page 195); Canterbury (page 213); West Coast (see page 213); Queenstown (page 269); Wanaka (page 271) and Fiordland (page 275). See also: flightseeing.co.nz, uflyextreme.co.nz, touristflightoperators.co.nz.

Jet boating

William Hamilton invented the first jet boat in New Zealand in 1954 and the country has never looked back. Not all are adrenaline-pumping trips with some being more scenic affairs. A 30-minute trip costs around $100.

North island: Rotorua (page 112), Motu River (from Opotiki, Wairakei Park, Whanganui River; **South Island:** Glenorchy (page 270), Shotover River in Queenstown (page 270). See also: dartriver.co.nz, shotoverjet.com, hukajet.co.nz, riverjet.co.nz.

Kayaking

New Zealand is a renowned playground for kayaking whether on river, lake or sea – even fiord. For novices, kayaking just takes just a wee bit of time to get used to, but before you know it, you'll be off and paddling. A word of warning – never share a canoe with a loved one. Within five minutes there will be a major argument about technique, threats of violence and floods of tears. If you find it to your taste (the silence, the solitude and the scenery can be heart-warming) then consider a multi-day trip. The best of these are in the Bay of Islands (page 83), Abel Tasman National Park (page 196) and, most recommended, Fiordland (page 275). You can hire your own kayak for about $20 per hour; a three-hour trip will cost about $150; a four-day affair from $550.

North Island: Bay of Islands, Whitianga, Lake Rotorua, Whanganui National Park; **South Island:** Havelock and Picton, Abel Tasman National Park, Fiordland. See also: alpinekayaks.co.nz, seakayak nz.co.nz, abeltasmankayaks.co.nz, seakayaknewzealand.com, nzkayakschool.com.

Mountain biking

New Zealand is, as you might expect, a paradise for the avid mountain biker. With its wide range of magnificent landscapes, the country offers numerous tracks, both long and short and mainly through native bush or commercial forest. Bike hire is readily available and quite cheap, so give it a go.

North Island: Whakarewarewa Forest Park (page 114), Rotorua (page 112), Taupo (page 119), Tongariro National Park (from Tongariro, Whakapapa or Ohakune (page 122); **South Island:** Christchurch (page 216), Hanmer Springs (page 227). Heli-biking from Wanaka (page 271) or Twizel (page 233) or Queenstown (page 269). See also: mountainbike.co.nz, bike-nz.com, vorb.org.nz, planet bike.co.nz, bikenz.org.nz.

Rafting

This is another must-do activity. The rapids are graded from I to VI. Although the 45-minute trips at about $95 are packed with adrenaline-pumping moments, the real experience only comes with a multi-day trip (four days costs around $795). The four-day trip down the wild and remote Motu in Eastland is among New Zealand's best outdoor experiences. The trips are well organized and safe; most even do the campfire cooking for you. If the multi-day trip is beyond your budget or timeline then the best experience is the 45-minute trip down the Kaituna Rapids near Rotorua. The highlight of this trip is the 7-m drop down the Okere Falls, the highest commercially rafted falls in the world.

Another option is river sledging. This is the simple but superb concept of rafting down a river on a bodyboard with little except a wet suit, flippers, a crash helmet and a PhD in lunacy. A 40-minute dunking will cost you about $100.

North Island: Wairoa, Rangataiki, and Kaituna rivers from Rotorua (page 112), Motu River (from Opotiki), Tongariro River (from Tokaanu and Turangi; **South Island:** Queenstown is a good base (page 269). See also: nz-rafting.co.nz, raft.co.nz, wetnwildrafting.co.nz, whitewaterrafting.co.nz.

Sailing

New Zealand, and Auckland in particular, is famous for sailing. Auckland is not called the 'City of Sails' for nothing. An estimated one in four of its inhabitants owns a recreational boat of some kind and this trend is echoed throughout the country.

At least a few hours out on the water are recommended and there are many opportunities including a hands-on experience aboard a former Americas Cup racing yacht, from $150. Multi- day trips are also an option giving you an insight into what sailing is all about.

North Island: Hauraki Gulf (page 78) and Bay of Islands (page 83). See also: sailnz.co.nz.

About the region

Skiing and snowboarding

New Zealand is the principal southern hemisphere skiing and snowboarding venue and although it is of course seasonal (May-Aug), the slopes are highly accessible. Packages are available that include lift pass, equipment hire and one or more lessons from $85-120.

North Island: Tongariro National Park (from Whakapapa and Turoa, page 122); **South Island:** Coronet Peak and the Remarkables near Queenstown (page 269), Cardrona and Treble Cone near Wanaka (page 271), Mt Hutt, near Methven. See also: nzski.com, snow.co.nz, brownbear.co.nz, nzsnow.com.

Tandem skydiving

Adrenaline aside, the beauty of taking the jump in New Zealand is the scenic factor. Once you have recovered from that falling feeling, the view of the land below hurtling towards you at 120 kph is unforgettable. Jumps range in height from 9000-15,000 ft. The latter will give you about 40 seconds of free-fall. Jumps cost from $275 and the price increases the higher you go, but it is well worth it.

North Island: Taupo (page 118); **South Island:** Wanaka and Queenstown (page 269). See also: skydivetaupo.co.nz, skydivewanaka.com

Wildlife encounters

Thanks to its almost perfect geographical isolation over the millennia much of the wildlife in New Zealand is of the bird variety. Owing to human intervention, the mainland is not the place it once was, but there are still plenty of opportunities to see the country's incredible and remaining birdlife firsthand. Offshore island reserves such as Tiritiri Matangi Island north of Auckland (page 79) and Kapiti Island north of Wellington (page 167), protect unique and endangered species like the takahe that were wiped out from the mainland. The birds are naturally very tame allowing you to get up close. Sadly, the kiwi is fast heading for extinction on the mainland and your best chance of viewing them is in the captive environment.

DoC's Mount Bruce Wildlife Centre in the Wairarapa, the yellow-eyed penguin viewing tours and the Albatross Centre on the Otago Peninsula (page 262), the penguins at Oamaru or Moeraki, the gannets at Cape Kidnappers (page 138) or Farewell Spit (page 202) are all recommended. The city zoos are also great places to see captive native wildlife at close range.

The New Zealand coast is world famous for its rich variety of marine mammals. Pods of dolphin can regularly be seen almost anywhere on the coast, from the large, common bottlenose to the tiny and endangered Hector's dolphin. New

Zealand is also on the main whale migration routes, making it relatively easy to encounter them. Kaikoura on the South Island is one of the world's best whale-watching locations. A 2½-hour whale-watching trip costs around $140. You can also view the whales from above by fixed-wing aircraft or helicopter from $145. A two-hour dolphin-swimming experience (30 minutes in the water) will cost around $150 (spectators half price). The endangered Hector's dolphin can also be viewed around Banks Peninsula in Canterbury.

North Island: Bay of Islands (page 83), Whakatane (page 132). Tauranga (page 131); **South Island:** Marlborough Sounds (from Picton, page 190), Akaroa (page 225), Kaikoura (page 228). Seal swimming at Abel Tasman (page 196). See also: whalewatch.co.nz, whaledolphintrust.org.nz, dolphin safari.co.nz, soundsair.com, whales.co.nz.

Wine tours

New Zealand produces some of the finest wines in the world and vineyards are a big attraction. The principal wine-growing regions are in (or on) the Waitakeres, Waiheke Island, Gisborne, Hawke's Bay and the Wairarapa in the North Island and around Blenheim, Nelson and Queenstown in the South. For more details, see Eating and drinking, (page 49).
    See also: nzwine.com, classicwinetrail.co.nz.

Zorbing

Last and by no means least is zorbing. This is a most bizarre concept that could only be the creation of incredible Kiwi ingenuity. Described as a 'bi-spherical momentous experience', it involves climbing into a clear plastic bubble and rolling down a hill. Sadly, the organized venture involves a short hill that takes about 10 seconds to roll down and relieves you of about $45 – a bit of a rip-off. But what you could do with your own zorb blows the mind. Incidentally, you can also do a wet run – joined inside the bubble by a bucket of water.

Tramping in New Zealand

Even before the National Geographic proclaimed the Milford Track as 'the world's best walk', New Zealand could, without doubt, claim to be the walking (tramping or hiking) capital of the world. Not only is it one of the principal pastimes for many New Zealanders, it is also the reason many visitors come to the country. There is a vast network of routes and literally thousands of kilometres of track the length and breadth of the country, from the well-formed and trodden highway of the famed Milford Track, to the sporadic trail and markers of the lesser-known Dusky. The range of habitats is immense, from remote coastlines and island traverses to rainforests, volcanic lakes and mountain peaks, with most penetrating national parks.

Under the administration and advocacy of the Department of Conservation (DoC) the tracks are superbly managed and all advertised tracks are clearly marked, well maintained and have designated campsites and huts offering clean water, basic accommodation, cooking facilities and toilets. Add to that the wealth of detailed information available; from route descriptions and access to up-to-date weather forecasts, it is little wonder that tramping is perhaps New Zealand's biggest and most uniquely precious tourist asset.

You are advised to consult the local DoC office before embarking on any of the major tramps regardless of experience and weather conditions and, if required, fill in an intentions sheet. Always make sure you are well prepared, equipped and of the required level of fitness. Unless you are experienced, tramping on the more remote and quieter tracks alone is not advisable.

The great walks

The most famous track is, deservedly, the magnificent Milford Track, a 54-km four-day trek that combines lake and mountain scenery. Also in the Te Waipounamu World Heritage Park are the Routeburn, Kepler, Dusky, Greenstone, Hollyford and the newest, the Hump Ridge Track. But these are only a few of many options. It would be easy just to recommend the likes of the Milford, Kepler and Abel Tasman, but a word of warning: many of the tracks are very busy and are now not so much tracks as public highways. The Milford, Kepler, Heaphy and Abel Tasman are considered the worst in this respect. Of course that does not mean that they should be avoided. They are still worth doing, and no less spectacular, but if you like a bit of solitude with your tramp, consider other options or at the very least go towards the start or the end of the tramping season (Oct to Apr). In the high season you must book accommodation sometimes weeks in advance.

Hut fees vary depending between $10-45 per night on category and the services and facilities provided. The general fee range per person is as follows. Some are mere shelters with just water and toilets while the Great Walks Huts (GW) huts have bunks with mattresses, basic cooking facilities, usually a log fire plus a clean water supply and long-drop toilets. Campsites associated with huts cost $15. An annual Hut Pass can be purchased for

$90. All Great Walk Huts must be pre-booked, sometimes weeks in advance, and all huts (except those run by guided walk companies) operate on a first-come-first-served basis. DoC campsites come under two categories; 'serviced', which cost $8-12 and 'standard' which cost $3-10. Camping is free for children under five. For detailed information about all the major tramping tracks and Great Walks, accommodation bookings and other info, contact the local DoC field centre or visit doc.govt.nz.

Day walks

The walking opportunities are endless and New Zealand is a walker's paradise. Most i-SITES or regional DoC offices compile lists of the most notable long and short walks in each region. There is everything from coastal or bush walks to historical trails.

Recommended one-day walks include the famed Tongariro Crossing (best accessed from Taupo or Turangi, (page 122); the Tarawera Falls (Rotorua); Whariki Beach near Farewell Spit (Golden Bay) (page 200) and the Rob Roy Glacier walk (Wanaka) (page 271). Walking boots are recommended on these and all day walks.

New Zealand's best photo locations

New Zealand is one of the most photogenic places in the world. Just walk in to any souvenir shop and the small forests of postcard racks and shelves laden with pictorials are testament to the country's awesome natural beauty.

Of course, a few years ago you may have been happy to settle for the odd book or postcard sent home with the old 'wish you were here' scrawled on the back. But now, with the digital revolution well and truly upon us, you are no doubt suitably armed and ready for action.

You may be the proud owner of a new digital compact or the latest DSLR. Regardless of your equipment or whether you're a pro, a keen amateur or a happy snapper, on your travels around New Zealand all you'll really want is to secure some great images and most importantly have a good idea of where to do so?

For most professionals and keen amateurs the pursuit of good imagery is an obsession. Indeed, it has to be. Taking great images is an art and always will be. But as already hinted, this is not about the profession, making money, the photographic revolution, or the obsession. It's not about in-depth techniques and not about whether your spiffy camera has an adjunct drinks cabinet (with ice). It's about getting to the right places and seeing New Zealand better. Making a few good images from precious moments in time and recording your memories with what you have and the most vital tool of all – your eyes.

So here is how we can hopefully do that. Within each of the six regions in the Around New Zealand section you will find a section that describes some of the best places to secure good images and some image examples. It may be cityscape, an event, a specific subject or some fine detail, but, regardless, it will be as creative and as Kiwi as possible.

Each location will have a set of symbols (see Guide to symbols box, opposite) which will provide you with specific detail such as 'accessibility' or the 'best time of day'. You can then decide whether to pursue the image or not, or indeed how long to spend doing so.

Tip…

For 20 top tips for better photography and to view a comprehensive list of New Zealand's best photo locations refer to the author's website, darrochdonald.com.

Guide to symbols

Type of subject
▲ Landscape
◍ Cityscape
☺ Cultural
✸ Event
◕ Wildlife
◔ Activity

Accessibility
⌇ Easy
! Moderate
∅ Hard

Degree of technical difficulty
📷 Easy
📷 Moderate
📷 Hard

Weather dependency
☀ Clear (requires at least partial blue skies)
◔ Showers
⌂ Indoors

Best time of day
☽ Dawn
☾ Dusk
✸ Night
◉ Time

❶ Detail from paua shell casing.
❷ A canoeist at Kaituna River, Rotorua.
❸ Two yellow-eyed penguins courting, Otago Peninsula.
❹ Maori carving, Rotorua.

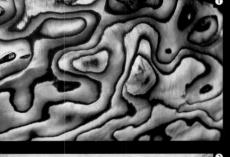

Contents

Auckland, Northland & Coromandel Peninsula

View of Rangitoto Island from Howick.

Introduction

Brush aside the jet lag and any preconceptions surrounding New Zealand and the inevitable expectations of mountain ranges, and Auckland will prove to be nothing other than a pleasant, if transitory, surprise. Here, from the top of the great hypodermic Sky Tower, you can marvel at how a metropolis almost the size of LA can really be so beautiful.

Eager to head for the hills and without delay, most polish the windscreen of the spiffy rental motor home and join the great Maui or Britz migrations south. But those with more time head north instead. It's a wise move. It might seem a bit disappointing that the region is so unimaginatively labelled Northland rather than something exotic like Whakaupaupawhawha, but, just you wait. Northland is dubbed the cradle of the nation and up there you will experience some of the best examples of Maoridom and get a true taste of just how beautiful New Zealand is. But just a taste, mind you.

Head south and it is rude not to go via the Coromandel. In the holiday season it is considered Auckland's principal stress buster. Here, beautiful coastal scenery gels with that laid-back atmosphere for which the country is famous and, for many, the peninsula is just the second chapter of a book you just can't put down.

What to see in...

...a long weekend
With a single day in Auckland don't miss the view from the Sky Tower. Also take a ferry over to Devonport and walk around North Head, or alternatively try a sailing trip on board a former Americas Cup yacht. Head south to the Coromandel Peninsula and check out Cathedral Cove near Hahei and the Driving Creek Railway.

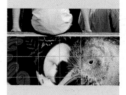

...a week
After a day or two in Auckland, head up to Northland and Paihia or Russell. Go on an island cruise and don't miss the Waitangi Reserve. The trip to Cape Reinga makes a fine day out from Paihia. Divers should visit Poor Knights Islands off Tutukaka.

Include a trip to the Waitakeres and west coast beaches of Bethells or Kare Kare, or to an offshore island from the city centre. If you love wine go to Waiheke, for wildlife try Tiri Tiri Matangi and for walks and views, the volcanic cone of Rangitoto.

Auckland's iconic Sky Tower is often lit at night.

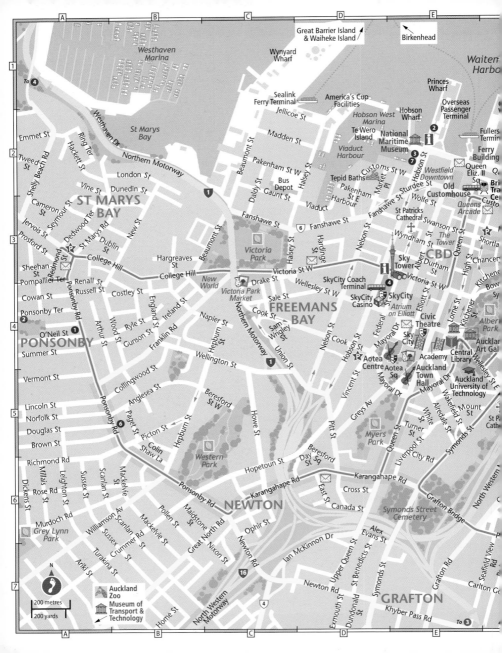

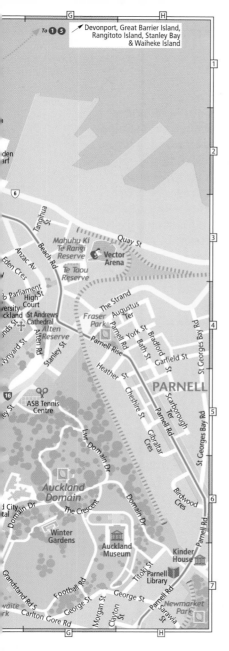

To ① ⑤ ↗ Devonport, Great Barrier Island,
Rangitoto Island, Stanley Bay
& Waiheke Island

Auckland listings

① Sleeping

1 **Esplanade Hotel** *1 Victoria Rd, Devonport* **G1**
2 **Great Ponsonby B&B** *30 Pomsonby Terr, Ponsonby* **A4**
3 **Manukau Top Ten Holiday Park**
   902 Great South Rd, Manukau City **E7**
4 **North Shore Motels and Top Ten Holiday Park**
   52 Northcote Rd, Takapuna **A1**

① Eating & drinking

1 **Dizengoff** *256 Ponsonby Rd, Ponsonby* **A4**
2 **Euro Shed** *22, Princes Wharf, Quay St* **E2**
3 **Kermadec** *1st floor, Viaduct Quay Building,*
   corner of Lower Hobson St and Quay St **E2**
4 **Orbit Restaurant** *Sky Tower, corner of Victoria St and*
   Federal St **D/E3**
5 **The Patriot British Pub** *14 Victoria Rd, Devonport* **G1**
6 **Ponsonby Fresh Fish and Chip Co** *127 Ponsonby Rd,*
   Ponsonby **B5**
7 **Soul Bar and Restaurant** *Viaduct Harbour* **E2**

Auckland

With a population of one and a quarter million, Auckland is Polynesia's largest city and by far the biggest in New Zealand. Thanks to its spacious suburban sprawl, Auckland covers more than 500 sq km – twice that of London and close to that of Los Angeles – but because the city is built on an isthmus and constantly fragmented by coastline, you are never far from water. As a result it thankfully lacks that overwhelming sense of humanity over nature. The sea pervades almost every aspect of Auckland life, from recreation to cuisine. Aucklanders own more recreational boats per capita than any other city in the world, earning it the affectionate nicknames of 'City of Sails'. Most sailing is done in Auckland's backyard: the beautiful aquatic playground and island-studded waters of the Hauraki Gulf is one of the most beautiful sailing venues in the world.

For the vast majority of visitors, Auckland will be their arrival point and their first introduction to the country. Many will treat it only as a gateway to better things, but they may be pleasantly surprised by what it has to offer. As well as sailing, you can go fishing, swimming or surfing; all within minutes of the city centre and, in some places, have the beach to yourself. The city also boasts some impressive man-made attractions such as the stunning 360° views from the hypodermic Sky Tower, and its bustling city centre streets and trendy suburbs are home to a thousand quality restaurants.

Sky Tower, Sky City & the Casino

Corner of Victoria and Federal streets,
T0800-759 2489, skycityauckland.co.nz.
Observation levels open Sun-Thu 0830-2230,
Fri-Sat 0830-2330, $28, child $11. Restaurant
open lunch 1000-1500, dinner from 1730,
weekend brunch 1000-1500, T09-363 6000.
SkyJump/SkyWalk, T09-368 1835, skyjump.co.nz.
Map: Auckland D3, p66.

It took almost three years for the Auckland skyline
to sprout its great 328-m hypodermic, opening in
1997 to a hail of publicity and – back then – a rather
sceptical public. But Aucklanders have grown to
love their Sky Tower – perhaps because it acts like a
beacon and can be seen from miles around. It is
indeed an awesome sight and, unless you hate
heights, you just have to go up it. As you might
expect it has spacious viewing decks and a
revolving restaurant from which you can enjoy the
360° views. In recent years, perhaps inevitably, it
has also become the focus for some typical Kiwi,
lunatic activities including a 192-m controlled
bungee known as the 'SkyJump', and the 'SkyWalk'
which involves a leisurely stroll round the pergola,
with a wee lean over the edge – like you do! (See
page 104).

The tower's rather nondescript 'grow-bag' is
called Sky City and claims to be Auckland's largest
multi-faceted entertainment and leisure
destination. The main casino provides all kinds of
gambling and gaming options, restaurants, bars
and live entertainment 24 hours a day and has no
doubt seen the ruin of many and the rapture of
few. Even if you are not a gambler it is well worth a
look. Less intimidating is the Sky City Theatre, a
700-seat, state-of-the-art entertainment venue,
staging national and international events and
productions. As well as the tower's Orbit restaurant
there are five other eateries offering everything
from Pacific Rim to Chinese, traditional buffet or
café-style options.

Tip...

Almost all your mapping needs can be met at
The Auckland Map Centre, National Bank Building,
209 Queen St, T09-309 7725, and for accommodation
booklets and information go to the AA, 99 Albert St,
T09-966 8919, aa.co.nz.

Sky Tower statistics

The Sky Tower was opened in 1997 and took two
years and eight months to build. At 328 m it is
the tallest man-made structure in the southern
hemisphere. The tower's shaft measures 12 m in
diameter and its foundations reach 15 m into the
earth. It houses the highest weather station, post
box and restaurant in the southern hemisphere.
The restaurant completes a 360° revolution every
60 seconds (though six would be far more fun). It is
designed to withstand a 8.0 earthquake and 200 kph
winds. Such winds would only create a 1-m sway of
the entire structure. There are 1257 steps to the Sky
Deck. The fastest recorded ascent during the annual
'Sky Tower Vertical Challenge' is five minutes, 57
seconds. In 1998, AJ Hackett made a 192-m bungee
jump from the main observation deck, the highest
jump ever attempted from a ground structure.

The 360° views from the Observation Deck of the Sky Tower.

Essentials

➊ Getting around Airport For airport information refer to aucklandairport.co.nz (T0800-247767). Auckland airport is 21 km southwest of the CBD. Transport to and from the airport is straightforward. The **Airbus**, T0508-247287, airbus. co.nz, is a cheap option leaving the airport every 20-30 minutes from 0600-2200 (from the city 0435- 2250), $15, child $6 one-way. Taxis wait outside the terminal and charge about $40 to the centre. The **Super Shuttle**, T0800-748885, supershuttle.co.nz, provides a door-to-door service from $30 one-way. There are no train services.

Bus & train station Train services and most central and suburban buses stop at the Britomart Transport Centre (BBT), centrally located between Customs and Quay streets near the waterfront (bottom of Queen St). Information can be obtained from the terminal itself, all major tourist information offices and by contacting **MAXX**, T09-3666400, T0800-103080, maxx.co.nz. This website also offers a convenient journey planner. There are several tourist-oriented passes, a one-day 'Discovery Pass' allowing unlimited travel on bus, ferry and train for $13, or a three-day 'Rover Pass' for $25 that includes the North Shore ferries. The excellent hop-on hop-off Auckland City Loop 'Link' bus (lime green) is an ideal way to get about the city centre and charges a flat fare of $1.60 for each journey. The national bus terminal is at the **Sky City Travel Centre**, 102 Hobson St, Auckland, CBD (below the Sky Tower), T09-583 5780, intercity.co.nz. Office hours (for sales) daily 0700-1950.

Ferry Almost all ferries depart from the historic Ferry Building on the waterfront, at Quay St. A limited commuter service to some waterside suburbs has been developed, but the vast majority of ferry traffic is tourist-based and operated by **Fullers**, T09-367 9111, fullers.co.nz. There are many excellent island or harbour locations, trips and tours to choose from.

Taxi Typical rates are around $2.75 base charge and then about $2 per kilometre. Taxis are widely available and can be flagged down, ordered by phone or picked up at numerous city centre ranks. Companies include **Auckland Co-Op**, T09-300 3000, cooptaxi.co.nz and **Alert Taxis**, T09-309 2000, alerttaxis.co.nz.

➕ Hospital Auckland Hospital, Park Rd, Grafton, T09-3670000.

↻ Post office Main post office and post restante, 24 Wellesley St, T09-379 6710, Mon-Fri 0800-1700. Postcode 1010. Additional branch at 23 Customs St, T09-302 1059, Mon-Fri 0830-1700, Sat 1000-1400.

➊ Tourist information There are visitor information centres (i-SITES) at both airport terminals. There are two main i-SITES in the CBD: Atrium, Sky City, corner Victoria and Federal streets, T09-367 6009, T0800-AUCKLAND, aucklandnz. com, daily 0800-2000; and the quieter Viaduct Harbour, next to the Maritime Museum, corner Quay and Hobson streets, T09-367 6009, Nov-Apr daily 0800-1700, May-Oct 0900-1730.

Waterfront

Map: Auckland, p66.

Radiating from the historic Ferry Building at the northern end of Queen Street, the waterfront is the place where the city of concrete becomes the City of Sails and where the locals would say it takes on its proper and distinct character. The waterfront has always been a focus of major activity. In the early years it was the point where exhausted immigrants first disembarked to begin a new life in a new land. Later, the immigrant ships gave way to the fleets of log-laden scows bringing kauri to the timber mills. Today, recreation has taken over, as modern ferries come and go, and towards the bridge, lines of expensive yachts rock together at the Westhaven Marina – the largest in the southern hemisphere.

The most rapid development is centered around the Viaduct Basin, which was formerly the hallowed home of the America's Cup Village. When New Zealand took the great yachting cup from the USA's tight grasp in 1995 it became an aquatic stadium of profound celebration.

New Zealand National Maritime Museum (Te Huiteananui-a-Tangaroa)

Corner of Quay and Hobson streets, Waterfront, T0800-725897, T09-373 0800, nzmaritime.org
Daily 0900-1700; $16, child $8. Guided tours 1030 and 1300. 'Ted Ashby Heritage Cruise' (1½ hrs) in summer Wed-Sun: $26, child $13, (includes museum entry).
Map: Auckland D2, p66.

Based on the waterfront it depicts a very important aspect of New Zealand's history and the maritime flavour of the City of Sails. Laid out chronologically, you begin with early Maori and Polynesian exploration and arrival before moving through to European maritime history, including immigration. Here, in the replicated living quarters of an early immigrant ship, complete with moving floor and appropriate creaking noises, you cannot help sympathizing deeply with the brave souls who made the journey. It is certainly a long way from sitting back in an Airbus 380 with a gin and tonic, iTunes and the latest Hollywood movie.

Moving on, you emerge into the galleries of New Zealand's proud yachting history, including the stories of New Zealand's participation and triumphs in the Louis Vuitton Cup, the Whitbread Round the World Yacht Race and, of course, the much-lauded Americas Cup. Much of this story is the personal résumé of the late Sir Peter Blake, New Zealand's most famous sailing son who was so tragically murdered in the Amazon in 2002. The centerpiece for the exhibition is the 1995 America's Cup-winning boat NZL32 – Black Magic. The museum also houses a café and shop with nautical gifts and memorabilia.

A number of cruises are also available from the museum, including the popular Ted Ashby Heritage Cruise, aboard the 57-ft traditionally built scow *Ted Ashby* and weekend excursions aboard the unfortunately named but nonetheless charming *SS Puke*. Note you can also experience a cruise on board former Americas Cup yachts with SailNZ (see page 105).

The Domain & Auckland Museum (Te Papa Whakahiku)

T09-3067067, aucklandmuseum.com.
Daily 1000-1700, $5 donation. Maori performance Jan-Mar 1100, 1200, 1330, 1430; Apr-Dec 1100, 1200, 1330; $25, child $12.50 (includes entry). Guided tours daily 1030, $10, child $5. Most city tour buses stop at the museum, as does the Link bus from the CBD. Map: Auckland H6, p67.

The **Domain** is one of Auckland's less obvious volcanic cones and New Zealand's oldest park. Originally another enclave and early Maori pa, it was formally put aside as a reserve by Governor Hobson in 1840. Within its spacious grounds are a number of historic and cultural features including the Auckland Museum.

An impressive edifice, the **Auckland Museum** houses some wonderful treasures, displayed with flair and imagination. Its most important collection is that of Maori taonga (treasures) and Pacific artifacts which, combined, is the largest such collection in the world. Other special attractions include an award-winning children's discovery centre, social and settlement history sections, natural history galleries, and 'Scars on the Heart', the story of New Zealanders at war, from the Maori Land Wars in the late 1800s to the campaigns in Gallipoli and Crete in the two world wars of the 20th century. The museum also houses a major national War Memorial.

If you are short of time make sure you see the Maori Court, a fascinating collection of pieces from woven baskets to lethal hand weapons carved from bone or greenstone, all centred round the huge 25-m Te Toki a Tipiri waka (war canoe) and a beautifully carved hotunui (meeting house). A commercial yet entertaining Maori concert is held three to four times daily and guided tours are available. There is a museum café is on the ground floor and a well-stocked museum shop.

Auckland Art Gallery (Toi-o-Tamaki)

Corner of Wellesley and Lorne streets, T09-3791 349, aucklandartgallery.co.nz.
Daily 1000-1700, free, $7 for temporary exhibitions; guided tours at 1400. Both galleries are in close proximity and within easy walking distance from Queen St. The Link bus stops right outside the gallery every 10-20 mins. Map: Auckland E4, p66.

The Auckland Art Gallery is essentially two buildings: one in Kitchener Street and the other on the corner of Wellesley Street and Lorne Street in

Auckland, the City of Sails.

and Lorne streets) hosts all current display exhibitions from the permanent collections. These include some of the better-known international masters, particularly 17th-century pieces, but from a national perspective it is the works by Charles Goldie and Gottfried Lindauer that are of particular interest. Goldie and Lindauer were early European settlers who specialized in oil landscapes and portraits of Maori elders in the 18th and 19th centuries. The works of Goldie are impressive to say the least, with their almost Pre-Raphaelite detail bringing the portraits to life, particularly the detail of the moko (Maori facial tattoos).

Also look out for works by Colin McCahon one of the nation's more contemporary and hugely respected New Zealand artists. **Reuben Cafe** (weekdays 0700-1600, Sat/Sun 0900-1530) is situated next to the New Gallery, with indoor and outdoor seating. Licensed.

City North

Devonport & North Head

The waterfront suburb is best accessed by ferry from Quay St, T09-367 9111, fullers.co.nz. Mon-Thu every 30 mins 0615-2030, then hourly until 2300, Fri-Sun every 30 mins 0610-0030, last sailing 0100; $10 return, child $5. The Devonport i-SITE visitor centre, 3 Victoria St, T09-446 0677, northshorenz.com, daily 0800-1700, can provide information on historic sights, the best short walks and places to stay.

Devonport's greatest asset is the fact that it is so near yet so far from the city centre, creating a distinct village feel. A 10-minute ferry ride from the city centre brings you immediately to the heart of this historic and picturesque little suburb. Victorian villas, craft shops, pavement cafés and pleasant short walks all lie in wait, dominated by its two extinct volcanoes, Mount Victoria and North Head, both of which offer great views. For a longer stay try one of its many quaint bed and breakfast hideaways or the Esplanade Hotel right on the waterfront.

the city centre. They combine to form the largest and most comprehensive collection of art in the country. The first building the Main Gallery (Kitchener Street) is over 100 years old and is currently undergoing major reconstruction. In the meantime the New Gallery (corner of Wellesley

If time is short your best bet is to take the short walk to North Head, which guards the entrance to Waitamata harbour. Follow the shore east along the pohutukawa-lined King Edward Parade from where you can then climb up and all around North Head and enjoy the commanding views back across the city and the Hauraki Gulf. The warren of underground tunnels and bunkers built amidst the hysteria of various potential invasions during both world wars provide added interest. Cheltenham Beach on the northern side is also a popular swimming and sunbathing spot in summer and one that gives the most spectacular and almost surreal view of the volcanic island of Rangitoto. On your return to the village, if you are feeling energetic, try to take in more great views from the summit of Mount Victoria.

City East

Mission Bay & Kelly Tarlton's Antarctic Encounter & Underwater World

23 Tamaki Drive, T09-531 5065, kellytarltons.co.nz. Daily 0900-1800, $29, child $15. Kelly Tarlton's operates a free shuttle between Sky City Atrium and Kelly Tarlton's daily between 0900-1700. Or, it is a scenic 6 km walk along the waterfront and Tamaki Drive.

The first reaction to this attraction is 'Err, so where is it?' The development is actually housed within what used to be Auckland City's sewage holding tanks beneath the car park and Tamaki Drive. It is a fascinating concept, and typical of the imagination, ingenuity and determination of New Zealand's most famous and best-loved diver, treasure hunter and undersea explorer, Kelly Tarlton, the founder and driving force behind the project. Sadly Kelly died just seven months after it opened.

The attraction is divided into three main parts: the Antarctic Encounter; Penguin Encounter; and Underwater World, all of which are pretty self-explanatory, entertaining and informative.

The highlight for many of course are the huge king penguins in their carefully maintained natural conditions. Such is the standard of the facility and the care of the birds that they breed happily and if you are lucky you will see, at close range, the huge and hilarious down-covered chicks.

Tamaki Drive

If you have your own vehicle it is worth continuing east along Tamaki Drive to Mission Bay and St Heliers. On a sunny afternoon, especially at the weekend, there is almost no better place to be in central Auckland than somewhere along Tamaki Drive. All along its 9 km length it is both a buzz of activity and a haven of relaxation. Bike and rollerblade hire is readily available along the route for $8-12 per hour.

Parnell & Newmarket

Map: Auckland H4-7, p67.

Trendy Parnell, 2 km east of the city centre, was once a rather run-down suburb, but in recent years it has undergone a dramatic transformation, which has seen it almost overtake Devonport and Ponsonby in the popularity and fashion stakes. It has the same 'village within a city' feel as Devonport, with tiny brick-paved lanes and boutique-style outlets, and boasts some of Auckland's finest galleries, shops and restaurants.

At the top of Parnell Rise is the **Auckland Cathedral of the Holy Trinity** (T09-303 9500, holy-trinity.org.nz, Mon-Fri 1000-1600, Sat and Sun 1300-1700, free), whose angular structure is aesthetically interesting but nothing compared to the beautiful stained-glass windows and 29-ton organ within. Guided tours and an audio-visual display are both available.

South of the cathedral, Parnell merges into the more modern commercial centre and suburb of Newmarket, which is best known for its shops, restaurants, cafés and entertainment venues.

Around the region

Auckland Zoo

Motions Rd, Western Springs, T09-360 3819, aucklandzoo.co.nz.
Daily 0930-1730, $18, child $9, 5 mins' drive from the centre; from the Great Western Motorway take the Western Springs off ramp and follow signs, free car parking. Or take Explorer Bus or Bus 045 from the city centre.

Set in pleasant parkland next to Western Springs and 6 km west of the city centre is New Zealand's premier wild animal collection. It has kept pace with the more conservation-minded function of zoos and is worth a visit. The zoo claims to be leading the way in the breeding of native species including kiwi and tuatara – both of which are on display. All the old favourites are also there – elephants (sometimes taken on walkabout around the zoo), giraffes, hippos, tigers and orangutans. Auckland Zoo has gradually developed some imaginative themed exhibits over the years, including the Newstalk ZB Rainforest where you feel more captive than the obscenely laid-back spider monkeys; Pridelands, the spacious home of the giraffe, lion and zebra with its adjoining Hippo River and Sealion Shores, a new state-of-the-art pinniped exhibit. KidZone provides the usual touchy-feelies with rabbits and other assorted furry friends. Several tours are also offered including the increasingly popular behind-the-scenes animal encounters, from $150, T09-360 4700.

Mount Eden

At 196 m, Mount Eden is the closest dormant volcano to the city centre providing great city views. The best time to come here is at dawn, especially on misty winter mornings, when it can be a photographer's delight, and you can avoid the coach-loads of visitors. At the southern base of the mount, **Eden Gardens** (24 Omana Av, T09-

Observation point, Mount Eden.

6388395, edengarden.co.nz, daily 0900-1630, $6, child free, concessions available, café 1000-1600), is a great place for lovers of all things green that grow. Mount Eden is a long walk from the city centre, and given the climb you might be better off taking Bus 274 or 275 from the BBT in the CBD.

Cornwall Park and One Tree Hill

Cornwall Park visitor centre, T09-630 8485, cornwallpark.co.nz.
Open 1000-1600, free. Café and free trail leaflet.

Just to the south of Mount Eden is Cornwall Park, famous not only for its crowning glory, the monument and the tree, but also the well preserved remains of a Maori pa on and around the summit. Kiwi Tamaki, the great chief of the Nga Marama, lived here during the mid-18th century with his thousands of whanau (family) and followers, attracted by the rich pickings of the region's coast and its fertile soils. His claim to the region ended after being routed by sub-tribes from the north and his people being decimated by a smallpox epidemic introduced by the Europeans. It was the Scot, Logan Campbell, the most powerful and well known of the new capital's residents, who eventually took ownership. Shortly before his arrival, a single Totara tree stood proudly on the summit. This had already given rise to the hill's Maori name, Te-Totara-a-Ahuameaning 'Hill of the single Totara'. Early settlers rudely cut down this tree in 1852 and it was Campbell who planted several trees in its place, including the lonesome pine you could see from miles around, until its demise in 2001.

At the base of the hill is a visitor centre in **Huia Lodge**, Campbell's original gatekeeper's house. It houses some interesting displays. Across the road is the simple and faithfully restored **Acacia Cottage** in which Campbell himself lived, though the building itself originally stood in the city centre and was relocated here in the 1920s.

One Tree Hill (before the removal of the pine).

Also within the park boundary at its southern end is the **Auckland Observatory** (Manakau Rd, T09-6241246, stardome.org.nz, times and events vary; standard viewing session with show $16, child $8). This is the official home of Auckland's stargazers, and also contains the Stardome Planetarium, a cosmic multimedia experience played out on the ceiling for the general public. Outdoor telescope viewing sessions and special events are also held, depending on what the weather and the heavens are up to. You can even adopt a star an interesting concept that will probably have you trying to find it again, for the rest of your life.

Around Auckland

Though you are doubtless like a sheepdog on a lead, just dying to be let off on your New Zealand adventure proper, bear in mind the Auckland region has much to offer beyond the suburbs and still within view of its mighty Sky Tower. Take a day or two to explore the myriad islands or rugged West Coast beaches and it will be time well spent. Your sense of the city will almost certainly change. Here you begin to realize how New Zealand's remarkable natural assets pervade everything, even a city of over one million people.

Waitakere Ranges at dawn.

Waitakere City

West Auckland, or **Waitakere City**, is made up of a number of diverse suburbs of little note the the tourist. At the fringe of the city is the pleasant little village suburb of **Titirangi**, which serves 'the gateway to the **Waitakeres**. The 'Waitaks', as they are affectionately known, are one of the region's biggest and most attractive regional parks, offering a 200-km network of walking tracks, many of which hide such scenic delights as large kauri trees, waterfalls and large dams. Before embarking on any outdoor activities in the area, visit the **Arataki Information Centre** on the hill at the southern end of Scenic Drive (6 km from Titirangi, T09-817 0089, T09-817 0077, arc.govt.nz, daily 0900-1700, 1600 in winter). Dominating its façade is an impressive Maori pou (carving), which lost its manhood a few years ago (though another was duly carved, and the glint in his little paua shell eye restored). Inside there are interpretative displays and all the information you will need about the area and its natural history.

Hellaby House

515 Scenic Drive, gardens.
Mon-Sat 1300-1600, Sun 1100-1700, free.

If you are limited for time and do not intend to visit the west coast beaches you should at least take the 28-km Scenic Drive that winds its way along the eastern fringe of the Waitakeres. It offers views across the city both by day and by night, with one of the best vantage points being from the garden of Hellaby House, just below the TV masts.

Tip...

Self-contained campervans are able to stay up to two nights in the Arataki visitor centre car park.

Tip...

If you do not have your own transport or want a rest from driving, try a tour out west with the Maori-owned and operated Potiki Adventures, T09-8455932, potikiadventures.co.nz.

Wineries

West Auckland is also one of the lesser-known wine-producing areas of the country, containing nearly 20 wineries with such famous names as Corbans, Coopers Creek and Nobilo. The northern areas of Waitakere City host most of these, especially in the Kumeu area. Most wineries offer tastings. Copies of the official Wine Trail and Wineries of Auckland leaflets can be secured at the main city i-SITES.

West Coast beaches

Wineries and Waitaks aside, what really draws people west are the wild west coast beaches at Whatipu, Kare Kare, Piha, Bethells and Muriwai. The most popular and accessible of these is the coastal enclave of Piha, with its excellent (yet dangerous) surf breaks and fishing spots. Muriwai Beach (the

The rugged west coast (Bethells) beaches.

most northerly) also hosts a breeding colony of gannets viewable from an observation deck.

But if you have time and fancy real solace, then head south to Whatipu, or north to Bethells, where a stroll along the beach will give you – perhaps for the first time – a sense of what New Zealand is all about. Welcome, at last to the nature made New Zealand, as opposed to the man-made. From here on it just gets better and better!

Hauraki Gulf Islands

For general information contact the Auckland (i-SITE) visitor centre, 137 Quay St, Princes Wharf, Downtown, T09-3796476.

The Hauraki Gulf is famed for its picturesque islands, which range in size from the 179-ha Motuihe to the 93-sq-km Waiheke. There is

significant contrast in their use and character as well as their geography.

There is no doubt that given a few days in Auckland you should visit at least one island. Which one really comes down to your interests beyond just pure aesthetics as all offer great views and beaches. If you are a wine lover then it would be rude not to visit Waiheke as it is home to some of the finest labels in the country including Goldwater Estate and Stonyridge. For walking, views and geological interest, let alone sheer convenience, head for Rangitoto. For wildlife there is no doubt Tiritiri Matangi offers a superb day out, while for a true island adventure take a few days to explore the wilds of Great Barrier.

Waiheke

Contact Fullers Ferries, Ferry Building, Quay St, T09-367 9111, fullers.co.nz. Fares from $32. For tourist information contact the Waiheke i-SITE visitor centre, 2 Korora Rd, in front of the Artworks Complex, Oneroa, T09-372 1234, Mon-Sun 0900-1700, waihekenz.com, tourismwaiheke.co.nz and gotowaiheke.co.nz. Close to the city, Waiheke is by far the most populated, so much so that it is often labeled 'just another suburb' of Auckland. Famed for its vineyards and blessed with a number of fine beaches, it has for decades been a favourite and convenient escape from the city for both residents and visitors.

Rangitoto

Contact Fullers Ferries, Ferry Building, Quay St, T09-367 9111, fullers.co.nz. Fares from $55.

Perhaps most obvious among the island family is Rangitoto with its atypical volcanic cone that dominates the horizon and although now fully clad in bush reveals some fascinating lava flows upon closer inspection via a network of walking tracks.

Takahe roam free on Tiritiri Matangi Island.

Great Barrier

Contact Fullers Ferries, Ferry Building, Quay St, T09-367 9111, fullers.co.nz. Fares from $130. Sealink (Subritzky Shipping), T0800-732546, T09-300 5900, sealink.co.nz, offer a vehicle (and passenger) service from 45 Jellicoe St, Freemans Bay, Auckland, but it is expensive. Note you can hire vehicles or take organized tours on the island. By air contact Great Barrier Airlines, Auckland Domestic Terminal (and at the airfield on the Barrier at Claris), T09-275 9120, T0800-900600, greatbarrierairlines.co.nz. From $109 one-way. Fly/cruise packages are also available, from $169. For tourist information the i-SITE Visitor Centre is in the post shop in Claris, T09-429 0033, T09-367 6009, greatbarrier.co.nz, daily 0900-1700. Also useful is greatbarrierisland.co.nz.

The second largest island in the group, Great Barrier, is 90 km from the city, and offers a true island escape and some superb scenery, walks and beaches.

Tiritiri Matangi

Contact 360-Discovery, T0800-3603472, T09-307 8005, 360discovery.co.nz. Runs a service from Auckland from Pier 3 (next to the Ferry Building) Wed to Sun at 0900, $66, child $29; or the same ferry from Z Pier, Gulf Harbour on the Whangaparaoa Peninsula, 45 mins later, $39, child $19.50. Trips return by 1600. For tourist information refer to tiritirimatangi.org.nz.

Two other islands in the Hauraki are the world-renowned wildlife reserves of Tiritiri Matangi near the Whangaparaoa Peninsula on the city's northern fringe, and the mountainous Little Barrier, which can be seen on a clear day to the north. Tiri is the most accessible and offers visitors an insight into what New Zealand used to be like, with abundant bird life and such enchanting avian odysseys as the takahe and spotted kiwi. Little Barrier is home to a few precious and well-looked-after kakapo – a large flightless parrot that with less than 100 remaining is one of the rarest birds in the world.

Northland

Northland is often called the 'birthplace of the nation' as it was here that the first Maori set foot in New Zealand, about AD 800, followed by the first European settlers over 800 years later. It was also here, in the Bay of Islands in 1840, that the Treaty of Waitangi was signed – the document that launched the relationship between two deeply contrasting peoples. This relationship is reflected in the calms and the storms of unsettled ocean currents that unite uneasily at New Zealand's northernmost point, Cape Reinga. Elsewhere, lost in time within the Waipoua Forest, making all that human history seem like yesterday, stands one of the few remaining ancient kauri trees: the centuries-old Tane Mahuta.

All in all, for the modern-day visitor, Northland must feature as one of the most aesthetically and historically interesting regions to visit in New Zealand and although psychologically, given that there is such a pull to the south, it may seem heading to Northland is the wrong thing to do, if time allows you will certainly congratulate yourself on the decision to go and on your sense of non-conformity.

Maori Po, Waitangi.

Warkworth & the Kowhai Coast

Although not geographically within Northland, Warkworth is for most a starting point and a gateway to the region. Most travellers, in their haste to reach the Bay of Islands, miss it out altogether, while others take the slower and more scenic route north, along the Kowhai Coast, via the vineyards of Matakana, then on to the scenic coastal settlements of Leigh, Mangawhai and Waipu. Whatever your intention, if you have time Warkworth and the pleasant coastal bays, peninsulas and islands to its east are certainly worthy of a stop.

About 4 km north of Warkworth is **Sheepworld** (T09-425 7444, sheepworldfarm.co.nz, daily 0900-1700, shows at 1100 and 1400, $12, with show $22, child $7/8) and if the foot falls heavy on the accelerator at the very prospect of such a place, then just hold off. It is actually quite entertaining and worthy of the stop. Kids are allowed to feed the lambs and you can get involved in some shearing. There is also a café – 'The Black Sheep' – well I never!

The countryside around Matakana, 8 km north of Warkworth on the main Warkworth to Leigh Road is increasingly famous for its vineyards. The i-SITE visitor centre in Warkworth can provide full wine trail details.

Further east other areas worth investigating are the **Tawharanui** (pronounced 'Ta-fara-nui') Coastal Park and the **Goat Island Marine Reserve** near Leigh. Tawharanui is quieter than most other parks and offers great beaches, walks and scenery, while at Goat Island you can view the assorted and colourful sea life by glass-bottom boat, T09-422 6334, glassbottomboat.co.nz.

Essentials

❶ **Getting there** Warkworth is 68 km north of Auckland, Whangarei 162 km and Paihia 233 km on SH1. Regional buses serve all the main centres with the principal operator being **Intercity** (Northliner), T09-583 5780, intercity.co.nz. There is no rail service.

❶ **Tourist information** Bay of Islands i-SITE visitor centre, The Wharf, Marsden Rd, Paihia, T09-4027345, T0800-363463, visitnorthland.co.nz.
Whangarei i-SITE visitor centre, Tarewa Park, 92 Otaika Rd, Whangarei, T09-438 1079, whangareinz.org.nz.
Warkworth i-SITE visitor centre, 1 Baxter St, Warkworth, T09-425 9081, warkworthnz.com.

Waipu

Labelled by many a kiwi kid as 'Whynot', poor Waipu does suffer a bit from its name. But what does Waipu really mean? It is Maori, of course: wai (water) and pu (song).

Waipu was founded in 1853 by a party of 120 Scottish settlers who were part of a group of 400 that originally left their homelands under the resolute leadership of the Reverend Norman McLeod. They did so in desperation during the terrible Highland Clearances, which resulted in mass migrations in the early 1800s. The small community is very proud of its Scottish heritage and no visit to Waipu would be complete without a look inside the **Waipu Museum and Heritage Centre** (T09-432 0746, waipumuseum.com, 0930-1630, $8, child $6). The museum walls are decked with photographs, and faces of early immigrants look down on cases full of personal effects from spectacles to spinning wheels. Logbooks listing the immigrant arrivals and the ships on which they arrived are being continuously updated and it really is a fascinating place.

Every New Year's Day since 1871 the Waipu Highland Games – the largest and longest-running in the southern hemisphere – gets into full swing with highland dancers, pipe bands and of course, kilted caber-tossers.

Around the region

Typical Northland coastline.

Whangarei

Given the obvious allure of the Bay of Islands to the north, with its promise of stunning scenery and a whole host of activities, few visitors pay much attention to Northland's largest town. However, if you do choose to linger here a while, you will find that it has a lot to offer.

Town Basin is an award-winning development that hosts a number of museums and galleries including the Clapham's Clock Museum (T09-438 3993, claphamsclocks.com, daily 0900-1700, $8, child $4) home to the biggest collection of timepieces in the southern hemisphere.

In the suburb of Maunu, 6 km west of town (SH14) is the Whangarei Museum, Clarke Homestead and Kiwi House (T09-438 9630, whangareimuseum.co.nz, daily 1000-1600, $10, $5 all sites). It is an indoor/outdoor complex with a colonial farming block and homestead and a modern building housing a number of taonga or Maori treasures, including a musket that belonged to the great northern warrior Hone Heke. The Kiwi House is one of the better examples in the country.

East of the city at Whangarei Heads is Ocean Beach one of Northland's finest: it's quiet, beautiful and, in a raging easterly wind, a place where the senses are bombarded with nature at its best. On the way you will begin to notice the prevalence of evocative Scots place names like McLeod's and Urquhart's Bay; all family names of the overspill Scots settlers from the Waipu enclaves.

Tutukaka Coast

Even if fishing and scuba-diving did not exist, the Tutukaka coastline would still deserve to be one of the finest coastal venues in Northland. But its rugged scenic bays are best known throughout New Zealand and beyond as the gateway and safe harbour to some of the best deep-sea fishing and diving in the world. The Poor Knights Islands, which lie 25 km offshore, are internationally significant both above and below the waterline, with a wide range of wildlife and vegetation. Most activity in the area takes place from Tutukaka with its large sheltered marina while the village of Ngunguru, 5 km before it, has most of the visitor and resident amenities. For dive operators, see page 105.

Tutukaka Coast.

Paihia is the main launching point for the Bay of Islands yet strangely upon arrival by road all you can see is one very little island just offshore. But, they are out there – all 150 of them. The Bay of Islands is one of the major tourist draws in the country, offering the visitor numerous water-based activities and superb coastal scenery. The area is also of huge historic significance in that it is the site of the first European settlement and the signing of the Treaty of Waitangi – the document that began the uneasy voyage of New Zealand's bicultural society. While the islands themselves are the main attraction, most are uninhabited and you can only stay at designated campsites. Most visitors stay on the mainland and take cruises to the islands. You can also explore them by kayak, yacht or sailing boat; go big-game fishing for marlin or shark; dive amidst shoals of blue maomao; swim with the dolphins; bask in the sun; or jump out of a plane.

Paihia & Waitangi

Paihia was the site of New Zealand's first church and missionary centre, but unless you have an inexplicable fetish for motels there is little in the way of sights, with the town acting primarily as an accommodation and amenity centre for tourists. Waitangi is a short walk north of Paihia and is a pleasant contrast. It's a site of celebrated national heritage as the Treaty of Waitangi was signed here in 1840 at the Treaty House, which is now a national museum and visitor centre for the Waitangi National Reserve.

Tip...

Most people take SH1 to the Bay of Islands, though a far more interesting route is via the Old Russell Road which leaves SH1 for the coast at Whakapara, about 26 km north of Whangarei. Welcome to rural Northland and the simple spirit of the north.

Tip...

While visiting Waitangi try brunch or a coffee at the Waikokopu Café in the Treaty Grounds.

Waitangi National Reserve
T09-402 7437, waitangi.net.nz
Daily 0900-1700. $20, child $5 self-guided, $35 including tour.

This is the heart of New Zealand's historical beginnings and a rather politically correct outline of events that led to the signing of the Treaty of Waitangi in 1840 and the significance of the document right up to the present day. The main focus of the reserve is the beautifully restored **Treaty House**, built in 1833-1834 and once home of British resident, James Busby, who played a crucial role in the lead-up to the treaty signing. The house is full of detailed and informative displays that help clarify the quite confusing series of events surrounding the creation of the treaty. Near the Treaty House the reserve boasts perhaps the most visited **Whare Runanga** (Maori meeting house) in the country. To call this, or any whare merely a house is rather an understatement. They are essentially artworks, with all the meaning, soul and effort therein and the Whare Runanga at Waitangi is a fine example.

From the Whare Runanga it is a short walk down to the shore where the **war canoe** Ngatokimatawhaorua is housed. This 35-m-long craft is named after the canoe in which Kupe, the Maori ancestor and navigator, discovered Aotearoa (New Zealand), and is launched every year as part of the Waitangi Day commemoration ceremonies hosted on and around the national reserve.

There are regular 30-minute Maori performances $15, child $5 (excludes entry). Another addition to the Waitangi experience is the **Culture North Treaty of Waitangi Night Show** (T09-4025990, culturenorth.co.nz, $60 all-inclusive, free pick-up), which is staged most evenings in summer and is recommended. It is genuine and so far lacking in the commercialism so rife in other tourist areas. This is the one must-do beyond the islands themselves.

Russell.

Russell

Russell can be reached by passenger ferry from Paihia Wharf, Oct-Mar every 30 mins 0720-2230, $6, child $3,or there is a vehicle ferry every 10 mins from Opua, 9 km south of Paihia, daily 0650-2200, car and driver $10, campervan $16, passenger $1, all one-way.

About 2 km across the bay from Paihia, yet still on the mainland, is the settlement of Russell. It enjoys a village feel and a rich history that eludes its frenetic, tourism-based neighbour. With the advent of the first European settlement, Kororareka quickly grew to be the base for whalers, sealers and escaped convicts and earned the sordid and notorious reputation as 'the hellhole of the Pacific'. The earliest missionaries tried their best to quell the unholy mob with mixed results. When the Treaty of Waitangi was signed in 1840, although it

was the largest European settlement in New Zealand, William Hobson, the then governor, decided it was not a good marketing ploy to give it capital status and instead bought land in what is now Auckland. To make matters worse, the treaty was seen by local Maori as a fraud and not as beneficial as was promised, with financial benefits in particular failing to materialize. Their scorn (led by the infamous chief Hone Heke) was focused on the Flagstaff near Russell, which proudly flew the Union Jack. Heke and his men duly cut it down, not once, but four times after which Kororareka was sacked and the first Maori Wars began. Once relative peace returned the authorities decided to make a new beginning and lose the notorious label, calling it Russell.

Today Russell, along with Kerikeri, is flaunted as the most historic village in New Zealand. The **Russell Museum** (2 York St, T09-4037701, russellmuseum.org.nz, daily 1000-1700, $7.50, child $2) has an interesting collection of early settler relics and, having being built to commemorate the bicentenary of Captain Cook's visit in 1769, features a host of information about the explorer including an impressive model of Cook's ship, *Endeavour*.

A short distance along the shore from the museum is **Pompallier House** (T09-403 9015, daily 1000-1700, $7.50, child $3.50). It is New Zealand's oldest surviving Roman Catholic building, built in 1842 as the printery, tannery and storehouse for the French Marist mission at Kororareka.

On the corner of Church Street and Robertson Street is the 1836 **Anglican Church**, which was one of the few buildings to survive the 1840s sacking and Maori war (bar a few visible musket ball holes) and remains the oldest church in New Zealand. For a grand view it is worth the steep climb to Flagstaff Hill (Maiki). Parts of the current pole were erected in the late 1850s over a decade after Hone Heke's admirable attempts at clear felling.

One kilometre north, the earth terraces of the ancient pa on the **Tapeka Point Reserve** make a pleasant walk, while **Long Beach**, 1 km behind the village, is also a pleasant spot and a fine venue on a hot summer's day.

Tip...

You might think it ridiculous to recommend a public convenience as a major attraction but if you have time, visit the Kawakawa 'Hundertwasser' Public Toilets in the centre of Kawakawa, 17 km south of Paihia. This marvellous and colourful creation of local artist Friedrich Hundertwasser who died in 2000, is now something of an icon and a monument.

Kerikeri

Travelling north from Paihia the rolling hills give way to corridors of windbreaks that hide the laden trees of citrus, grape and kiwifruit for which the area is famous. The word keri means 'dig', and it was here, in pleasant little Dig Dig, that the first plough cut into New Zealand soil in 1820. Along with Russell, Kerikeri is rich in Maori and early European history with the **Kerikeri Basin**, 2 km northeast of the present town, being the nucleus of New Zealand's first European colonization.

For a sense of history and atmosphere head straight for the Basin past the main commercial centre. There the road falls to meet the babbling Kerikeri River and the dominant and attractive **Stone Store** (daily 1000-1700, $3.50). This was New Zealand's first stone building and was completed in 1835. The first Anglican bishop George Selwyn used it as a library in the early 1840s and later as an ammunition store during conflicts between

Ngapuhi chief Hone Heke, before assuming its intended purpose as a general mission store. Today it is neatly laid out as testimony to that function with a museum on its top floor.

Almost immediately next door is the two-storey Kemp House or **Mission House** (daily 1000-1700, $5, combined entry with Stone Store $7.50, children free). This is the oldest surviving building in New Zealand (at the very young age of 188). It was established by pioneer missionary Samuel Marsden on land offered to him by the great local Maori warlord Hongi Hika, who accepted 48 felling axes for the land and also offered Marsden and his staff protection from invading tribes.

Overlooking both buildings is the more ancient **Kororipo Pa**, which served as chief Hongi Hika's more basic domain (until, not surprisingly, he had a European-style house built nearby in the 1820s).

The Kerikeri Basin offers a number of pleasant short walks along the river, the most notable of which takes in the 27-m **Rainbow Falls**. You can also take a one-hour heritage steamboat cruise aboard the *SS Eliza Hobson* (T09-407 9229 steamship.co.nz, Sun-Fri 1400, $30 child $15).

As well as its fruit, Kerikeri is also famous for its arts and crafts. Ask for the free leaflet **Kerikeri Art and Craft Trail** at the Kerikeri visitor centre (Cobham Rd, T09-4079297, kerikeri.co.nz, Mon-Fri 0900-1700, Sat 1000-1200).

Stone Store, Kerikeri.

The Rainbow Warrior

Matauri Bay has always been a popular holiday spot, but assumed additional national fame when the wreck of the Greenpeace vessel *Rainbow Warrior* was laid to rest off the Cavallis in 1987. The famous flagship was bombed by French secret service through an act of terrorism in Auckland in 1985. The idea was to prevent her leading a protest flotilla to the French nuclear test grounds on the Pacific atoll of Mururoa. Her sunken hull, 3 km offshore, provides a home to countless sea creatures while an impressive memorial on the hill overlooking the islands near the beach pays tribute to the ship, her crew (one of which was killed) and the continuing cause for a nuclear-free region. The incident sparked an international outcry and New Zealanders are in no hurry to forget, or forgive. There is an echo of Maori history, spirit and support in the bay with the waka (war canoe) *Mataatua II* located near the campground. The history of this legendary canoe led to the local tribe, the Ngati Kura, offering the remains and the mana (spirit) of the modern day *Rainbow Warrior* a final resting place. The wreck is now a popular diving spot.

A memorial to the Greenpeace ship *Rainbow Warrior*, blown up by terrorists in Auckland, 1985.

North to the Cape

Provided you have your own transport, the roads that branch off SH1 to the coast north of Kerikeri offer stunning coastal scenery and some secluded beaches that are well worth visiting. About 15 km north of Kerikeri the road loops to the coast taking in settlements and hideaways including Matauri Bay where you can soak up some views of the Cavalli islands and pay homage to the Greenpeace vessel *Rainbow Warrior* that was laid to rest just offshore in 1987 after it was sunk by terrorists in Auckland in 1985 (see box above). A small memorial sits on the hill overlooking the islands.

Rejoining SH1 again near Whangaroa you then meet the sweeping shores of Doubtless Bay with its mainly retirement communities of Mangonui, Coopers Beach and Cable Bay, before cutting across the picturesque Karikari Peninsula on your way to the last significant northern outpost and predominantly Maori enclave of Kaitaia.

It's a fact...

The northern tip of New Zealand is steeped in Maori legend and tradition. The name Reinga means 'Place of Leaping' and it is here, according to Maori lore, that the souls of the dead depart Aotearoa to the afterlife.

Kaitaia & the Aupouri Peninsula

The Aupouri Peninsula forms the northernmost tip of New Zealand and satisfies that strange human desire to reach the very end of everything. Like some long sandy pier, people naturally gravitate and rush as if late for an appointment for an obligatory photo with the lighthouse and a signpost to famous cities with distances that bend the mind. And to further satisfy that sense of 'what now?' an organized trip is made truly memorable with a blast down Ninety Mile Beach on the peninsula's western flank. It is, in fact, less than 90 miles and nearer to 90 km. Clearly, whoever first measured it was northbound and in a bit of a rush.

Kaitaia at the base of the peninsula is the main rural service centre for the Far North. It is predominantly Maori with a smattering of Dalmatian blood – mainly Croats who came during the kauri gum boom years of the late 1800s. For the tourist it provides a gateway to Cape Reinga and you can join the various coach trips north from here.

With your own wheels it will take about 1½ hours to reach the cape from Kaitaia. The road is sealed all the way, but watch your speed – many a budding Lewis Hamilton in their Maui campervan has come to grief along this stretch. Although Ninety Mile Beach is classified as a highway, you are not advised to take anything other than a 4WD vehicle onto the sand. For those in rental cars (which are not insured on the sand) who cannot resist the temptation to do so, be warned: it will probably all end in tears. If you are short of time the best way to see the peninsula is to join the many coach tours from Paihia, Mangonui or Kaitaia.

Cape Reinga Lighthouse.

Around the region

For most visitors, sadly, the visit to this amazing area will be all too brief and revolve around Cape Reinga and the lighthouse. The views from the hill above the lighthouse are stunning and in stormy weather you can see the Tasman Sea and Pacific in an uneasy union, and as far as the Three Kings Islands, 57 km offshore. The northland coastline has claimed over 140 vessels and many lives since 1808, with the majority falling foul around the cape. The lighthouse was built in 1941 and contains the lens from the original lighthouse built on Motuopao Island to the south. Beside the lighthouse is the obligatory multi-destination signpost for that vital digital memento. Hello Mum!

The Hokianga & Kauri Coast

From Ahipara (west of Kaitaia) the road turns south via Herekino to Narrows Landing on the Hokianga Harbour. There you meet the ferry to **Rawene** (T09-405 2602, daily 0730-1930, light vehicles $15, foot/car passengers $3) and the heart of Hokianga.

There is little to hold the visitor in Rawene except the laid-back **Boatshed Café and Gallery** (T09-405 7728) and the historic 1868 Clendon House the former residence of James Clendon, a local dignitary.

To the east of Rawene and 14 km north of the small settlement Taheke (off SH12) is one of Northland's newest natural tourist attractions, though at almost three million years old, new is hardly an apt description. The **Wairere Boulders** (McDonnell Rd, Horeke, T09-401 9935, wairereboulders.co.nz, daily, $10, child $5) can loosely be described as a valley of ancient basalt rocks formed by ancient pyroclastic flows that have since eroded and become stacked upon one another, creating a strange geological labyrinth, or stream of rocks. Allow three hours.

Cape Reinga sand dunes.

Sand dunes at the entrance to the Hokianga Harbour, Omapere.

Opononi & Omapere

Back in Rawene you join the SH12 to Opononi and Omapere and all points south to Dargaville. These two converging waterfront villages are the main resorts in the Hokianga. The villages and the harbour entrance are dominated by the impressive bare sand dunes that grace its northern shore. They rise to a height of 100 m and at sunset glow with an orange radiance. It was here in the Hokianga Harbour, in the 10th century, that the great Polynesian explorer Kupe is said to have first set foot in Aotearoa (New Zealand) from his homeland of Hawaiki. Other than that, both Opononi and Omapere were somewhat insignificant until the appearance of a solitary wild dolphin in 1955. Opo, as she was christened, won the hearts of the nation and subsequently put little Opononi on the map. Most activity in Opononi and Omapere revolves around the two hotels, particularly the Omapere Tourist Hotel with its deck over looking the harbour.

The small **Omapere Museum** (0930-1630, free) housed above the information centre, has some interesting historical stories, pictures and items, of which the original and highly entertaining 'Tally Ho' video about Opo the dolphin stands out. There are some fine coastal walks in the area and the i-SITE can advise (T09-405 8869).

The Waipoua Forest

Just south of Omapere you bid farewell to the coast and the Hokianga and enter kauri country. Waipoua, Mataraua and Waima forests make up the largest remaining tract of native forest in Northland, and the Waipoua and Trounson kauri forests contain 300 species of tree including the great kauri with two of the finest examples and living monuments to these magnificent and awe-inspiring trees. The Waipoua Forest is home to the largest remaining individuals, including the much-loved and ancient **Tane Mahuta** or 'Lord of the Forest'. For lovers of life and for those who have a healthy respect for nature, to visit this great tree is something of a pilgrimage. For those who have never really thought about it, it

is a fine place to start. Look for the signs and car parks. The **Waipoua Forest visitor centre** (DoC, off SH12 towards the southern end of the park, T09-4393011, doc.govt.nz, daily 0900-1700) contains a museum and provides information.

About 30 km south of Waipoua and 10 km towards the coast is the aquatic summer playground of the **Kai Iwi Lakes.** This is a favourite Northland holiday spot for those wanting to enjoy the combination of endless beach and surf, together with the more sedate inland waters of the three main lakes.

Dargaville & Kaipara Harbour

Just south of the lakes is **Dargaville**, once a bustling port and the largest town on the west coast of Northland. It straddles the banks of the Wairoa River, a tributary of the mighty **Kaipara Harbour.** With a combined coastline of over 3200 km, the Kaipara is one of the largest natural harbours in the world. Irish timber merchant Joseph Dargaville founded the town in 1872, when the district was already the enclave of a large group of Dalmatian settlers. Kauri timber was the name of the game and for many years and it was an important export centre. Today it serves as the main centre for the farms with their barren fields on which the great kauri once stood, and the river transports very little except ducks. The region as a whole is also known as the kumara capital of the country producing the best of this sweet potato introduced by the early Polynesian navigators. The main attraction in the region – and one of the best in Northland – is the **Kauri Museum** (Church Rd, T09-431 7417, kauri-museum.com, daily 0900-1700, $15, child $3) near the village of Matakohe, 45 km south of Dargaville. The museum houses a number of imaginative displays that offer a detailed insight into the natural history of the kauri and man's exploitation and love affair with the great tree.

From Matakohe the SH12 meets the main SH1 at Brynderwyn (26 km). From there it is a 114-km journey south to Auckland.

Coromandel Peninsula

The Coromandel Peninsula offers varied and spectacular coastal scenery, rugged mountain bush and a relaxed lifestyle that has, during the summer holidays, drawn Aucklanders south for decades.

The west coast, bounded by the Firth of Thames, is the most undeveloped side of the peninsula. It has a ragged coastline of islands and pebble beaches, lined with some of the best examples of pohutukawa trees in the country. For three weeks in December, with their olive evergreen leaves that crown the gnarled trunks, they flower in a radiant mantle of crimson, earning them the label of New Zealand's Christmas tree.

In contrast, the east coast is a plenitude of beautiful bays and sandy beaches, with Cathedral Cove and New Chums Beach being two of the most celebrated in the North Island. Here you will find most of the population, from the transitory tourist in the holiday townships of Whitianga and Whangamata to the rich retiree in the rather sterile resorts of Matarangi and Pauanui.

Between the two coasts a dominating backbone of bush-clad mountains make up the Coromandel Forest Park, with its wealth of walks and historic logging and mining remains. In summary, if you have the time, put the Coromandel firmly on the travelling agenda.

Thames

T07-868 8514, goldmine-experience.co.nz.
Daily 1000-1600, $10, child $5, includes tour
underground.

The town of Thames is at the western base of the
Coromandel Peninsula at the mouth of the
Waihou River and fringe of the Hauraki Plains.
Behind the town rise the bush-clad hills of the
Coromandel Forest Park. Thames serves as the
gateway to the peninsula, either north to
Coromandel town and the west coast, or across
the heart of the forest park to Tairua and the east
coast. It is the largest town on the Coromandel
and was one of the largest towns in New Zealand
during the peak of the kauri logging and gold
mining eras of the late 1800s, though you would
not guess it now. Other than essential services
there is little in the town to hold the tourist back,
except perhaps a few historic buildings and the
old Gold Mine and Stamper Battery.

Coromandel Forest Park
T07-867 9080, doc.govt.nz.

The Kauaeranga Valley is the main access point to
the **Coromandel Forest Park**. The forest was, in the
late 1800s, one of the most extensive kauri logging
areas in the North Island. At the head of the valley
(13 km east of Thames) there is a DoC visitor centre,
from where you can plan numerous short, day or
multi-day walks taking in mining relics.
The coast road from Thames to Coromandel Town
is scenic but very windy and quite dangerous so
take your time. On the way, the **Rapaura
Watergardens** (6 km up the Tapu–Coroglen Rd,

Tip...
You can also visit Coromandel Township on a day-
cruise from Auckland Tuesday, Thursday, Friday
and Saturday with 360 Discovery, T0800-888006,
360discovery.co.nz. From $89, child $49, full tour $136.

Essentials

⌕ Post office 72 Albert St, Whitianga.
ⓘ Tourist information Thames i-SITE visitor centre,
206 Pollen St, Thames, T07-868 7284, thamesinfo.co.nz.
Coromandel i-SITE visitor centre, 355 Kapanga Rd,
Coromandel, T07-866 8598, coromandeltown.co.nz
Whitianga i-SITE visitor centre, 55 Albert St, Whitianga,
T07-866 5555, whitianga.co.nz.

Pohutukawa tree in bloom.

Around the region

T07-868 4821, rapaurawatergardens.co.nz, 0900-1700, $12, child $6) are worth a look, with lots of lily ponds. It also has a café and self-catering lodge ($275), or cottage ($165) accommodation.

Coromandel Township

T07-866 8703, drivingcreekrailway.co.nz. Trains run daily at 1015, 1400, also 1245 and 1515 in summer, $20, child $11, family $50.

Coromandel Township has a wonderful bohemian village feel and a warm atmosphere. The locals, many of whom are artists, are friendly and contented souls who walk about with a knowing smile, as if they are well aware they have come to the right place. Again, gold and kauri in the late 1800s were the attraction, and some old buildings remain, though sadly not the beautiful native bush that once cloaked the hills. Just north of the town one of New Zealand's most famous potters, Barry Brickell, has created – along with many fine works from his kiln – a quirky **Driving Creek Railway**. It is a delight and a construction of budget engineering genius, together with artistic creativity and environmental sensitivity.

The 309 to Whiti

T07-866 7191, waiauwaterworks.co.nz. Daily 0900-1700, closed in winter, $12, child $6.

The old 309 road, which starts just south of Coromandel Town, winds its way 22 km to Whitianga and has a number of attractions along the way. The first stop on the 309, 4.5 km from Coromandel, is the charming **Waiau Waterworks**, which is a garden full of fascinating whimsical water sculptures and gadgets. This is Kiwi ingenuity and imagination at its wonderfully eccentric best.

A short distance up the road from the waterworks there is a track on the left that takes you a further 2 km to the start of the Castle Rock Walk (standard cars will be fine, walk 1-2 hrs return). The aptly named **Castle Rock** (490 m) is a particularly knobbly-looking volcanic plug that commands a wonderful view of the northern end of the peninsula.

Just over 7 km up the 309 are the **Waiau Falls** (15-min walk). Less than a kilometre further is the Kauri Grove, a stand of ancient kauri (20 min walk). From here you can return to Coromandel Town or carry on to Whitianga.

North to Colville and the Cape

North of Coromandel Town, the Colville Road rejoins the coast at Papa Aroha (Land of Love) and Amodeo Bay. From these charming bays you will be able to feast your eyes on Mount Moehau, which at 893 m is the highest mountain in the north of the North Island. The summit is sacred to Maori and tapu (out of bounds) but you can access it in part along a very pleasant riverside walk at Te Hope Stream.

Note also the wonderfully old and gnarled **pohutukawa trees** that grace the shoreline in this area. These are some of the best examples in the country, and in December flower in a gorgeous crimson mantle. From this point you are entering perhaps the most remote and scenic area of the Coromandel Peninsula with an atmosphere all of its own. The beach at **Waitete Bay**, 5 km north of Amodeo Bay, is a cracker and a favourite haunt in summer. From here the road climbs over the hill and falls again to the historic settlement of Colville, with its amazingly well-stocked **general store** (T07-8666805, Mon-Thu 0830-1700, Fri 0830-1730, Sat/Sun 0830-1700) Next door, the Colville Café is a great place for lunch.

North of Colville you can continue to the cape along the Port Jackson Road. After negotiating numerous idyllic pebble bays, the road eventually climbs round the northern tip of the cape and falls steeply to **Port Jackson** and Fletcher Bay where the road ends. From here you can enjoy great views of Great Barrier Island, seemingly only a stone's throw away across the Colville Channel.

New Chumbs beach, Coromandel.

Coromandel Town to Whitianga

From Coromandel Town the SH25 winds its way east, over the ranges, offering fine views, before descending steeply to Te Rerenga and Whangapoua Harbour. Whangapoua village, 4 km north of the junction at Te Rerenga, is essentially made up of holiday homes and beaches that come alive in the summer months. A 30-minute walk north from the road end in Whangapoua is New Chums Beach, which is one of the best beaches in the Coromandel. The fact that you cannot drive there and have to negotiate the headland by foot seems to protect its beauty. Even in bad weather it is worth the walk. Another fine beach where you can escape the crowds is **Opito Bay**, accessed via Kuaotunu 17 km north of Whitianga.

Whitianga

Whitianga is a very popular holiday town on the shores of beautiful Mercury Bay, which was given its planetary name by Captain Cook during a spot of astronomy on his brief visit in 1769. 'Whiti' (pronounced 'fitty') has much to offer, including a number of fine beaches within walking distance of the town. It also acts as a convenient short-cut access point, across the narrow Whitianga Harbour entrance and **Ferry Landing**, to two fine smaller resorts – Cooks Beach and Hahei. Although there is an abundance of activities to choose from, Whiti is most famous as a sea- and big-game fishing base and a trip on the water is recommended.

There are a number of short walks in the area and the i-SITE can advise. The **Shakespeare Cliff Scenic Reserve** accessed via the ferry and Ferry Landing is recommended for its great bay views.

Whiti also has a couple of excellent **bone carving** studios (see page 106), which offer the opportunity to carve your own bone pendant – traditionally from whale bone but now typically from beef bone.

Cathedral Cove, Hahel.

Tip...

By far the best time to visit Cathedral Cove is at sunrise.

Hahei, Cathedral Cove & Hot Water Beach

Hahei is a wonderful little unspoiled coastal settlement, 35 km by road from Whitianga. A shorter route is via the ferry from Whitianga. Both Hahei and Cooks Beach have wonderful beaches especially Hahei Beach as it looks over a wealth of islands and rock outcrops. But the real jewel in the region's crown, indeed perhaps for the whole peninsula, is the amazing Cathedral Cove, which guards the Te Whanganui-A-Hei Marine Reserve. Access is by boat or a half-hour walk. The track starts from a glorious lookout point just north of Hahei on Grange Road.

About 15 km south of Hahei is Hot Water Beach where you can dig a hole in the sand to access natural hot water. You can only do this for about two hours each side of low tide. No spade? The Hot Water Beach Store hires them out for a small fee.

Opoutere & Whangamata

Opoutere is one of the Coromandel's best-kept secrets. It has a quiet and magical atmosphere with sweeping white-sand Ocean Beach, guarded by the Wharekawa Harbour and a narrow tract of forest. At the tip of the sand spit is the Wharekawa Wildlife Refuge where oystercatchers and rare New Zealand dotterel breed in summer. The beach can be accessed from the car park around the corner from the Opoutere Youth Hostel (YHA).

Just south of Opoutere is the town of Whangamata, which is the main surfing venue on the Coromandel. The often-busy beach is over 4 km long, but a far quieter option is Whiritoa Beach and lagoon, 12 km south. It also offers a lovely bush walk, heading north. Whangamata is also a base for trips to the outer islands, including Mayor Island.

Waihi

Waihi was once host to 1200 mines producing half of the country's gold and earning it the reputation as the most famous mining town in New Zealand. Between 1878 and 1952 the town produced over 174,000 kg of gold and 1 million kg of silver. Today the most impressive evidence of the town's mining history is the enormous open-pit **Martha Mine**, which sits like a huge, but strangely discrete bomb crater right in the centre of town. From a lookout behind the **Waihi VIC** (Upper Seddon St, T07-863 6715, waihi.org.nz, daily 0900-1700), you can watch huge earth-moving trucks relentlessly winding their way in and out of the massive terraced hole.

Given the town's 'rich' history the **Waihi Arts Centre and Museum** (54 Kenny St, T07-863 8386, waihi.co.nz/arts/museum, Mon-Fri 1000-1600, Sat-Sun 1330-1600, $5, child $3) is well worth a look. It displays an array of mining memorabilia and interesting working models, including a miniature stamping battery. Inevitably you leave a lot wiser about the incredible 175-km-long network of tunnels that insidiously lies beneath your feet.

Nearby, the Ohinemuri River winds its dramatic way west, through the **Karangahake Gorge**, where there are a number of interesting walks and mining relics (DoC leaflet available from the VIC). A vintage steam train, the **Goldfields Railway** (T07-863 9020, waihirail.co.nz, trains leave from Wrigley St, daily at 1000, 1145, 1345, $15 return, child $8; café at Waikino station, daily 1000-1600), runs 6.5 km and 30 minutes into the gorge from Waihi to Waikino. If you want to go to the beach, head for the popular surfers' hangout at **Waihi Beach**, 11 km to the east. A pleasant 45-minute coastal walk at the northern end of the beach will take you to the very pretty Orokawa Bay.

Tip...

Before you leave Whangamata (from the north) be sure to duck in to Whangamata Traders, 114 Port Rd, where the copious and multifarious second-hand and antique goods are an attraction in themselves.

Best photo locations

❶ Auckland: Sky Tower
Page 69
An obvious photo target, but most often as the platform and not as subject itself,given the magnificent 360° views on offer from the observation deck. By all means head to the top for some keepsakes, but you will find the windows compromise the results and there is a limit to the creativity.

Far better are images of the tower itself from both near and far. The base of the tower presents numerous possibilities especially with a wide angle and at night when it is lit up. Another good vantage point at night is from the eastern (Albert Park) end of Victoria St East. Try some slow exposures.

During the day look for reflections of the tower in the plate glass buildings of the CBD. Contrast can be found between old buildings and the tower along Ponsonby Road, again at night. From afar try Mount Donald McLean in (road to Whatipu Beach) or along Scenic Drive, both in the Waitakeres.

❷ Devonport & North Head
Page 72
Devonport offers some excellent vantage points of the city, particularly at dawn from North Head

or Mount Victoria. Another great view of the city centre is from the very end of Stanley Point Road. It is particularly good on a Wednesday about 1800 when the yachts are doing their mid-week rum-racing.

❸ Northland: Waitangi
Page 83
The Treaty Grounds present a wealth of opportunity to gather cultural based imagery, but sensitivity is paramount. Adhere to protocols and do not take photos if signs or staff indicates it is insensitive to do so.
It is a good time to think about angles and close ups. Search for abstracts and experiment.

❹ Coromandel: Cathedral Cove
Page 95
Bar Wharariki (Golden Bay) this is probably the most photographed beach in New Zealand and with good cause. But do not let that put you off. It is imperative to arrive just before sunrise when you should be alone. If the tide is in your favour there will be few footprints in the sand and you will have the entire 'creative canvas' to yourself – perfect. If you have company try figurative silhouettes from within the arch looking out, but underexpose slightly to bring out the shadows.

① ⑪/⚡/📷/☀️/⏱️1000

② ▲/⚡/📷/☀️/⚡

③ ▽/⚡/📷/☀️/⚡

④ ▲/⚡/📷/⊕/🌙⚡

Sleeping

Auckland

Esplanade Hotel $$$$-$$$
1 Victoria Rd, Devonport,
T09-445 1291,
esplanade hotel.co.nz.
Map: Auckland, G1, p67 (off map).
One of Auckland's oldest hotels, dominating the promenade with fine views of the harbour. Due to its position (15 mins from the city centre by car, or a 10-min ferry ride from the CBD) it's a good place to get away from the centre and enjoy Devonport's 'village within a city' atmosphere. All rooms are en suite, with the spacious harbour view suites being the most sought after. Sky TV and Wi-Fi. Classy in-house restaurant with an open fire in winter adds to the charm. Tariff includes breakfast.

Great Ponsonby B&B $$$
30 Ponsonby Terr, Ponsonby,
T09-376 5989, greatpons.co.nz.
Map: Auckland, A4, p66.
Undoubtedly one of the best in the city, this B&B is a restored villa in a quiet location only a short stroll to the funky Ponsonby Road. Range of tastefully decorated en suite rooms and studios with a colourful Pacific influence. Enthusiastic, knowledgeable owners and a friendly dog and cat. The fantastic breakfasts are all cooked to order, using only fresh ingredients.

Great Ponsonby B&B.

Motor parks
Manukau Top Ten Holiday Park $$$-$
902 Great South Rd, Manukau City, T09-266 8016, manukautop10.co.nz.
Handy for the airport or for those heading south.

North Shore Motels and Top Ten Holiday Park $$$-$
52 Northcote Rd, Takapuna, T09-418 2578, nsmotels.co.nz.
Map: Auckland, A1, p66 (off map).
The most popular holiday park in the city but around 35 km from the airport, offering lodges, motel and cabin accommodation as well as the usual reliable Top Ten motor camp facilities. Five minutes to the beach.

Northland

Whangarei
Whangarei Top Ten Holiday Park $$$-$
24 Mair St, T09-437 6856, whangareitop10.co.nz.
This motor park has the best facilities and is the most convenient in Whangarei.

Tide Song $$
Taiharuru Estuary, Beasley Rd, Onerahi, T09-436 1959, tidesong. co.nz.
Excellent, peaceful B&B offering a self-contained two-bedroom loft and a double ensuite in a bush and seaside setting 30 minutes east of Whangarei.

Paihia

Haruru Falls Resort Panorama (and motor park) $$$-$

Old Wharf Rd, 6 km northwest of Paihia, T0800-757525, harurufalls.co.nz.

Standard apartment, hotel rooms and motel units, powered sites, pool, restaurant and bar all within view of the Haruru Falls. Courtesy shuttle to Paihia.

Allegra House $$

39 Bayview Rd, T09-402 7932, allegra.co.nz.

Conveniently located in the heart of Paihia with fine views across the bay to Russell and beyond, this modern home offers the choice of conventional B&B accommodation or a spacious self-contained apartment with an extra en suite if required. There are two B&B rooms that can accommodate single, twin or double. Both have TV, tea and coffee-making facilities and a fridge. Owners are fluent in both German and French. Internet and off-street parking. Minimum two-night stay.

Russell

The Duke of Marlborough $$$

Waterfront, Russell, T09-403 7829, theduke.co.nz.

Right on the waterfront and oozing all the gracious charm its 150-year location deserves, 'The Duke', as it is affectionately known, offers some welcome relief from the tourist hype of Paihia. The recently refurbished modern rooms perhaps deflect from the establishment's historic charm, but there is no denying the quality, with some affording fine bay views and a large bath or spa. The cosy bar and à la carte restaurant offers a fine place to relax. When you're here, it's difficult to believe, the village was once called the Hell Hole of the Pacific. Continental breakfast included, cooked breakfast extra.

Arcadia Lodge $$$-$$

10 Florence Av, Matauwhi Bay, T09-403 7756, arcadialodge.co.nz.

Lovingly restored, historic Tudor house with three characterful, spacious suites, great breakfast.

North to the Cape

Kauri Cliffs Lodge $$$$

Matauri Bay, T09-407 0010, kauricliffs.com.

One of the top 100 lodges in the world set on 2500 ha near Matauri Bay, Northland. Superb luxury facilities, memorable views and an international standard golf course. Tariffs also remain within the realistic as opposed to the ridiculous. If you really want to spoil yourself in Northland and can swing a golf club then this is the venue.

Carneval Ocean View B&B $$

360 SH10, Cable Bay, T09-406 1012, carneval.co.nz.

Perched on a hill overlooking Doubtless Bay this modern B&B provides a fine base from which to explore the Aupouri Peninsula. Fresh ensuites with contemporary decor offering either garden or ocean views. Organized trips to Cape Reinga and a range of other aquatic based activities can be arranged.

Matauri Bay Holiday Park $$-$

Matauri Bay (30 km north of Kerikeri), T09-405 0525.

Tight on the beach near the Rainbow Warrior memorial hill, which sadly affects the view, but a great spot nonetheless. Powered sites, self-contained chalets and general store. Dive trips a speciality.

Kaitaia & the Aupouri Peninsula

Motor parks

Waitiki Landing $$-$
SH1, 20 km south of the Cape, T09-409 7508.
Cheap powered tent sites, bunks and ensuite cabins. Camp kitchen. Restaurant on site.

YHA Ahipara Motor Camp and Backpackers $$-$
168 Takahe St, Ahipara (14 km southwest of Kaitia), T09-409 4864, ahiparamotorcamp.co.nz.
Good option for campervans, tents, backpackers or self-contained cabins. Camp kitchen.

The Hokianga & Kauri Coast

Copthorne Hotel and Motel $$
SH12, Omapere, T09-405 8737, omapere.co.nz.
A fine spot next to the beach and the wharf. Modern hotel rooms with kitchenette, TV and internet. Pool, restaurant and bar.

Motor parks

Kauri Coast Top Ten Holiday Park $$$-$
Trounson Park Rd, Kaihu (30 km north of Dargaville), T09-439 0621, kauricoasttop10.co.nz.
Best motor park between Opononi and Dargaville. Powered sites and cabins in a site next to the river. Clean and modern. Guided night tours to Trounson Kauri Reserve in summer to hear kiwi, see glow-worms and native eels, $20.

Coromandel Peninsula

West Coast

Pottery Lane Cottages $$$-$$
15 Pottery Lane, Coromandel, T07-866 7171, potterylncottage@xtra.co.nz.
Two good-value, self-contained cottages in a garden setting and within a short stroll from the village centre. The first has a separate double and twin room while the second is smaller and open plan. Both have character and are tastefully decorated. There is also a loft room with kitchenette. Off-street parking.

Motor parks

Miranda Holiday Park $$$-$
Front Miranda Rd (30 km west of Thames), T07-867 3205, mirandaholidaypark.co.nz.
Although some distance before Thames this is an excellent motor park with above-average facilities, plus its own hot pool. Will get your visit to the Coromandel off to a good start.

Coromandel Holiday Park $$-$
636 Rings Rd, Coromandel, T07-866 8830.
Centrally located with good facilities and modern cabins.

East Coast

The Church $$
87 Beach Rd, Hahei, T07-866 3533, thechurchhahei.co.nz.
The accommodation takes the form of attached wooden studio units, separate studio or self-contained cottages surrounding a church (restaurant) and surrounded by private gardens. Two of the self-contained cottages have an open fire adding to the cosy ambience.

Opoutere Youth Hostel (YHA) $$-$
389 Opoutere Rd, Oputere, T07-865 9072.
A fine peaceful place to stay with great facilities, short walks nearby, and a lovely view across the harbour.

Motor parks

Hahei Holiday Resort (motor park) $$$-$
Harsant Av, Hahei, T07-866 3889, haheiholidays.co.nz.
Right on the beach is this fine and spacious facility with self-contained (beachfront) lodges and backpacker accommodation. Camp kitchen.

Mill Creek Bird and Campervan Park $$-$
365 Mill Creek Road, Whitianga, T07-866 0166, halcyonheights.co.nz
If you love animals and/or have kids this is ideal. Peaceful and friendly with more than 400 birds of 40 species to view. Located a few kilometres south of Whitianga. Powered sites and B&B rooms with en suite.

Eating & drinking

Euro $$$

*Shed 22, Princes Wharf, Quay St,
T09-309 9866.*
Daily for lunch and dinner,
brunch Sat-Sun from 1030.
Map: Auckland, E2, p66.
A waterfront restaurant designed
to capture the sailing crowd,
with a boast of being the 'best of
the best'. It has a very luxurious
interior with a large mesmerizing
clock projected onto the wall,
and offers new and imaginative
cuisine in the revered Pacific Rim
style. Licensed, outdoor dining
available.

Kermadec $$$

*1st floor, Viaduct Quay Building,
corner of Lower Hobson St and
Quay St, T09-3090412,
kermadec.co.nz.*
Mon-Fri for lunch and dinner.
Map: Auckland, E2, p66.
Perhaps the best restaurant in
town, and arguably the best
seafood venue. Tickle your taste
buds with the many delights of
the Pacific Ocean as well as more
traditional fare. There are two
private rooms in a Japanese-style
decor that contain small ponds.
Don't miss the seafood platter.
Licensed and BYO.

Orbit Restaurant $$$-$$

*Sky Tower, corner Victoria St and
Federal St, T09-363 6000.*
Brunch Sat/Sun 1000-1500,
lunch Mon-Fri 1130-1430,
dinner daily 1730-2230,
lunch Thu-Sun.
Map: Auckland, D/E3, p66.
More than two-thirds of the way
up the Sky Tower, this restaurant
has the best view of any in the
city, if not the entire hemisphere.
The restaurant itself revolves of
course, apparently once every
hour, though every six seconds
would be far more fun.
Contemporary Pacific-rim cuisine
and extensive NZ wine list. The
Observatory is the other option
in the Sky Tower and offers
buffet-style fare. Licensed.

Ponsonby Fresh Fish and Chip Co $$

*127 Ponsonby Rd, Ponsonby,
T09-378 7885.*
Daily 1100-2130.
Map: Auckland, B5, p66.
A Ponsonby institution. Although
the portions have gradually
decreased in size, the quality has
pretty much stayed the same. Try
the local Pacific fish. Always busy,
and it is takeaway only, so expect
to place an order then return
about 20 minutes later. Good
vegetarian burgers.

Soul Bar and Restaurant $$

*Viaduct Harbour, T09-356 7249,
soulbar.co.nz.*
Daily for lunch and dinner.
Map: Auckland, E2, p66.
Much to the chagrin of the local
competition, owner and chef

Judith Tabron ensured that Soul was the place to be during the America's Cup and its reputation lives on. Doubtless, the open-air decks overlooking the harbour had much to do with that and of course the bar is the main attraction, but the food is also excellent and affordable. Internationally renowned guest chefs add to its appeal.

The Patriot British Pub $$
14 Victoria Rd, Devonport, T09-445 3010.
Map: Auckland, G1, p67 (off map).
Sure, 'When in Rome…' as the saying goes, but if you are European and weary of all things new, want a good beer, or a hearty breakfast or rapport with ex-pats then head here on a sunny Sun or weekend evening.

Dizengoff $$-$
256 Ponsonby Rd, Ponsonby, T09-360 0108.
Daily 0700-1700.
Map: Auckland, A4, p66.
A quintessential Auckland café that attracts a wide-ranging clientele, making it a great spot for people watching. The breakfasts (especially the salmon and eggs on toast) are delicious. Unlicensed.

Northland

Auckland to the Bay of Islands

Kamakura Restaurant $$$
29 The Strand, Russell, T09-403 7771, kamakura.co.nz.
Mon-Sun 0600-late.
Waterfront dining at arguably the Bay of Island's best restaurant. Pacific Rim with Asian influences. Book a window table and watch the sunset.

A Deco $$$-$$
70 Kamo Rd, Whangarei, T09-459 4957.
Lunch Wed-Fri, dinner Tue-Sat.
As the name suggests, an art deco property housing an award-winning restaurant. Imaginative and beautifully presented Pacific Rim cuisine.

Salt Brasserie $$$-$$
78-94 Marsden Rd, Paihia, T09-402 6199.
One of the more reliable options in Paihia offering Pacific Rim, Asian and Classic European-style cuisines. Situated overlooking the lonesome Motumaire Island. Try the seafood tasting platter as a starter.

Bob Café $$-$
29 Bank St, Whangarei, T09-4380881.
Mon-Fri 0800-1800, Sat 0730-1500, Sun 0900-1500.
Convenient and quality coffee or lunch stop while heading through town. Licensed.

Waikokopu Café $$-$
Waitangi National Reserve, T09-4026275.
Daily 0900-1700.
Undoubtedly one of the best places for daytime eating in and around Paihia with pleasant surroundings and a highly imaginative menu including the sumptuous 'Whalers Breakfast'. BYO and licensed.

North to the Cape

Carrington Club Restaurant and Karikari Estate Café $$$-$
Maitai Bay Rd, T09-4087222, heritagehotels.co.nz/ Carrington-Resort.
Lunch and dinner.
Bookings advised.
It is a bit of a drive to this five-star golf/vineyard resort on the Karikari Peninsula, but the food, wine and scenery are worth it. Fresh local seafood a speciality complimented by award-winning wines from the winery. For lighter meals during the day you may also consider the Karikari Estate Cafe.

Mangonui Fish and Chip Shop $$-$
Beach Rd, Mangonui, T09-4060478.
Open 0800-2100.
A northland institution set waterside just north of the village and a popular stopping point for those on day trips to the cape.

Entertainment

Coromandel Peninsula

West Coast
Driving Creek Café $$-$
*180 Driving Creek Rd,
Coromandel Town,
T07-866 7066.*
Daily 0900-1700.
Independent and not an adjunct to the railway complex. Laid-back, arty café largely demonstrative of the township itself. Good coffee, home baking and organic cuisine. Internet.

Peppertree Restaurant and Bar $$-$
Coromandel Town, T07-866 8211.
Daily from 0900.
Reliable fine dining option in Coromandel with a lunch and mainly seafood dinner menu. It has a pleasant interior, bar and outdoor eating area. On summer evenings book in advance.

East Coast
Café Nina $$-$
Behind the i-SITE visitor centre at 20 Victoria St, Whitianga, T07-866 5440.
Daily from 0800 and 1730 for dinner.
The finest café in town. Small and bustling, it covers a range of healthy and imaginative dishes.

Eggsentric Café and Restaurant $$-$
Purangi Rd, Flaxmill Bay (1 km east of Ferry Landing), Whitianga T07-866 0307, eggsentriccafe.co.nz.
Tue-Fri 1000-late, Sat/Sun 0900-late.
Without doubt the most colourful place around and at times the liveliest, whose artistic and multi-talented owners put on organized and often impromptu musical performances and poetry readings. Licensed and BYO.

The Church $$
87 Beach Rd, Hahei, T07-866 3797, thechurchhahei.co.nz.
Closed Sun/Mon.
One of the region's most popular restaurants set in a restored turn-of-the-20th-century church.

Auckland

For the latest live music, theatre and cinema listings for Auckland check the daily and especially the weekend *New Zealand Herald*, nzherald.co.nz, or eventsauckland.com and nzlive.com. The free publication *What's Happening* is also a very useful guide, and is available from the visitor information centre. For ticketing and nationwide entertainment listings refer to the online service ticketek, ticketek.co.nz. For Festivals, see page 42.

The Edge
T0800-289842, the-edge.co.nz.
A conglomerate of Auckland's main venues offering the top international performance events. It combines the Aotea Centre, The Civic, the Auckland Town Hall, and Aotea Square. The event schedule leaflets are available from all the main information centres.

Sky City
For detail T0800-7592489, skycityauckland.co.nz. The cinemas are at Sky City Metro, 291-297 Queen St, T09-979 2400.
The largest entertainment venue in Auckland with its showpiece casino (open 24 hrs), but there is plenty more with a theatre and a 12-screen cinema.

Shopping

Activities & tours

If you are looking for products specific to New Zealand, whet your appetite by visiting the New Zealand Trade Centre, 26 Albert Street, Auckland City, T09-366 6879, nztc.co.nz. Although you cannot actually buy things here, it will give you an insight into what is available.

Auckland

Otara Market

Otara town centre car park, 18 km south of the city centre, T09-274 0830.
Every Sat 0600-1100.
Thought to be the largest Maori/Polynesian market in the world.

Victoria Park Market

Opposite Victoria Park, just a few mins' walk west of the city centre, victoria-park-market.co.nz.
It provides seven days a week shopping with a variety of outlets from shops to stalls that expand into the car park on Saturday. There are a wide variety of products with a market theme, a number of good cafés, a food hall and a pub, all in pleasant surroundings.

Coromandel Peninsula

Moko Art Gallery

24 Pye Place, Hot Water Beach, just opposite the main car park, Coromandel, T07-866 3367, moko.co.nz.
The arts and crafts are top class, reasonably priced and very Kiwi.

Auckland

Bungee & sky jumping

Bridge Climb and Bungee

Harbour Bridge Experience (Bridge Climb), Westhaven Reserve, T09-3612000, ajhackett.com.
1½ hrs from $120. Bungee $120.
The Auckland Harbour Bridge has – not surprisingly – been utilized by Mr Hackett for both bungee and bridge climb. The verdict? If you are going to Sydney this is of course nothing compared to their Harbour Bridge walk, also if you are going to Queenstown, save your money until then. Otherwise go for it!

Sky Jump and Sky Walk

T0800-759586, skyjump. co.nz. From $195 (maximum weight 125 kg).
This is the original and much-talked about jump from just above the restaurant of the Sky Tower. But there is a catch (thankfully, or sadly, depending how you look at it). Given the incredible jump height of 192 m, not to mention the surroundings, it is not possible to jump conventionally with an elastic cord attached to the ankles and to do the yoyo bit. Obviously if you did, in this scenario, you would probably end up plastered against somebody's window. That said, at 20 seconds and 75 kph it is should still get the adrenaline-pumping. Sky Walk is the latest Sky Tower

adventure that involves walking around the tower's pergola (or ring) on a 1-m walkway with 192-m drop and nothing but thin air on either side. An overhead safety tether travels above. From $135, combo $260.

Cruises & sailing
360-Discovery Cruises
T0800-888006, 360discovery.co.nz.
Offer a range of harbour cruise options as well as day trips to Kawau Island, Tiritiri Matangi and the Coromandel Peninsula.

Explore NZ
T09-359 5987, sailnz.co.nz.
Offer excellent sailing trips as well as whale and dolphin viewing and swimming. Their SailNZ operation offers basic cruises on, or match races between authentic Americas Cup racing yachts, the NZL 40 and NZL 41, from $150 (racing from $195, child $175).

Fullers
Fullers Cruise Centre, Ferry Building, waterfront, T09-367 9111, fullers.co.nz.
The main ferry operator offering everything from two-hour harbour cruises to island transportation and stopovers. They can also arrange wine tours of Waiheke.

Tours
Potiki Adventures
T09-845 5932, T0800-6923836, potikiadventures.co.nz.
Excellent Maori-themed adventure tours, with a range of fixed or custom activities from hiking to marae stays. Their Auckland Orientation Trip (8 hrs from $195) is a fine introduction to the city, region and country from the Maori perspective.

Northland

The minute you arrive in Paihia you are under pressure to book, book, book and buy, buy, buy. There is a huge range of water-based tour and activity options. Most of the day excursions options to Cape Reinga are also booked from here. The best thing to do is to take your time and to take advice from the unbiased VIC before venturing into the booking mall on the waterfront. The main player is Fullers Great Sights: T09-402 7421, T0800-653339, dolphincruises.co.nz, which offer tours around the islands with Cape Brett's famous Hole in the Rock being the main highlight. Trips generally involve combinations of activities from simple sightseeing to island stops, lunch cruises and swimming with dolphins. Coastal Kayakers: T09-402 8105, coastal kayakers.co.nz, offers half- or full-day guided trips (some up

river to Haruru Falls) and also the excellent three-day experience. Three days on a remote bay with a kayak to explore the islands can be a great adventure, and is a chance to encounter dolphins.

Diving
Dive Tutukaka
T09-434 3867, diving.co.nz.
The main dive company for the Poor Knights Islands, internationally recognized dive sites. Offer dive courses, snorkeling, kayak, and whale- and dolphin-watching activities. Full dive day (2 dives) from $225.

Golf
Kauri Cliffs Golf Course
Kauri Cliffs, Matauri Bay Rd, T09-405 1900, kauricliffs.com.
One of the most scenic golf courses in the country, but expensive at over $200 a round.

Waitangi Golf Club
T09-402 7713, waitangigolf.co.nz.
An excellent 18-hole course.

Walking
Cape Brett Walk
One of the finest walks in Northland following the ridge of Cape Brett to the lighthouse and DoC Cape Brett Hut. With a clear view across the Bay of Islands, it provides some spectacular coastal scenery. It will take an entire day (about 8 hrs) to walk the 20 km to the hut though if you cannot face the return journey, book a water taxi back to Rawhiti from just below the hut with T0800 387 892, islandshuttle.co.nz. To attempt the walk and stay in the hut you must first pay a hut fee of $10 and a track fee of $30 at the DoC visitor centre in Russell, T09-403 9005. For organized trips contact Cape Brett Walkways, T09-403 8823, capebrettwalks.co.nz.

Coromandel

Bone carving
Bay Carving
Next to the museum on the Esplanade, Whitianga, T07-866 4021, dreamland.co.nz/ baycarving.
Open 0900-1600, evenings by appointment.
A very well equipped bone-carving studio and provides expert tuition (2-3 hrs from $40-80).

Kayaking

Cathedral Cove Sea Kayaking
Hahei, T07-866 3877, seakayaktours.co.nz.
Based in Hahei, offers kayak hire and half- or full-day kayak trips from $85 with all equipment provided. Courtesy transport to/ from Whitianga Ferry.

Transport

Tours

Cave Cruzer
T0800-427893, T02-586 6744, cavecruzer.co.nz.
A rigid inflatable that can take you on a range of tours around the bay from one to three hours ($40-90), taking in the main coastal sights including Cathedral Cove.

Hahei Explorer Tours
Hahei Beach, T07-866 3910, glassbottomboatwhitianga. co.nz/haheiexplorer.
If you want to experience Cathedral Cove from the water, this is an excellent trip. Daily scenic trips on board a nippy inflatable cost $65, child $40, for 2 hours. The tour also takes in caves and a blowhole not accessible by foot.

All the main centres in Northland and on the Coromandel Peninsula are served by **bus** and i-SITES can assist with bookings. There are no rail services.

Coromandel Peninsula

Intercity offers coach services to and from the Coromandel. The i-SITE visitor centre in Thames or Whitianga act as agents. A number of bus tour companies offer shuttle, personalized or specialist tour options, including: **Go Kiwi Shuttles**, T07-866 0336, go-kiwi.co.nz, Auckland to Thames from $27, Whitianga from $36, shuttle plus tours and charter; and **Coromandel Explorer Tours**, T07-866 3506, coromandeltours.co.nz, day tour from $250, two-day from $420 (plus accommodation), four-day tours from $820 (plus accommodation).

Contents

Central North Island

Introduction

The TVZ, or Taupo Volcanic Zone, is one of the most active in the world and has been shaping the natural and (more recently) the human history of Central North Island for thousands of years. Perhaps the region's most obvious feature is Lake Taupo (the country's largest), home to a bustling tourist town and renowned not only for its world-class trout fishing, but also a host of adventure activities.

Evidence of ancient and ongoing volcanic activity is apparent throughout the region, but nowhere more so than in the Tongariro National Park. Steeped in Maori legend and spirituality, New Zealand's oldest national park boasts the active volcanoes of Ngauruhoe and Ruapehu – the North Island's highest peak, which erupted in spectacular fashion as recently as 1996. When the mountains are in a less aggressive mood the park provides excellent skiing and tramping opportunities, including the great Tongariro Crossing, considered one of the best day hikes in the country.

With its own inventory of volcanic features and rich Maori heritage Rotorua has served as one of the country's major tourist destinations for over 200 years.

Given the time constraints, the vast majority of people head south through the centre via Rotorua, but both the east and west coasts also have much to offer. Ultimately, if you choose carefully, you can create the perfect mix of activity, relaxation and cultural insight.

What to see in...

... a long weekend
Travelling through the Central North Island south to Wellington there are essentially three route choices. The recommended option is to head to Waitomo for a cave adventure, then Rotorua for one night, Taupo (taking in Waiotapu) on the way and then south, through the scenic Tongariro National Park to Wellington. Second is to head down the west coast from Waitomo via Taranaki to Wellington. Alternatively from Coromandel, take in Whakatane (White Island), East Cape to Napier and then the Wairarapa to Wellington.

...a week
Spend more time in Rotorua and then via Taupo and (if the weather allows) attempt the Tongariro Crossing (full day). Or take the chairlift up Ruapehu's slopes and take in the views or (in summer) a high-altitude hike from there. Taupo is also good for tandem skydiving.

Maori 'po' depicting a warrior, Rotorua.

Rotorua & around

Of all the places in the Bay of Plenty, nature has indeed given Rotorua 'plenty'. The natural thermal wonders first attracted the Maori in the 14th century and later the Europeans, who quickly developed them in to a world-renowned tourist attraction. But nature has not always been so kind. The violent eruption of the Tarawera volcano in 1886 led to the loss of 150 lives and temporarily wiped out the tourist industry. Now, over a century later, Rotorua is deserving of its 'most visited' tourist status. The city and the region probably offer more unusual sights and activities than anywhere else in New Zealand. And although, like Taupo, it is famous for its thermal and volcanic features, lakes and fishing, the region offers a multitude of other activities. Here you can join in a Maori concert or hangi (feast), plummet over a 7-m waterfall in a raft, bike, walk and (of course) throw yourself down the infamous luge.

Lake Rotorua & Ohinemutu

Lake Rotorua is the largest of the 17 lakes in the Rotorua thermal region and is, not surprisingly, a flooded volcanic crater. A feature of many of the launch trips based on the city's lakefront is the bush-clad nature reserve of Mokoia Island, scene of the classic love story of the Arawa princess Hinemoa and her suitor Tutanekai. As well as island trips the lake is a top venue for recreational activities including boating, waterskiing, flight-seeing and, above all, trout fishing.

Situated on the lakefront within the city is the former Maori settlement and thermal area of Ohinemutu. The focal point of the village is the Tamatekapua marae, a beautifully carved wharerunanga (meeting house), erected in 1939.

Just opposite the marae is the Tudor-style St Faith's Church built in 1910 (daily 0800-1700, free). Its interior pillars, beams, rafters and pews are beautifully carved with Maori designs, and on a sandblasted window overlooking the lake a Maori Christ is portrayed, dressed in a korowai (chief's cloak). There are still boiling pools near the church that are frequently used by locals for cooking.

Government Gardens & the Rotorua Museum of Art and History

Queens Drive, Government Gardens, T07-350 1814, rotoruamuseum.co.nz.
Daily summer 0900-2000, winter 0930-1700, $12, child $5.50. Guided tours hourly 1000-1600. Shop and a café.

Fringing Lake Rotorua are the elegant Government Gardens with their well-manicured bowling greens and croquet lawns, ponds and scented roses, creating a distinctly Edwardian, colonial atmosphere. They provide the perfect setting for the Rotorua Museum of Art and History housed in the once world-famous Bath House. Built in 1908, it was designed along the lines of the European spas and attracted hundreds of clients the world over who hoped to take advantage of the thermal waters' therapeutic and curative powers. In one

Essentials

❶ **Getting around** Baybus (T0800-4229287, baybus.co.nz) is the principal local bus company, the main stop is on Pukuatua Street. Several local shuttles vie for business in providing daily transportation to the main attractions from around $25 return including **Geyserlink**, T0800-0004321, gyserlink.co.nz. Contact the i-SITE for full listings.

The i-SITE serves as the principal bus arrival and departure point. The in-house travel centre administers local and national bus, coach, air and rail ticketing, which has its own travel centre T0800-768678.

❸ **ATM** ATM and currency exchange facilities at the i-SITE and all major banks are represented in the centre of the town.

❹ **Hospital** Lakes Prime Care, 1165 Tutanekai St, T07-348 1000, 0800-2200 (also 24-hr duty doctor).

❺ **Pharmacy** Central Pharmacy, 1245 Haupapa St, T07-348 6028.

❼ **Post office** 1189 Hinemoa St, Mon-Fri 0730-1700, Sat 0830-1600, Sun 1000-1500 (Post Restante).

❶ **Tourist information** Tourism Rotorua Travel and Information (i-SITE), 1167 Fenton St, T07-348 5179/ T0800-768678, rotoruanz.com, daily 0800-1800, is one of the oldest and busiest tourist offices in the country. There is a travel centre, a currency exchange office (0800-1730), toilets, showers, a shop, and a café.

Bubbling mud pool, Te Puia.

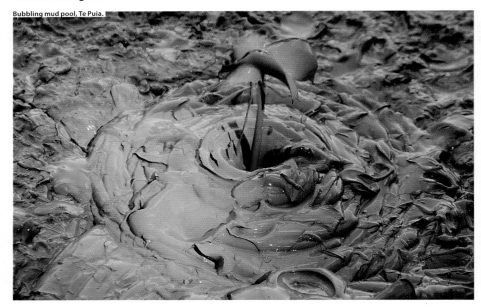

wing of the museum you can see some of the original baths, changing rooms and equipment, together with old photographs. Elsewhere, given the rich local Maori history, it is not surprising to find a superb collection of Te Arawa taonga (treasures) and displays that feature the great Tarawera eruption of 1886. Not to be missed is the excellent audio-visual display entitled Rotorua Stories (every 20 mins) that has its own surprises.

Polynesian Spa

Lakeside, 1000 Hinemoa St, T07-348 1328, polynesianspa.co.nz.
Daily 0800-2300, from $20, child $6.

Rain or shine this is a Rotorua 'must do' and, although often very busy, it is a delight. There is a luxury spa complex and hot springs and pools, private spa pools, a family spa, shop and café. A range of massage treatments are also available. The best times to go are at lunch and dinnertime when the tour buses are elsewhere.

Te Puia (Whakarewarewa)

Fenton St (3 km south of the city), T07-348 9047, tepuia.com.
Summer daily 0800-1800, winter 0800-100, $40, child $20, guided tours depart hourly. Maori concerts 1015, 1215, 1515, tour and concert $50, child $25. Te Po evening performance and feast, $95, child $47.50. General admission and Te Po $130, child $65. There is a shop and a café on site.

For many, Europeans especially, this is their first exposure to thermal features and all things bubbly mud! 'Whaka' (pronounced 'Fuckka') – or brand name 'Te Puia' – now claims to be New Zealand's premier Maori cultural centre and is certainly the most commercial. The complex includes the functional Rotowhio Marae, the modern and thriving Maori Arts and Crafts Institute and of course a number of natural thermal features. The star attraction is the much-celebrated Pohutu the country's largest geyser, and also boiling pools, silica terraces and lots of bubbling mud.

Lady Knox Geyser in full flow, Waiotapu.

The Rotowhio Marae with its fully carved wharenui (meeting house) hosts daily cultural performances and a longer performance entitled Te Po in the evenings that includes a hangi (feast). There is a deliberate and entertaining element of interactivity with visitors. The Maori Arts and Crafts Institute was established in 1963 to ensure that the traditional artist aspects of Maori culture are not lost. A viewing platform allows visitors to see students at work in the woodcarving studio.

Waiotapu

Off SH5 (29 km south of Rotorua and not to be confused with Waimangu Thermal Valley 4 km before it), T07-3666333, geyserland.co.nz. Daily 0830-1700, $30, child $10.

Waiotapu is, without doubt, the best thermal park in the region, with an almost surreal and colourful range of volcanic features, from mud pools and silica terraces to the famous and beautiful Champagne Pool. The full self-guided walk around the park will take about two hours and take in features with such evocative names as the Devil's Home and Thunder Crater. Without doubt, the highlight of the park is the Champagne Pool, a 62-m-deep flooded volcanic vent, the base of which boils the water to a surface temperature of around 74°C. Hot stuff.

Many time their arrival with the daily 1015 eruption of the Lady Knox Geyser, which is signposted on the Waiotapu Loop Road (off SH5). Just before the geyser, again on the Loop Road, are a number of wonderfully melodious and globulous mud pools that are separate from the park itself.

Devils Home, Waiotapu.

The scenic gondola at Skyline Skyrides.

Skyline Skyrides

Fairy Springs Rd, T07-347 0027, skylinesskyrides.co.nz.
Daily 0900-late. Gondola $24, child $12; gondola
and 3 luge rides $45, child $35.

Everyone who is fit and able and visits Rotorua
should call into the Skyline Skyrides to take a ride
up the mountain in the gondolas and have a go on
the infamous luge, which basically involves
throwing yourself down a concrete course on a
plastic tray with wheels and primitive brakes.
Sounds mad? Absolutely! Other more conventional
activity options include helicopter trips, mountain
biking and then once the adrenalin has settled,
there is always the scenic restaurant, with its
memorable views across the city and the lake.

Hell's Gate & the Waiora Spa

*SH30, Tikitere (15 km from Rotorua), T07-345 3151,
hellsgate.co.nz.*
Daily 0900-2030, from $30, child $15. Park entry,
mud bath and spa from $115. Massage from $80.

Even without the very saucy looking, scantily clad
couple daubing each other in mud on all the
promotional material, the aptly named Hell's Gate
thermal reserve and Waiora Spa is a thoroughly
steamy affair. The 10 ha of thermal features are set
on two levels separated by a tract of bush. With all
that mineral rich bubbly mud about it would seem
rude not to create a mud spa and there are a
number of attractive options from massage or
sulphur spas, to the wonderfully messy and
therapeutic mud facials, scrubs and (best of all)
private mud baths. Who could resist?

Trout pool at Rainbow Springs.

Rainbow Springs & Kiwi Encounter

Fairy Springs Rd, SH5 north (5 km), T07-350 0440,
rainbowsprings.co.nz.
Open 0800-2130, $26, child $15. Kiwi Encounter
T07-350 0440, kiwiencounter.co.nz, 1000-1700,
$28, child $18. Rainbow Springs and Kiwi
Encounter Combo $40, child $20.

The main attraction at Rainbow Springs are shoal
of local trout, combined with other wildlife treats,
including some very tame native birds in a
free-flight aviary. The underwater viewing area is
particularly popular. There are farm animal shows
and a café on site.

Opposite the Rainbow Springs complex is the
Kiwi Encounter complex. As the name suggests the
attraction comes in the form of that truly enigmatic
creature and national icon the kiwi, and this is
undoubtedly one of the best captive-breeding
displays in the country.

You will certainly see live kiwi, but that aside,
the experience is only augmented by a view
through to the husbandry area where you can see
staff tending to incubating eggs, or, if you are very
lucky, chicks (Nov to Mar).

Tip...

For an (as yet) free bathe in natural hot waters try
Kerosene Creek that emanates from the lakes down
Old Waiotapu Road south of Rotorua (signposted
off SH5 and then 2 km to marked Kerosene Creek
parking area). Best time is around 1000 when
everyone is heading for the Lady Knox Geyser
eruption. Also, do not leave valuables in the car and
make sure you lock it. DO NOT swim in the lake.

Sign at Kiwi Encounter.

Taupo & around

For those heading south from Auckland, Taupo is really the first place that begins to satisfy the imagination in terms of what New Zealand is 'supposed' to look like: wide open spaces with distant snow-capped mountains and clear blue lakes. As you come over the hill into the town on a clear day the huge expanse of Lake Taupo dwarfs the distant volcanoes of the Tongariro National Park.

Because of its position in the centre of the North Island, Taupo is the commercial headquarters for the central districts of Taupo and Ruapehu, as well as a major tourist resort. The town is very pleasant, busy and friendly, nestled close to the source of the Waikato River (the longest in the country), and lies on the northernmost bank of the huge lake, once a mighty volcanic crater. The region has a multitude of activities to enjoy. Trout fishing is the main attraction, but you can also try the more adrenalin-pumping pursuits of bungee jumping and tandem skydiving, as well as mountain biking, golf, sailing and walking.

Thermal features create their own dangers in Taupo.

On a calm day the 619-sq-km lake – the largest in the country-can be almost mirror-like, disturbed only by the wakes of boats and ducks. But it wasn't always like this. Lake Taupo is in fact the tranquil remains of one the biggest volcanic eruptions the planet has created in the last 5000 years. In AD 186 the caldera spewed out over 100 cu km of debris at up to 900 kph, covering almost the entire North Island in up to 10 m of ash. Hard to imagine. Now, however, the placid waters are famous for their copious trout and are the domain of the serious angler. The lake is also used for numerous other water-based activities including sailing, cruising, windsurfing and waterskiing. The i-SITE visitor centre can provide the numerous operator listings including local fishing charters and guides.

Most of the longer cruises take in the **Maori rock carvings** which is essentially a huge face complete with moko (tattoos) that can only be seen from the water and adorn an entire rock face in Mine Bay, 8 km southwest across the lake. Although impressive, they were only created in recent years, which does dampen the excitement.

Just west of the town centre the **Waikato River** (the longest in the country) begins its 425-km journey to the Tasman Sea and winds its merry way north behind the town and towards the **Huka Falls** and **Wairakei Park**.

Hot pools

The **AC Baths** (at the top of Spa Rd, T07-3760350, taupovenues.co.nz/ac baths.asp, daily 0600-2100, $6.50, child $2.50), is one of two thermal pool complexes in Taupo where you can soak away any troubles in a range of outdoor, indoor and private spa pools while the kids do their thing on the hydro-slide. The other less frenetic complex is the **Taupo DeBretts Springs Resort** (just off SH5, which heads west from SH1, T07-377 6502, taupohotsprings.com, daily 0730-2130, $15, child $4), along the lake front at the southern edge of town. Their facilities include a massage and beauty-treatment centre.

Essentials

❶ **Getting around** Hot Bus, T0508-468287, hotbus.co.nz, is a hop-on/hop-off service that links most major attractions including the hot pools, Huka Falls and the Craters of the Moon, with an hourly service from the i-SITE visitor centre, 0900-1600, from $15 return. A number of operators service the Tongariro National Park and Tongariro Crossing, daily via Turangi, including **Tongariro Expeditions**: T07-377 0435, thetongarirocrossing.co.nz and **Alpine Hotbus**: T0508468287, alpinehotbus.co.nz. **Taupo Taxis**, T07-3785100.

Bus station Regional buses arrive and depart from the **Travel Centre**, 16 Gascoigne St, T07-3789032 and/or the i-SITE Visitor Centre, Tongariro St.

⊕ **Hospital** Kotare St, T07-376 1000; Taupo Medical Centre, corner of Heu Heu and Kaimanawa streets, T07-3784080.

✚ **Pharmacy** Mainstreet Open Late Pharmacy, corner Tongariro St and Heuheu St, Taupo, T07-3782636, 0900-2030.

➋ **Post office** 46 Horomatangi St, T07-378 9090, Mon-Fri 0830-1700, Sat 0900-1400.

❶ **Tourist information** Taupo i-SITE Visitor Centre, 30 Tongariro St, SH1, T07-376 0027, laketauponz.co.nz, daily 0830-1700, has all the usual information and a good range of maps. It also handles DoC enquiries and offers specialist information available on the Tongariro Crossing with up-to-date weather forecasts.

Wairakei Park

North of Taupo, Wairakei Park straddles the great Waikato River and is home to a range of attractions. Paramount is the thundering Huka Falls (signposted from the SH1, accessed via the Huka Falls Rd). Arguably the most spectacular in the North Island they are the result of the Waikato River being forced through a cleft of solid rock only 15 m wide, before falling 7 m into a cauldron of aquatic chaos and foam. Believe it or not some utter lunatics have attempted the ultimate adrenalin buzz of riding the Huka by canoe. The last time it was attempted, in 1994, two canoeists went down. One made it in about 60 seconds. The other disappeared in the torrent and reappeared minus canoe, and life, 40 minutes later.

Around the region

Maori 'whare' at the Wairakei Terraces.

The walking tracks that lead both north and south along the river from here are worthy of a trek on foot or mountain bike. Just up river is the exclusive retreat of Huka Lodge that frequently hosts visiting dignitaries.

Carrying along the Huka Falls Loop Road (north) you can take a small diversion to admire the view looking back at the falls, before arriving at the **Volcanic Activity Centre** (T07-3748375, volcanoes. co.nz, daily 1000-1700, $10, child $5).

It's well worth a peek, if only to get an inkling of the scale and magnitude of the natural powers that lie beneath your feet. The Taupo district is in the heart of one of the most active volcanic zones in the world, the details of which are well presented in the centre. There are models and displays, all with appropriate shaking and rumbling noises and of course close monitoring of current status.

At the roads terminus **Prawn Park** (T07-3748474, prawnfarm.co.nz, daily 0900-1630, $15, child $10) is hailed as the world's only geothermal prawn farm, where you can join an informative tour or sample some in the Prawn Farm Restaurant.

Alongside Prawn Park are the headquarters of **Huka Falls Jet** (T07-3748572, hukafallsjet.com, from $95, child $55) offering an adrenalin-filled trip to view the base of the Huka Falls with the obligatory 360° spins. Trips depart daily every 30 minutes from 0830 to 1700 on demand.

Back on SH1 and almost directly across it, you can access the **Craters of the Moon Volcanic Reserve**. This is a very steamy affair somewhat akin to taking a stroll through a smoldering bush fire. From almost every conceivable crack and crater along the 50-minute boardwalk, steam quietly billows into the air, with only the faintest hiss giving you an indication of the forces that lie below. Friendly thermo-volunteers selling thermo-souvenirs staff the reserve and the car park and they will kindly keep a hot eye on your car.

A further 7 km north is the **Wairakei Terraces** (T07-378 0913, wairakeiterraces.co.nz, 0900-1700, $18, child $9), which takes a historical and cultural look back in time when the Pink and White terraces, destroyed during the great Tarawera eruption of 1886, were one of the region's most famous volcanic feature. Of equal if not more interest is the **geo-thermal field** behind the complex where huge feeder pipes draw from the subterranean wells and form part of the region's clean green power station.

To complete a convenient circuit back into town you can continue up SH1 and on to SH5 for about 2 km, before turning right, following the signs to Aratiatia. This will take you to a dam on the Waikato that tempers the flow of the **Aratiatia Rapids**, a similar gorge to the Huka Falls, but more jagged. The dam gates are opened at 1000, 1200 and 1400 daily in winter (plus 1600 in summer). **Rapids Jet** (T0800-727437, rapidsjet.com, 4 trips daily, from $90, child $50) are located at the base of the falls on Rapids Road. It's an entertaining trip beginning with a spin upstream to the base of the

Limestone caves at Orakei Korako.

controlled rapids and power station, then downstream through a series of rapids with plenty of 360° spins along the way.

Orakei Korako Thermal Reserve

Head north from Taupo on SH1 for 27 km, turn right onto Tutukau Rd for 13 km, then left on to Orakei Korako Rd, T07-378 3131, orakeikorako.co.nz. Open 0800-1630, $31, child $12.

About 40 km north of Taupo is one of the least visited, but best thermal parks in the country. From the lakeside visitor centre only plumes of steam and a colourful silica terrace across the water give any indication of the numerous interesting volcanic features awaiting you. Once delivered at the terraces by boat you are free to roam the self-guided tracks of the reserve. There is a bit of everything here including algae-covered silica terraces, boiling pools, geysers and bubbly mud.

Tongariro National Park

Tongariro National Park is New Zealand's oldest national park, and the fourth oldest in the world. In 1887 Horonuku Te Heuheu Tukino, the then paramount chief of Ngati Tuwharetoa, gave the central portion – essentially the volcanoes of Ruapehu, Ngauruhoe and Tongariro – to the nation. In more recent years the park has been substantially increased in size to cover an area of 75,250 ha, taking in the forest, tussock country and volcanic desert to the east. The slopes of Ruapehu serve as the principal North Island base for skiing in winter and in summer the park offers excellent walking opportunities, including the Tongariro Crossing, hailed as the best one-day walk in the country.

Mount Ngauruhoe dominates the Tongariro Crossing, Tongariro National Park.

All of the national park's sights are, of course, natural and dominated by the three majestic volcanic peaks of Ngauruhoe, Ruapehu and Tongariro. Although all three mountains are active volcanoes they are quite different in size and appearance.

The symmetrical cone of Ngauruhoe (2291 m) is the youngest of the three volcanoes. Its classic cone shape is due to its relative youth, but also because it has a single vent, unlike Ruapehu and Tongariro. Although Ruapehu has been far more active recently, Ngauruhoe has, over the years, been considered the most continuously active, frequently venting steam and gas and, occasionally, ash and lava. Its last significant eruption occurred in 1954. About 16 km south of Ngauruhoe is the majestic shape of Ruapehu, with its truncated cone, perpetually snow-covered summit peaks and crater lake. It is the North Island's highest mountain, at 2797 m, and over the course of the last century has seen the most violent activity of all the three volcanoes. Between 1945 and 1947, due to a number of eruptions blocking the overflow, the waters of the craterlake rose dramatically. On the stormy Christmas Eve of 1953, without warning, the walls of the crater collapsed and a mighty lahar (volcanic rock and water debris) rushed down the Whangaehu River, wiping out the rail bridge near Karioi. The night train to Auckland arrived moments later and 153 lives were lost. It erupted more recently in September 1995, miraculously without loss of life, and the same thing happened a year later, wiping out the possibility of a ski season for both Whakapapa and Turoa. Ruapehu attracts thousands of visitors each year who come to ski or climb, or enjoy its numerous tramping tracks. Both the summit and Crater Lake of Ruapehu are popular climbs and are, in part, easily accessible via the Whakapapa Ski Field chairlift. The climb to the crater and back takes about seven hours (four hours if you use the chairlifts). Whatever your intentions, always obtain all the necessary information before attempting this climb, go well prepared and do not go alone.

Essentials

❶ **Getting around** The park is bordered along its north and western sides by the SH47 and to the east by SH1 – the famous Desert Road. Whakapapa Village, at the northern base of Ruapehu, serves as the park's main headquarters.

A number of local operators service the Tongariro National Park and Tongariro Crossing, daily via Turangi, Whakapapa and National Park, including (from Taupo) **Tongariro Expeditions**: T07-377 0435, thetongarirocrossing.co.nz; **Alpine Hotbus**: T0508468287, alpinehotbus.co.nz and (from Ohakune) **Maitai Shuttles**: T06-385 8724, wwwtongarirocrossingtransport.co.nz
Bus station The i-SITE in Turangi is the principal bus arrival and departure point. They can assist with local and national bus and coach ticketing.

❶ **Tourist information** Turangi i-SITE visitor centre, Ngawaka Pl, just off SH1, T07-3868999, laketaupo nz.com, ruapehunz.com, daily 0830-1730.
DoC Whakapapa, Whakapapa Village on SH48, T07-892 3729, doc.govt.nz, whakapapa.co.nz, mtruapehu.com, daily 0800-1700 has a wealth of information on the park, interesting displays, maps and weather reports.
Ruapehu i-SITE visitor centre, 54 Clyde St, Ohakune, T06-385 8427, ohakune.info, visitruapehu.com, Mon-Fri 0900-1700, Sat-Sun 0900-1530 (summer).

Ruapehu is home to two main ski fields: Whakapapa on its northwestern flank (serviced by Whakapapa village) and Turoa on the southwestern flank (serviced by Ohakune). Whakapapa is home to the area's most prominent man-made feature, the gracious Bayview Chateau Hotel built in 1929.

Tongariro, at the northern fringe 3 km north of Ngauruhoe, is a fairly complex, flat-topped affair and the lowest at 1968 m. Of the three mountains it is the most benign. From a purely aesthetic point of view its most attractive features are the aptly named Red Crater (which is still active) and the small Emerald Lakes at its base. Nearby are the contrasting Blue Lakes of the central crater and the Ketetahi Springs (hot, but no access is allowed), which emerge on its northern slopes.

A well-trodden section of the Tongariro Crossing.

Tip...

For a live webcam of Ngauruhoe
or Ruapehu visit geonet.org.nz/
volcano/animations/ngauruhoe.
html; and geonet.org.nz/volcano/
animations/ruapehu.html.

Tongariro Crossing

Providing the weather is kind, there is no doubt that the views and the varied volcanic features certainly make this excellent walk a memorable one. But to call it a walk is really an understatement: at about 16 km in length with some steep climbs and the odd bit of scrambling, it is really a mountain hike that can take up to 10 hours. In winter it can be impassable and even in summer it can be dangerous, so despite what you may have heard, don't underestimate it. Having said that, provided you are fit, well prepared and the weather is looking good, you should not pass up the opportunity. One other word of warning. In summer and on a clear day don't expect to be alone; the track now has to handle more than a 1000 people a day, which can spoil it a little.

The walk can be tackled from either north or south, with a number of diversions on the way. The usual recommendation is to start from the Mangatepopo Car Park (off SH47 on the park's western edge) at dawn, and walk the 16 km straight to the SH47A at the park's northern edge (walk terminus) by late afternoon. Much depends on your transport and whether you are tied in to organized drop-offs or are independent. If relying on the various shuttle buses unfortunately in summer you really cannot escape the crowds. However, if you have your own transport try ascending from the northern flank (Ketetahi). Start one hour before dawn (with a head torch) and then you will reach the great vistas at dawn and essentially be alone. The ant trails of people start appearing on the southern horizon about ten in the morning.

From south to north (Mangatepopo) the track makes a gradual ascent towards the southern slopes of Tongariro, while the steep slopes and lava flows of Ngauruhoe loom to the northwest. Sandwiched between the two mountains the track is then forced to make a steep ascent up the Mangatepopo Saddle. Before this ascent there is the option of a short diversion to the Soda Springs – a series of cold springs that emerge from beneath an old lava flow, surrounded by an oasis of greenery. Once you have negotiated the Saddle you enter Tongariro's South Crater. The views of Ngauruhoe from here are excellent (and the especially fit can take in the summit diversion from here). A short climb then leads to the aptly named Red Crater and the highest point on the crossing (1886 m). Following the rim of this colourful (and, in the odd place, steaming) crater you are then treated to a full artist's palette, with the partial descent to the Emerald Lakes, which make food colouring seem bland. (The minerals from Red Crater create the colours in the water). Just beyond Emerald Lakes the track branches right to Oturere Hut, or continues to Ketetahi Hut across the Central Crater and alongside Blue Lake, another water-filled vent. The track then straddles the North Crater taking in the stunning view north across Lake Taupo, before making a gradual zigzag descent to the Ketetahi Hut. The hut sits alone on the slopes at an altitude of about 1000 m, like a first-class real estate property: location, location, location and a real view. (It is the busiest and most popular hut in the park. If you have booked your stay in the hut bear in mind it operates on a first-come first-served basis, so get there early.) The huts all have mattresses, gas cookers (summer only), water supplies and toilet facilities. In the busy seasons wardens can provide information and weather reports. The hot Ketetahi Springs are on private Maori land only a few hundred metres away. Years ago a soak in the pools of the stream armed with a gin and tonic was a highlight of the walk. But sadly disagreements between DOC and the local Iwi mean the springs and stream are now out of bounds. From Ketetahi it is a two-hour descent through native bush to the SH47A access point. For more information contact the DoC Whakapapa visitor centre, page 123.

Waikato & the Waitomo Caves

The Waikato is one of the country's richest agricultural areas, where the eponymous river – the longest in the country – snakes its way through a landscape of green rolling hills and fields. The Waikato, the homeland of the Tainui people – one of the largest tribes in the land – is rich in Maori history, as well as being home to the current Maori queen and head of state. The first Maori king was elected here in 1858 and the subsequent formation of the Maori King Movement, in direct opposition to rule under the British monarchy, led to much bloodshed. After almost a year of fierce battles and confrontation the British finally quashed the Kingites, who fled to southern Waikato, which is now also known as King Country. Today, peace reigns, but the memory lives on.

Waikato also boasts New Zealand's fourth largest city, Hamilton. Although not a major tourist destination, the Waikato is a region with considerable diversity from the famous surf beaches on its coast to the jewel in the crown of the King Country, the Waitomo District, a wonderland of limestone caves and subterranean activities that deservedly make it one of the North Island's premier tourist attractions.

Hamilton

Perched on the serpentine banks of the famous Waikato River, 129 km south of Auckland, Hamilton is the main service centre for the rich fertile agricultural region of the Waikato. Being so close to the major tourist destinations of Auckland and Rotorua, the city struggles to attract visitors for any length of time as it has few major attractions. It is, however, ideally located for explorations around the Waikato Region and can be used as base for exploring the North Island. Visitors stopping briefly in the city can enjoy a visit the celebrated museum, gardens and free-flight aviary of Hamilton Zoo.

Waikato Coast

With the well-advertised attractions of Waitomo and its caves, the Waikato Coast seldom features very high on the average travelling agenda. Indeed, after some unique subterranean adventures most simply pass through the Waikato on the way south, or east to the capital of all things thermal – Rotorua. But for those with more time, who wish to ride a world-class left-hand break, or who simply wish to get off the beaten track, then the Waikato Coast offers some pleasant surprises. The small laid-back coastal village of **Raglan**, 50 km west of Hamilton, offers a palpable sense of relaxation, not to mention plenty of the near legendary surf breaks. Further south, a diversion off SH1 to the remote coastal village of **Kawhia**, and back via the **Marakopa Falls** to Waitomo, can be a relaxing, scenic and often solitary highlight.

Essentials

❶ **Getting around** Both SH1 and the main Auckland to Wellington trunk rail line run through the heart of the Waikato. In Hamilton regional buses arrive and depart from the Transport Centre (and i-SITE), corner of Bryce and Anglesea streets, T07-834 3457/T07-839 3580. For information on local bus services, contact **Busit**, T0800-42875463, busit.co.nz. The train station is on Fraser Street, in Frankton T0800-872467, tranzscenic.co.nz. To get to the Waitomo Caves by bus, the **Waitomo Shuttle**, T0800-808279, $12 one-way, operates a regular service from 0900-1730, between Otorohanga and Waitomo. The **Waitomo Wanderer** T03-477 9083/T0508-926337, waitomotours.co.nz, $45 ($75 return), runs a daily service from Rotorua. It departs Rotorua at 0745 and arrives in Waitomo at 1000, departing Waitomo again at 1545. All the major bus companies offer transport and tours to the glow-worm cave from Auckland and Rotorua; shop around for the best deal. If coming by car or motor home, note there is no fuel available in Waitomo village.
❷ **Post office** 36 Bryce St, Hamilton, T07-8382233, Mon-Fri 0800-1700, Sat 0900-1200.
❶ **Tourist information Hamilton i-SITE visitor centre**, Hamilton Transport Centre, corner of Bryce and Anglesea streets, T07-839 3580, visithamilton.co.nz, waikatonz.co.nz, Mon-Thu 0715-1730, Fri 0715-1845, Sat 0900-1645, Sun 0930-1845.
Otorohanga i-SITE visitor centre on the main SH3 drag at 21 Maniapoto St, T07-873 8951, otorohanga.co.nz, Mon-Fri 0900-1730, Sat-Sun 1000-1600.
Waitomo Museum of Caves i-SITE visitor centre, T0800-474839/T07-878 7640, waitomo.org.nz and waitomo-museum.co.nz, daily 0845-1930.

An academic cow, Hamilton.

Around the region

Otorohanga

The small agricultural service town of Oto, as it is better known, fancies itself as the gateway to the caves and boasts one of the best kiwi houses and displays of native New Zealand birds in the country at the **Otorohanga Kiwi House and Native Bird Park** (Alex Telfer Drive, T07-8737391, kiwihouse.org. nz, daily 0900-1630, $16, child $4).

But before heading off to Waitomo or making a beeline for the kiwi house it is also worth looking at the **Kiwiana Displays** at various points along the main street. They are very well presented and chronicle a range of kiwi icons, heritage and heroes from Sir Edmund Hillary to rugby and Pavlova. The i-SITE visitor centre has a locations leaflet, which comes with a quiz.

Tip...

Of the two high-profile caves the Aranui Cave offers a far more realistic and sedate experience.

Waitomo & the caves

Heading south, beyond the gentle meanderings of the Waikato River and the uninspiring urban vistas of Hamilton, the rest of the Waikato is typical of the North Island countryside with deliciously green, gently rolling hills replete with plump and contented dairy cows. However, in these parts, perhaps more than anywhere else in the country, looks are deceiving since beneath the hooves and the haystacks exists a very different world more suited to the stuff of mystical dreams and wild adventures. As Rotorua is to bubbly mud or Kaikoura is to whales, then southern Waikato and Waitomo are to subterranean caves, rivers and glow-worms. There is easy access to a labyrinth of incredible limestone caves and underground river systems and to all the unique activities that go with them. Where else for example can you abseil 100 m into the 'Lost World' or float through the 'Haggas Honking Holes'?

Typical karst (limestone) scenery, Waitomo.

Waitomo Walkway

If the idea of disappearing underground for a few hours wearing a wetsuit, a rubber ring and a miner's torch holds little appeal then try The Waitomo Walkway (3 hrs return). No wetsuit, no rubber ring, no worms with glowing bottoms, just a good pair of walkie boots. It begins opposite Glow-worm Cave and follows the Waitomo Stream, taking in a number of limestone features before arriving at the Ruakuri Scenic Reserve. This reserve encompasses just a good short walk that is hailed as one of New Zealand's best. Although it does not deserve quite that billing, it is well worth it, with a circular track taking in interesting caves and natural limestone bridges, hidden amongst lush, native bush. At night, just before the path crosses the stream, you can see a small 'scintilla' of glow-worms. These are the only glow-worms you'll see around here for free.

Entrance to Aranui Cave, Waitomo Walkway.

The district of Waitomo ('wai' water and 'tomo' hole) is one of the North Island's biggest tourist attractions. Below ground there is an astonishing network of over 360 recorded caves in the area, the longest over 14 km. If you don't mind getting wet, you should promise yourself that you will try at least one of the amazing underground activities, beyond the highly commercial tour of the Glow-worm cave. Wherever you go, it is pretty unforgettable. All the various companies are based in or around the small village of Waitomo. Waitomo Museum of Caves i-SITE visitor centre is at the heart of operations and almost all the above-ground attractions; below-ground activity operators, booking offices and tourist amenities are within walking distance. Although compact it can be confusing, so the best bet is to absorb the information at the i-SITE and take your time. There are numerous and often very similar activities on offer. Let the staff book on your behalf, or go to the relevant tour operator for more information. The i-SITE has internet access and currency exchange. There is also an ATM outside.

The Lost World.

Tip...

If you can afford it try the seven-hour Lost World Epic (Waitomo Adventures). With a 100m abseil and five hours underground this has to be one of the best and most unusual full-day activity trips in the country T0800-924866/ T07-878 7788, waitomo.co.nz.

Bay of Plenty & East Cape

When Captain James Cook explored this particular stretch of the country's coast in the 18th century he christened it the Bay of Plenty. Back then a mere stretch of the legs on terra firma was no doubt enough to attain such a label. But now, for us modern-day navigators, the obvious question remains – so, is it?

Well, if statistics are anything to go by the answer is categorically yes. By population, the Bay of Plenty is the North Island's fastest-growing region, with the real estate figures of Tauranga now generally accepted as being a barometer to the health of the national economy. Of course inland Rotorua steals most of the attention – and the visitors – but if you have time to spare, a little exploration along the coast here can be rewarding, especially given the almost irresistible attraction of White Island, which is currently the most active volcano in the country.

The svelte statue of Wairaka guards the entrance of Whakatane Harbour.

Tauranga

Tauranga has enjoyed tremendous growth in recent years. With the combination of location, climate, attractive beaches and the many associated activities, as well as its proximity to the delights of Rotorua, it has much to offer both the native and the tourist. Dominating the scene is the harbour and the volcanic dome of Mount Maunganui to the north, which guards its precarious entrance. Nowadays there are almost as many cruise liners as there are merchant ships, and the town's tourist allure seems almost set to overtake its popularity with the locals.

The main historical attraction in Tauranga is the **Elms Mission House** (T07-577 9772, theelms.org. nz, Wed, Sat, Sun 1400-1600, $5) set amidst pleasant grounds on Mission Street on the Te Papa Peninsula, on the site of the original mission.

Of a more contemporary nature is the chic new **Tauranga Art Gallery** (corner of Willow and Wharf streets, T07-578 7933 art gallery.org.nz), which is well worth a look around.

Mount Maunganui

Six kilometres north of Tauranga and dominated by the Mount, the town of Mount Maunganui is graced by golden beaches and maintains an irresistible appeal to kiwi holidaymakers. In winter the streets and beaches are almost empty, but in summer and particularly over the New Year, the town is a tourist battleground with the Mount crowned with an army of view junkies and the beach with battalions of soporific sunbathers. Mount Maunganui itself (known as 'Mauao' or **'The Mount'**) is 232 m high and dominates the coastal horizon at the narrow entrance to Tauranga Harbour. There is a network of pathways that criss-cross the Mount, offering a range of pleasant walks to suit all levels of fitness. The summit climb takes about 45 minutes, while the 3.5-km base track walk is a less demanding option and also offers some good views. At the base of the mount is the **Mount Maunganui Hot Salt Water Pools** (Adams Av, T07-5750868, Mon-Sat 0600-2200, Sun

Essentials

❶ **Getting around** Tauranga, 210 km southeast of Auckland and 83 km north of Rotorua. Regional buses arrive and depart from the i-SITES in Tauranga and Whakatane; all handle bookings and ticketing. **Bayline Coaches** (Bay Hopper), T07-578 3113/T0800-422 9287, baylinebus.co.nz is the local suburban bus company operating regular daily services to Rotorua, Mount Maunganui and east as far as Opotiki.
❷ **Post office** 17 Grey St, T07-577 9911, Mon-Fri 0830-1700, Sat 0900-1600, Sun 1000-1500
❶ **Tourist information** Tauranga **i-SITE visitor centre**, 95 Willow St, T07-578 8103, bayofplentynz. com, Mon-Fri 0830-1730, Sat-Sun 0900-1700. **Mount Maunganui i-SITE visitor centre**, Salisbury Av, T07-575 5099, Mon-Fri 0900-1700, Sat/Sun 0900-1600. **Whakatane i-SITE visitor centre**, corner of Quay Drive and Kakahoroa Drive (east of the centre), T07-308 6058, whakatane.com, Dec-Feb Mon-Fri 0800-1800, Sat/Sun 0900-1700. Mar-Nov Mon-Fri 0800-1700, Sat/Sun 1000-1600. **Opotiki i-SITE visitor centre**, corner of St John and Elliot streets, T07-315 3031, opotikinz.com, daily 0800-1700.

Surfs up at Ocean Beach, Mount Maunganui.

0800-2200, from $6, child $3), where therapeutic salt water is heated to 39°C in a number of large communal and private pools.

From the narrow neck of the Mount, **Ocean Beach** begins a stretch of sand that sweeps, almost uninterrupted, east to Whakatane.

Around the region

White Island, the country's most active volcano.

White Island, the country's most active volcano.

Tip...
To see a live webcam of White Island's crater log on to geonet.org.nz/volcano/activity.

Whakatane

Whakatane is the principal town in the eastern Bay of Plenty, at the mouth of the Whakatane River. It has a vibrant atmosphere that is often lacking in many New Zealand towns of the same size. Whakatane is rich in Maori history, with settlement taking place before the great migrations of the 14th century. For the modern tourist Whakatane serves principally as a gateway to visit the active volcano White Island, which can, on a clear day, be seen 50 km offshore, steaming away merrily. The other major activities are swimming with dolphins, fishing, diving (again off White Island) and, to a lesser extent, walking in the Urewera National and Whirinaki Forest parks.

Ohope

Just 8 km over the hill from Whakatane, heading east, is the 11-km-long sandspit called Ohope Beach, guarding the entrance to the Ohiwa Harbour. Principally a beach resort, it is a fine place to while away a few hours in the sun, swimming, sunbathing or just watching White Island billow with steam in the distance.

White Island

A distinctly steamy affair White Island (Whakāri) is one of New Zealand's most active cone volcanoes built up by continuous volcanic activity over the past 150,000 years. What makes it more remarkable is that about 70% of the volcano is under the sea, making this massive volcanic structure one of the largest in New Zealand. Captain Cook christened it White Island in 1769 purely due to its appearance. But he apparently did not come close enough to confirm, or even realize it was a volcano.

As well as a fascinating natural and geological history it also has a fascinating human history that revolves principally around sulphur mining, which began on the island in 1885. Quite what mining sulphur must have been like on an active volcano in the late 1800s blows the mind (if you'll pardon the pun). This was surely the domain of either desperate or greedy men. In 1914 part of the crater wall collapsed and the resulting landslide destroyed the sulphur mine and miners' village with twelve lives lost and that, as they say, was that. Along with the fascinating and colourful natural features that range from steaming vents, fumarole and that wonderful 'what if' feeling, what remains of the buildings from that era are now a major tourist attraction. The island is now privately owned and became a private scenic reserve in 1953. Daily tours allow more than 10,000 people to visit White Island every year and GeoNet constantly monitors volcanic activity. The most recent eruption was in 2000 when a new vent developed and began to emit ash. An eruption then occurred late in July, which covered the crater area in scoria, also displacing the main craterlake and forming a new explosion crater 150 m across. Of course these days although subtle changes can occur at any time and you can never say never, it is perfectly safe to visit and were any major eruption imminent all the monitoring would almost certainly provide ample warning. One thing however that is a tad amusing is that all visitors must wear a hard hat.

You can visit the island by boat or by helicopter. The principal (and very good) water-based tour company is Pee Jays (15 Strand East, Whakatane, T07-3089588, T0800-733529, whiteisland.co.nz). They offer excellent five-to six-hour volcano trips with around two hour on the island. Lunch and refreshments provided. It will often deviate off schedule if dolphins are spotted, $175. Bookings essential.

By helicopter try **Vulcan Helicopters**, T0800-804354, vulcanheli.co.nz. Three-hour tour, one hour on the island, from $455.

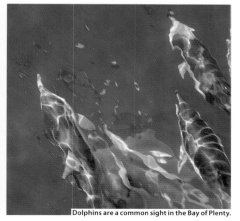

Dolphins are a common sight in the Bay of Plenty.

East Cape to Gisborne

Those with a healthy imagination and good sense of geography will recognize East Cape as the heel of the upside-down boot that is New Zealand. East Cape is the least-visited area in the North Island. This is due not so much to its isolated location but its geography. Almost the entire peninsula is sparsely populated, remote and mountainous. Indeed, much of the Raukumara Range, which makes up most of its interior, remains impenetrable by road, with only wild rivers like the Motu and Mata carving their way through the wilderness. Many make the trip to experience a sunrise at the Cape Lighthouse and satisfy themselves they are one of the first on that day to see it. Of course whether you can depends on the cloud cover but it does add a unique aspect to the trip.

Further south and back to civilization the coastal town of Gisborne prides itself on being the first place Captain Cook set foot in New Zealand in 1769 and in modern times good surf breaks and winemaking. Inland from Wairoa (south of Gisborne) and the enchanting Mahia Peninsula, are the dense forests of the Te Urewera National Park, a place of almost spiritual beauty and particularly famous for its Great Walk, which circumnavigates its most scenic jewel, Lake Waikaremoana.

The best way to explore the Cape is undoubtedly to drive the 331 km of SH35 from either Opotiki to Gisborne or vice versa. Although the trip can be done comfortably in two days, taking longer will allow you to soak up the laid-back atmosphere and explore the numerous bays and beaches as you go.

Before embarking on the trip pick up the detailed road guide from the Opotiki i-SITE (corner St John and Elliott St, Opotiki, T07-315 3031, infocentre@odc.govt.nz / opotikinz.com, open Mon-Fri 0800-1600, Sat-Sun 0930-1330).

One of the several Captain Cook monuments in Gisborne.

Gisborne

The agricultural service town, port and coastal resort of Gisborne attracts many visitors in search of the sun, eager to jump on a surfboard or explore the East Cape. Being the most easterly city in the country, Gisborne prides itself on being the first city in the world to see the sunrise. It is also the first place that Captain Cook set foot in New Zealand in October 1769. Given that it might be rude not to visit **Cook's Landing Site and National Historic Reserve** next to the main port and the base of Titirangi (Kaiti Hill). To get there, cross to the east bank of the river, which flows through the centre of the town. The reserve marks the spot where Cook first set foot to a hostile response from local Maori. Above the reserve the Kaiti Hill provides great views across the city and the second of three Cook memorial edifices. Set in trees at the foot of the hill to the east is the **Te Poho-O-Rawiri marae**, which was built in 1930 and is one of the largest carved meeting houses in the country.

To see the third Cook memorial and a statue of Cook's cabin boy, Young Nick (who is credited as being the first to sight land), head to the beachside reserve on the southern bank of the river. These statues are of particular interest simply because of their location with the backdrop of the port and huge steel-hulled cargo ships, which prove we have come a long way since the tall ships and crow's nests.

For a comprehensive insight in to local and regional history head for the **Gisborne Museum** (Tairawhiti) (Stout St, T06-867 3832, tairawhitimuseum.org.nz, Mon-Sat 1000-1600, Sun 1330-1600, donation).

There are an ever-increasing number of **vineyards** around the region producing the notable vintages. Contact the i-SITE visitor centre for details, 209 Grey Street, Gisborne, T06 868-6139.

For information relating to Lake Waikaremoana and Te Urewera National Park contact the DoC visitor centre, T06-837 3803, doc.govt.nz.

Urewera National Park & Lake Waikaremoana

Te Urewera is daunting and mysterious; a place of almost threatening beauty. The national park encompasses the largest area of native bush in the North Island and is the third largest national park in the country. The main focus of the park is Lake Waikaremoana, the Sea of Rippling Waters, while the track, which circumnavigates it, the Lake Waikaremoana Circuit, is one of the most popular walks in the North Island. The area has a fascinating natural and human history and the vast park is home to a wealth of wildlife: some native and welcome including kiwi, kaka and kokako (one of New Zealand's rarest and most endangered birds). The hub for amenities and accommodation surrounds the motor camp and DoC visitor centre in Waikaremoana. There you can plan some excellent short bush walks, or if time allows the full circuit; a 46-km walk of moderate difficulty, that can usually be completed in three to four days. It can be walked at any time of year and has excellent hut facilities, but permits must be obtained from the DoC Aniwaniwa visitor centre, SH38 at Lake Waikaremoana, T06-837 3803, urewerainfo@doc. govt.nz, daily 1000-1700. Staff can assist with the limited but surprisingly good accommodation options and also handle walk information, fees and hut bookings.

Wairoa is the eastern gateway to the Te Urewera National Park and sits on the coast at the junction of SH2 and SH36, roughly halfway between Gisborne (98 km) and Napier (118 km). Access to Lake Waikaremoana and the heart of the park is 61 km via the hardy SH38. From Waikaremoana it is then a further 75 km to Murupara, or 137 km to Rotorua. If accessing the park from the east call in at the Wairoa i-SITE visitor centre, Cnr SH2 and Queen Street, T06-838 7440/0800 924762, wairoanz.com.

Fire down below

As you no doubt have discovered by now New Zealand has some intriguing names that, political and cultural correctness aside, can reduce grown adults in to the epitome of giggling puerility. Let's face it every country has them, from Bottoms in England to Titty Bong in Australia. In New Zealand the obvious is the correct pronunciation of 'Whaka' of course but let's not even go there. Then there's Waipu. But, alas, here in Waikaremoana, you are really going to have to at least try to maintain a semblance of order. Nothing silly about Waikaremoana of course, Sea of Rippling Waters seems eminently romantic, even marvellous. But what about Te Urewera? It means 'burnt penis' or 'singed genitals' and derives from a rather harrowing local tale of a Māori chief who died after rolling over in his sleep while lying too close to a camp fire.

To Whaiti-Nui-A-Toi Canyon, Whirinaki Forest Park, Te Urewera.

Napier & Hawke's Bay

Napier is the principal town in Hawke's Bay and the largest on the east coast. It is a bright, dynamic place with the pleasant vibe of a Mediterranean coastal town. On the surface it enjoys the perfect relationship with nature: the rich fertile land and the warming sun making it the wine-producing capital of the North Island. However, it paid a heavy price in 1931 when an earthquake almost razed the town. Undeterred, the proud and determined people used this to their advantage and set about its rebuilding with an internationally recognized collection of art deco buildings thought to be amongst the finest in the world. Here, even the McDonalds is art deco.

Craggy Range Vineyard.

Marine Parade

Most of Napier's attractions lie along Marine Parade, which in itself creates an impressive perspective with its long promenade lined with Norfolk Pines and old wooden houses (the few that survived the earthquake). The Marine Parade Walkway starts at the northern end of Marine Parade. It features a number of art deco sculptures in a beachside garden setting and links several waterfront attractions that combine to create an almost European ambience.

First up, at the northern end heading south is the **Ocean Spa complex** (T06-835 8553, Mon-Sat 0600-2200, Sun 0800-2200, $8, child $6, massage from $35). It has hot pools, private spas, health and beauty therapies, and a café.

Almost immediately to the south of the spa complex gardens again predominate with a floral clock, the Tom Parker Fountain and **Pania of the Reef** statue. The fountain is just your average garden fountain by day but by night comes alive with a multi-coloured aquatic light show, while Pania is a small, attractive statue of a Maori maiden, with her legend of love described accordingly in a shower of the fountain's mist.

Heading south is the art deco Colonnade and Sound Shell. The Colonnade was once used for dancing and skating. Opposite the Sound Shell, which is occasionally used for open-air concerts, is the **Hawke's Bay Museum** (9 Herschell St, T06-8357781, hbmag.co.nz, daily 1000-1800, $10, children free), which offers a wide range of exhibits relating to the history and art of the region in modern surroundings. Nga Tukemata (The Awakening) presents the art and taonga of the local Maori and a rare presentation of evidence that dinosaurs once existed in New Zealand. Special attention is afforded to the earthquake of 1931. Relics from the rubble accompany audio-visual descriptions and touching memories of survivors.

Dominating the corner of Emerson Street and Marine Parade are the art deco Tower (The Dome) and the art deco Masonic Hotel.

Essentials

❶ **Getting around** Napier is on SH2, 321 km north of Wellington. The junction with SH5 and SH2 is about 6 km north of the town and from there it is 117 km to Taupo. Buses arrive and depart from the **Napier Travel Centre**, Munroe St, T06-835 2720, 0830-1700. All major buses companies serve Hastings too. The i-SITE visitor centre acts as ticketing agents.
Gobus, T06-835 8833, gobus.co.nz, offers service in Napier and to Hastings and Havelock North.
❷ **Post office** Napier PostShop, 151 Hastings St, T06-835 3725, open Mon-Fri 0800-1700, Sat 0930-1230.
❶ **Tourist information** Napier i-SITE visitor centre, 100 Marine Parade, T06-834 1911, visit us.co.nz/hawkesbaynz.com, open daily 0900-1700. **DoC**, 59 Marine Parade, T06-834 3111, napier-ao@doc.govt.nz, Mon-Fri 0900-1615. It has information about Cape Kidnappers Gannet Colony (plus tide times).
Hastings i-SITE visitor centre, Westerman's Building, corner of Russell and Heretaunga streets, T06-873 5526, hawkesbaynz.com and hastings.co.nz, Mon-Fri 0830-1700, Sat-Sun 0900-1700.

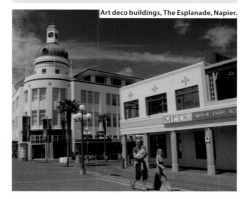

Art deco buildings, The Esplanade, Napier.

Back on the seaward side of Marine Parade past the modern i-SITE visitor centre and Sunken Gardens is **Marineland** (T06-834 4027, marineland.co.nz, daily 1000-1630, $11, child $5.50; Swim with the Sea Lion, daily sessions $50; Penguin Recovery Workshop at 1300, $16) where seal displays are combined with ongoing programme of wild penguin and gannet rehabilitation.

Art deco architecture

The main attraction of Napier is its famous art deco and Spanish Mission architecture created after the devastating 1931 earthquake. On foot, the two central streets, Emerson and Tennyson, have many examples. On Emerson Street is the ASB Bank with its incorporated Maori designs and fine doorway, while on Tennyson Street the highlights are (from east to west) the Daily Telegraph Building, restored Municipal Theatre and the Deco Centre (art deco shop). Further afield is perhaps the most attractive building of all, the façade and entrance of the 1932 National Tobacco Company at the corner of Bridge and Ossian streets. Although somewhat distant from the town centre (in the port area of Westshore), it is worth the diversion. The building is even more impressive at night, when it is beautifully and imaginatively lit. Also worth seeing is the art deco McDonalds 'McDeco' in the suburb of Taradale (Gloucester St). For more comprehensive insight you can join a walking tour or pick up self-guided walking or driving leaflets from the i-SITE.

The art deco McDonalds in Taradale.

Continuing south you then encounter the intriguing Millennium Sculpture created by local artist David Trubridge. The work is carefully lined up to where the sun rose at the dawning of the new millennium. Nearby The **National Aquarium of New Zealand** (T06-834 1404, national aquarium.co.nz, open daily 0900-1700, $16, child $8.30, behind-the-scenes tours $25, child $12, tank dives from $50) hosts an eclectic mix of native and non-native water and land creatures, from the enchanting seahorse to the iconic kiwi. The design of the building is quite clever, creating the impression that one is descending into the depths. Several remarkably toothy inhabitants will also have any unsuspecting herpetophobe breaking into a cold sweat.

Cape Kidnappers

Cape Kidnappers, the jagged white peninsula that marks the southern boundary of Hawke's Bay, is famous for its colony of gannets. These large, elegant seabirds have lots of attitude and, weighing in at about 2 kg with deadly 15-cm beaks

designed to spear fish, they have every right to it. In the summer months, up to 15,000 gannets gather at Cape Kidnappers to breed, forming the biggest mainland colony in New Zealand, and one of the biggest in the world. Perhaps given their attitude and armoury, gannets are not particularly fearful of anything or anybody, which makes them very approachable, particularly when grouped together and guarding their own little breeding patch. The tourist visiting season runs from October to late April, with the best time to view being early November and late February.

There are two tours available to see the gannets. One operator negotiates the beach and the tides below the peninsula by tractor, the other goes overland (see page 153). The tractor-trailer affair is very entertaining for young and old and recommended. Provided the tides are right you can walk the 10 km to the colony yourself. The walk and beach tractor trip starts from the Clifton MotorCamp. 19 km southeast of Napier.

Hawke's Bay Vineyards

Given the climate and the soil in the Hawke's Bay area, it was inevitable that it would not take long for the first grapevine to be planted by the first Europeans settlers. Since then, the vines and the industry have boomed, making Hawke's Bay second only to Marlborough as the country's top wine-producing region. There are over 40 wineries in the area so unless you are a connoisseur, knowing which to visit can be a dilemma. Thankfully the free Hawke's Bay Winery Guide leaflet gives details of what each vineyard offers. Some like the **Sileni Estate**, (Maraekakaho Rd, Hastings, T06-879 8768, selini.co.nz).

have stunning architecture, others like **Craggy Range** (253 Waimarama Rd, Havelock North, east of the village, T06-873 7126, craggyrange.com) set in the shadow of Te Mata Peak enjoy admirable surroundings; some like the **Mission Estate** (end of Avenue Rd, Taradale, T06-844 2259, missionestate. co.nz), are very old, while others are particularly famous, more established, or have fine restaurants or cafés. Most offer sales and tastings. You can either embark on a tour according to your own choice and itinerary, or join a number of organized tours. If you know little about wines, and New Zealand wine in particular, an organized tour is advised (see page 153).

Hastings

Hastings is a lively, sprawling, mainly agricultural service centre 21 km south of Napier and, like Napier, it was devastated by the 1931 earthquake, with the loss of 93 lives. In rebuilding the town the architects echoed Napier's art deco and Spanish Mission styles, much of which can clearly be seen in the town centre. The two best examples are the **Westerman's Building** that now houses the i-SITE visitor centre on Russell Street and the recently refurbished HB Opera House on Hastings Street. During the summer the town is a blaze of colour for the annual Blossom Festival, when row upon row of hanging baskets line the streets providing a tourist attraction in itself and winning the town

much praise around the country. Many remain year-round. Modern-day attractions in Hastings include the **Hawke's Bay Exhibition Centre** (201 Eastbourne St, T06-876 2077, Mon-Fri 1000-1630, Sat-Sun 1100-1600, usually free depending on exhibitions), which serves as the region's premier arts venue offering a varied programme of national and international touring exhibitions. Science and history also feature and there is an in-house café. If your visit to the town coincides with a Sunday the weekly **Farmers Market** at the Hawke's Bay Showgrounds, Kenilworth Rd, 0830-1230, provides an ideal opportunity to meet locals and purchase fresh produce.

Havelock North & Te Mata Peak

Havelock North is a very pleasant little village nestled amongst vineyards and orchards towards the coast and in the shadow of the 399-m Te Mata Peak. The view from the summit of Te Mata on a clear day is a 'must-see' and it is easily reached by car via the village and Te Mata Peak Road. Weather permitting, it is also a popular spot for paragliding (see page 153).

Paragliding from Te Mata Peak, Havelock North.

Taranaki & Wanganui

In many ways Taranaki is more mountain than region. The awesome 2518-m snow-capped volcanic cone of the same name seems to dominate everything and, even shrouded in mist, it is strangely omnipresent. Although many have enjoyed the volcano, it has also caused a number of deaths, and they say it is due for another eruption. However, whether you look at it with reverence or fear, it will always be the region's defining feature.

The largest town in the region is New Plymouth, a proud, prosperous and modern centre that lies in the shadow of Mount Taranaki on the northwest coast. Although a little bit out of the way, those who make the effort to visit the region will not be disappointed. As well as the superb scenery and range of activities on or around the mountain itself, the region boasts a fascinating history, fine parks, gardens, arts and crafts and a coastline internationally recognized for its excellent surfing.

Further south and east is the Wanganui Region, scythed almost in half by the Whanganui River, the longest navigable river in the North Island. Steeped in history, and supporting a rich watershed of remote hills adorned with native bush, much of the region is protected within the boundaries of the Whanganui National Park, a popular spot for kayakers and trampers, who leave civilization behind for days on end.

New Plymouth

Based on resources of rich agricultural land and natural gas and oil supplies, lively New Plymouth enjoys considerable prosperity and is the main service town and population base of the Taranaki Region. The town, and the entire district, is dominated by the mountain, which seems to dictate the general mood, like some huge meteorological barometer. On a clear day, when the mountain radiates, its sheer size and stature are mirrored proudly in the town and the region. But, when shrouded in mist and rain, the area feels dull and somber. As well as being a fine base from which to explore the recreational delights on and around the mountain and the region as a whole, New Plymouth itself has an excellent art gallery, some interesting historic buildings and a fine marine and public park.

The rather flash **Taranaki Museum and Library (Puke Ariki)** (Egmont St, T06-759 6060, pukeariki. com, Mon, Tue, Thu, Fri 0900-1800, Wed 0900-2100, Sat/Sun 0900-1700, free, temporary exhibitions $6) houses an interesting collection of Maori artifacts and displays, mixed with the usual pioneer exhibits and wildlife specimens. Obviously the great mountain features heavily and this is an opportunity to learn of its importance to the region, if not its power.

One of the town's most celebrated institutions is the **Govett-Brewster Gallery** (corner of Queen and King streets, T06-759 6060, govettbrewster. com, daily 1030-1700, free). The interior is on three levels and looks very modern, befitting its reputation as the premier contemporary art gallery in the country. The gallery doyen is Len Lye, a poet, writer and multimedia artist who specialized in pioneering animation work in the 1930s. His best-known work is the **Wind Wand** on the waterfront near the museum. Created for the millennium celebrations it is a 45-m, 900-kg kinetic sculpture that is designed to sway gently in the breeze. The bulb at the end is lit at night to enhance this effect. New Plymouth is famous for its extensive and feature-filled parks, the oldest and

Taranaki coastline.

finest of which are **Pukekura Park and Brooklands Park**, which merge together. On the southern edge of the city near the ugly towers of the power station and the port is the **Sugar Loaf Island Marine Park** with its eroded, volcanic rock islands. It is home to fur seals and a variety of nesting seabirds. Boat trips to visit the park and view the wildlife are available. The shoreline of the park is part of an interesting 7-km Coastal Walkway, the highlight of which is the climb up **Paritutu Rock**.

Around the region

Mount Taranaki at dawn from Lake Mangamahoe.

Around New Plymouth

Carrington Road (off Victoria Rd) heads southwest out of New Plymouth towards the mountain. It has a number of sights including **The Pukeiti Rhododendron Trust Gardens** (2290 Carrington Rd, T06-752 4141, daily 0900-1700, winter 1000-1500, $15, $10 in winter). This is a 4-sq-km garden surrounded by bush that is world-renowned for its beautiful displays of 'rhodies' and azaleas, which are best viewed in the spring/summer and especially during the Rhododendron Festival in late October. There is a restaurant, and a shop selling plants and souvenirs.

If you continue on Carrington Road you will join the network of roads that surround the mountain. There is a fine walk and views of the mountain on the Stony River and Blue Rata reserves.

There is something you simply must do on your visit to New Plymouth (weather permitting) and that is to soak up the beauty and serenity of

Lake Mangamahoe. Just 10 km southeast on SH3, this scenic reserve is one of the very best places where you can see a reflection of the mighty mountain on water. After enjoying the lake itself, head to the road end and take the right hand track up the steps to the lookout point. From here at sunset, or anytime when the mountain is clear, the view is magnificent.

If you fancy doing the 175-km trip around the mountain, it involves at least a full day via the Surf Highway 45 and SH3. But on a clear day the mountain will be good company throughout, and there are a number of interesting places to see and visit on the way including the **Cape Egmont Lighthouse**, about 3 km down Cape Road. Although the lighthouse is closed to visitors it is still of interest. Back on SH45, you can enjoy the scenery or explore the many side roads until you reach Opunake and Manaia, which is the place to leave SH45 if you want to get a bit more intimate with the mountain at **Dawson Falls**. You can also stay there if you wish to attempt the summit walk and there is a DoC visitors centre to obtain the detail (Manaia Rd, Kaponga, T06-7560990). At Dawson Falls there are also some good short-walk options.

Mount Egmont (Taranaki) National Park

Weather permitting, no trip to Taranaki would be complete without getting close to the mountain. At 2518 m, Mount Taranaki is a classically shaped, dormant volcano formed by the numerous eruptions of the last 12,000 years. The most recent happened 350 years ago and they say she is now overdue, with the potential to go off at any time. But don't worry these days there would be plenty of warning.

The main access points to the park and the mountain are at North Egmont (Egmont visitor information centre), Stratford (East Egmont) and Manaia (Dawson Falls). East Egmont is accessed via Pembroke Road, which heads 18 km towards the mountain from Stratford. Dawson Falls is at the end of Upper Manaia Road, via Kaponga on the southern slopes of the mountain, 24 km from Stratford. If you do not have your own transport, Taranaki Tours (T06-757 9888, taranakitours.com), offer shuttle services to the mountain from New Plymouth (particularly north Egmont), from $40 return.

Before attempting any major walks on the mountain you should read all the relevant information. The i-SITE visitor centre in New Plymouth can provide basic information, while the DoC office (both in town and on the mountain) can fill in the detail with walking information, maps and weather forecasts.

The 140-km of walks take from 30 minutes to four days and are well maintained. The tracks vary in difficulty, but all are easily accessible from the main access points and information centres above. The forest and vegetation is called 'goblin forest' (due to its miniature hobbit-style appearance as the altitude increases) and the entire mountain is drained by myriad babbling streams.

Wanganui & the Whanganui River National Park

Wanganui lies at the mouth of the Whanganui River roughly halfway between New Plymouth and Wellington.

Proud of its river and once a bustling port, Wanganui is now principally an agricultural service town and the southern gateway to the Whanganui River National Park. The town boasts a rich heritage and retains some fine buildings as well as a reputable museum and many parks and gardens. In summer the main street is ablaze with a thousand hanging baskets of flowers and throughout the year the restored steamboat **Waimarie** plies the great river, reminding both locals and visitors of days gone by.

From Wanganui the river it begins its 290-km journey inland, carving its way through some of the most remote and inaccessible country in the North Island. Negotiable by waka (canoe) and steamboat for much of its length, the region is rich in both Maori and European history, from the first days of early exploration and settlement through to the river's renaissance as a tourist and recreational attraction. Although the park is hard to access (which is undoubtedly part of its charm), there is the opportunity to explore the historical sites of the river and enjoy its atmosphere. You can do this, in part on its banks by road and walking tracks, or on the river itself by jet boat or kayak.

Central North Island

❶ Rotorua: Maori
Page 112

As the cultural capital Rotorua offers plenty in the way of Maori based imagery from commercial performances to fence posts.

A word of warning however. Common sense and sensitivity is required at all times. Do not enter any private property and when it comes to impromptu shots of Maori always ask first.

Exterior shots of the Tamatekapua marae and St Faiths Church at Ohinemtu are often productive (see page 113) as are the carvings bordering and within Government Gardens (itself a great photo venue especially at dawn or dusk, page 113). If you attend a commercial Maori performance (there are many on offer) you will have the opportunity to take photos of proceedings. If indoors try to get a seat at the front and discreetly use slow exposures hand held without flash (1/4-1/8 of a second) of the performance group. This can often result in unusual images.

Again, if in doubt, ask.

❷ Waiotapu & Waikite
Page 115

Waiotapu is a wonderful venue for photography with the obvious highlight the mesmerizing Champagne Pool. Wideangle lenses are of course best and it needs to be in full sunlight. The 'Artists Palette' also presents opportunities and don't forget abstracts. Think near, not just far – but do not stray from the walkways.

Also do not miss the mud pools just north of the park. You can spend hours there getting that perfect globulous mud shot and all the time thinking 'thank God for digital'.

While you are in the area it is also well worth capturing some images at the Waikite Springs (nature trail) about 6 km west. You can then reward yourself with a hot pool.

❸ Wairakei Valley: Taupo
Page 119

The Wairake Valley presents numerous possibilities. Two of the best venues are:

The Craters of The Moon thermal reserve A very steamy affair and free. Within reason try to capture that quintessential boardwalk, person and steam combo – it takes patience.

The Geothermal fields (left off SH1 at the Wairakei Terraces) Another fascinating place especially just before sunset, again it costs absolutely nothing.

❹ Tongariro National Park
Page 122

You just can't take your eyes off Ngauruhoe can you? That almost perfect volcanic cone with shades of red in summer and shrouded in its white blanket in winter. There are endless vantage points to photograph both Ngauruhoe and Ruapehu, but by far the best way to do so and to secure some world-class volcanic landscape photography is to do the Tongariro Crossing (see page 125). The weather will have to be clear (or clearing) and you must try to get up to the plateau around dawn (which means a very early start and the lower part of the track negotiated by head torch). Beyond that advice is not necessary. Short of a lack of memory cards you can't go wrong. Always go prepared and in company.

❺ Mount Taranaki
Page 143

Isn't it beautiful! Needless to say dawn and dusk are the best times and sometimes a bit of weather is required. Try the lookout and reflections at Lake Mangamahoe (10 km southeast left off SH3). Egmont Road (13 km southeast and right off SH3) that heads into the North Egmont (DoC) Visitor Centre is a happy hunting ground. Also try using the Waiwhakaiho River (that runs alongside Egmont Road) as a foreground.

Sleeping

Rotorua & around

The Princes Gate $$$

*1057 Arawa St, T07-348 1179,
princesgate.co.nz.*
Conveniently located between
the city centre and Government
Gardens, the 1897 Princes Gate is
a boutique hotel with plenty of
character. Wide range of rooms,
some fully self-contained, and
replete with four-poster beds
and bath. An in-house bar/
restaurant, sauna and thermal
pools all add to the appeal.

Treks YHA Backpackers $$-$

*1278 Haupapa St, T07-349 4088,
yha.co.nz.*
A fine modern establishment
carefully considered in layout
and design, well facilitated with a
spacious kitchen and living area
and tidy ensuite doubles.

Motor parks
Rotorua Thermal Holiday Park $$$-$

*Old Taupo Rd, T07-346 3140,
rotorua thermal.co.nz.*
Well-maintained, spacious and
sheltered motor park with a wide
range of accommodation
options from standard self-
contained units to standard and
en suite log cabins, powered and
non-powered sites. Camp
kitchen, TV lounge, small shop,
licensed café and free hot pools.
Also within walking distance of
the Whakarewarewa (Te Puia)
Thermal Reserve.

Waikite Valley Thermal Pools and Camp Ground $

*Waikite Valley Rd, Rotorua,
T07-333 1861, hotpools.co.nz.*
A gem of a motor camp located
32 km south of Rotorua off SH5
and attached to the Waikite
Thermal Pools complex. Basic
but adequate facilities including
powered sites, camp kitchen and
free entry to pools. It is also just
7 km from the Waiotapu Thermal
Reserve.

Taupo & around

Terraces Hotel $$$

*Napier-Taupo Highway, T07-378
7080, terraceshotel.co.nz.*
First established in 1889 this
hotel on the edge of the town
has standard rooms, studio
suites, bar and restaurant that
combined offer both class and
character. The added attraction
is the Hot Springs and Spa Resort
only a short stroll away.

Action Downunder YHA Hostel $$-$

*56 Kaimanawa St, T07-3783311,
yha.co.nz.*
A very tidy YHA associate with
great modern rooms and
facilities including family and
double ensuites with personal
computer and internet – a rare
find. Off-street parking,
impressive kitchen facilities,
outdoor big-screen movies, spa,
gym and bike hire.

Motor parks
De Brett's Thermal Resort $$$-$

*Napier/ Taupo Highway (SH5),
T07-378 8559, debrettsresort.co.
nz.*
A well-facilitated five-star motor
park located right opposite the
hot pools complex at the edge
of town. Standard and self-
contained cabins, studio and
family units and lodges. Powered
and non-powered sites, camp
kitchen and TV lounge.
Concession rates to thermal
pools are an added incentive.

Wairakei Thermal Valley Motor Camp $

Wairakei, T07-374 8004.
Basic camping with powered
sites and camp kitchen 9 km
north of Taupo and 1.5 km from
SH1. The appeal here is the
peaceful location and the small
menagerie of visitor loving
animals roaming free. Missing
your pets? Here is the solution.

Bayview Chateau $$$$-$$

Whakapapa Village, T07-892 3809, chateau.co.nz.
Perhaps the most famous hotel in the North Island, the Bayview provides traditional luxury in a grand location. Visible for miles around, the hotel sits like a beacon in the heart of the national park. Elegance in keeping with its age (1929) combined with traditional modern facilities, including an excellent restaurant, a bar, café, pool and even a golf course.

Powderhorn Chateau $$$

Corner of Mangawhero and Thames streets, Ohakune, T06-385 8888, powderhorn.co.nz.
Alpine-style accommodation base especially for skiing in winter. Choice of lodge-style suites, an apartment, a heated swimming pool and a small casino. Warm and lively atmosphere in the bar and two in-house restaurants. Ski and bike hire is also available.

Motor parks

Whakapapa Holiday Park $$-$

Whakapapa Village, T07-892 3897, whakapapa.net.nz.
Standard motor park and backpacker accommodation with basic facilities but set in the heart of the village and riverside close to all amenities.

Waitomo Express and Hobbit Motel $$$

1177 Waitomo Valley Rd, Waitomo, T07-8786666, woodlynpark.co.nz.
If it is the unusual you are looking for, look no further than Barry Woods at Woodlyn Park (1 km down Waitomo Valley Rd) and his converted train carriage, hobbit motel, or ex-Second World War aircraft and patrol boat accommodation. Most are self-contained.

Solscape $$$-$

Located 7 km west of Raglan village centre at 611 Wainui Rd, T07-825 8268, solscape.co.nz.
Again, if you're looking for something completely different this really is the only place to stay in Raglan. The owners have gone to great pains to relocate and renovate an array of railway wagons as colourful accommodation units from dorm to self-contained. Smaller cabooses (cabin houses) and a choice of three fully self-contained cottages (2 with open fires), powered and tent sites are also available. Bay views and a veritable menagerie of animals add to the appeal.

Motor parks

Waitomo Caves Top Ten Holiday Park $$$-$

Waitomo T07-878 7639, waitomopark.co.nz.
A modern, convenient and very friendly motor camp right in the heart of the village. Spacious, great facilities including internet, pool and spa.

Bay of Plenty

Harbour City Motor Inn $$$-$$

50 Wharf St, Tauranga, T07-571 1435, taurangaharbourcity.co.nz.
Modern motel, ideally located in the heart of Tauranga. Stylish studio and two-bedroom units with spa. Sky TV and parking.

White Island Rendezvous $$$-$$

15 Strand East, T0800-733529, T07-308 9500, whiteisland.co.nz.
Part of the Pee Jay White Island tour operation, so ideal if you are taking the tour. Modern waterfront motel with a full range of units from standard to deluxe with spa, a fully self-contained apartment and cottage. Sky TV and internet ports. Café open 0630-1700.

Motor parks
Top Ten Papamoa Beach Holiday Resort $$$-$
535 Papamoa Beach Rd, T07-572 0816, papamoabeach.co.nz.
One of many options and a good base near Mt Maunganui. Beachfront location with a wide range of accommodation options and facilities.

East Cape to Gisborne
Waiwaka B&B and Snapper Bach $$
Located 2 km north of Te Kaha and 12 km from Whanarua Bay, East Cape T07-325 2070, waikawa.net.
Modern self-contained two-bedroom bach and separate bed and breakfast ensuites in a peaceful spot. TV, BBQ, cooking facilities, internet.

Motor parks
Waikanae Beach Holiday Park $$$-$
Grey St, Gisborne, T06-867 5634, gisborneholidaypark.co.nz.
This is the best-equipped and most centrally located motor camp in town. Short walk to the beach and i-SITE visitor centre.

Morere Hot Springs Accommodation $$$
SH2, Morere, (52 km south of Gisborne) T06-837 8824, morerehotsprings.co.nz.
Lodge (6 bedrooms) plus two character self-contained cabins and cottage. Just a short stroll from the hot springs.

Papamoa Beach Resort.

Napier & Hawke's Bay

Black Barn (Vineyard) Retreats $$$$
Havelock North, T06-877 7985, blackbarn.com.
A superb selection of luxury lodge retreats or cottages, from eight to two bedroom, fully self contained and set in the heart of the vineyard.

Motor parks
Kennedy Park Top Ten Motel and Holiday Park $$$-$
Storkey St, T06-843 9126, kennedypark.co.nz.
Popular, well-established and facilitated motor park and the closest to the town centre.

Taranaki & Wanganui

The Nice Hotel $$$
71 Brougham St, New Plymouth, T06-758 6423, nicehotel.co.nz.
A small luxury boutique hotel well placed for the town centre and all amenities. Each of the eight rooms is themed according to its outlook and reflects the town's history or contribution to the arts. As well as stylish design, the rooms offer all the comforts. The popular restaurant is relaxed.

Anndion Lodge $$-$
2 km from the centre, 143 Anzac Parade, Wanganui, T06-343 3593, anndionlodge.co.nz.
Top-quality option pitched between a modern backpacker hostel and a motel. Offers modern and tidy riverside accommodation, with rooms ranging from super-king to dorms at reasonable prices. Well facilitated with spa, internet, off-street parking.

Motor parks
Egmont Eco Leisure Park $$-$
12 Clawton St, New Plymouth T06-753 5720, egmont.co.nz.
Set in native bush with lodge, cabins powered and tent sites, fully equipped camp kitchen. A short walk from the town centre.

Eating & drinking

Bistro 1284 $$$
1284 Eruera St, T07-364 1284, bistro1284.co.nz.
Tue-Sat from 1800, booking advised.
A 1930s wooden townhouse with a congenial atmosphere and causing something of a stir locally having won the city's best restaurant award four years running. Minimalist and imaginative Pacific Rim menu with NZ venison and lamb a speciality. For entrée don't go past the roast kumara and honey soup with yoghurt and rocket.

Landings Café $$
537 Spencer Rd, Lake Tarawera, T07-362 8502.
Daily from 0900.
Book for dinner.
Set on the shores of Lake Tarawera with uninterrupted views over both mountain and lake. Affordable and casual café style dining, excellent service and a cosy open fire in winter. There is also a garden bar for those lazy summer evenings.

Fat Dog $$-$
1161 Arawa St, T07-347 7586.
Sun-Wed 0800-2100, Thu-Sat 0800-2130.
Consistently rated as the best café in town, always busy and friendly with a mixed clientele. Quirky decor, local artwork, an imaginative blackboard menu and yes, the odd fat dog.

The Brantry Restaurant $$$
45 Rifle Range Rd, Taupo, T07-378 0484.
Owned and operated by local sisters Prue and Felicity Campbell the Brantry is fast earning a reputation as one of Taupo's best. Set in a stylishly refurbished 1950s town house you can enjoy the intimacy of the cellar room or the buzz of alfresco in summer. Beautifully presented and affordable contemporary NZ cuisine and an extensive wine list. Perhaps try the set three-course option and for sweet the divine Tiramisu.

L'Arte Mosaic café and Sculpture Garden $$
225 Marapa Rd, Acacia Bay (2.5 km off Acacia Bay Rd right on to Marapa Rd), T07-378 2962.
Wed-Sun 0900-1600.
A magical little café that has grown around the work and imaginations of local clay artist Judi Brennan. Her signature quirky clay garden decor adorned with colourful mosaics and the work of other local artists are a delight and the food and coffee is also well worth the trip. Try the famous 'eggs benny'.

Knoll Ridge Café $$-$
Top of the Bruce Rd (take the chairlift!), Whakapapa, T07-892 3738. Chairlift $21, child $11.
Open 0900-1600 (last lift down 1600 in summer).
This is the highest café in the North Island, at the top of the main chairlifts of the Whakapapa ski field. Not only a good place to head if you fancy a coffee with a view, but the ride is wonderful and you can take a walk to the ridgeline for even better views. For conditions, refer to mtruapehu.com.

Scott's Epicurean $$
181 Victoria St, Hamilton, T07-839 6680.
Daily Mon-Fri from 0700 for breakfast, lunch. Sat/Sun from 0830 for brunch.
Hamilton is renowned for its wide range of quality eateries and it is hard to choose, but this long-established funky little café with its imaginative lunch/brunch menu is hard to resist.

Waitomo Caves Tavern $$
Near the i-SITE visitor centre, Waitomo Village, T07-878 8448.
The great place to go for cheap and basic pub grub and a pint with the locals. A fine opening line is 'So, why do glow worms' bottoms glow'!

Listings

Bay of Plenty

Harbourside Restaurant $$$
The Strand, Tauranga, T0800-721714, harbourside-tga.co.nz.
Open 1130-late.
Enjoys a loyal following and the reputation as Tauranga's best restaurant. Located as much on the water as beside it, at the southern end of the Strand, it offers an excellent and imaginative all-day blackboard and à la carte menu, with an emphasis on the NZ contemporary classics and local seafood.

Astrolabe $$$-$$
82 Maunganui Rd, Mount Maunganui, T07-574 8155, astrolabe.co.nz
Open for breakfast, lunch and dinner.
Named not after a space ship, but a shipwreck, this classy combination restaurant, bar and café offers breakfast, lunch and dinner with a range of fine and imaginative traditional dishes. Live bands often play at weekends.

East Cape to Gisborne
The Wharf Café $$$-$$
60 The Esplanade, The Wharf, Gisborne, T06-868 4876, wharfbar.co.nz.
Daily 0900-late.
This is not very expensive but still at the high end, very popular, with wide-ranging menu with European, Pacific Rim and Asian combinations. Nautically themed and a great waterside setting overlooking the marina.

Colosseum Café and Wine Bar (Matawhero Wines) $$
Riverpoint Rd, Matawhero, T06-868 8366.
Open Mon-Sat.
Excellent vineyard option attached to the Matawhero Vineyard where established vintner Denis Irwin has, since the mid-1970s, earned a fine reputation for his *gewurztraminers*. Also produced are Chardonnay, Cabernet Sauvignon, Merlot and Pinot Noir.

Mission Estate $$$
198 Church Rd, Taradale, T06-845 9354, missionestate.co.nz.
Daily for lunch and dinner, booking essential.
This is the country's oldest winery and one of a number of vineyard restaurants. Has a solid reputation for quality contemporary cuisine with European influences. Outdoor seating available in summer.

Café Ujazi $$-$
28 Tennyson St, Napier, T06-835 1490.
Daily from 0800.
The local favourite in Napier. Good coffee, good vibe and a comprehensive blackboard menu. Vegetarian a speciality.

Peak House Restaurant $$-$
Te Mata Peak Rd, Havelock North, T06-877 8663, peakhouse.co.nz.
Wed-Mon 1000-1600.
Perched 300 m up Te Mata Peak this is a great lunch or afternoon tea venue with a fantastic view.

Andre L'Escargot $$$
37-43 Brougham St, New Plymouth, T06-758 4812.
Mon-Sat from 1700.
This is long-established regional favourite offering award-winning, fine French-style cuisine in a congenial setting. Now offers affordable Bistro Chic set menus for around $50.

Vega Restaurant $$$-$$
49 Taupo Quay, Wanganui, T06-349 0078.
Lunch Tue-Sun, daily for dinner.
Classy establishment set in a converted warehouse near the river. It has earned a reputation as the city's finest, especially for seafood. Excellent wine list.

Entertainment

Te Po at Te Puia (Whakarewarewa)
Fenton St, T07-348 9047, tepuia.com.
Te Po evening performance and feast, $95, child $47.50.
Rotorua is arguably the best place to experience a Maori cultural performance in New Zealand, but beware; they can be horribly kitsch and commercial. One of the better experiences is the Te Po evening performance at Te Puia. It is commercial but well polished and of course there is a hangi-style meal included, as well as a tour of the famed thermal features.

Woodlyn Park
1177 Waitomo Valley Rd, T07-878 6666, woodlynpark.co.nz.
$23, child $13. Shows at 1130 and 1330.
This is the above-ground entertainment must-see in Waitomo, if not the region. A typical example of Kiwi imagination, ingenuity and that simple can-do mentality. The show, hosted by ex-shearer Barry Woods or staff, is an informative, interactive (and at times comical) interpretation of old and modern-day Kiwi country life, and is hard to describe. It involves a clever pig, a not so clever pig, an axe, a homemade ingenious computer, dogs, sheep, a 'kiwi bear' and pants. Enough said – you'll just have to go and see for yourself.

Festival & events
Art Deco Weekend
Held on the third weekend of Feb, Napier stages its annual Art Deco Weekend, a not-too-serious celebration of the art deco style. Locals dress in the deco style, classic cars grace the city streets and everyone enjoys the wining, dining, jazz, dancing, film, and theatre.

Costume and the old wheels on show at the art deco festival, Napier.

Activities & tours

Rafters negotiate the Tutea Falls, Kaituna River, Rotorua.

Volcanic Air Safaris
Waterfront, T07-348 9984, T0800-800848, volcanicair.co.nz.
Has a fleet of fixed-wing and float plane aircraft as well as helicopters that take in all the local sights from $60-795.

Taupo & around

Taupo Tandem
Taupo, T07-377 0428, T0800-275934, taupotandemskydiving.com.
One of three companies in New Zealand's capital of the tandem skydive.

TroutLine
Taupo, T07-378 0895, troutline nz.com.
Fully guided, dawn trout fishing trip on the lake from $80-120 depending on numbers.

Tongariro National Park

Mokai Gravity Canyon
Taihape (look for signs 7 km south of the town), T06-388 9109/ T0800 802864, gravitycanyon.co.nz.
The Mokai Canyon site on the Rangitikei River near Taihape boasts three extreme adventure activities. The 1-km flying fox, an 80-m bungee and a 50-m freefall on a bridge swing. Great even for spectators.

Rotorua & around

Kaitiaki Adventures
T07-357 2236, T0800-338736, sledge-it.com.
River Sledging and rafting trips down the Kaituna River with the opportunity to learn about Maori culture on the way. Raft trip includes the highly entertaining 7-m drop of the Okere Falls, from $85.

Planet Bike
T07-346 1717, planet bike.co.nz.
Offers organized trips or independent hire for the renowned Whakarewarewa Forest tracks. Try the half-day raft and bike combo trips from $90. Independent bike hire also available, from $35 for two hours, $55 per day.

Whakapapa and Turoa Ski fields

Full winter program and facilities but also interesting summer activities. See mtruapehu.com.

Waitomo Adventures Ltd

Waitomo Village, T07-878 7788, T0800-924866, waitomo.co.nz, waitomowalk.com.

Fine company offering a wide range of caving adventures including the seven-hour Lost World Epic.

Hibiscus Surf School

Maunganui, T07-575 3792, surfschool.co.nz.

Two hours from $80.

Pee Jays

15 Strand East, T07-308 9588, T0800-733529, whiteisland.co.nz.

The best sea-based operator for the five- to six-hour White Island volcano tour from $175. Bookings essential.

Wet 'n' Wild Rafting

T07-348 3191, wetnwild rafting.co.nz.

Offers one of the North Island's best wilderness rafting expeditions, the multi-day trip down the remote Motu River, from $795.

Airplay Paragliding

Havelock North, T06-845 1977, 0274512886, airplay.co.nz.

For those wishing to take to the sky over Te Mata Peak, paragliding flights and courses are available from $140.

Gannet Beach Adventures

Clifton, T06-875 0898, T0800-426638, gannets.com.

The oldest company and very entertaining. This four-hour tour leaves daily (Oct-May) from Clifton Beach by tractor and allows about 1½ hours with the gannets, from $38, child $23.

Grant Petherick Wine Tours

T06-876 7467, flyfishingwinetours.co.nz.

Quality, personable tours of the Hawke's Bay vineyards.

Waka Tours

Raetihi, Whanganui River National Park, T06-385 4811, wakatours.com.

Three-day guided Canadian canoe trip down the Whanganui River with a Maori cultural and environmental edge, including a stay and hangi at the Koriniti Marae, from $650.

Transport

There are domestic **airports** at Hamilton, Rotorua, Tauranga Taupo, Napier and New Plymouth. All the main centres are well served by south/north bound **bus services** from Auckland via Hamilton or Tauranga. Waitomo is served from Auckland, Hamilton, Otorohanga, Taupo and Rotorua. The main i-SITES can assist with schedules and bookings.

There is a daily **train service** from Auckland to Wellington stopping at Hamilton, Otorohanga (for Waitomo) and Ohakune.

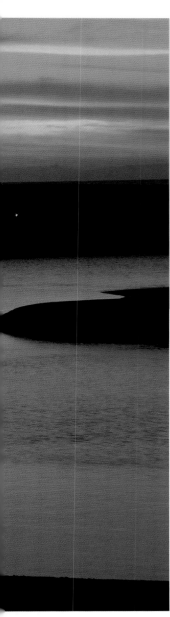

Contents

Wellington & around

Sunset from Lake Ferry Wairarapa with the Kaikoura Range in the distance.

Introduction

W hen it comes to tourism Wellington perhaps echoes the dilemma of the Australian capital, Canberra. It's a bit like the youngest, smallest child sitting between the two older, more popular and spoiled siblings – both gloating. In Australia, of course, the two most venerated are Sydney and Melbourne. In New Zealand they are Auckland and Christchurch. But the great thing about Wellington is that it has fostered no insecurity about its position, neither geographical nor in the popularity stakes. On the contrary, it has developed its own perfectly attractive and robust identity and a personality that goes far beyond its considerable and primary responsibility for running the country, or serving as the gateway to the South Island.

East of the city the rash of wineries around Martinborough and the scenic drive to Cape Palliser are just two of the great attractions of the Wairarapa Region, while Kapiti Island to the north offers a fascinating insight in to the country's unique and once prolific birdlife.

What to see in…

…a long weekend
Spend two days concentrating on Wellington sights bearing in mind that Te Papa will take up a full day in itself. Try to eat out at least once while in Wellington. For the remaining day head west to the Wairarapa taking in the vineyards of Martinborough and the Waiohine Gorge swing bridge, or spend a day on Kapiti Island.

…a week
With the extra few days spend two nights in the Wairarapa (one in Martinborough) and spend a day exploring the coast road to Cape Palliser. A day trip to Castlepoint is another option. Then head back east to Palmerston North and ultimately Wellington via the Manawatu Gorge (SH3) and the Te Apiti Wind Farm (Ashhurst). Again, it you are at all wildlife minded, try to arrange a day trip to Kapiti Island.

The Putangirua Pinnacles, Wairarapa.

Wellington

If you can defy that inevitable eagerness to board the ferry and don't mind dodging the odd suit, you certainly won't regret it. Wellington offers a wealth of things to see and do from the impressive icons of Te Papa (Museum of New Zealand) and the incongruous Beehive, to cable-car rides and kiwi spotting. Also, with more restaurants per capita than just about any city on earth, it is the ideal place to sample some of the best of Australasia's Pacific Rim cuisine.

Essentials

⟳ Getting there The scenic 85-km journey across Cook Strait takes three hours. There are currently two services: the **Interislander** (T0800-802802/T04-4983302, interislander.co.nz) and the smaller of the two companies **Bluebridge** (T0800-844844/T04-4716188, bluebridgeco.nz).

The latter has older vessels, tend to be cheaper and is the best choice if you are looking for character and a more traditional ferry experience. In adverse weather conditions the crossing can be a bit of an ordeal with one crossing in 2006 taking a nauseating 10 hrs. Sailings will be cancelled if conditions are considered too dangerous, but this is rare. Advance booking in advance is advised at all times, but especially in December/January. Most major i-SITES and travel agents can organize bookings and tickets. A free shuttle bus to the Interislander terminal (2 km) is available from the Wellington railway station (Platform 9), 30 mins before each scheduled ferry departure.

Various day/limited-excursion, family and group fares and standard discounted fares are available but must be booked in advance and are subject to availability. Like most travel bookings these days the internet will secure the best deals. At peak periods (particularly Dec/Jan) discounts are rarely available. Fares for passengers range from a standard vehicle with two passengers from about $265 one-way, a motor home with 2 passengers $365 and 2 passengers no vehicle $53 per person.

$ ATM All the major banks with ATMs are represented in the CBD especially along Willis St and Lambton Quay.

⊕ Hospital Wellington Hospital, Riddiford St, T04-385 5999.

✛ Pharmacy Medical Centre Building, 729 High St, T04-939 6777. Corner Victoria and Harris Streets, T04-3812000.

⌒ Post office 94-98 Lambton Quay, T04-472 3301. Mon-Fri 0830-1700. Post Restante, 43 Manners St, 6011, T04-473 5922, Mon-Fri 0800-1730, Sat 1000-1330.

❶ Tourist information Wellington i-SITE visitor centre, corner of Wakefield and Victoria streets, T04-802 4860, wellingtonnz.com, Mon-Fri 0830-1800, Sat-Sun 0930-1700. **Palmerston North and Destination Manawatu i-SITE visitor centre**, The Square, T06-350 1922, manawatunz.co.nz, daily 0900-1700. **Martinborough i-SITE visitor centre**, 18 Kitchener St, Martinborough, Wairarapa, T06-306 9043, wairarapanz.com, daily 0900-1600.

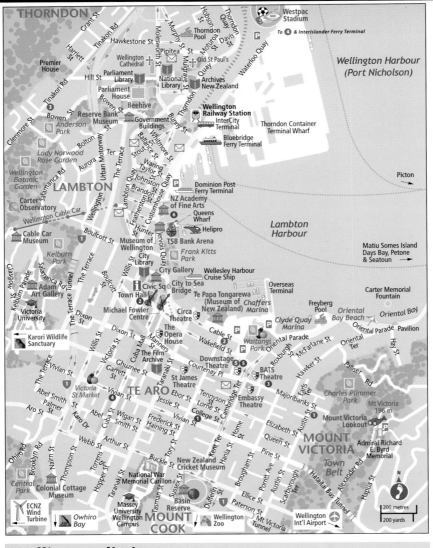

Wellington listings

Sleeping
1. Austinvilla B&B *11 Austin St, Mt Victoria*
2. Museum Hotel-Hotel De Wheels *90 Cable St*
3. The Shepherds Arms Hotel *285 Tinakori Rd, Thorndon*
4. Top-Ten Hutt Park Holiday Park *95 Hutt Park Rd, Hutt Park*
5. Wellington YHA *292 Wakefield St*

Eating & drinking
1. Café L'Affare *27 College St*
2. Café Lido *opposite the i-SITE*
3. Kai *21 Marjoribanks St*
4. Logan Brown *192 Cuba St*
5. Monsoon Poon *12 Blair St*
6. Shed 5 *Queen's Wharf*

Mount Victoria Lookout

Most of Wellington's major attractions are within walking distance or a short bus ride from each other. An ideal spot to get your bearings is the 196-m Mount Victoria Lookout southeast from the city centre. The view is spectacular at sunrise and after dark. Although from a distance the wooded sides of the mount hardly seem in character with the film trilogy *Lord of the Rings* it proved both a convenient and aesthetically suitable location for several scenes depicting The Shire in the first film, the Fellowship of the Ring.

Thorndon & the Parliamentary District

The suburb of Thorndon, to which the Parliamentary District essentially belongs, is the oldest and most historic in Wellington.

The Parliamentary District is centered on and around Bowen Street, in the Lambton Quarter just west of the rather grand-looking railway station. You will be immediately struck by the rather odd and aptly named **Beehive**, which houses the various government offices full of workers, the odd swarm of killers and, until recently, the Queen bee herself – Helen Clarke – one of the nation's longest-serving Prime Ministers. Designed by British architect Sir Basil Spence, and built in 1980, the honeyless hive is either loved or hated. Parliament's visitor centre (T04-817 9503, parliament.nz) is in the ground floor foyer of the Beehive. Far more aesthetically pleasing is the 1922 **Old Parliament House** (Mon-Fri 0900-1700, Sat 0930-1600, Sun 1130-1600; regular tours are available and you can also see parliament in session). While in the vicinity of Parliament House take a peek or stop for lunch in the **Backbencher Pub**, across the road on Molesworth Street facing the High Court. Adorning the walls are some superb cartoons and Spitting Image-style dummies of past and present prime ministers.

Just a short stroll from the Backbencher Pub on Lambton Quay is the historic **Old Government Buildings** built in 1876 to house the Crown Ministers and public servants of the day. The

building was designed to look like stone but actually constructed of wood and is the second largest wooden building in the world (the largest being the Todaiji Temple in Nara City, Japan). It now houses the Victoria University's Law Faculty.

Also in the Parliamentary District is the **National Library Gallery** (5 Molesworth St, T04-474 3000, Mon-Fri 0900-1700, Sat 0900-1300) with its impressive collection of research books, colonial photographs and in-house gallery. It also has a shop and a café. **The Archives New Zealand** (10 Mulgrave St, Thorndon, T04-499 5595, archives. govt.nz, Mon-Fri 0900-1700, Sat 0900-1300, free), have within its hallowed walls a number of important historical documents including the original and controversial Treaty of Waitangi.

Also of historical and literary note in Thorndon is the birthplace of **Katherine Mansfield** (25 Tinakori Rd, T06-473 7268, katherinemansfield. com, Tue-Sun 1000-1600, $5.50). Mansfield is generally hailed as New Zealand's most famous writer. The house and gardens have been faithfully restored and there is an interesting video portrait of the writer.

Civic Square & the waterfront

Civic Square, just behind the i-SITE visitor centre has some interesting architectural features and is often used for outdoor events. The recently redeveloped **City Gallery** (T04-8013021, citygallery. org.nz, daily 1000-1700, free) is located here and given Wellington is considered the artistic heart of the nation, the gallery strives (successfully it would seem) to present a regular programme of the very best of contemporary visual arts.

From Civic Square it is a short walk across the very arty **City to Sea Bridge**, which connects the square with the waterfront. The bridge sprouts a number of interesting sculptures that celebrate the arrival of the Maori in New Zealand.

The waterfront has become a major focus in the city for its museums, aesthetics and recreational activities.

Te Papa Museum of New Zealand.

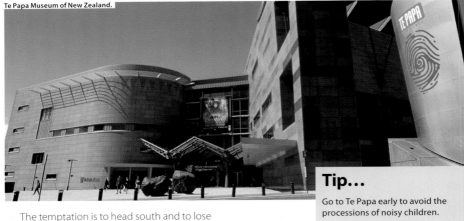

Tip...

Go to Te Papa early to avoid the processions of noisy children.

The temptation is to head south and to lose oneself in the impressive Te Papa Museum of New Zealand, but it is worth heading north first, past Frank Kitts Park and the wharf to the **Museum of Wellington City and Sea** (T04-472 8904, museumofwellington.co.nz, daily 1000-1700, free).

Being in such close proximity to Te Papa, you might think its attempts to compete and woo visitors was an exercise in futility, but this museum is actually superb and, in its own way, competes favourably with Te Papa. As the name suggests, the emphasis is on local history, with a particular maritime bent. Of note are the Wahine Ferry Disaster Gallery and the state-of-the-art holographic display on Maori legends. The Wahine was a passenger ferry that came to grief at the harbour entrance in 1968 with the loss of 51 lives.

Te Papa Museum of New Zealand

55 Cable St, T04-3817111, tepapa.govt.nz.
Daily 1000-1800, Thu 1000-2100, free, (around $15 for temporary exhibitions). Allow at least half a day at the museum. One-hour 'Introducing Te Papa Tours' available Nov-Apr daily on the hour 1000-1500, $11; Apr-Oct 1015 and 1400. Specialist tours (including a Maori Experience Tour) are available at a cost.
Map: Wellington, F5, p160.

To the south of Civic Square and gracing the harbour's eastern bank is the unmistakable Te Papa Museum of New Zealand – Wellington's biggest tourist attraction. As if the exterior was not enough, the interior is also mind-bending. Heavily publicised Te Papa has faithfully represented the nation's heritage since 1998, at an initial cost of $317 million. Since then over twice the population of the nation itself (9.3 million) have passed through its doors and few have been disappointed.

In Te Papa they say there is something for everybody and this does seem to hold true. As expected, there is a heavy emphasis on Maori heritage, taonga (treasures) and biculturalism, mixed with the inevitable early settler material, contemporary displays of all things Kiwi and 'Toi Te Papa' – an exhibition of 130 New Zealand artworks.

More recently it was the turn of the natural history section to grab the headlines with the arrival and display of the world's largest specimen of colossal squid. The half-ton, 10-m long specimen arrived at the museum in March 2007, after being captured in New Zealand waters a month before.

Given entry to the museum is free, it is a good idea to have an initial quick recce and return later for a more in-depth investigation to avoid the almost inevitable information overload.

There is an excellent shop on the ground floor, but the café is less than impressive.

Botanic Gardens, Cable Car & Cable Car Museum

The main entrance is on Glenmore St in Thorndon, T04-499 1400, wellington.govt.nz.
Gardens open dawn till dusk, free.
Cable car, T04-472 2199, runs every 10 mins, Mon-Fri 0700-2200, Sat-Sun 0830-2200, $5, child $2 return.
Map: Wellington, E4, p160.

Wellington's Botanic Gardens are really quite magnificent and by far the best way to visit them is via the Cable Car at 280 Lambton Quay. First built in 1902 and now a tourist attraction in itself, the almost completely subterranean single line has cables that haul the two lovely red carriages up and down, with four stops on the way. When your carriage glides in quietly to the summit (Kelburn) station you step out into the gardens and are immediately rewarded with a fine view across the city. **The Cable Car Museum** (T04-475 3578, cablecarmuseum.co.nz, daily 0930-1730, free) is also located at the summit and houses some lovingly restored cars and interpretive displays.

Beyond the museum there are 26 ha of specialist gardens, radiant flowerbeds, foreign trees and native bush to explore. Not surprisingly one of the most popular spots is the **Lady Norwood Rose Garden** where you can muse upon the names and fragrances of more than 300 varieties form a budding pink 'Little Willy' to the rather disheveled 'Nancy Reagan'.

The gardens also play host to the recently redeveloped **Carter Observatory** (T04-472 8167, carterobservatory.org). It has static displays, planetarium shows and audio-visuals.

You can also find a very fragrant and relaxing café next to the rose gardens (Mon-Fri 1100-1500, Sat-Sun 1000-1600).

Zelandia & The Karori Wildlife Sanctuary

Waiapu Rd, Karori, T04-920 9200, visitzealandia.com.
Daily 1000-1700, from $14, child $6.

The Karori Wildlife Sanctuary is a great conservation success story and a tribute to an army of devoted volunteers. In 1994 an area of 250 ha was set aside and protected with a predator-proof fence. This was of course a challenge and an expensive one at that, but was done to hopefully repeat the efficacy of New Zealands offshore islands. Now, with the eradication of non-native pest species within the boundary of the fence, the benefits for both native flora and fauna are plain to see. Reintroduced species like kaka (native parrot) and the 'living fossil' tuatara are making a solid comeback and birdsong is returning to native bush that once lay silent. The sanctuary has over 30 km of bush walks to explore its many features from the lake to specialist feeding stations. A new visitor centre is currently under construction with state-of-the-art interactive exhibitions that tell the story of New Zealand's unique natural history from the day before humans arrived through to the groundbreaking conservation techniques of today. It will also house a shop and café. There are guided tours daily and also at night to view or hear nocturnal wildlife, including the resident kiwi, from $60, child $30, pick-ups from the i-SITE.

The lake at Karori Sanctuary.

Half-day drive: Oriental Bay to Owhiro & the Weta Cave

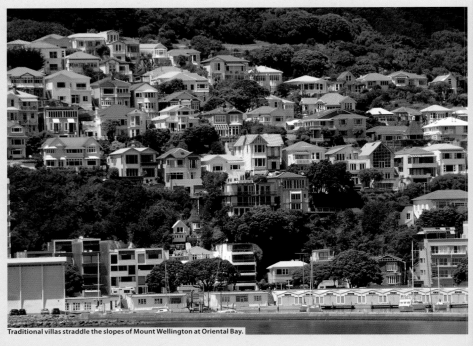

Traditional villas straddle the slopes of Mount Wellington at Oriental Bay.

A sleeping New Zealand fur seal, Red Rocks, Owhiro Bay.

f you have your own vehicle there is a very pleasant drive around the Miramar peninsula with its pleasant bay suburbs and coastal scenery.

Start from Oriental Bay and follow the road round to the airport then take Shelley Bay Road around the next headland to Palmer Head and Scorching Bay on the edge of Seatoun. There are some good beaches in the area, suitable for sunbathing and swimming. Note this is also the home of little blue penguins that come ashore to roost at night, often under the old waterside houses. While in Miramar it is worth calling in at the Weta Cave (corner of Camperdown Rd and Weka St, Miramar, T04-380 9361, wetanz.com/cave, open daily 0900-1730, free). Weta Workshops was founded in part by Peter Jackson and was the group of incredibly talented creative's responsible for the characters, props and special effects for films like *Lord of the Rings*, *King Kong* and most recently *The Hobbit*. The Weta Cave is a small museum that takes a detailed look at the Weta Workshops phenomenon including screened interviews with its founders and artists. There are also some of the famous – or infamous – characters, props and displays from the movies and a shop selling Weta-designed clothing, jewellery and mementos.

On the way back to the city from Owhiro Bay west of the airport, try to take in the eclectic metal and junk creations of Carl Gifford's Stonewall Co (287 Happy Valley Rd, T04-971 8618, stonewallco. net.nz). Call at the house for sales and permission to view at close hand.

There is also a New Zealand fur seal colony at Red Rocks which is accessed via the quarry track at the western end of Owhiro Bay (4 km), but if you are short of time, don't worry you will see plenty more on the shores of the South Island or Cape Palliser (see page 175).

Kapiti Coast & Palmerston North

Just north of Wellington, SH1 slices its way through the hills of a major fault-line and passes the rather dull town of Porirua before joining the picturesque Kapiti coastline. For the next 30 km the small coast and inland settlements of Paekakariki, Waikanae and Otaki are shadowed by Kapiti Island on one side and the Tararua Forest Park on the other. Kapiti Island is well worth a visit while Paekakariki, Paraparaumu and Waikanae offer a number of interesting local sights and activities. Otaki is the principal access point to the Tararua Forest Park.

Rubbing shoulders with kaka on Kapiti island.

Paraparaumu & Waikanae

Paraparaumu is the principal township on the Kapiti Coast and has close ties with Wellington both as commuter town and as a seaside resort popular during the summer months. There are two main beaches, Raumati to the south and Paraparaumu Beach to the north. All the usual facilities are here and the town also serves as the gateway to Kapiti Island. A little further north on SH1 is the small satellite town of Waikanae, which also prides itself on its fine beach. Paraparaumu's main claim to fame came in 2001 when Tiger Woods was lured with a rather attractive $2 million to play at the New Zealand Open golf challenge on its world-class golf course, T04-902 8200.

Kapiti Island

Native pigeon (keruru), Kapiti Island.

Kapiti Island is a very special place; not only is it a delight to visit but it's like going back in time to when New Zealand was an unspoiled paradise. Lying 5 km offshore from Paraparaumu, it is 10 km long, 2 km wide and is now one of the most important reserves in the country protected and nurtured by DoC. It took a huge budget and six years of hunting and poisoning in the 1980s to rid the island of 22,500 possums, while further exhaustive helicopter poison drops in the 1990s have been successful in keeping rats at bay. After numerous plant and animal re-introductions, the results are the first signs of regeneration and hints of what once was. Here you are in nature's territory – not human. You can walk on a number of well-kept tracks through proper New Zealand bush. Inquisitive birds like robin, saddleback and stitchbird flit about your head, while weka and takahe poke about for insects disturbed by your feet. At night you can hear kiwi, or share the coastal path with little blue penguins that do not run in fear, but merely stick their heads in the grass and croak at you with their little white bottoms sticking in the air. And at dawn, if you are very lucky, you can hear one of the most beautiful bird songs ever to grace human ears – that of the endangered kokako.

Bulls

The small agricultural service town of Bulls stands off the junction of SH3 and SH1, midway between Wanganui and Palmerston North. Blink and you'll miss it, but take a closer look and you may be surprised to learn that the township was not named after our four-legged friends, but after James Bull, who was one of the first settlers in 1858. By all accounts he was quite the entrepreneur and created so much of the town's infrastructure that in 1872 the government approved the replacement of the original name for the settlement – Rangitikei – with Bulls. However, our James has a lot to answer for. In the desperate effort to put Bulls on the map, the community has gone to ridiculous lengths to incorporate its name into every one of its amenities. Take a look around and you'll find the i-SITE visitor centre, which is 'Inform- a-Bull', the chemist which is 'Dispense-a-Bull, the fire station 'Extinguish-a-Bull', the police station 'Const-a-Bull' and the church, which is 'Forgive-a-Bull', and so it goes on. However, there are a few major omissions including, as you head out on SH3, a sign saying 'Antiques and Collectibles' – clearly owned by a right misera-bull. Annoyingly, this is very infectious, and for days you will find yourself suffering from this 'Voca-Bull-ary' affliction. Some may find Bulls entertaining, but others may find such behaviour total bullocks.

All access and landing permits must be pre-booked well in advance with DoC (18 Manners St, Wellington T04-3847770, doc.govt.nz, Mon-Fri 0900-1630, Sat-Sun 1000-1500). Only 50 people can land per day; permits cost $11, child $5 (available on-line).

Paekakariki

Paekakariki is a tiny seaside village, popular with train enthusiasts. But before looking at locos take the 3-km diversion up to the viewpoint on Paekakariki Hill Road. On a clear day there are great views of Kapiti Island and the coast right up to Wanganui. At the village railway station train buffs will enjoy the **Paekakariki Rail & Heritage Museum** (pspt.wellington.net.nz, open Sat and Sun), where devoted enthusiasts have restored a number of vintage trains, some of which still huff and puff along the tracks. A few kilometres further north is the **Wellington Tramway Museum** (Queen Elizabeth Park, T04-292 8361, $9.50, child $4, open weekends 1100-1630), where historical displays look back at one of Wellington's former modes of transport. Several trams are currently in operation in Queen Elizabeth Park and rides are available. The beach at Paekakariki is also worth a look and typical of the area with its piles of driftwood, a deposit from the South Island's West Coast.

Palmerston North

On the banks of the Manawatu River and in the heart of flat, rural Manawatu is the pleasant university and agricultural service town of Palmerston North. Although set away from SH1, Palmy can provide a good base from which to explore the southern half of the North Island and is an important gateway west, through the impressive Manawatu Gorge, to the Wairarapa and Hawkes Bay. Other than Massey University, which is the second largest in the country, the town is perhaps most famous for its rugby museum, a place of almost spiritual significance, where many New Zealand rugby fanatics come on a pilgrimage to pay homage to their All Black heroes.

New Zealand Rugby Museum

87 Cuba St, T06-358 6947, rugbymuseum.co.nz. Mon-Sat 1000-1200 and 1330-1600, Sun 1330-1600, $5, child $2.

Established in 1969, it was the first of its kind in the country and contains the largest collection of rugby memorabilia including shirts, caps, photographs and programmes. There are also videos and detailed accounts of every All Black game since 1870 available for specialist research. If you have a particular question there is a wealth of fanatics on hand to fill you in on every pass, ruck and maul.

Te Manawa Science Centre, Museum & Art Gallery

396 Main St, T06-355 5000, temanawa.co.nz.
Daily 1000-1700, free entry to some galleries.

Te Manawa is a progressive and modern centre that integrates the usual social, cultural and artistic heritage with hands-on science displays. It is split into three main parts, the museum, gallery and science centre, all of which are worth visiting. There are some interesting Maori taonga and a few nationally significant artworks by contemporary gurus like Colin McCahon and Ralf Hotere. The gallery often hosts national touring exhibitions.

Te Apiti & Tararua Wind Farms

Well before arriving in Palmy you will no doubt have seen the small forest of white blades that make up the Te Apiti and Tararua Wind Farm on the ranges east of the town. With almost 200 turbines this is one of the largest wind farm sites in the southern hemisphere and a great testimony to clean, renewable energy in New Zealand. It is well worth going to take a closer look and you can do so in the heart of the Te Apiti site via the town of Ashhurst. From Palmerston North, turn off SH3 at Ashhurst and follow the Saddle Road signs. A visitor car park underneath one of the turbines has views of the wind farm and an information display.

It's a fact...

The 55 turbines of Te Apiti are 70 m in height and the blades 35 m; combined they create enough power for 45,000 homes.

If you do not have your own transport you can join a quad bike tour (see page 181). From Ashhurst you may consider returning to Palmerston North via the **Pohangina Valley Tourist Route**, which takes in a combination of rural scenery, gardens, craft outlets and the town of Feilding. The i-SITE visitor centre can provide details.

The Wairarapa

The Wairarapa is one of the least-visited regions in the North Island. Most visitors miss it out in their rush to reach Wellington via SH1, which lies to the west beyond the natural barrier of the Ruahine and Tararua ranges. If that simple fact is not appealing enough, the remote and stunning coastal scenery and relaxed atmosphere will, if you make the effort to visit, confirm that this is a place worth getting to know. The highlights, other than the delights of rural towns like Martinborough, which lie like a string of pearls along SH2, are the ever-increasing number of quality vineyards, a terrific range of country B&Bs and the coastal splendour of Castlepoint and Cape Palliser, the North Island's most southerly point.

Taumatawhakatangihangakoauauotamat eaturipukakapikimaungahoronukupokai whenuakitanatahu

Try reading that while driving, in fact, try reading it at all. By all accounts this is the longest place name in the world – and you thought it was that ludicrous train station in Wales. It is Maori (obviously), has 85 letters and roughly translated, it means *'The place where Tamatea, the man with the big knees, who slid, climbed and swallowed mountains (known as land eater) played his flute to his loved one'*.

Well what a boy. For the sake of it, it is worth the trip to see the ludicrously latitudinous sign that points at – won't write it again – but it does involve a bit of a hike and you should kick back and enjoy the back country drive either north or south and take a look (indeed stay) at the charming little coastal enclaves of Herbertville and/or Castlepoint en route. To get to the sign from Waipukurau (north), take the SH52 coast road towards Porangahau. The sign is a few kilometres south of Porangahau on SH52 to Wimbledon. SH52 re-emerges on SH2 at either Eketahuna or Masterton. This will allow you to take in the stunning Castlepoint on the way.

Castlepoint

It is a major diversion to get to this remote coastal settlement (65 km from Masterton) but the trip is well worth it. Castlepoint is considered to be the highlight on the Wairarapa's wild and remote coastline and it certainly deserves the honour. At the eastern end of the main beach a stark rocky headland, from which sprouts the Castlepoint Lighthouse, sweeps south to enclose a large lagoon. The picturesque bay, which is itself a popular spot with surfers and swimmers, is dominated at its southern entrance by the aptly named 162-m Castle Rock, which can be accessed from the southern end of the bay. The lighthouse can be accessed across the sand tombolo, which connects it to the mainland via a boardwalk. Just below the lighthouse there is a cave that can be explored at low tide, but beware – Maori legend has it that it is the hiding place of a huge menacing octopus.

It's a fact…

Although 'Taum… etc, etc, etc' is officially the longest place name according to the *Guinness Book of Records*, unofficially (and reputedly) there is in fact a longer one in Thailand, a place called 'Krungthepmahanakorn-amornratanakosinmahintarayutthaya-mahadilokphopnopparatrajathaniburi-romudomrajaniwesmahasatharnamorn-phimarnavatarnsathitsakkattiyavisanuk-amprasit'. What does it mean? You tell us!

Masterton

The chief commercial centre for the Wairarapa Region, Masterton gives Te Kuiti in the Waikato (the 'sheep-shearing capital of New Zealand') a run for its money in the big woolly event stakes. The Golden Shears is the major date in the local young farmers' calendar and offers moderate fame and fortune to the fastest clipper around. It is held at the beginning of March and lasts about four days.

Alongside the i-SITE visitor centre, corner Dixon and Bruce Streets (T06-3700900, wairarapanz.com) is the **Aratoi Wairarapa Museum of Art and History** (T06-370 0001, aratoi.co.nz, daily 1000-1630, donation), which admirably showcases many aspects of the area's social, cultural and natural history, as well as rapidly blossoming into the main focus for local contemporary artists. There's also a good in-house café. Alongside Aratoi is the **Shear Discovery National Shearing and Woolhandling Museum** (12 Dixon St, T06-378 8008, sheardiscovery.

Around the region

co.nz, daily 0900-1700, $5, child $2). Developed in two relocated former woolsheds it offers 'a fine round-up' of the shearing and weaving process and showcases the champions of the prized annual Golden Shears contest. Also within walking distance is the much-loved and celebrated **Queen Elizabeth Park**, first planted in 1878.

Pukaha Mount Bruce National Wildlife Centre

30 km north of Masterton on SH2 T06-375 8004, mtbruce.org.nz.
Daily 0900-1630, $8, children free.

This centre is the flagship of DoC's conservation and endangered species breeding programme. Although much of what happens at Mount Bruce takes place behind the scenes (and involves dedicated staff acting as surrogate mothers), the public can see many species otherwise rarely seen.

There is something very special about sitting on the veranda of the café, sipping a coffee and overlooking an enclosure with a takahe (a charming prehistoric-looking purple bird, not dissimilar to a large chicken) going happily about its business in the knowledge that there are only 200 or so left in the world. Likewise, taking a stroll through the native bush, to see other enclosures hiding stitchbirds and kokako, all of which you will probably never see again in your lifetime.

There is a nocturnal kiwi house that rates among the best in the country and leaves you in no doubt as to the numerous threats which this national icon faces in the modern world. Other highlights include the eel feed at 1330 and the kaka feed at 1500. The latter should certainly not be missed. Within the main building there are some fine displays, a shop and a café.

Feeding time with the Kaka (native parrot), Mount Bruce National Wildlife Centre.

Carterton, Waiohine Gorge & Greytown

Located 22 km west of Carterton and at the entrance to the **Tararua Forest Park** the Waiohine Gorge is well worth a visit for the scenery itself, let alone the walks on offer and the heart-stopping **swing bridge**, one of the longest in New Zealand. The road is signposted just south of the town on SH2. Eventually an unsealed road connects you with the riverbank, which gradually rises high above the river gorge. At the road terminus you can embark on a number of walks all of which involve the initial negotiation of the swing bridge that traverses the gorge at a height of about 40 m. If you do nothing else at Waiohine, a few trips back and forth on the bridge is great fun. Although it is perfectly safe, jelly has less wobble.

While in Carterton you may like to visit the **Paua Shell Factory** (54 Kent St, T06-379 4222, pauashell. co.nz, daily 0800-1700, free), one of the few places in the country that converts the stunningly beautiful paua (abalone) shells into jewellery and souvenirs. Further south Greytown, one is the prettiest of the Wairarapa settlements best known for its antiques, art and craft shops and roadside cafés. It's a great spot to stop for a coffee or lunch.

Martinborough

Martinborough is located towards the coast from SH2, 16 km southeast of Greytown. First settled by nationalistic Briton John Martin in the late 1880s, the village square and the streets running off it form the shape of the Union Jack. With names like Kansas, Texas and Ohio, it is clear that Martin had as much a love of the US as he did his homeland. Described as a unique 'wine village', with over 20 vineyards within walking distance of the square, and blessed with as many charming B&Bs, it is a favourite romantic haunt for Wellingtonians in search of a weekend away. The local i-SITE visitor centre is at 18 Kitchener St, T06-306 5010, wairarapanz.com, daily 0900-1600, can provide all the vineyard detail and a Vintage Village Heritage Walk leaflet that will pinpoint sites of historical interest. The most dominant is the grand and recently restored Martinborough Hotel that is just one of many excellent places to stay. It also has a good restaurant.

Day drive: the coast road to Cape Palliser

The day-long drive to see the Cape Palliser Lighthouse epitomizes the Wairarapa region and is highly recommended. On the way you can take in the bizarre rock formations of the Putangirua Pinnacles, the charming coastal fishing village of Ngawi and a colony of enchantingly languid fur seals, before the road terminates at the steps of the lighthouse. To get there from Featherston or Martinborough make your way down Lake Ferry Road, towards Lake Ferry. Just before the village turn left for Ngawi. From here the lighthouse is about 40 km.

After about 15 km look out for the Putangirua Pinnacles car park. The pinnacle formations are a series of gravel spires and turrets and have reached a new level of popularity after being used as a backdrop in the *Lord of the Rings* film trilogy. They are about an hour's walk down a streambed, so take proper footwear. Don't miss the viewpoint accessed from the main pathway.

From the car park the road continues, hugging the cliffs before opening out across a wide coastal plain, with a beautiful shore of rock and sand, well known for its excellent surfing.

The coastal village of Ngawi soon comes into view and you will be struck by the collection of old tractors and bulldozers on the beachfront with rigs supporting a raft of fishing boats of all shapes and sizes.

From Ngawi the red and white tower of the lighthouse can soon be seen. On the rocks just before it is a colony of New Zealand fur seals though you will probably smell them before you see them. Like fat, brown barrels they doze the day away amongst the boulders turning scratching and wanton flatulence in to an art form. All they're missing is a TV, a beer and a remote control. Take a closer look, but do not go nearer than 10 m. If you do, their soporific attitude will evaporate in an explosion of rippling blubber as they charge towards the surf.

From the seal colony it is only a short distance to the lighthouse with its steep climb of steps and rewarding views. How many steps? Go on, count! This is the southernmost tip of the North Island. Once you return to Lake Ferry Road it is worth the short diversion to see Lake Ferry itself. The beach, which must endure its fair share of wild weather, is a favourite venue in summer for fishing. The hotel serves good beer and food.

Best photo locations

❶ Te Papa & The Beehive
Pages 161 and 162

Time for some architectural photography. While Sydney has its Opera House and Auckland its Sky Tower, Wellington has Te Papa (page 161) and the Beehive (page 162). Sure, the Beehive is more odyssey than awe, but there is no doubting Te Papas' impact or its potential for photography.

Perhaps the best way to incorporate both buildings (and others) is to spend a few hours walking from Oriental Bay (just east of Te Papa) along the waterfront to the Parliamentary District (page 161) then return through the CBD or via the Botanical Gardens and Cable Car (page 163). Other highlights along the way are Civic Square and the City to Sea Bridge and the historic Railway Station.

Again, often the key is to source more unusual shots with low or unusual angles (often in conjunction with a wide-angle lens). Also look for detail within the subject and abstracts. Sometimes an image can still represent the whole faithfully with just one element.

❷ Te Apiti and Tararua Wind Farms
Page 169

Wind turbines offer a compelling photographic subject either en-masse or singularly. But much of the success depends on the weather and the clouds. Dark stormy skies are good but the best backdrops arewispy cirrus clouds that emphasise the 'wind' factor. So, here it is all about timing and weather. The best location is the viewpoint among the turbine via Ashhurst.

❶ 1500

❷ 1500

❸ Cape Palliser & Lake Ferry
Page 174

Give yourself a whole day to explore and photograph the scenic drive from Martinborough to Cape Palliser (page 174).

❸ ▲/•/◉/☻/☺1500

First stop are the Putangirua Pinnacles. Beyond the viewpoint encapsulating the entire scene and when you are in amongst them they present a real challenge to photograph, or to capture their essence. A wide-angle is necessary and preferably blue sky. You will also need company in order to represent scale. For once the middle of the day is best when light gets in to the nooks and crannies.

Next stop Ngawi with its retired and colourful tractors used to launch fishing vessels, some of which have seen better days. They are actually more difficult to capture than you expect. It is a classic example of the image telling a story as opposed to just being a shot of a colourful tractor – good luck. Just before the Cape and lighthouse spend some time at the seal colony. But be careful, do not approach any seal within 6-m and do not get between them and the sea. Again patience is required. If move very slowly and let them get used to you, the shots will come.

The lighthouse has obvious photographic appeal, especially from the headland above it, but again take care.

❹ ▲/•/◉/☻/☺1600

❹ Waiohine Gorge
Page 173

Now for some fun. First, forget about photography and return to childhood for a wee while going back on forth on the swing-bridge.

Fun, eh! Now for some images. The best shots are from below (there is a path from the car park down to the riverbed). Get in to position looking up find your composition and wait for figures to cross. A blue sky is best with some cloud, but a white background ruins the shot.

Sleeping

Wellington

Museum Hotel-Hotel De Wheels $$$$-$$$

90 Cable St, T04-802 8900, museumhotel.co.nz.
Map: Wellington, p160.
A modern boutique establishment ideally located across the road from Te Papa and in the heart of the café, bar and restaurant areas. It oozes class and along with all the standard facilities also has fully self-serviced luxury apartments.

The Shepherds Arms Hotel $$$-$$

285 Tinakori Rd, Thorndon, T04-472 1320, T0800-393782, shepherds.co.nz.
Map: Wellington, p160.
Conveniently located historic hotel within walking distance from the city and botanical gardens, offering a wide range of boutique accommodation from singles or doubles to King Suite with spa and four-poster. There is also a good restaurant and bar with a open fire and parking.

Wellington YHA $$-$

292 Wakefield St, T04-801 7280, yha.org.nz.
Map: Wellington, p160.
Deservingly popular with a wide range of rooms (some with ensuite bathrooms and TV, excellent facilities and helpful friendly staff. All this just a stone's throw from Courtenay Quarter's cafés and restaurants, a major

supermarket and Te Papa. The only drawback is the lack of off-street parking.

Self-catering
Austinvilla B&B $$$

11 Austin St, Mt Victoria, T04-385 8334, austinvilla.co.nz.
Map: Wellington, p160.
Set in a villa on the slopes of Mount Victoria and with views across to the city this is a great self-contained B&B option. Two separate fully self-contained units with private entrance, within walking distance of Courtenay Place.

Motor parks

There are no motor parks in Wellington itself. The best and nearest are in Lower Hutt. You might also like to consider the motor park at Paekakariki.

Top-Ten Hutt Park Holiday Park $$$-$

95 Hutt Park Rd, Lower Hutt, T04-568 5913, huttpark.co.nz.
Around 20 minutes from the city centre. Standard Top Ten facilities with a full range of accommodation options, from two-bedroom motel-style units, to non-powered campsites. Camp kitchen, spa and internet.

Paekakariki Holiday Park $$-$

180 Wellington Rd, T04-292 8292, paekakarikiholidaypark.co.nz.
Above-average facilities and good location close to the beach

and adjacent to Queen Elizabeth Park. 40 minutes to ferry outside rush hour.

Kapiti Coast & Palmerston North

Plum Trees Lodge $$

97 Russell St, Palmerston North, T06-358 7813, plumtreeslodge.com.
Well-appointed, self-contained and within walking distance to the town centre.

Palmerston North Holiday Park $$-$

133 Dittmer Drive, Palmerston North, T06-358 0349, holidayparks.co.nz/ palmerstonnorth.
A bit dated but has all the necessary facilities and is located in a peaceful spot next to the river and Esplanade Park.

The Wairarapa

Peppers Martinborough Hotel $$$$

The Square, Martinborough, T06-306 9350, peppers.co.nz.
The historic 1882 Martinborough Hotel adds character and sophistication to this Wairarapa village. The elegant, luxury en suite rooms are individually designed and named after some of the region's first settlers.

Eating & drinking

White Swan Country Hotel
$$$$-$$$
*Main St, Greytown, T06-304
8894, thewhiteswan.co.nz.*
Offers a choice of seven rooms.
There are also suites and studios
in a separate wing to the rear of
the hotel. Restaurant and bar.

Duckback Cottage $$$
*9 Broadway St, Martinborough,
T06-306 9933,
duckbackcottage.co.nz.*
Self-contained cottage with
open fire and three bedrooms.
Within walking distance of
all amenities.

Motor parks
Castlepoint Holiday Park
and Motels $$-$
*Jetty Rd, Castlepoint, T06-372
6705, castlepoint.co.nz.*
Well off the beaten track in a
stunning location. Spacious
motor park with adequate
amenities right next to the
beach. Wide range of
accommodation options from
tent sites to tourist flats. Modern
self-contained motel units are
also available in the village.

Martinborough Village
Camping $$-$
*Corner of Princess and Dublin
streets, Martinborough,
T06-306 8946,
martinboroughcamping.com.*
Quality motor park with cabins,
powered and tent sites all with
shared facilities. Wi-Fi and bike
hire for vineyard tours.

Wellington

Wellington prides itself on its
thriving café and restaurant
scene. The Courtenay Quarter is
where most are located with a
number of pubs offering fine,
reliable and mainly international
or Pacific Rim cuisine. Cuba Street
has numerous inexpensive
restaurants, funky cafés and
takeaways, while Queen's Wharf
is a favourite haunt at lunchtime.

Logan Brown $$$
*192 Cuba St, T04-801 5114,
loganbrown.co.nz.*
Lunch Mon-Fri, dinner daily.
Map: Wellington, p160.
A well-established, multi
award-winning establishment,
offering international cuisine in
the old historic and spacious
banking chambers.

Shed 5 $$$
*Queen's Wharf, T04-499 9069,
shed5.co.nz.*
Daily from 1100.
Map: Wellington, p160.
A fine evening venue, but
popular during the day and at
weekends. The menu is mainly
seafood or Mediterranean.

Café Lido $$
*Opposite the i-SITE,
T04-4996666.
Mon 0730-1500, Tue-Fri
0730-late, Sat-Sun 0730-late.*
Map: Wellington, p160.
One of the most popular in the
city and always busy especially

for breakfast. A fine place to mix
with Wellingtonians and watch
the world go by.

Café L'Affare $$
27 College St, T04-385 9748.
Mon-Fri 0700-1630, Sat
0800-1600.
Map: Wellington, p160.
Well worth the extra walk. It is a
thriving coffee business as well
as an excellent café, full of
atmosphere. As you might
expect, the coffee (and even the
smell of the place) is sublime.

Kai $$
*21 Majoribanks St
T04-801 5006.*
Mon-Sat from 1730.
Map: Wellington, p160.
A truly Maori eating experience
and it doesn't come much better
than this. Small and friendly, with
a range of traditional Maori
dishes from kumara pies (Pacific
sweet potato) to kuku (steamed
green-lipped mussels) all for a
reasonable price.

Monsoon Poon $$
12 Blair St, T04-803 3555.
Mon-Thu 1100-2300, Fri
1100-2400, Sat 1700-2400, Sun
1700-until the chefs get tired.
Map: Wellington, p160.
Considered the pick of the
Asian restaurants, offering a
wide range of dishes from Thai
to Vietnamese. The chefs do
their thing in full view of the
spacious dining floor. Lively bar,
great atmosphere.

Entertainment

Shopping

Although Aucklanders would disagree, Wellington probably has the edge when it comes to a good night out. As well as a large number of pubs and clubs, there are numerous venues including large concert halls such as the **Michael Fowler Centre**, offering rock and classical, and noted theatres such as the **Westpac St James** and **Circa** offering contemporary drama, dance and comedy.

For listings ask at the VIC or check the daily newspaper *The Dominion Post* or the tourist paper *Capital Times*. Useful websites are: feelinggreat.co.nz or wellington nz.com. Tickets for major events can be bought from **Ticketek**, Michael Fowler Centre, 111 Wakefield St, T04-384 3840, ticket ek.co.nz, i-SITE sometimes offers discounts on theatre tickets

The Embassy Theatre

10 Kent Terrace, at the bottom of Courtenay Place, T04-384 7657, deluxe.co.nz.
This deserves special mention due to its giant screen (one of the largest in the southern hemisphere). It was also used to host the premieres of Kiwi director Peter Jackson's *Lord of the Rings* trilogy.

Festivals & events
International Rugby Sevens Tournament
(Feb/Mar)
T04-389 0020, nzisevens.co.nz.
The world's best rugby sevens teams run around like loonies at the Westpac Stadium.

New Zealand International Arts Festival
(Feb/Mar)
T04-473 0149, nzfestival.nzpost.co.nz/2010.
This is a biennial event (next in 2010) and Wellington's most celebrated. It lasts for three weeks and is currently the country's largest cultural event with a rich and varied pageant of music performers, drama, street theatre, traditional Maori dance, modern dance and visual arts.

World of Wearable Art Awards (Sep)
T03-548 9299, worldofwearableart.com.
A unique Kiwi arts affair that has grown from strength to strength from humble beginnings in the country's arts capital, Nelson. This is your once in a lifetime chance to see models dress as a banana, or a boat, or in something made of copious sticky back plastic and toilet roll holders. Anything is possible and it is incredibly creative. Even former PM Helen Clarke once hit the catwalk donned in a fetching kind of paua shell little number – sort of.

Wellington is a fine city for shopaholics. The main shopping areas are Lambton Quay, Willis, Cuba and Courtenay streets. For quality souvenirs try the shop at Te Papa (see page 162).

As you might expect, Cuba Street's wide variety of cafés and restaurants are echoed in the nature of its shops. Whether it is 1970s clothing, second-hand books, utter kitsch, a pair of skin-tight pink plastic pants or an erotic device (batteries not included), this is where to go. It is always good fun to muse even if you do not indulge yourself. Along Lambton Quay, nicknamed The Golden Mile, the retail highlights are the elegant boutique shops of the Old Bank and the unfortunately named Kirkcaldie and Stains, Wellington's answer to Harrods.

Activities & tours

Tours
Flat Earth Tours
T04-9775805, T0800-775805, flatearth.co.nz.
An excellent tour company offering an exciting range of tours with the quintessential 'capital' edge, from a Wild Wellington Tour that focuses on local native wildlife; a Maori Treasures Tour that offers demonstrations of art and crafts (with an opportunity to create an artwork of your own); a Classic Wine Tour to the Wairarapa and of course the inevitable Lord of the Rings tour. Other options include sightseeing and a city arts tour. Tours are half or full-day and start from around $65.

Zest
T04-4791778, zestfoodtours.co.nz.
This operator offers a package for small groups of self-confessed gourmands, whipping up the ingredients of local knowledge and fascinating ventures behind the scenes to create a fine tour experience. Walking option 0930-1330, from $195.

Boat trips
Boat transport to Kapiti Island is available through Kapiti Marine Charter, T04-297 2585, T0800-433779, kapitimarinecharter. co.nz and **Kapiti Tours Ltd**, T04-237 7965, T0800 527 484, kapititours.co.nz, from $55, child $30. Boats depart from the Kapiti Boating Club, Paraparaumu Beach. **Kapiti Island Alive**, T06-362 6606, kapitiislandalive. co.nz, offer Maori-themed day trips to the northern end of the island, departing 0900 or 1430 with one-hour guided walks ($20). Overnight kiwi-spotting trips are also a possibility but book well ahead.

Transport

Wellington offers **air**, **train** and nationwide **bus** services. Palmerston North has air and bus services. The Wairarapa is served by regional bus and train services contact **TranzMetro** T0800-801700, tranzmetro.co.nz. The main i-SITES can assist with bookings. For ferry crossings to South Island see page 159.

Wellington is 658 km from Auckland. The principal route is via SH1. Martinborough is 65 km via SH2, the principal route to the Wairarapa and the east coast. Wellington airport has regular services to all the main domestic centres and is located in Miramar, 6 km south of the centre, T04-3855100, wellingtonairport. co.nz. The taxi fare into town is about $35. Shuttle buses can be shared for about $15, T0800-748885. The Airport Flyer is an express bus service that runs from the airport to the centre of Wellington every 15 minutes, $8. For $12 the 'StarPass' will give you unlimited travel for one day on Airport Flyer, Valley Flyer & GO Wellington services.

Wellington bus services are operated by **Metlink**, T0800-801700, metlink.org.nz.

Regional buses arrive and depart from the train station, Bunny Street, (Intercity, T04-385 0520).

The train station is next to the quay on Bunny Street. **TranzScenic** operates the daily 'Overlander' service from Auckland, T0800-872467/ T04-495 0775, tranzscenic.co.nz. **TranzMetro** T0800-801700, tranzmetro.co.nz, offers regular daily services from the Wairarapa including Martinborough (bus link) and Masterton direct.

Contents

French Pass, Marlborough Sounds.

Marlborough & Nelson

Introduction

The regions of Marlborough and Nelson have all the classic New Zealand ingredients – mountains, lakes, golden beaches and great tramping tracks – all safe, within the boundaries of its national parks and warmed by the sunniest climate in the country. If that wasn't enough, they also have a relatively low population density. Those who are lucky enough to live here are a diverse bunch, from the farmers, fruit growers and winemakers in the valleys, to the artists and alternative lifestylers in the quiet creative havens of the Marlborough Sounds and smaller rural towns like Takaka.

Despite the appealing lifestyle and obvious attractions, few foreigners have heard of this region. Most simply pass through on their way to the tourist honeypots further south, stopping only briefly in Picton, the main ferry port on the South Island.

The region has an interesting history and exhibits evidence of Maori settlement from as early as the 14th century. But the most famous early historic association was with Captain James Cook, who visited the Marlborough Sounds on each of his three voyages in 1770, 1773-1774 and again in 1777. Clearly, he too, loved the place. He was particularly fond of Ship Cove near the mouth of Queen Charlotte Sound, which he visited five times; a monument in Ship Cove commemorates his visits. As you might expect, Cook is responsible for many place names in the area.

What to see in...

... a long weekend
Arrive early and take a half-day wine tour from Picton (page 190) then drive to Havelock for a cruise on the sounds to the mussel farms. Overnight in the area and sample the mussels for dinner (page 208) Next spend the day exploring Nelson. Day three head to Motueka and do a cruise or a cruise/walk in the Abel Tasman.

... a week
From Picton walk part of the Queen Charlotte Track and stay overnight in the Sounds. Following day explore the Wairau Valley vineyards. Try green-lipped mussels with your vintage. Day three drive to Nelson via the scenic drive to French Pass. Spend a day exploring Nelson including the World of Wearable Art Museum. With the three remaining days either try a walk/kayak in the Abel Tasman, or a day water taxi/walk combo followed by two days in Golden Bay including the walk to Wharariki Beach.

Te Waikoropupu Springs, Takaka, Golden Bay.

Marlborough

As the ferry slides into port at Picton, Queen Charlotte Sound seems like a giant foyer and your sense of anticipation surrounding what lies beyond goes in to overdrive. The vast convoluted system of drowned river valleys, peninsulas and islets that make up the Sound's 1500 km of coastline are often dubbed New Zealand's 'little slice of Norway' and throughout its watery maze you can enjoy stunning scenery, cruising, tramping, kayaking, wildlife watching or just a few days' peaceful relaxation. The two main tourist bases for the Sounds are Picton at the terminus of Queen Charlotte Sound, and also Havelock at the terminus of Pelorus Sound. From these you can organize activities, or catch water taxis to the numerous accommodations that are scattered, out there – somewhere!

There are only two access points and tricky road networks out into the root-like systems of terra firma. The first is at Linkwater on the Queen Charlotte Drive between Picton and Havelock – itself a very pretty, but winding drive. From there you can access the bays of Kenepuru and Queen Charlotte Sounds as well as Endeavour Inlet, where Captain Cook came ashore. The second is at Rai Valley with access to points on the Tennyson Inlet and to French Pass. Alas, the Sounds are not a place to watch the clock, or rush. If you do not have much time, settle for a water-based trip from Picton or Havelock and perhaps a night's stay at one of the many excellent and remote accommodations. Or, if you are Nelson-bound, take a day to explore the road to French Pass with its stunning views and tidal maelstrom.

Essentials

◉ **ATM** There are ATMs at the Ferry Terminal and in all the main centres.

⊕ **Hospital** Nelson Hospital, Tipahi St, T03-546 1800.

✛ **Pharmacy** Emergency pharmacy, corner of Hardy and Collingwood streets, Nelson, T03-548 3897.

↻ **Post office** Mariners Mall, High St, Picton, T03-573 6900, Mon-Fri 0830-1700; Nelson PostShop, 209 Hardy St, T03-5467818, open Mon-Fri 0800-1700; Sat 0930-1230.

❶ **Tourist information** Picton i-SITE visitor centre, The Foreshore, T03-520 3113, dest inationmarlborough. com, daily 0830-1800 (1700 winter). **Blenheim i-SITE visitor centre**, Railway Station, SH1, T03-577 8080, destinationmarlborough.com, winemarlborough.net.nz, daily 0830-1830; winter Mon-Fri 0830-1800, Sat-Sun 0900-1600. **Nelson i-SITE visitor ventre** corner of Trafalgar and Halifax streets, T03-548 2304, nelsonnz.com, Mon-Fri 0830-1700, Sat-Sun 0900-1600. **Golden Bay i-SITE visitor centre**, Willow St, Takaka, Golden Bay, T03-525 9136.

View over Pelorus Sound, Marlborough Sounds.

Wineries around Blenheim

A comprehensive list of the wineries is beyond the scope of this guide, but some wineries of particular note are listed below. The best time to visit the vineyards is in April when the heavily laden vines are ripe for the picking. See also Winery tours, page 210.

Allan Scott Estate
Jackson's Rd, T03-572 9054, allanscott.com, daily 0900-1700.
Established in 1973, producing fine Sauvignon, Chardonnay and Riesling wines. The Twelve Trees restaurant, is a deservedly popular lunch venue, open daily from 0900.

Cloudy Bay
Jackson's Rd, T03-520 9147, cloudybay.co.nz, tastings and tours daily 1000-1700.
An internationally famous label with a loyal following particularly for its Sauvignon Blanc.

Herzog
81 Jeffries Rd, T03-572 8770, herzog.co.nz, daily 1100-1500.
Not only fine wine (particularly Pinot Noir) but also one of the best winery restaurants, October-mid May. Exceptional international wine list.

Highfield Estate
Brookby Rd, T03-572 9244, highfield.co.nz, daily 1000-1700.
Fine wine, architecture and the best view of the lot from its rampart tower. Reputable indoor/outdoor restaurant open daily for lunch 1130-1530.

Hunters Wines
Rapaura Rd, T03-572 8489, hunters.co.nz.
Another of the larger, most popular labels and home to one of the world's most renowned female vintners, Jane Hunter. Also noted for its gardens and café (open weekdays 1030-1630).

Johanneshof Cellars
SH1, Koromiko, 20 km north of Blenheim, T03-573 7035, johanneshof.co.nz, summer Tue-Sun 1000-1600.
Cellar tour $8. Boutique vineyard famous for its underground 'rock cellars', lined with both barrel and bottle.

Montana Brancott Winery
Main South Rd (SH1), just to the south of Blenheim, T03-578 2099, montanawines.com, daily 0900-1700.
It is almost rude not to visit this, the largest wine producer in the country. The new visitor centre is very impressive and there are half-hourly tours (1000-1500), tastings, a restaurant with outdoor seating and a classy shop. This is also the venue for the now world-famous Marlborough Food and Wine Festival in February (see page 209).

Prenzel Distillery
Sheffield St, Riverlands Estate, T03-520 8215, prenzel.com.
Something different – New Zealand's first commercial fruit distillery producing a range of fruit liqueurs, schnapps, and brandies.

Seresin
85 Bedford Rd, Renwick, T03-572 9408, seresin.co.nz, summer daily 1000-1630, winter Mon-Fri 1000-1630.
Noted not only for its wine, but also its artwork. That has to be one of the best logos of any label.

Te Whare Ra
56 Anglesea Street, Renwick, T03-572 8581, te-whare-ra.co.nz.
Small family-run boutique operation with a fine reputation and a wide range.

Tip...

While you are in the Marlborough Sounds try some
locally farmed and steamed green-lipped mussels –
without doubt the best-tasting mussels in the world.
Better still wash them down with a glass of local wine.

Around the region

Picton Foreshore and the Interislander ferry, Marlborough Sounds.

It's a fact...

Havelock was once the boyhood home of one of New Zealand's most famous sons, Ernest Rutherford – the man who split the atom.

Marlborough Sounds

Although most of what the Sounds has to offer is easily accessed by boat, it is also possible to explore much of it on foot. There are two popular tramping tracks, the 71-km, three- to five-day, **Queen Charlotte Track** and the lesser-known 27 km, two-day **Nydia Track**.

The Queen Charlotte can be tackled in several ways, by foot (of course), but also in combination with mountain bike and/or kayak. There are DoC huts and plenty of independent accommodation establishments to suit all budgets along the way and you can even have your pack delivered en route by water taxi. Again all the fine detail is available from the i-SITE. The Nydia is more rugged and far less facilitated, which may of course suit the more traditional tramper.

Picton

The pretty township of Picton, gateway to the Marlborough Sounds and the South Island is in summer a buzz of activity with eager visitors coming and going by ferry, car and train, or heading out in to the Sounds in all manner of crafts. But in winter it reverts to its more familiar role as a sleepy port, the ferry terminal café frequented by rotund lorry drivers on the ol'familiar inter-island run dripping ketchup as they demolish a mushy meat pie. There are a few sights in Picton, nothing spectacular. Remember you are on the South Island now, where sights become the domain of the nature-made, not the man-made. For most new arrivals, quite rightly, the first major sight is the activities board in the visitor centre. Cruising, dolphin watching, island trips, kayaking, mountain biking, tramping or just plain 'where's the best hammock with a view' – it's all on offer and the range is a little daunting.

Perhaps while you are thinking about it you should take a muse at the **Edwin Fox Maritime Museum** (T03-5736868, daily 0900-1700, $6) between the ferry terminal and the town centre. There the remains of the 1853, once fully rigged East India Trading ship is being lovingly restored to a reminder of her former glory by the Edwin Fox Society. The vessel, which is (apparently) the ninth oldest ship in the world and the only remaining example of her type, was a troop carrier in the Crimean War before being commissioned to bring immigrants to Australia and New Zealand.

In front of the museum is the **EcoWorld Aquarium & Terrarium** (T03-573 6030, ecoworldnz. co.nz, daily 0900-1700, day pass $17, child $9). As one of the few aquariums in the country it is perhaps worth a look, but more fun for kids. A range of displays house the usual characters including an octopus called Larry, some seahorses, rays, the local 'living fossil' – the tuatara (reptile) and last but by no means least a big tank of squid soup.

Blenheim & the Marlborough vineyards

Although it is depressingly flat and unremarkable looking, Blenheim, Marlborough's largest town, is a popular tourist base, primarily for those intent on sampling the region's fine wines. Most of the wineries lie just to the west of town and around the satellite village of Renwick 12 km west, on the fertile soils of the **Wairau Plains**. Marlborough is New Zealand's largest wine-growing region and forms the start (or finish) of the **Classic New Zealand Wine Trail** that tipples its way through Wellington and the Wairarapa to the Hawes Bay, classicwinetrail.co.nz.

There are over 50 wineries around Blenheim and Renwick producing highly acclaimed Chardonnay, Riesling, Cabernet Sauvignon, Merlot, Pinot Noir, sparkling Methode Champenoise and some of best Sauvignon Blanc in the world. Montana sowed the first seeds of success in the early 1970s and is now the largest winery in the

Sometimes the old techniques are best – Marlborough vineyard.

country. Three decades on, Montana has been joined by other world-famous names like Cloudy Bay and Villa Maria and has become a major national export industry.

Like Hawke's Bay in the North Island, the wineries have been quick to take advantage of the tourist dollar, with most offering tours, tastings (free or small charge) and good restaurants. Although the competition in Marlborough is fierce, the region's vineyards lack the architectural splendour or variety of Hawke's Bay. Perhaps they just leave the wine to do the talking.

If you are a complete novice it's a good idea to join one of the many excellent tours on offer. They generally last a full or half-day, taking in the pick of the crop and the widest variety of wine types. There is always an informative commentary, often a lunch stop and, of course, numerous tastings included in the package. If you know a bit about wines and have particular tastes, many tour operators will create a personal itinerary. If you wish to explore by yourself, there are plenty of maps and leaflets at the i-SITE visitor centre.

Nelson & around

Nelson is known as the sunniest place in the country and one of the most desirable places to live. It is lively and modern, yet steeped in history, its people down to earth and unpretentious thanks in no small part to a large contingent of artisans. Surrounding it, all within 100 km, are some of the most beautiful coastal areas and beaches in New Zealand, not to mention three diverse and stunning national parks, where you can experience some of the most exciting tramping tracks in the South Island, plus a host of other activities. Little wonder then that the Nelson region is one of the top holiday destinations in the country.

Mural, Nelson waterfront.

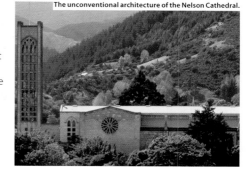
The unconventional architecture of the Nelson Cathedral.

Civic Tower

There is one sight that must be mentioned straight away, if not out of despair, then in order to highlight that nature-made versus man-made issue mentioned throughout this book. Have you ever seen a building as ugly as Nelson's Civic Tower – across the road from the visitor information centre – you can't miss it? Is that not, without doubt, the most hideous-looking building you have ever seen beyond a public convenience? An utter mess of concrete and steel, covered with aerials and radar. Even the pigeons boycott that one. Enough said.

Nelson Christ Church Cathedral

Daily in summer 0800-1900, winter 0800-1700, tours available and entry by donation.

Although Nelson was one of New Zealand's earliest and largest settlements, there is little architectural evidence. Of obvious notoriety, but hardly historical (having being finally completed in 1965), is the Nelson Christ Church Cathedral. Dominating the southern end of town it has an intriguing almost strangely unconventional design and contains some fine stained-glass windows and a 2000-pipe organ.

Nelson Provincial Museum

Corner Hardy and Trafalgar streets, T03-548 9588, museumnp.org.nz.
Exhibitions Mon-Fri 1000-1700, Sat-Sun 1000-1630, $5, child $2.

For the best sense of history head for the Nelson Provincial Museum, which serves as the region's principal museum and contains all the usual suspects covering life from Maori settlement to the present day using an imaginative and dynamic range of well-presented displays.

Nelson galleries

With over 300 artists resident in the town arts and crafts feature heavily in the list of attractions. A copy of the *Nelson Art Guide* is a great memento in itself and available from most bookshops. The **Te Aratoi-o-Whakatu or Suter Gallery** *(208 Bridge St, T03-548 4699, thesuter.org.nz, daily 1030-1630, $3, child 50c)* heads the list of major art galleries. Located next to Queen's Gardens, it boasts four exhibition spaces that showcase both permanent and temporary historical and contemporary collections. There is also a café, cinema and theatre on site that runs a programme of musical and theatrical performances.

There are many other galleries in the area displaying a vast array of creative talent. Of particular note is **Höglund Art Glass** (Korurangi Farm, Landsdowne Rd, Richmond, T03-544 6500, hoglund.co.nz, daily 0900-1700, tours from $15), home to the Hoglund Glass Blowing Studio. Here the internationally renowned pieces are created for sale and show in the gallery. There is also a café and the entire set-up is located in a pleasant park-like environment. Also worth a visit is the **South Street Gallery** *(10 Nile St West, T03-548 8117, nelsonpottery.co.nz).* This is the historical home of the Nelson Pottery where 25 selected potters of national and international renown create their various wares. The street itself is also noted for its 16 working-class historical cottages built between 1863 and 1867.

WOW

The most lauded tourist attraction in the Nelson area is the **World of Wearable Art and Collectable Cars** (95 Quarantine Rd, Annesbrook, just north of the airport, T03-547 4573, wowcars.co.nz, daily 1000-1830, 1700 in winter, from $18, child $10).

Set in a 1-ha site the complex has two galleries. The first is the Wearable Art Gallery showcasing the historic Wearable Art Garment collection. There is a fully scripted show that uses mannequins rather than live models but with all the usual elements of sound and lighting. The original concept was first initiated in 1987 as a gallery promotion by local sculptor Suzie Moncrieff and is easy to describe. Choose a theme, make the most remarkable and creative costume imaginable, from any material or media and get a bonny lass to show it off. But such a basic description could never do justice to the results, the story of how it all came about, or, indeed, how it has all developed since – you just have to see it for yourself. This is a remarkable synergy of art and fashion and a true tribute to the creative imagination.

The second gallery has an impressive collection of classic cars formerly on view in the town centre.

Around Nelson

Tahunanui Beach & Rabbit Island

Upon arrival you might think for a region famous for its beaches Nelson lets the side down and is bereft of one, but it isn't. Tahunanui Beach is just a few kilometres southwest of the town centre and is particularly well known for kite-surfing. Slightly further afield (20 km) towards Motueka (SH60) are the beaches and forest swathe of Rabbit Island. This seemingly never-ending beach offers a far quieter and expansive alternative.

It's a fact...

A viewpoint above the Nelson Botanical Gardens is claimed as the geographical centre of New Zealand. Access off Milton Road (one-hour return).

Nelson Lakes National Park

The slightly under-rated Nelson Lakes National Park 90 km south of Nelson protects 102,000 ha of the northernmost Southern Alps range. Its long, scenic and trout-filled lakes – Rotoroa and Rotoiti – cradled in beech-clad alpine ranges, hiding beautiful tussock valleys and wildflower-strewn meadows, dominate the park. Although a quick look at the lakes are all that most people see of this park, the ranges and river valleys offer some superb walking. The two most noted tramps are the 80-km, four- to seven-day Traverse-Sabine Circuit and the excellent two- to three-day Robert Ridge/Lake Angelus Track. There are a number of very pleasant short walks from 20 minutes to two hours that extend into the park from St Arnaud or Lake Rotoroa. The principal base for the park is the pretty village of **St Arnaud**, which nestles at the northern end of Lake Rotoiti. Almost all accommodation, services, major park access and activities are located here including the DoC Nelson Lakes National Park visitor centre (T03-5211806, doc.govt.nz, daily 0800-1900 seasonal), providing comprehensive displays and information, as well as offering advice on local accommodation and water taxi transport.

Murchison

A further 65 km along SH6 from St Arnaud delivers you in Murchison at the head of the Buller Gorge and junction of the Matakitaki and Buller rivers. It is a service centre for the local farming community and for many, the gateway to the west coast from the north. Although once an important gold-mining town (and famous for being nearly wiped out by a violent earthquake in 1929), it is today a quiet place, primarily of interest to the tourist as the base for a number of interesting activities including rafting and kayaking. It is also the haunt of the odd serious tramper intent on exploring the remote southern wilderness of the Kahurangi National Park.

Across the Buller River near Murchison.

Sunset at the Waimea River mouth, Mapua.

Nelson to Motueka

From Richmond, 14 km southwest of Nelson, SH60 follows the fringe of Nelson Bay west to Motueka. This route – often labelled as Nelson's Coastal Way – is the realm of vineyards, orchards, arts and crafts outlets and some pleasant seaside spots. One such spot worth a look, particularly around lunch or dinnertime, is Mapua. A congenial little settlement at the mouth of the Waimea Inlet (and just a short diversion off SH60), it has a few interesting art and craft shops, a small aquarium and one of the best restaurants in the region, The Smokehouse, which does good fish and chips.

Wineries are also a big feature in the Nelson Region and particularly the Moutere Valley and although the fine winemakers perhaps suffer from the reputation and sheer scale of their much-hyped neighbours in Marlborough, the wine they produce can be of a very fine quality. For more information on Nelson Region wineries consult the i-SITE visitor centre in Nelson or Motueka for a list of some of the better-known wineries.

Motueka

Motueka itself is a rather unremarkable little place, but set amidst all the sun-bathed vineyards and orchards and within a short distance from some of the most beautiful beaches in the country, it seems to radiate a sense of smug satisfaction. Once a thriving Maori settlement, the first residents were quickly displaced by the early Europeans, who were also intent on utilizing the area's rich natural resources. Today Motueka is principally a service centre for the numerous vineyards, orchards and market gardens that surround it, or for the many transitory tourists on route to the Abel Tasman National Park and Golden Bay. With such a seasonal influx of visitors Motueka is also a place of contrast, bustling in summer and sleepy in winter. One thing you will immediately notice on arrival is its almost ludicrously long main street – so long you could land a 747 on it and still have room for error.

Around the region

Kaiteriteri & Marahau

Kaiteriteri and Marahau (the gateway to the Abel Tasman National Park) are both accessed from SH60 just north of Motueka. Kaiteriteri (13 km) is a very pretty village with two exquisite beaches of its own and is a popular holiday spot. The main beach is the departure point for scenic launch trips, water taxis and kayak adventures into the park. If you do nothing else in Kaiteriteri, allow yourself time to take in the view from the Kaka Pa Point Lookout at the eastern end of the beach. There is a signpost with destinations and distances that will remind you how far you are from home – and how close to paradise. Breakers Beach below, looking east towards the park, is truly idyllic – and yes, who does own that house?

Marahau a further 6 km east of Kaiteriteri, is principally an accommodation and activity base at the main access point to the national park. There is a good range of accommodation options, a number of water taxi and activity operators and a café to satisfy the needs of hungry trampers.

Abel Tasman National Park

The Abel Tasman is the smallest national park in New Zealand, and one of the most beautiful, protecting 23,000 ha of some of the finest coastal scenery and beaches in the country. Rolling hills of native bush fall to azure-coloured clear waters and a 91-km coastline, indented with over 50 beaches of golden sand. It is a paradise for trampers and sea kayakers and boasts the famous and increasingly popular 51 km two- to five-day Coastal Walkway. The park is also home to the Tonga Island Marine Reserve – the preserve of all manner of sea life including some friendly and inquisitive fur seals.

Opened in 1942 after the tireless efforts of conservationist and resident Perrine Moncrieff, the park was named after the Dutch navigator Abel Tasman who first sighted New Zealand in 1642. Many of the place names are accredited to the explorations and subsequent mappings in 1827 by the French explorer (and man in possession of an extraordinarily grand name) Jules Sebastian Cesar Dumont d'Urville.

Viewpoint looking towards the Abel Tasman National Park, Kaiteriteri.

A word of warning: this small stretch of coastline, with its picturesque sandy bays and well-worn coastal walking track is one of the most popular natural attractions in the country. As such, it seldom disappoints, but don't expect to find much solitude here. In summer it can all get a bit silly and the park now attracts four times as many people as it did a decade ago (now 120,000)!

Other than the obvious waterborne sightseeing trips the various services and schedules offer casual walkers or day-trippers the option of being dropped off at one beach to be picked up later at the same, or at another. For trampers this can also provide numerous options to walk some or all of the Coastal Walkway. Note also that some operators will tow kayaks, giving you the option to kayak, walk or indeed retire from the track early. Bags and backpacks can also be carried independently, but this tends to be in conjunction with organized trips. The choice and combinations are vast, so study what is available prior to your arrival. The Motueka i-SITE (Wallace St, in the town centre, T03-528 6543, abeltasmangreenrush.co.nz,

daily 0800-1800/0800-1630 winter) provides the best, most up-to-date and most importantly, non-biased information on the park. The DoC visitor centre (Nelson T03-546 9339) or the field centre in Motueka (corner of King Edward and High streets, T03-528 1810, doc.govt.nz, Mon-Fri 0800-1630), has maps and leaflets for the entire region and can book huts for the Abel Tasman Coastal Walkway. You could also call into Abel Tasman Wilson's Experiences (265 High St, T03-528 2027/T0800-223582, abeltasmanco.nz), which operates beachfront lodges, launch cruises, water taxi, guided/non-guided sea kayaking and walking; it can provide maps, tide information and help with itinerary planning.

Day walk: Torrent Bay to Marahau

If you are short of time or cannot stand the sight of a paddle, the following day-walk will provide a pleasant taste to what the Abel Tasman is all about. They are also not too strenuous and have the added fun of getting your feet wet.

Torrent Bay to Marahau: 14 km; three to six hours.

From Marahau take an early morning water taxi to Torrent Bay, $40. Although there is an alternate high-tide route around Torrent Bay – try to make sure your arrival at Torrent Bay coincides with low tide so you can make the direct crossing. Take in the immediate delights here, then take the Coastal Track heading south, for which you need to take off your boots and then follow the markers across the estuary. Return boots to feet and find the track again that climbs the small headland before falling to the exquisite Anchorage Bay Beach. Then, from halfway up the beach, climb the hill, not forgetting to look back at the stunning view. Take the side track (15 mins) from the top of the hill down to the

incredibly cute (and hopefully quiet) Watering Cove. Climb back up to the coastal track and continue south. If you have time, check out Stillwell Bay and certainly walk along Appletree Bay (re-access to main track at the far end of the beach). From there complete the walk past Tinline Bay to the Marahau entrance point. If the tide is in your favour, you can cross the bay directly just beyond Tinline Bay (where the path descends to beach level). Fall exhausted and happy in to the Park Café, reward yourself with a pint of beer, a glass of wine or the full seafood fettuccine.

Golden Bay

Beyond Motueka SH60 makes the steep ascent of Takaka Hill to the quieter, far more laid-back realms of Golden Bay. Beyond the great hill, the small arty township of Takaka offers a fine introduction to the region, while the nearby Pupu Springs possess an almost palpable sense of peace, and an extraordinary clarity. Then, skirting the shores of Golden Bay, via the former gold rush town of Collingwood, SH60 finally terminates at the surreal sandy sweep of Farewell Spit, with the unforgettable beauty of Wharariki Beach within walking distance. All in all, it can prove a memorable diversion and the scenery and general atmosphere of this little corner of the South Island can act like a natural tranquillizer from the people overload experienced around the Abel Tasman National Park.

Sea stacks framed by a cave, Wharariki Beach, Golden Bay.

Takaka

Takaka was founded in 1854 and is the principal business and shopping area for Golden Bay. In summer it is a bustling little place and year round the residence of a colourful and cosmopolitan palette of arts and crafts people. There are a number of interesting attractions around the town including Pupu Springs and Rawhiti Cave. The township also serves as the gateway to the northern sector of the Abel Tasman National Park.

The biggest attraction in the immediate area are the beautiful and crystal-clear **Te Waikoropupu** or **Pupu Springs** administered by DoC. (north of Takaka left off SH60). Borne of the Takaka Marble Aquifer, the turquoise waters of the 'Pupu Springs' bubbles out at an average rate of 13.2 cu m per second, creating a lake that is the clearest of any freshwater body outside Antarctica. To the Maori, the springs are considered taonga – a treasure, and wahi tapu – a sacred place to be revered. It is a peaceful, beautiful place that has a palpable and rare sense of purity lost in the parks and reserves in the more populous nations of the world.

Also close to Takaka are the weird and wonderful limestone (karst) formations of the **Labyrinth Rocks** (3 km outside town, Labyrinth Lane, Three Oaks, T03-5258434, daily 1200-dusk, $7). It is not a cave system so is great for kids.

Also worth a day of exploration is the **Totaranui Road** via the beachside village of Pohara, Wainui Bay and the Northern sector of the Abel Tasman National Park. Features along the way include the Abel Tasman Memorial on the headland just beyond Tarakohe, the Wainui Falls (an easy 40-min walk) and of course Totaranui itself with its picture postcard orange sand!

Bencarri Farm (6 km south of Takaka, signposted off SH60 on McCallum Rd, T03-525 8261, bencarri.co.nz, daily 1000-1730, $12, child $6) is something of a novelty with its tame eels – yes, eels – reputed to be the oldest in the country with some individuals still enjoying a daily snack after 80 years of residence. Bencarri Farm also has a host of more congenial touchy-feely animals including

llamas and some homesick Scottish 'Heelan coos'. There is a good café on site (open 1000-late).

Collingwood

Collingwood was formerly known as Gibbstown and was (believe it or not) once a booming gold-mining town that was promoted as an eminently suitable capital for the nation. But that dream turned to dust when the gold reserves were laid waste and a fire almost destroyed the entire village. Rebuilt and renamed Collingwood in honour of Nelson's second-in-command, fire struck again in 1904 and yet again as recently as 1967 when the town hall, hotel and two shops were reduced to ashes. Despite its fiery past, Collingwood still retains a few historical buildings, including the former courthouse, which is now a café where you can sentence yourself to a lengthy tea break.

South of Collingwood, in the attractive Aorere River Valley and back on the limestone theme, are the privately owned **Te Anaroa** and **Rebecca Caves** (Caves Rd, near Rockville, T03-524 8131, 1-hr guided tours of the Te Anaroa Caves available; dual cave tours of 2-3 hrs are also available $15, child $6). The Te Anaroa Caves are 350 m in length and include the usual stalactite and stalagmite formations and fossilized shells, while the Rebecca Caves are best known for their glow-worms. At the end of Cave Road are two limestone rock monoliths known as the Devil's Boots (presumably because they are upside-down).

Farewell Spit

Access on the spit is restricted so an organized tour is the only way to truly experience this weird and wonderful place. You can also book and join the Farewell Spit tour en route to the spit at the visitor centre, or see tour operators, page 211.

The spit, which is only around 20 m at its highest, is formed entirely from countless tons of sand ejected into the northerly ocean currents from the numerous rivermouths scattered all the way up the west coast. Both Cape Farewell and Farewell Spit were noted by Tasman in 1642 (no doubt a little shorter than it is now) and named by Cook when he left the shores of New Zealand in 1770. It is a dynamic, almost desert-like landscape, with sparse vegetation struggling to take root in the dry and constantly shifting sand. The majority of the spit is a DoC nature reserve and the vast mud flats that it creates along its landward edge are one of New Zealand's most important wading-bird habitats. Over 100 species have been recorded around the spit, with some migrating flocks of well in to the thousands, providing a memorable sight. Hundreds of black swans also use the food-rich mud flats of Golden Bay, and there is also a small colony of rapacious gannets at the very end of the spit.

The lighthouse, at the very tip of the spit, was first erected in 1870. It has an interesting history and was replaced due to rotting timber.

At the base of the spit and just beyond the last small settlement of Puponga is the **Farewell Spit Visitor Centre** (T03-5248454, daily 0900-1700). It stocks a range of leaflets and has a number of displays surrounding the spit, its wildlife and the rather sad and repetitive whale strandings in Golden Bay. The café sells a range of refreshments and snacks and has a deck overlooking the bay and the spit itself. Most of the established walking tracks leave directly from the centre.

Pillar Point with Farewell Spit in the distance.

Tip...

If you cannot afford to go out on the spit and do not have time to walk to Wharariki Beach, or simply want to get a better impression of its scale from afar, the best place to view it is from the elevated hills around the Pillar Point Light Beacon, accessed by foot from Wharariki Road and Puponga.

Wharariki Beach

Wharariki Beach has to be one of the most beautiful beaches in the country. Perhaps it is its very remoteness that makes it so special, but add to that its classic features – including caves, arches and dunes – and you have near perfection. It is so beautiful you almost find yourself feeling a corrupting sense of guilt at leaving your lone footprints on its swathes of golden sand. You can access the beach by road from Puponga via Wharariki Road (20-min walk) or make it the highlight on a longer and stunning coastal walk from Pillar Point Lighthouse. Note that swimming here is very dangerous. Horse treks to and on the beach are also available.

Day walk: Pillar Point to Wharariki Beach coastal walk

Pillar Point to Wharariki Beach: 13 km; six to eight hours.

From Puponga, follow Wharariki Beach Road to the turn-off (right) up to Pillar Point Light Beacon ('Blinking Billy'). Note this is a rough non-signposted road. Park your vehicle at the base of the hill below the light beacon. Climb the hill to Pillar Point and enjoy your first proper view of Farewell Spit before heading further north towards the Old Man Rock (155 m) along the crest of the hill. Take in the views of the spit and Golden Bay before retracing your steps to Pillar Point. From Pillar Point follow the sporadic orange markers south through a small tract of manuka trees. From there follow the markers and the cliffs taking in all the cliff-top views to Cape Farewell. Keep your eyes peeled for fur seals, whose plaintive cries will probably reach the senses first. Continue south along the cliffs before descending to Wharariki Beach. If the tide is in your favour, walk its entire length and investigate the many caves and rock corridors along its length. Once at the base of Pilch Point (at the very end of all the beaches) retrace your steps to Pillar Point.

Kahurangi National Park

Kahurangi is New Zealand's second largest national park, after Fiordland. It is a vast and remote landscape of rugged alpine ranges and river valleys, the most notable being the Heaphy, which meets, in part, the park's most famous tramping route, the **Heaphy Track**. One of the most interesting features of the park is its ancient geology. It contains some of the country's oldest rock landforms, with spectacular limestone caves, plateau, arches and outcrops. Kahurangi is home to over half of New Zealand's native plant species (over 80% of all alpine species) and over 18 native bird species, including the New Zealand falcon, the great spotted kiwi and the huge New Zealand land snail.

The low-level 82-km Heaphy Track takes four to six days and is noted for its diverse habitats, open areas and beautiful coastal scenery (western end). It is usually negotiated from west to east and the western trailhead starts about 15 km north of Karamea, while the eastern, starts 28 km south of Collingwood. Take insect repellent with you.

For information on the park and its tramping tracks consult the DoC or i-SITES in Nelson, Motueka or Takaka.

Best photo locations

**❶ Marlborough: Wairau Valley vineyards Tower
Page 186**

The linear abstracts of vines in conjunction with rolling hills, some elevation (and if you are lucky a little early-morning mist) can create some great abstracts both in winter and spring when the vines are at there greenest. Harvest time is of course the best time for colour and for close-ups of the grapes themselves. As usual around dawn and late in the day will create the best colour saturation. Elevated views of vines can be secured from tower at the Highfield Estate, or from SH1 south to Seddon. For images of actual vintage operations your best bet are the small boutique vineyards around the Moutere Valley north of Nelson.

**❷ French Pass
Page 186**

As spectacular as the Marlborough Sounds are it is difficult to capture their essence, especially with a paucity of time. If time is short and you are Nelson-bound then at the least take the Queen Charlotte Drive to Havelock stopping (carefully) at the various viewpoints en route.

Of course a scenic flight at dawn would be productive, but perhaps the best bet for impacting imagery is to drive to French Pass. There are many good vantage points along the way with one of the best about 4 km short of the Pass itself. The best light occurs late in the day and at sunset, so you may have to stay in French Pass, which of course gives you the added advantage of the following dawn. Keep your eye out for cargo ships making the passage through the strait. It is an experience in itself and as far as images are concerned you could just about manage a portrait of the captain on the bridge!

**❸ Farwell Spit & Wharariki Beach
Page 202**

Although a trip along the spit itself is fun, at such low levels there is little on offer photographically that says 'sand spit' and an elevated view is far better. For photography there really is only one option here and all going well the coastal walk from Pillar Point to Wharariki Beachcan be one of the most photographically productive and rewarding anywhere in the country. There is so much on offer here, from views of Farewell Spit, to sea cliffs, caves, dunes and stacks, even the odd horse galloping along the beach. This is quintessential New Zealand, so enjoy and at some point don't forget to put the camera down and take it all in for its own sake.

**❹ Abel Tasman National Park
Page 196**

Like the Marlborough Sounds, don't expect miracles. Note most of the iconic shots of the Abel Tasman National Park are from the air and with good reason. It is difficult to capture its essence from low levels often with only one beach or vantage point to work with. There are plenty of lovely (yet uninspiring) bush walking and beach shots on offer, but to be truly successful you need some luck with the activity of other trampers or kayakers. The best imagery is often secured at the northern end of the park, particularly at Totaranui where the sand is a deep orange colour. Another good spot is the tidal crossing at Awaroa Bay where trampers are often up to their waists in water. Plan accordingly… Both locations can be accessed by car via Takaka, or by water taxi.

① ▲/✦/◉/☀/◉1000

② ▲/◊/◉/☀/☀

③ ▲/✦/◉/☀/◉1500

④ ▲/✦/◉/☀/☀

Sleeping

Marlborough

Marlborough Sounds
Bay of Many Coves Resort $$$$
Queen Charlotte Sound, T03-579 9771, bayofmanycovesresort.co.nz.
Represents the Sounds at its best. Remote seclusion yet all the comforts of a modern award-winning resort. Classy studio units and apartments with memorable views across the sound, café, restaurant and a wide range of activities from kayaking to heli-fishing.

Hopewell $$$-$
Kenepuru Sound, T03-573 4341, hopewell.co.nz.
Excellent establishment in a remote location on Kenepuru Sound, providing the perfect blend of value and comfort. Although accessible by road from Havelock North or Picton it is a tortuous drive. A water taxi is recommended and adds the overall experience, or you can fly direct from Wellington (Soundsair) to the local airfield from where you can be picked up. A range of options from a self-contained cottage to doubles and four-shares. Attractive grounds right down to the water's edge. Outdoor spa overlooking the sound, internet, kayaks and plenty of water-based activities, with fishing trips a speciality.

Lochmara Lodge (Backpackers) $$-$
Lochmara Bay, Queen Charlotte Bay, T03-573 4554, lochmara lodge.co.nz.
A deservedly popular eco-oriented backpacker hostel with a great, laid-back atmosphere. Dorm and private studio chalets (some ensuite). If you can remove yourself from a hammock there is a spa, licensed restaurant/café, open fire, free kayak and windsurf hire. Excellent in-house eco-trips to Motuara Island.

Picton
The Broadway Motel $$$
113 High St, T03-573 6563, broadwaymotel.co.nz.
Centrally located and handy for the ferry terminal the Broadway is one of the most modern motels in the town. Spotless standard units, some with spa and balcony.

The Gables $$$-$$
20 Waikawa Rd, T03-573 6772, thegables.co.nz.
Good value with three rooms and two self-contained cottages.

Motor parks
Blue Anchor Top Ten Holiday Park $$$-$
78 Waikawa Rd, T0800-277444, pictontop10.co.nz.
An excellent award-winning holiday park. It is well located within walking distance of the town, has tidy cabins and tourist flats and great facilities. It gets crowded, especially if you're camping, so arrive early.

Alexanders Holiday Park $$-$
Canterbury St, Picton T0800-4742866, T03-5736378, alexanderspicton.co.nz.
If the Blue Anchor is busy, or you want a more peaceful (but older) site try Alexanders Holiday Park on the southern edge of town. It has plenty more space and great (but older) camp kitchen facilities.

Blenheim & the Marlborough vineyards
Hotel D'Urville $$$$
52 Queen St, T03-577 9945, durville.co.nz.
Quality boutique hotel in a former bank in the heart of the town centre. Award-winning restaurant attached.

Cranbrook Cottage $$
Giffords Rd, T03-572 8606, cranbrook.co.nz.
Without doubt one of the most characterful self-contained cottage B&Bs in the region. Set among the vines and fruit trees, the 135-year-old renovated cottage provides plenty of privacy. Breakfast delivered to the door each morning.

St Leonards $$
18 St Leonards Rd, T03-577 8328, stleonards.co.nz.
Beautifully appointed self-contained accommodation sleeping up to six, in three

vineyard cottages (one of which is a former stables) and a homestead annexe. Open fires, potbelly stoves and claw-foot baths add to a cosy, homely atmosphere. Great value.

Chartridge Park $
SH6 (3 km south of Havelock), T03-5742129.
A superb peaceful and low-key little motor park with two great-value cabins and a bunkroom. Small camp kitchen and games lounge with TV.

Nelson & around

Nelson

Te Puna Wai $$$$-$$$
24 Richardson St, Port Hills, T04-548 7621, tepunawai.co.nz.
An immaculate villa-style B&B set overlooking the bay in the Port Hills area. Three luxury ensuite rooms, two of which can be combined to form a spacious apartment. Great views, open fire, classy decor and hosts that go the extra mile.

Accents on the Park $$-$
335 Trafalgar Sq, T03-548 4335, trafalgaraccommodation.co.nz.
In a word: exceptional. A beautifully renovated Victorian villa with a distinct air of class. A full range of well-appointed rooms from ensuite to shared dorms with all the usual facilities and a lovingly constructed basement lounge bar with open fire and plenty of character.

Nelson City Holiday Park & Motels $$-$
230 Vanguard St, T03-548 1445, nelsonholidaypark.co.nz.
Closest quality park to the city centre. Full range of units and cabins, powered sites, camp kitchen.

Nelson to Motueka
Jester House $$$$
15 km south of Motueka on the Coastal Highway (SH60), T03-526 6742, jesterhouse.co.nz.
Something totally different and without doubt the most original accommodation in the region. Quite simply, this could be (and probably will be) your only opportunity to stay in a giant boot.

Rowan Cottage Organic B&B $$$
27 Fearon St, T03-528 6492, rowancottage.net.
Studio with good facilities and character amidst a proudly nurtured organic garden.

Motor parks
Mapua Leisure Park $$$-$
33 Toru St, T03-540 2666, nelson holiday.co.nz.
An excellent camp, set amidst pine trees and sheltered surroundings, at the river mouth. It has numerous pretty areas to camp in, powered sites, cabins, chalets, sauna, pool and spa. There is also a small café and bar on the beach and internet.

Kaiteriteri & Marahau
Abel Tasman Ocean View Chalets $$$-$$
305 Sandy Bay Marahau Rd,T03-527 8232, accommodationabeltasman. co.nz.
Neat, self-contained one- to two-bedroom cottages and studio units set on the hillside overlooking the bay, about 500 m from the main village.

Abel Tasman National Park
Torrent Bay Lodge $$$
T03-528 7801, abeltasman.co.nz.
Owned and operated by Abel Tasman Wilson's Experiences offer an excellent standard of modern, mid- to upper-range accommodation as part of a walks or kayaking package from two days/one night to five days/ four nights.

Old McDonald's Farm and Holiday Park $$$-$
Harvey Rd, at the entrance to the Abel Tasman Park, T03-527 8288, old macs.co.nz.
A large but sheltered, well-facilitated holiday camp complete with various animals, including two friendly and extremely dozy kune pigs. There are plenty of sheltered tent and powered sites and a range of well-appointed self-contained units, cabins and a backpacker's dormitory. Small café and shop on site and internet. Within walking distance of the Park Café.

Eating & drinking

Golden Bay

Adrift $$$-$$
10 km south of Collingwod, 52 Tukurua Rd, Tukurua, T03-525 8353, accommodationgoldenbay.com.
Excellent self-contained, beachside luxury cottages, designed for two but accommodating three. Plenty of privacy, beautiful surroundings and great hosts.

Innlet and Cottages $$
Main Rd, Pakawau, on the road to Farewell Spit, T03-524 8040, goldenbayindex.co.nz/theinnlet.
Oozes character and is in a lovely bush setting offering dorms, twins and doubles and charming self-contained cottages, studio apartment and a flat that sleep three to six. Bike hire available and excellent harbour/rainforest kayak trips, guided or self-guided. Internet.

Motor parks
Pohara Beach Top Ten Holiday Park and Motels $$$-$
Abel Tasman Drive, Pohara, T03-525 9500, pohara.com/paradise.
The best motor camp with tent, powered sites, modern timber kitchen cabins and full facilities all next to the beach, 10 km north of Takaka.

Marlborough

Picton
Le Café $$
London Quay, T03-573 5588.
Daily for breakfast, lunch and dinner.
Perhaps the best bet, it has a good atmosphere and is well placed on the waterfront.

Blenheim & the Marlborough Vineyards
Hotel D'Urville $$$
52 Queen St, Blenheim, T03-577 9945.
Daily 0600-2400.
The place for fine dining in Blenheim itself.

Herzog $$$-$$
81 Jeffries Rd, Wairau Valley, T03-572 8770, herzog.co.nz.
Daily, lunch from 1200-1500 and dinner from 1800.
Just one of many fine winery restaurants.

Raupo Riverside Café $$
2 Symonds St, Blenheim, T03-577 8822.
Daily 0730-1900.
Eco-oriented and located on the banks of the Taylor River in the heart of Blenheim.

The Cork and Keg $$
Inkerman St, Renwick, T03-572 9328.
Sick of vineyards? Try this character English-style pub and brewery with its all-day pub-grub menu.

The Mussel Pot Restaurant $$
73 Main Rd, T03-574 2824.
Daily 1030-2100.
Great mussels and chowder.

Nelson & around

Nelson
Hopgoods Restaurant and Bar $$$
284 Trafalgar St, T03-545 7191.
Quality locally sourced cuisine, with much of it organic.

The Boat Shed $$$
350 Wakefield Quay, T03-546 9783, theboatshedcafe.co.nz.
Daily for breakfast, lunch and dinner.
Fresh, local seafood a speciality.

Lambrettas Café Bar $$
204 Hardy St, T03-545 8555, lambrettascafe.co.nz.
Open 0900-late.
A popular, good value café specializing in all things Italian.

Nelson to Motueka
The Smokehouse Café $$
Mapua, T03-540 2280, smokehouse.co.nz.
Daily for lunch and dinner.
Known for its smoked fish. Also has takeaway fish and chips.

Motueka
Hot Mamma's Café and Bar $$
105 High St, Motueka, T03-528 7039.
Sun-Thu 0900-2200, Fri/Sat 0900-0100.

Good licensed café and in the evening a good vibe with musos.

Kaiteriteri & Marahau
Park Café $$
Harvey Rd, Marahau,
T03-527 8270
Daily from 0800 (closed May-Aug).
Just at the southern (main) entrance to the park. Fine blackboard fare, a bar, good coffee and internet.

Golden Bay

Mussel Inn $$$-$$
Onekaka, half way between Takaka and Collingwood on SH60, T03-525 9241, musselinn.co.nz.
Open 1100-late.
Good pub grub with great-value mussels and good beer.

Courthouse Café $$
Corner of Gibbs and Elizabeth streets, Collingwood, T03-5248025.
Daily 0830-late (seasonal).
Sentence yourself to tea and scones at this former courthouse.

Wholemeal Café $$
Commercial St, Takaka, T03-525 9426, wholemealcafe.co.nz
Daily 0730-late.
Good coffee, breakfasts, health-conscious blackboard menu and excellent service.

Entertainment

Marlborough

Festivals
Marlborough Wine Festival
(2nd Sat in Feb)
T0800-000575, bmw-wine marlborough-festival.co.nz.
A lively celebration of the region's gourmet food and wines. Live music provided.

Nelson Arts Festival
(2nd Sat in Feb)
A week-long celebration showcasing many forms of artistic expression.

Shopping

Marlborough

Weka Gallery
SH6, Havelock, T03-571 6322.
Worth a look, representing some of the Sounds diverse talent.

Nelson & around

Nelson Market
Montgomery Square every Saturday, 0800-1300. Local arts and crafts.

Golden Bay

Golden Bay Museum and Gallery
Takaka, T03-525 6268,
Daily 1000-1600, closed Sun in winter, $1.
Showcases the cream of local arts and crafts talent.

Activities & tours

Marlborough

Beachcomber Fun Cruises
London Quay, T03-573 6175, T0800-624526, beachcombercruises.co.nz, and Endeavour Express, based in both Endeavour Inlet and at the Waterfront in Picton, T03-573 5456, boatrides.co.nz.
Wide-ranging cruise services and packages.

The Cougar Line
London Quay, Picton, T0800-504090, T03-573 7925, queenchar lottetrack.co.nz
One-way transfers, multi-day walk packages; mountain-biking packages and a daily 'Track Pass' that will drop you off at Ship Cove and pick up at Anakiwa, from $95. Offers half- or full-day cruise walks from $55.

Dolphin Watch Ecotours
Picton Foreshore, T03-573 8040, naturetours.co.nz.
Offers a wide range of eco-based tours to Ship Cove and Motuara Island Bird Sanctuary above and beyond its conventional dolphin swimming and viewing trips.

Marlborough Sounds Adventure Company
London Quay, Picton, T03-573 6078.
Guided and self-guided walks of the Queen Charlotte Track. It also offers kayaking trips and a three-day walk/paddle/mountain bike adventure from $585.

Marlborough Travel
Havelock, T03-577 9997,
greenshellmusselcruise.co.nz.
Offers the Greenshell Mussel
Cruise: a cruise through the
Pelorus and Kenepuru Sounds.
Daily departures from Havelock
at 1330 (Nov-Mar) including a
visit to a mussel farm where you
can enjoy mussels with a glass of
wine, from $110, child $35.

Marlborough Wine Tours
Blenheim, T03-578 9515,
marlboroughwinetours.co.nz.
Tour of up to eight wineries.
Flexible itinerary depending on
taste, from $43-$79. UK
wine-delivery service.

Soundsair
T0800-505005, soundsair.com.
Extraordinary number of
flight-seeing combinations and
options that include one night's
lodging, lunch, day walks and
cruises from $150-400.

Sounds Connection
T03-573 8843,
soundsconnection.co.nz.
Another alternative based
in Picton.

Sounds Natural
Havelock, T275-382203,
soundsnatural.co.nz.
Really want to go au naturelle?
Full or multi-day 'clothing
optional' guided trips to remote
private locations from $95.

Wine-Tours-By-Bike
Blenheim, T03-577 6954
winetoursbybike.co.nz.
This is the common-sense
method of visiting the wineries
by bike. Half day from $40, full
$55, guided tour $25 per hour.

Nelson & around

Abel Tasman Aqua Taxi
Marahau, T03-527 8083,
T0800-278282, aquataxis.co.nz.
Has an office and café (where
you also board your boat). Prices
are reasonable and competitive.
An average fare to Totaranui at
the top end of the park will cost
from $40 one-way. Most water
taxis depart between 0830 and
1030 from Motueka, Kaiteriteri
and Marahau with additional
sailings in the early afternoon
(1200 and 1330), depending on
the tides.

Abel Tasman Wilson's Experiences
265 High St, Motueka, T0800-
223582, T03-528 2027,
abeltasmanco.nz.
Operates beachfront lodges,
launch cruises, water taxi,
guided/non-guided sea
kayaking and walking; it can
provide maps, tide information
and help with itinerary planning.

Bay Tours
48 Brougham St, T03-548 6486,
baytoursnelson.co.nz.
Flexible with wine and art tours a
speciality, from $78.

Creative Tourism
Nelson, T03-526 8812,
creativetourism.co.nz.
For $55-110 you can try your
hand at a range of contemporary
or traditional crafts from bone
carving to organic brewing.

Happy Valley Adventures
194 Cable Bay Rd, Nelson,
T03-545 0304, happyvalley
adventures.co.nz.
Back-country guided quad bike
rides, taking in some superb
views. Interesting eco-based
commentary. An excellent wet
weather option. From one to four
hours $75-150, standard tour $95
for 2½ hours. Also Skywire a
four-person flying-fox that runs
1.6 km across the valley,
reputedly at 120 kph, from $85.
Transportation available.

Kahu Kayaks
Sandy Bay Rd, Marahau, T03-527
8300, T0800-300101,
kahukayaks.co.nz.
One of many companies based
around the southern section of
the park. Good local knowledge,
but compare prices and options.
Freedom rentals available.

Kitescool
Nelson, T021-354 837,
kitescool.co.nz.
Kitesurfing is huge in Nelson
with the winds over Tahunanui
Beach often creating the perfect
conditions. Lessons from $150.

Skydive Abel Tasman
Mouteka Airfield, 16 College St,
T03-528 4091, T0800-422899 ,
skydive.co.nz.
If the weather is in your favour
you can do a tandem skydive
from 3,600 ft ($279).

Tasman Bay Air Nelson
T03-528 8290, flytasmanbay.co.nz.
Flights across both Kahurangi
and Abel Tasman National Parks.
A truly memorable experience.

U-Fly Extreme
Motueka Airfield, College St,
T03-528 8290, T0800-360180,
uflyextreme.co.nz.
Fun to the extreme aboard a
Pitts-Special Biplane. A
once-in-a-lifetime opportunity
to actually fly an aerobatic
aircraft yourself, from $285
(20-min flight). Remarkably easy,
safe, good value for money.

Vertical Limits
34 Vanguard St, Nelson,
T03-545 7511, verticallimits.co.nz.
Open Mon-Thu 1200-2100,
Fri-Sun 1000-1800.
Offers some excellent half- or
full-day rock-climbing trips to
some notable venues in Golden
Bay, $65-130. Tandem paragliding
is another option. It also has a
climbing wall, from $16.

Golden Bay

Cape Farewell Horse Treks
Puponga, Farewell Spit, T03-524
8031, horsetreksnz.com.
Some of the most scenic routes
in the country, including
Wharariki Beach (3 hrs, $115).

Farewell Spit Tours
6 Tasman St, T03-524 8257,
T0800-808257, farewellspit.com.
This is, as the name suggests, the
original tour operator and has
been taking people out on to
the spit for over 60 years. Range
of themed eco-oriented options
lasting 6½ hours.

Golden Bay Kayaks
Pohara, Golden Bay, T03-525
9095, goldenbaykayaks.co.nz.
Popular and slightly different
with trips in both the Abel
Tasman National Park and
Golden Bay region.

Transport

Picton, Blenheim and Nelson all
offer **air** and nationwide **bus**
services including Golden bay
and the West Coast. The main
i-SITES can assist with bookings.
For ferry crossings to South
Island see page 159. The
TranzScenic operates the daily
TransCoastal service from Picton
to Christchurch, T04-4950775
T0800-872467, tranzscenic.co.nz.

Blenheim is 28km from Picton,
Kaikoura 157 km and
Christchurch 336km on SH1.
Nelson is 110 km via SH6. Nelson
and Blenheim airports serve the
main national centres, while
Picton receives flights from
Wellington with **Soundsair**,
T03- 520 3080/T0800-505005,
soundsair.com, eight times daily,
from $89 one-way. The
Interislander and **Bluebridge**
ferries dock at the ferry terminal
in Picton 500 m north of the
town centre (for ferry detail see
page 159). There are many bus
companies that serve Picton to/
from the south or west including
Intercity, T03-520 3113/T03-573
7025, intercitycoach.co.nz. Buses
drop off or pick up at the railway
station, ferry terminal or outside
the i-SITE visitor centre. The main
booking agent is the i-SITE visitor
centre. The Picton train station is
on Auckland Stand is the
terminus for the daily
TranzCoastal service to/from
Christchurch, T03-573 8857/
T0800-872467, 0900-1700,
tranzcoastal.co.nz. It arrives daily
at 1213 and departs at 1300, from
$59-100. This trip is famous for its
coastal scenery.
    Buses to and throughout the
Nelson region, including the
Abel Tasman National Park can
be booked at the Nelson i-SITE
visitor centre.

Contents

Canterbury & the West Coast

Giant chess, Cathedral Square, Christchurch.

Introduction

Canterbury is the largest region in the South Island, extending from the Pacific Ocean and the Canterbury Plains in the east to the Great Divide and Southern Alps to the west, and from the Kaikoura Ranges in the north to the Waitaki River in the south. Central Canterbury is the hub of the South Island and its capital, Christchurch, is the country's second largest city. Aesthetically and historically it is also the most Anglican having being one of the first areas on the South Island settled by the British in 1850.

North Canterbury is home to Hanmer Springs, a relaxing thermal resort, while beyond that is Kaikoura, famous for its whales and a veritable 'Who's Who' of sea life. In South Canterbury, via Fairlie and Burke's Pass, you enter MacKenzie Country. Here you will find the region's most stunning and diverse scenery, culminating in Pukaki Lake and New Zealand's highest peak, Mount Cook (3754 m).

West of Christchurch, beyond the curtain of mountains, is the 'wild' West Coast. Reached precariously via the portals of Lewis or Arthur's Pass it offers a glut of breathtaking scenery and for many the experience of New Zealand that truly satisfies all the hype – provided of course that the equally wild weather behaves itself.

What to see in...

... a long weekend
With only three days arriving from the north via road, it really is an 'either or'. Either head down the West Coast from Nelson, or from Picton head south via the east coast with a stop in Kaikoura to Christchurch. Then go south to Wanaka via the MacKenzie Country and Lindis Pass.

... a week
Take in Kaikoura, Christchurch, and/or Hanmer Springs, then the West Coast via Lewis or Arthur's Pass, or alternatively remain on the east and head south via the MacKenzie Country.

Note the trip down the West Coast is very weather dependent and you are advised to have a plan B should it be looking grim. Very often when it is wet on the West Coast it can be fine or dry on the east. MacKenzie Country is in the rain shadow of the West Coast.

View across Lake Pukaki to Mount Cook.

Christchurch & Banks Peninsula

Dubbed the Garden City, Christchurch is known as being the most English of New Zealand's cities. Reminders of these roots are everywhere from the formal blazers and straw hats of the city's school children to the distant chorus of 'howzat' from its myriad cricket pitches on lazy summer Sunday afternoons. Without doubt the key to its charm is the immense, tree-lined Hagley Park that borders its centre and has over the decades remained remarkably intact. With the park, its trees and the pretty Avon River that threads it all together, the aesthetics of Christchurch verge on the adorable. But natural aesthetics and its obvious English colonial feel aside, Christchurch has developed its own very Kiwi-orientated atmosphere. It has the buzz and vitality of Auckland, the cosmopolitan town feel of Wellington and it shares a pride in its heritage and architecture that only Dunedin can beat.

In 1850 the 'first four ships' (as they became known) – the *Charlotte Jane*, *Randolph*, *Sir George Seymour* and *Cressy* brought 782 colonial souls to the then whaling base of Lyttleton, which had already been established on the Banks Peninsula. Even before their arrival, the Canterbury Association (formed in Britain in 1849) had already christened the great settlement-to-be, Christchurch.

Essentials

⊘ ATM There are ATMs and currency exchange available at the airport and the i-SITE visitor centre. All the major banks are represented in the CBD.

⊕ Hospital Southern Cross Hospital, 131 Bealey Av, T03-9683100.

⊕ Pharmacy 555 or 748 Colombo St.

⤴ Post office Cathedral Sq (Post Restante), T0800-501501, Mon-Thu 0800-1800, Fri 0800-2000, Sat-Sun 1000-1600.

❶ Tourist information Christchurch i-SITE visitor centre, Old Post Office Building, Cathedral Sq (West), T03-379 9629, christchurchnz.com, christchurchinformation.co.nz, localeye.co.nz, Mon-Fri 0830-1700, Sat-Sun 0830-1600. There are also i-SITES in the international (T03-353 7783/4) and domestic (T03-353 7774/5) airport terminals.

The Avon river, Christchurch city.

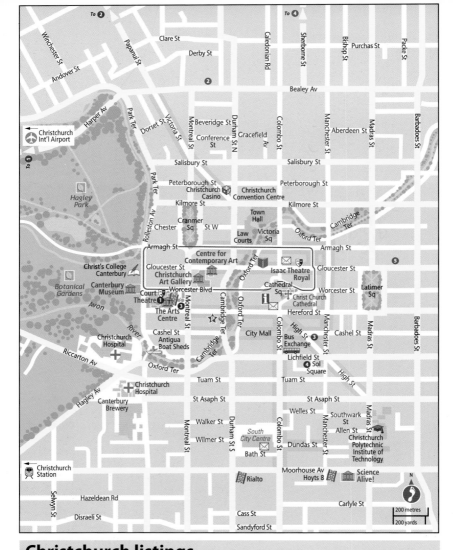

Christchurch listings

⊙ Sleeping

1 Airport Christchurch Motel *55 Roydvale Av*
2 Hambledon *103 Bealey Av*
3 Hotel So *165 Cashel St*
4 Meadow Park Top Ten Holiday Park
5 Stonehurst *241 Gloucester St, Latimer Sq*

⊙ Eating & drinking

1 Annie's Wine Bar and Restaurant
  Corner Rolleston Av and Hereford St
2 Charlotte Jane Hotel *110 Papanui Rd*
3 Dux de Lux *41 Hereford St*
4 Fat Eddie's *Unit 10, Sol Sq, Tuam St*

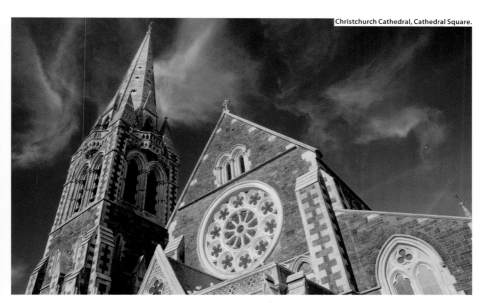
Christchurch Cathedral, Cathedral Square.

Cathedral Square

Map: Christchurch, p218.

Dominated by the Gothic-revival Anglican **Christ Church Cathedral** (T03-366 0046, 1-hr tours Mon-Fri 1100 and 1400, Sat 1100, Sun 1130, free), Cathedral Square is considered the heart of the city and its main focus point, but it is not without contention. Most Cantabrians feel the square (which had a major makeover in the late 1990s) is an aesthetic disaster and certainly, it does seem hopelessly out of character with the rest of Christchurch. Perhaps here in the Garden City of all places it suffers from the scourge of the average old-school antipodean architect – a severe disregard for trees. However, current aesthetics aside, the main feature worth looking at in the square is of course the cathedral itself. It houses a number of interesting memorials and boasts an interior design that is an interesting and eclectic mix of Maori and European. The spire can be climbed in part, offering a panoramic view of the city. The square is also home to the statue of John Robert Godley the founder of the Canterbury Association and essentially Christchurch itself and the Four Ships Court, a memorial to the 'first four ships' that stands outside the 1879 Old Post Office (which now houses the Christchurch). Accessed through the i-SITE is the **Southern Encounter Aquarium and Kiwi House** (T03-3597109, southernencounter.co.nz, daily 0900-1630, from $16, child $6), which seems remarkably out of place but still houses an interesting collection of local sea creatures and the obligatory kiwi exhibit.

It's a fact...

Given Christchurch's strong and outwardly obvious English links, it is perhaps ironic that the first European settlers on the Canterbury Plains were in fact Scottish. Brothers William and John Deans arrived before 'the first four ships' in 1843, calling the land they purchased from local Maori Riccarton after their hometown in Central Scotland.

Around the region

Avon River

Though hardly the Mississippi this little river is without doubt one of the city's greatest assets. Meandering from the northwest tip of the four avenues through Hagley Park and the Botanical Gardens, it cuts furtively through the city centre, before finally continuing its journey through the city's eastern suburbs to the sea. The river is particularly attractive in autumn when poplar and weeping willows are radiant in golden hues. On the eastern bank of the river, just beyond Cathedral Square is the 1917 statue of Scott of the Antarctic beside the river – a reminder that Christchurch is a principal gateway to the Antarctic.

Beside the Worcester Street Bridge and at the 1882 **Antigua Boat Sheds** (2 Cambridge Terr, T03-366 0337, punting.co.nz, daily 0900-2100, winter 1000-1600, 30 mins, $20, child $10), you will find bases for punting, a congenial mode of river transport that hails from the university towns of Oxford and Cambridge in the UK. Apart from anything else this presents an opportunity to meet a real punter…

Located 3.5 km west of the city centre on the banks of the Avon are **Riccarton Bush** and **Riccarton House (Putaringamotu)** (16 Kahu Rd, T03-341 1018, riccartonhouse.co.nz; tours Sun-Fri 1400, $15). Set in 12 ha of parkland, the historic Riccarton Estate was once the home of the Scots pioneers and brothers William and John Deans (the first European settlers on the Canterbury Plains). It features the faithfully restored and furnished original 1843 **Deans cottage** (open daily) in which they first lived, and the grand Victorian/Edwardian **homestead** (Mon-Fri 1300-1600) that was built by the next generation from 1856 to 1874. There is a café on site.

Further downstream is **Mona Vale** (63 Fendalton Rd, T03-348 9660, daily Oct-Apr 0930-1700, May-Sep 0930-1600), a beautiful Elizabethan-style homestead and gardens, built in 1905 on the land first settled by the Scots Dean brothers in 1843. While the homestead itself is now a fine restaurant and café, the 5.5-ha grounds boast

a spectacular array of features including a lily pond, rhododendrons, azaleas and exotic trees, all set in reverence to the river. The gardens can be reached by punt, and guided tours are available.

Hagley Park

T03-941 7590.
Daily Sep-Apr Mon-Fri 0900-1600, Sat-Sun 1000-1400.
Map: Christchurch, p218.
Amazingly intact after all the years of development, Hagley Park (over 200 ha) is divided in two portions by Riccarton Avenue and comprises pleasant tree-lined walkways, sports fields and, in its central reaches, the **Botanical Gardens** (0700-dusk, Conservatory Complex 1015-1600) enclosed by a loop of the Avon River. Well maintained and with a huge variety of gardens from herb to rose, they provide a great escape from the buzz of the city year round. Autumn sees the gardens at their most colourful. There is an information centre and café housed in old Curators House off Rolleston Avenue.

Arts centres

Two entities along Worcester Street, one old and one new dominate the arts scene in the city.

The Christchurch Art Gallery (Te Puna O Waiwhetu) (T03-941 7300, christchurchartgallery. org.nz, daily 1000-1700, Wed 2100, free with a charge for major exhibitions) was upon its completion in 2003 immediately christened by some cynics as 'a warehouse in a tutu'. It is actually supposed to be 'evoking the sinuous form of the koru and the River Avon that flows through Christchurch', but whether you love it or frown at it with over 3000 sq m of exhibition space, it can certainly accommodate a formidable 5500 permanent works. Beyond its almost mesmerizingly colourful 'grand stair' you will find a dynamic range of contemporary exhibitions and an many of the famous New Zealand names including Charles Goldie, Colin McCahon and Ralph Hotere. There is also a retail outlet and the obligatory café/bistro.

The Arts Centre (2 Worcester Blvd, T03-3660989, artscen tre.org.nz, tours daily from 1030-1530), was once the site of the original University of Canterbury. The old Gothic revival buildings now house an excellent and dynamic array of arts and crafts, workshops, galleries and sales outlets, as well as theatres, cinemas, cafés, restaurants and bars. It is well worth a visit, particularly at the weekend when it hosts a lively arts and crafts market.

Nearby, **The Centre for Contemporary Art** (66 Gloucester St, T03-366 7261, coca.org.nz, Tue-Fri 1000-1700, Sat-Sun 1200-1600, free) is also worth visiting. There are five galleries and over 50 exhibitions per annum; much of the art is for sale.

Canterbury Museum & Christ College

Rolleston Av, T03-366 5000 cantmus.govt.nz. Daily 0900-1730 (winter 1700), entry is free but there are charges for the Exhibition Court and Discovery Centre ($2); guided tours also available. Map: Christchurch, p218.

Housed in a grand 1870 neo-Gothic building and founded in 1867, the regions largest museum is well worth a visit, the undoubted highlights being its impressive Maori collection and the Hall of Antarctic Discovery. In keeping with other museums in the country, it also hosts a dynamic Discovery Centre for kids. The Exhibition Court displays a changing programme of travelling national and international exhibitions. There is also a fine in-house shop and a café overlooking the Botanical Gardens.

Around the region

Just north of the museum is **Christ College Canterbury**, which is without doubt New Zealand's most famous historic school. Built in 1850 it is an aesthetic and architectural delight, and in the late afternoon spills forth suitably clad and 'proper' scholars.

International Antarctic Centre

38 Orchard Rd, (near the airport, signposted), T03-353 7798, iceberg.co.nz.
Daily Oct-Mar 0900-1900, Apr-Sep 0900-1730; $48, child $30 provides unlimited entry all day to the Indoor Attraction, NZ Penguin Encounter and unlimited Hagglund rides. Guided tours are available or you can self-guide with the help of 'snow-phones' ($6). The city-airport bus (from Cathedral Sq) stops here and runs every 30 mins.

> **66**
> Had we lived I should have had a tale to tell...
> **99**
>
> *Robert Falcon Scott,*
> *Ross Ice Shelf,*
> *Antarctica 29 March, 1912.*

Since the days of Scott and Shackleton, Christchurch has been a principal 'gateway to the Antarctic'. Today, an area alongside the airport is a working campus to which a formidable array of buildings can attest. From here you can often see the US Hercules sitting waiting to head off into the wild blue and very cold yonder. The International Antarctic Centre is the public face of operations and was opened in 1992. Though somewhat pricey it offers an excellent introduction to the great white continent and overall it is both informative and fun, with an excellent array of displays from the historical to the modern day. Highlights include the **Snow and Ice Experience**, a room kept at -5°C, replete with manufactured snow and ice and most recently, **Penguin Encounter** comprising a small group of mainly rehabilitated and permanently disabled little blue penguins – a species that is, ironically, far more at home around the golden beaches of Australasia than the icebergs of Antarctica. From the displays you then emerge into the well and unusually stocked Antarctic shop and the South Café and Bar – more likely for a stiff whiskey than a double-scoop ice cream.

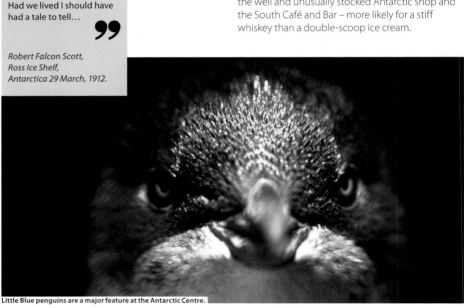

Little Blue penguins are a major feature at the Antarctic Centre.

In addition to the centre's indoor activities is the Antarctic Hagglund Rides, which are free. The Hagglund is a tracked vehicle that was originally used on the Scott and McMurdo bases. During the 15-minute ride you are taken to see some of the major facilities of the centre before experiencing the all-terrain abilities of the vehicle.

Wildlife attractions

Christchurch has two main wildlife attractions both located near the airport.

Orana Park *(743 McLeans Island Rd, 10 mins from the airport, T03-3597109, oranawildlifepark.co.nz, daily 1000-1700, from $24, child $8)*, New Zealand's largest captive wildlife reserve, is set in 80 ha of parkland. It has native and international wildlife with an emphasis on African animals, including meerkats.

Willowbank Wildlife Reserve (60 Hussey Rd, off Gardiners Rd, T03-3596226, willowbank.co.nz, daily 1000-2200, $25, child $10) focuses primarily on native wildlife and farm animals. The reserve has a successful kiwi-breeding programme and one of the better kiwi exhibits in the country. Weekends are best avoided, however, as it gets busy. The reserve is also base for the **KoTane Maori Experience** (daily at 1730, 1830-1830 winter, $48, child $24 performance only; $65, child $30 performance and tour; $110, child $55 performance and traditional New Zealand dinner).

Tamaki Heritage Village

Ferrymead Park Drive, Ferrymead T03-366 7333; maoriculture.co.nz.
From $126, child $73.

Set within an era of dramatic change in New Zealand's history, this is an interactive evening experience called "Lost in our Own Land". It re-lives the impact of colonization upon the Maori people. A Maori village, fortified Pa and colonial village come to life with dramatic performances and you then feast upon a selection of traditional Maori hangi and colonial banquet food. The evening is capped off with a steam train journey.

It's a fact...

Permanent European settlement actually began with the arrival of the French at Akaroa on the Banks Peninsula in 1840 and the British in Lyttleton three years later. In effect, it was this pre-emptive settlement strike by the French that spurred the British to initiate the Treaty of Waitangi and effectively place New Zealand under British sovereignty and subsequent rule. Had they not, today, the Sky Tower in Auckland would perhaps be of the Eiffel variety and its residents would say 'poisson-frit', not 'fush and chups'.

Christchurch (Port Hills) Gondola

10 Bridle Path Rd, T03-384 0700, gondola.co.nz.
Sun-Wed 1000-180, Thu-Sat 1000-2100, $22, child $10. The Best Attractions Shuttle Bus leaves from the visitor centre at 1000, 1400 and 1600 or the No 28 bus from the Bus Exchange.

The Christchurch Gondola is worth the trip. The base terminal is in the Heathcote Valley 10 km southeast of the city via Ferry Road. From there gondolas whisk you 945 m to the top of the Port Hills (1500 m) and the Summit Complex. The complex has all the expected shops and a café but also offers viewpoints from which you can gaze down to Lyttleton and across the Banks Peninsula, or beyond the Canterbury Plains, to the Southern Alps. You can embark on a number of walks from the complex including one that explores the crater rim.

The Tamaki Heritage Village.

Half-day scenic drive:
Lyttleton, the Gondola and Banks Peninsula views

If you are short of time the following half-day drive offers some memorable views of the city and the Banks Peninsula and gives you a far better sense of place than the flat milieu of the city and the plains that surround it.

From the city centre head southeast along Moorhouse, then Ferry Roads towards Sumner. Then take Tunnel Road (SH74) to Lyttelton. Once through the tunnel take some time to look around Lyttelton. Lyttelton i-SITE visitor centre, 20 Oxford St, T03-328 9093, lytteltonharbour.co.nz, daily 0900-1700, can provide detailed information and a self-guided historical-walks leaflet.

Although visiting cruise liners and container ships now mask Lyttleton Harbour's history, this was the place where the 'first four ships' arrived in 1850. It was also the port that Captain Scott and Lieutenant Shackleton used as their base to explore the Antarctic and is still regularly used by Antarctic service and tourist vessels. From Lyttelton head east around the hills on Sumner Road, then once you turn back inland head up left on Summit Road. Summit Road winds its way up and along the Port Hills offering great views across the city north and west. You can also access various viewpoints looking south over the peninsula including the Gondola complex.

Continue west along Summit Road until it drops to Dyers Pass Road. Before descending back in to the city it is worth taking in the view from Coronation Hill Reserve that overlooks the Cashmere Valley and Lyttelton Harbour. The curiously named building Sign of the Kiwi was opened in 1917 as a tearoom and inn and is one of a chain of similar buildings, built by local politician Henry Ell, in the early 1900s and used as staging posts along a hillside tourist route. The Sign of the Takahe a little further back towards the city is now a fine-dining restaurant. From there just follow your nose back in to the city centre.

View across Lyttleton Harbour, Banks Peninsula.

The gondola slides over the scenic Summit Road, Banks Peninsula.

Banks Peninsula

Jutting out into the Pacific Ocean from Christchurch is the Banks Peninsula. Captain Cook was the first European to discover the peninsula, but he actually thought it was an island (which it actually once was) and charted it as such, bestowing on it the name Banks Island after his ship's naturalist Sir Joseph Banks. Distinctly out of character with the (now) connected and flat alluvial Canterbury Plains, it is a refreshing and rugged landscape of hills and flooded harbours formed by two violent volcanic eruptions. The two largest harbours, which now fill the craters and shelter their namesake settlements, are **Lyttleton** to the north and **Akaroa** to the south. These settlements provide an interesting excursion from Christchurch, with Akaroa a long but scenic 85 km drive and Lyttleton – 12 km away via the Lyttleton Tunnel – being by far the more accessible.

Other than the hill and harbour scenery, both places offer historic sites, and activities such as dolphin watching. The bays and waters that surround the peninsula are home to the world's smallest and rarest dolphin, the Hector's dolphin. The two- or four-day trek on the Banks Peninsula Track from Akaroa is also a popular attraction.

The Akaroa visitors centre, 80 Rue Lavaud, T03-304 8600, akaroa.com, daily 0900-1700, is an independent information office, with helpful staff, who will share their knowledge regarding the village and more out-of-the-way places.

Around Christchurch

From Christchurch SH1 heads north and is embraced by the Hurunui hills. At Waipara, SH7 heads northeast to Hanmer Springs and the West Coast via the Lewis Pass, while SH1 continues north to Kaikoura and eventually Blenheim. In landlocked Hanmer activities include skiing, rafting, horse trekking and mountain biking. All these activities are in addition to the more obvious and soporific attraction of its hot pools in the thermal resort. Kaikoura, in contrast and almost miniaturized in the shadow of the Kaikoura mountain ranges, is equally abuzz with activity. But here the emphasis is most definitely on the colder waters of the ocean and its inhabitants. At Kaikoura you can view an impressive list of sea creatures including albatrosses, seals, dolphins and of course Kaikoura's very own whales.

If you're heading south from Christchurch, SH1 passes through the flat heartland of the Canterbury Plains to Timaru. With so much stunning scenery elsewhere in New Zealand, it is often labelled as the least exciting drive in the country; only the occasional glimpse of the distant Southern Alps far to the west and the odd wide pebble-strewn riverbed crossing, breaks the monotony of the endless roadside windbreaks and expansive fields.

Hanmer Springs

Amuri Av, T03-315 7511, T0800-442663, hanmersprings.co.nz.
Daily 1000-2100, $14, child $7 (same-day return pass $16, child $8).

The name derives from the name of Canterbury pioneer Thomas Hanmer who no doubt had a lifelong struggle with his 'M-n-Ns'. Hanmer has long been popular with Kiwi holiday-seekers, and is now a top national tourist venue. Its biggest attraction is of course its impressive **Thermal Reserve**, which is (arguably) the best in the country.

The springs were first discovered by the Europeans in 1859 and later became a commercial venture and public attraction; in 1907, the first facilities and a hotel formed the beginnings of the resort and, subsequently, the town as a whole. The resort has enjoyed an impressive expansion and improvement in recent years, and has various pools including open and landscaped, freshwater, swimming and a children's play pool – all connected by steaming boulder streams. The mineral-rich waters range in temperature from 30-47°C. Also on site are a massage and beauty clinic, private pools, saunas, a steam room, a licensed café and a picnic area.

Hanmer is also a very popular base for mountain biking and walking in the Hanmer Forest Park. The town offers a wide range of modern accommodation, some good restaurants and numerous other activities from bungee jumping to horse trekking and is particularly beautiful in autumn when the forest and tree-lined streets are flush with golden hues and falling leaves.

For detailed information call in at the Hanmer Springs i-SITE visitor centre, next to the thermal reserve, 42 Amuri Av, T03-3150020, T0800-442663, visithanmersprings.co.nz.

Taking a dip at Hanmer Springs north of Christchurch.

Lewis Pass

From Hanmer Springs SH7 crosses the northern ranges of the Great Divide (Southern Alps) to the west coast via the Lewis Pass (864 m), Maruia Springs (another smaller thermal springs resort), Springs Junction and the former mining town of Reefton (130 km).

The name Lewis derives from Henry Lewis (surveyor) who came across it in the early 1860s but well before that the Ngai Tahu Maori of Canterbury used this route to access the west coast in search of pounamu (greenstone). Having negotiated the pass on their return, they are said to have dispensed with their slaves – alas not with a 'thanks lads, see you next year', but a brutal death followed by a feast of their various bodily parts. Alas, perhaps right there and then corporations and capitalism were created!

Although not as dramatic as Arthur's Pass (see overleaf) further to the south the Lewis offers some lovely scenery and a few good walking opportunities along the way. It also boasts a mountain with one of the most unusual names in the country. There are many with wonderful names, but frankly 'Mons Sex Millia' has to take the biscuit. Of course the translation is a real balloon burster; it actually means 'six peaky bits' – or words to that effect!

Kaikoura

So you want to see Moby Dick and friends? Well, you have certainly come to the right spot. Kaikoura is aesthetically stunning and is also home to a wealth of sea creatures. They are all here: Moby, Flipper, Keiko, Jaws. Okay, not quite. But for the wildlife enthusiast the Kaikoura Coast is on a par with the Otago Peninsula for richness and accessibility to some of New Zealand's biggest and most famous wildlife icons. This is due to the topography and depth of the ocean floor: just south of Kaikoura, a trough comes unusually close to the coastline creating an upsurge of nutritious plankton soup, giving rise to the many creatures with which we are more familiar further up the

Not all the whales at Kaikoura are in 3D.

food chain. At the very top of course is the majestic and much-victimized king of them all – the whale. But here you can also get up close and personal with many others including dolphins, seals and those mighty masters of flight – albatrosses.

Prior to your arrival consider what you want to see and how. You can see whales by boat or from the air, you can swim with dolphins and seals, go diving, kayaking or fishing. But a word of warning; factor in an extra day in case of inclement weather. Like the West Coast it can be very frustrating imagining yourself partaking in all these great activities only to end up in a café watching rain drops in street puddles. Also, in the high season you will need to book whale watching or dolphin swimming in advance, see page 252.

Tip...

The Kaikoura i-SITE visitor centre, West End, T03-319 5641, kaikoura.co.nz can provide non-biased detail on the full range of options.

Peninsula Walk Kaikoura

The two-hour return 'Peninsula Walk', which links the two settlements is excellent and recommended. You can either walk along the cliff-top or the shoreline (depending on the tide) and start at the Point Kearn car park (at the end of Avoca St), or alternatively at the South Bay car park. You will encounter seals, lots of interesting rock pools, and some superb coastal scenery.

The Kaikoura Peninsula offers some fine walks and views.

Arthur's Pass

The Arthur's Pass visitor information centre (DoC) is in the heart of the village on the southern side of SH73 (T03-318 9211, doc.govt.nz, daily 0900-1600). It has various displays about the national park, a video ($1), walks information and all local accommodation and service details. But before embarking on any long walks or tramps check the weather forecast and ask about up to date track conditions. For train travel, see page 253.

The route (258 km) to Greymouth and the west coast via SH73 from Christchurch across the Great Divide and the northern ranges of the Southern Alps is one of the most celebrated scenic drives and rail journeys in the country. It is most notable perhaps for its sheer range of dramatic South Island landscapes from the flatlands of the Canterbury Plains to the east, through the rugged mountain peaks and braided rivers in its centre, to the lush coastal valleys and lakes to the west. On the way the Craigieburn Forest and Arthur's Pass National Parks offer some excellent walking, tramping, rock climbing and skiing opportunities.

Arthur Dudley Dobson, a pioneer surveyor, was the first to explore the route in 1864. Due to the gold boom a basic road was built within a year of his observations, but the rail link that later served the coal and timber trade took a further 60 years to complete.

Timaru

Timaru i-SITE visitor centre, 2 George St, T03-688 6163, southisland.org.nz/timaru.asp.

The port city of Timaru, halfway between Christchurch and Dunedin, provides a refreshing stopover on SH1, or a convenient starting point from which to head west, via SH8, to the MacKenzie Country, Mount Cook and Queenstown. The city is pleasant, boasting the popular Caroline Bay beach near the town centre, a few good parks, the region's main museum, a reputable art gallery and a few unique attractions, including some ancient seventh-century Maori rock art.

The South Canterbury Museum

Perth St, T03-684 2212, Tue-Fri 1000-1630, Sat-Sun 1330-1630, free.

The main regional museum and contains some interesting exhibits on local maritime history, Maori rock art and the exploits of local farmer and wannabe aviator Richard Pearse (1877-1953). In April 1903, at the tender age of 26, Pearse created history by making the first-ever powered flight in a 'heavier-than-air-man-carrying aeroplane'. His flight, though neither long nor spectacular, was a world first and was completed nine months before the better-known and much- celebrated flight by the American pioneer aviator Orville Wright of the famous Wright brothers. However, unlike the celebrated Wright brothers, Pearse died an

Scenic drive:
Mount Sunday and the Rangitata River Valley

Until recently there were basically two main reasons tourists headed for the hills west of Christchurch. The most obvious reason was to reach the west coast via SH73 and Arthur's Pass, while the other was to ski the popular Mount Hutt ski fields near Methven. However, since the release of the *Lord of the Rings* trilogy, there is now another very good reason in the surprising form of a large and conspicuous lump of rock. Mount Sunday, which sits predominantly in the Rangitata River Valley and in stark contrast against the mountainous skyline of Southern Alps, became the perfect filming location and set for Edoras and Meduseld, King Theoden's grand hall in the realm of Rohan. Although the set is long gone, it remains one of the most scenic drives in the region and, even without all the hype, was always a great place to visit. There are organized tours available from Christchurch (see page 251) or you can go it alone. Ask at the Christchurch i-SITE visitor centres for detailed directions.

Mount Sunday in the Rangitata Valley was used as the set for Edoras in the *Lord of The Rings* film trilogy.

It's a fact...

unrecognized recluse in a psychiatric hospital in Christchurch. A full replica of his impressive flying machine is on display in the museum. Other relics of Pearse's flying inventions are held at the **Pleasant Point Railway Museum** (18 km northwest of Timaru (SH8), T03-6862269, pleasantpointtrail.org.nz).

MacKenzie Country

The area known as the MacKenzie Country refers mainly to the flat expanse of tussock grasslands that make up the watersheds of the Tekapo and Gray rivers beyond Fairlie and south to Omarama. It is a strange barren landscape, devoid of trees and almost analogous to the plains of heartland USA. There is nowhere else like it in New Zealand and it bears little semblance to the lofty peaks that rise from around its edge. The name MacKenzie was bestowed upon it through the almost legendary sheep rustling activities of Scottish pioneer James 'Jock' MacKenzie.

Lake Tekapo

In the heart of MacKenzie Country is Lake Tekapo, a pretty little place, famous for its lakeside church and an ever-watchful little collie dog. However, over the last five years or so Tekapo has suffered somewhat from the rapacious development so evident throughout the central South Island and spreading north from Queenstown. Already parts of the village are looking horribly like a Christchurch suburb and it seems 'the money' has arrived, which is enough to have the little collie heading for the hills with its tail between its legs.

Just about everybody who visits Lake Tekapo pays homage to the **Church of the Good Shepherd**, which sits alone, in a picture-postcard position overlooking the lake. Built in 1935 it remains a functional place of worship, but sadly its modern-day function is almost entirely aesthetic, and the minister, who is in attendance almost daily, must tend a very superficial and transitory flock (the vast majority of whom fall out of tour buses and come only to worship the Lord Digital, Kodak and Text SMS). Whatever you do, go early in the morning or late in the day to avoid the hordes. A few pew lengths from the church is a statue of a collie sheepdog; a simple tribute to the shepherd's best friend.

If you have time (and a rugged vehicle) the unsealed roads on either side of Lake Tekapo are well worth exploring. The road to the west passes Lake Alexandria and Lake McGregor both of which are very peaceful (and full of trout), before winding its way north to terminate at the Godley Peak Station.

Dominating the scene at the western end of Tekapo Village is **Mount John**, which at 300 m offers great views and a suitable home for the University of Canterbury's Astronomical Observatory. Open to the public its popular **Earth and Sky** (T03-680 6960, earthandsky.co.nz; observatory tours 1100-1500, 40 mins from $30, child $15; stargazing summer 2200, winter 2000, 2 hrs from $75, child $45; café open 0900-1700) offers daytime guided tours and night stargazing. Weather permitting, the stargazing tour is fascinating and offers a great opportunity to see such heavenly bodies as the Alpha-Centuri, Southern Cross, Scorpius and, if you're really lucky, Kylieminorearendi. Even if you cannot join the tours the café is well worth a visit for the views.

Back down to earth and at the base of Mount John is Tekapo's latest attraction the **Alpine Springs, Spa & Winter Park** (6 Lakeside Drive, T03-680 6550, T0800 23538283, alpinesprings.co.nz, open daily 1000-2100; hot pools from $16, child $9; ice-skating $14, child $11; snow tubing $15, child $11; combo deals available). The facility offers three hot pools and several private hot tubs that look out over the lake and range in temperature from 36-40°C. The day spa offers the standard facilities and treatments including sauna, steam

Swing bridge across the Hooker River, Hooker Valley walk, Mount Cook.

room and massage. The Winter Park comprises an ice rink for skating, ice hockey and curling events and outside a snow-tubing run, in effect a 100-m-long artificial snow slope with purpose-built contours for snow tubing.

Mount Cook National Park

Some 50 km south of Lake Tekapo and 8 km north of Twizel, the famed SH80 skirts the western banks and azure waters of **Lake Pukaki** to pay homage to Aoraki (Mount Cook). Before entering the chancel you are first advised to admire the cathedral from afar from the southern banks of the lake. There is a car park, information centre and lookout point from which, on a clear day, the mountain beckons. Unless you are really pressed for time, or the weather is foul, it really is sacrilege not to make the scenic 55-km drive to **Mount Cook Village**. Located so close to the base of the mountains and **Hooker and Tasman Glacier** valleys, it is like a miniature toy-town which acts as the gateway to

national park. This 70,696-ha park has to be one of the most spectacular in New Zealand, and the scenery is second only to Milford Sound. With the 3754-m peak of **Mount Cook** as its altar, its robust ministers include Tasman (3498 m) and Mount Sefton (3158 m), surrounded by a supportive choir of 19 peaks all over 3000 m. Rising up to this great chancel are the vast and impressive Hooker and Tasman glaciers, which not only created the long nave but once blocked the very porch. All this natural architecture makes for world-class scenery and mountaineering. Indeed, it was here that Sir Edmund Hillary first started a career that was to reach its 'peak' on the summit of Everest in 1953. And once here, it seems a terrible waste not to explore the park from even closer quarters.

Glentanner Park, 32 km towards the mountain serves as a motor park and scenic flight-seeing base (T03-4351855, glentanner.co.nz). If the weather is fine you are advised to stop here and consider the scenic flights and other activities on offer, perhaps over a coffee, in its café overlooking the mountain. Note other fixed-wing flight-seeing options are available from the Mount Cook airport 7 km east of the village (see below). If you are in a motorhome and intend to stay in the valley overnight, Glentanner can be home – there is good basic DoC campsite in Mount Cook Village but no fully facilitated motor park.

Upon arrival in Mount Cook Village (a further 23 km) you will be immediately struck at how ordered and dull in colour it is. This is not an accident, since the settlement comes within the boundary of the park and is therefore strictly controlled. The only real exception to this is the **Hermitage Hotel**, which many claim to be the most famous in New Zealand (while others hail it merely as a blot on the landscape).

There are a wide range of activities on offer that focus mainly on the Hooker and Tasman Glacier valleys and lakes, from short and multi-day walks/ tramps, to kayaking and mountain biking. The airport (7 km) also serves as base for Mount Cook Ski Planes, a superb flight-seeing option that offers the exciting prospect of a snow-landing high up amidst the peaks on the Tasman Glacier.

Another great (and cheaper) option is the overnight tramp to the **Mueller Hut** which sits in an idyllic position (1768 m) on the ridge of Mount Oliver (1933 m) behind Mount Cook Village. Although a strenuous climb requiring a fair level of fitness, proper planning and equipment, it is a classic excursion. If you stay overnight in the Hut, the views at sunset and sunrise over the Hooker and Mount Cook especially are simply world class. In total it is a stiff four-hour climb each way. A further one-hour return will see you at the top of Mount Oliver, which, rumour has it, was the first peak in the region that Sir Edmund Hillary climbed.

For more park information, hut bookings, all activities and accommodation options within in the park visit the DoC visitor centre (just below the Hermitage, Larch Grove, T03-4351186, mtcooknz. com, daily 0830-1800; winter 0830-1700). For comprehensive regional information the Lake Pukaki Visitor Centre, SH8, T03-4353280, mtcooknz. com, open daily 0900-1800, can also assist.

Twizel

The town of Twizel was purpose-built in the 1960s to provide a home for workers involved with the Waitaki power scheme. Today, though a little soulless perhaps, it is a well-placed base for a host of activities mountain climbing, kayaking, mountain biking, skiing, horse trekking and hiking. It's also a place to see one of the rarest wading birds in the world – the Khaki, or **Black Stilt**. Thanks primarily to man's introduction of non-native predatory species, like the weasel and stoat, numbers have been decimated and currently total less than 100 wild birds. A guided visit to the viewing hide 3 km south of the village is available through DoC, late October-mid April (weekdays only in winter), 0930 and 1630, $12.50, child $5; contact Twizel DoC, Wairepo Rd, Twizel, T03-4350802, doc.govt.nz.

For comprehensive information on activities contact the Twizel visitor information centre, (Market Place,T03-4353124, twizel.com, daily Oct-Apr 0900-1800; May-Sep 1000-1600).

Omarama

Located at the head of the Waitaki Valley (from Oamaru) and north of the scenic Lindis Pass (from Wanaka and Queenstown), Omarama provides a convenient overnight stop and finishing (or starting) point from which to explore the MacKenzie Country. There are a number of local activities that may detain you, including fishing and water sports on lakes Benmore, Aviemore and Ohau. Omarama is also world renowned for gliding. Other than the obvious appeal of the local lakes, the **Clay Cliffs** between Omarama and Twizel are worthy of investigation, and echo the bizarre eroded rock and gravel formations of the Pinnacles in the Wairarapa, North Island. To reach them turn off SH8 west towards the mountains on Quailburn Road, 3 km north of the village (signposted), 15 km. There is a small charge ($6) at the gate to the cliffs.

The West Coast

The west coast of the South Island is a land of extremes: extreme climate, extreme geography, extreme ecosystems and, above all, extreme scenery. It is a place of majestic beauty. Bounded on one side by the Tasman Sea and on the other by the heady peaks of the Southern Alps, it encompasses a narrow stretch of land that accounts for only 8% of the total landmass of New Zealand. Between these boundaries lies a quarter of all New Zealand's native forest, a lush and predominantly impenetrable landscape copiously watered by an average annual rainfall of more than 5 m. The boundaries of five of the country's 14 national parks breach the west coast region. Two of these, Paparoa National Park and the Westland National Park, it can call its very own, with the latter boasting the huge Fox and Franz Josef glaciers.

The settlements in the region, strung along the 600-km length of SH6, from Karamea in the north to Jackson's Bay in the south, are not attractive places and stand in stark contrast to the beauty surrounding them. Nature, thankfully, has never made it easy for man to live here nor plunder its resources. The modern-day West Coast is sparsely populated, housing less than 1% of the country's total population. Indeed, there are fewer people living here now than in the late 19th century.

Most visitors tackle the West Coast from North to south and either via the Buller Gorge from Nelson, Lewis Pass from Hanmer or Arthur's Pass from Christchurch. As usual what you see and what you do here will depend on time, but unfortunately you must now add another more crucial factor – the weather. Beware, for many, the West Coast can alter the perception of what proper rain really is and what 'rain stopped play' really means.

A giant sandfly guards the Bushmans Centre, Pukekura.

Tip...

Before heading over to the West Coast and certainly before booking a flight over the glaciers, it is worth looking at the detailed weather resource at metservice.co.nz and the forecast charts at metvuw.com for the latest synopsis.

Westport

For regional details contact the Westport i-SITE visitor centre, 1 Brougham St, T03-7896658, westport.org.nz, daily 0900-1800, winter 0900-1600.

Westport, the west coast's oldest town, is not a pretty place. On first acquaintance, its flat expanse of unimaginative, orderly and treeless blocks are uninspiring to say the least. But if the place lacks soul, its people do not. They retain the proud and stoic traditions of the old pioneers and coal miners: the down-to-earth working-class attitude, the warm welcome and the humour. Westport is often used as an overnight base before heading north to Karamea and the Heaphy Track or south towards Greymouth. There, however, are a few attractions and activities that may detain you, including rafting on the **Buller River** and a large fur seal colony at **Cape Foulwind** (11 km).

The **Coaltown Museum** (Queen St South, T03-7898204, daily 0900-1630, $10, child $5) has an interesting range of displays covering the history of coal mining in the region, while the **West Coast Brewery** (10 Lyndhurst St, T03-789 6253, free tastings Mon-Sat) offers tastings of various heady brews including the popular 'Good Bastards'.

Karamea

From Westport, SH67 heads north to Karamea (100 km), a former 'frontier' settlement of Karamea, perched on its namesake river mouth and overshadowed by the rising peaks of the **Kahurangi National Park**. It is a pleasant and peaceful place and most often used as a base for the famed **Heaphy Track**, which begins at the road terminus 15 km north. Walking part of its first section offers a great day walk. Karamea also has

Around the region

Oparara Arch, Oparara Basin near Karamea.

It's a fact...

If you arrived on the West Coast via the Buller Gorge and thought it was a little precarious, you had it easy. In 1846 English-born surveyor and explorer Thomas Brunner took three months to negotiate the gorge and on 17 June 1929 there was an earthquake measuring a massive 7.8 on the Richter scale.

Punakaiki & the Paparoa National Park

From Westport SH6 begins its relentless 600-km journey south, down the length of the west coast. The pretty coastal enclave of Punakaiki sits on the coast and the boundary of the Paparoa National Park 60 km south of Westport and 50 km north of Greymouth. Designated in 1987, Paparoa covers a relatively small area (by New Zealand standards) of 30,000 ha and features a predominantly karst (limestone) topography. From mountain to coast, the park has everything from limestone bluffs to dramatic overhangs and caves. The most visited feature in the park are the pancake rocks and blowholes of **Dolomite Point** accessed from Punakaiki (20 minutes). There are some notable walks including the **Truman Track**, which begins beside SH6, 3 km north of Punakaiki. It is a beautiful 15-minute stroll through coastal rainforest and nikau palms that delivers you peacefully on the sands and rocky outcrops of Perpendicular Point.

Kayaking and horse trekking are two other popular activities in the area.

For detail contact the **DoC Paparoa National Park visitor centre** (SH6, Punakaiki, T03-731 1895, doc.govt.nz, punakaiki.co.nz, daily 0900-1800, winter 0900-1630).

some lesser-known sights nearby that are quite simply superb, in particular the limestone caves and arches of the **Oparara Basin**. Bones have been discovered in the caves belonging to the now extinct moa and the New Zealand eagle that had a 3-m wingspan. If you have time (or even if you do not, make the time) go and see them.

For detail and directions contact the **Karamea i-SITE Visitor Centre and Resource Centre**, Bridge St, just as you come into the village, T03-7826652, karameainfo.co.nz, daily 0900-1700. It also has internet, can organize activities and issues DoC hut passes.

Tip...

Heading north or south be sure to fill up your tank in Greymouth or Westport as there is no petrol station in Punakaiki.

Renderusinsanitus

Meet Renderusinsanitus. There is no collective noun that adequately describes Renderusinsanitus (as they call it on the West Coast) - that heinous, insect equivalent to Hannibal Lecter – the New Zealand sandfly. Venture anywhere west of the main divide of the South Island and you will, without fail, not only encounter vast squadrons of them but also unconsciously enter into a state of perpetual war against them. And sadly it is a war that you cannot ever hope to win. Their staggering thirst for blood added to their tactical superiority, fighting skills and sheer numbers make them a formidable force indeed.

However, they say that to have the slightest chance of winning a war you should 'know thine enemy' – so here goes. There are not one, but 13 species of sandfly (or blackfly) in New Zealand. Well that's a good start. Fortunately though, only two of the species actually bite, but unfortunately, you are still hopelessly outnumbered. You may (or indeed may not) be surprised to learn that it is only the female that bites. Apparently they need a good feed of blood in order to go shopping..err..sorry..lay their eggs.

And why is it that the moment you enter the great outdoors it takes about three milliseconds before the entire sandfly Luftwaffe are upon you? Well, apparently, you are instantly detected by a combination of breath, odour, movement, shape, colour and temperature. Yes, you look awful and smell. Biting is at its peak just after dawn or before dusk on warm, overcast, low pressure days, especially when humidity is high. Great. Your only saviour is wind – natural as opposed to your own, even though you will find yourself trying anything to repel them – a strong breeze affects their strike rate. It is due to the high rainfall that sandflies are so prevalent on the West Coast and in Fiordland.

So how can you bite back? Is there anything other than a small thermo-nuclear device that is effective against the enemy? You will find a number of expensive insect repellents readily available throughout the region. Those that contain DEET (a rather strong chemical, to say the least) are the most effective. Whatever you do, do not let them deter you from going to experience the West Coast. Besides, if it was not for the sandfly, just think how much more spoilt the west coast would be by human habitation. Perhaps the cloud is, in fact, all silver lining.

Greymouth & around

From Punakaiki the coast road continues its relentless route south, treating you to some fine coastal scenery, before turning inland through Runanga to meet the Grey River and the west coast's largest commercial centre – Greymouth. The Grey River Valley receives some of the heaviest rainfall in the country and on more than one occasion the town has been badly flooded. On initial acquaintance Greymouth seems to share the drab aesthetics of most northern west coast towns and certainly lives up to its uninspiring name. That said, the people of Greymouth are welcoming, friendly and certainly not short of heart or colour. Today, the town is mostly used by tourists as a short stopover point or supply base for further investigations of the coast. It is also the terminus of the **TranzAlpine** (TranzAlpine, T0800-872467, tranzscenic.co.nz) scenic train journey through Arthurs Pass from Christchurch – a major attraction

in itself. There are a few local attractions and some exciting activities on offer from whitewater and cave rafting to quad biking and brewery tours. Inland from Greymouth, the small satellite towns of **Blackball** and **Reefton** are the main highlights along the watershed of the Grey River Valley and provide further evidence of the regions gold and coal mining past. It was in Blackball in the early 1900s that the Labour and Trade Union movements were first formed in New Zealand. Further south the peaceful surroundings of **Lake Brunner** are a stark contrast to the highly commercial '**Shantytown**' a working replica of an 1880s gold mining settlement.

For information contact the **Greymouth i-SITE visitor centre** corner of Mackay and Herbert streets (T03-7685101, greydistrict.co.nz, Mon-Fri 0830-1900, Sat 0900-1800, Sun 1000-1700. Travel Centre, railway station, 164 Mackay St, T03-768 7080).

Around the region

Driftwood litters the beaches of the West Coast.

Hokitika

More gold passed through Hokitika (or 'Hoki') in the 1860s than any other town on the coast. Between 1865 and 1867, over 37,000 hopefuls arrived requiring a staggering 84 hotels to put them all up in. In those heady days it seemed only the river itself could hold the town back. At one point during the gold rush there was at least one grounding every 10 weeks – and 21 in 1865 alone. Like everywhere else of course the gold soon ran out and old 'Hoki' slipped into rapid decline. But today gold has been replaced by that other precious resource – tourism. It is now the craft capital of the west coast and summer sees crowds of visitors arrive by the busload, to watch glass-blowing and greenstone carving and to browse in its numerous galleries concentrated along Tancred Street.

Inland from Hokitika (14 km) is the picturesque **Lake Kaniere**, a popular haven in summer for swimming, watersports, picnicking and walking. Also accessed directly from Hokitika (33 km) via the settlements of Kaniere and Kokatahi (end of Kowhitirangi and Whitcombe Road) or, alternatively, via Lake Kaniere (loop road to Kokatahi) is the picturesque and moody **Hokitika Gorge**. Other than the impressive scenery the highlight here is the swing-bridge that after heavy rains, makes the crossing an exciting prospect.

For regional information contact the **Westland i-SITE visitor centre** (Carnegie Building, corner of Hamilton and Tancred streets, T03-755 6166, hokitika.org.nz, west-coast.co.nz.nz, daily in summer 0830-1800, winter Mon-Fri 0830-1700, Sat-Sun 1000-1600).

South to Franz Josef

South from Hokitika the influence of humanity decreases dramatically and the aesthetics begin to reflect the sheer dominance of nature. Mountain ranges climb steadily on the eastern horizon towards the heady peaks of the Westland National Park and to Mount Cook itself. Small villages like Ross and Harihari cling precariously to a history of gold mining and demonstrate in size alone how much nature rules these parts, and hopefully always will. For many this is where the real west coast begins.

Pukekura & the Puke Pub

T03-7554144, pukekura.co.nz.

About 18 km south of Ross is the small settlement of Pukekura, population 2.

It began as a hotel on the stage coach trail south, had a saw mill for a while in the 1950s before Peter Salter and his partner Justine Giddy establishment the **Bushman's Centre** in 1993. The place is instantly recognizable and notorious for the giant **sandfly** that hangs with menace from its walls. As well as a fine café (with its superb 'road kill soup of the day') and shop it has a great little

Hardly Eureka! Gold panning, West Coast.

It's a fact...

The land beneath the township of Ross has never been mined and a Ministry of Commerce geologist estimated in 1993 that gold deposits of about $700 million lie under the towns.

Honourable Roddy

In 1909, towards the end of the great West Coast gold rush, two lucky miners (names unknown) struck it mighty big. Their find, later named the 'Honourable Roddy', after the erstwhile Minister of Mines, was a nugget weighing in at a very healthy 3.1 kg. As you might expect, the nugget immediately took on a life of its own, at first being paraded from bar to bar then sold and sold again. Then – reputedly – after a short stint as a doorstop, it was bought by the government in 1911 as a coronation gift for King George V. Sadly, this act of generosity proved its demise. After a life above ground, the Royals melted it down for use as a gold tea service at Buckingham Palace. Or that is what we are led to believe. A replica is now on view at the Ross information centre, 4 Aylmer St, T03-7554077, ross.org.co.nz.

interactive museum ($4), where you can learn about bush craft, meet live possums (one that have not been turned in to pies that is), stroke a pig, then wantonly throw sharp knives and axes at the wall. It's brilliant. Other activities based at the centre include horse trekking and gold panning.

Across the road from the centre is the famed (and unfortunately named) Puke Pub where you can do your bit for conservation and indulge in a possum pie.

Whataroa

Whataroa, 35 km southwest of Harihari, provides an opportunity to see the revered white heron or **kotuku** congregated at their sole New Zealand breeding rookery. The birds are only in residence from mid-October to mid-March. **White Heron Sanctuary Tours** (T03-753 4120, T0800-523456, white herontours.co.nz, tours $110, child $45, page 252). offers a 2½-hour tour by jet boat to access the hide that overlooks the colony.

While in Whataroa don't miss the **Kotuku Gallery** (Main St, T03-753 4249) regarded as one of the best Maori galleries in the country.

Okarito

Okarito, a small coastal settlement and former goldfields port, is 13 km off SH6 and 15 km south of Whataroa. This beautiful little paradise, set beachside next to the vast 3240-ha **Okarito Lagoon** backed by stunning views of the Southern Alps, is not surprisingly the favourite haunt of many a New Zealander. Thankfully most people shoot past the road junction from SH6 in their rush to see their first glacier – Franz Josef – 29 km to the south. But for those who take the time and the diversion, they will be rewarded not only with Okarito's simple do-nothing appeal, but also some excellent walking, kayaking and birdwatching opportunities. There is no public transport to Okarito and no shops in Okarito so take your own supplies. Across the road from the obviously historic and incredibly cute youth hostel is the almost unsightly **obelisk** commemorating Abel Tasman's first sighting of New Zealand, somewhere off Okarito in 1642. For a walk try the steady climb (1½ hours) via the old, but well-formed, pack track through native bush to the **Okarito Trig**. On a clear day it affords a stunning view across the bush-clad hills to the Southern Alps.

The Glacier Region

To add to New Zealand's majestic scenery and ecological surprises, the two gigantic and dynamic monoliths of ice – Franz Josef and Fox Glaciers – provide a dramatic sight. They are the brightest jewels in the highly decorated crown of the Westland and Mount Cook national parks, joined, yet separated on the map, by the jagged summits and peaks of the Southern Alps and the Great Dividing Range. In summer there are two moods to the neighbouring villages of Franz and Fox. When the sun shines they are a frenetic buzz of activity: from the moment the sun peeks over the mountains, the skies fill with the sound of aircraft, the roads swarm with tour buses and the streets fill with expectant tourists, consumed with the desire to get to the glaciers, walk on them and photograph them. And yet, when the clouds gather (which is often) and the rain descends (or rather crashes down), the pace of everything slows, dramatically: the air hangs heavy with silence, the streets fill with puddles and the tourists' glum faces stare out from behind café windows. The average annual rainfall in the area is 5 m, over 180 rain days, and at Franz and Fox it's amazing just how much the weather and two multi-million, ton blocks of ice can dictate. However, it's not all bad, there are many clear, sunny days too – an average of 1860 sunshine hours annually, more than in many other regions in New Zealand. Plan to give yourself at least two days in the area and always book your accommodation well in advance. If you have scenic flights booked, these can be forwarded if it's cloudy.

Franz Josef Glacier.

viewpoint on **Sentinel Rock** (a remnant of previous glacial erosion) is perhaps the best place to view the glacier from afar; it is easily accessed from near the main car park (20 mins). But perhaps the best way to view the glacier and the peaks that crown it is from the air and there are numerous **scenic flight** options available. If the weather is fine do not miss the opportunity to do so. At the very least take a heli-flight that involves a snow landing. To experience the silence up there is as memorable as the scenery.

Franz Josef i-SITE visitor centre, Main Road, Franz Josef, T03-752 0796, doc.govt.nz has displays, information on walks and up-to-date weather forecasts. On Main Road numerous outlets also provides local information, arrange transport and offer activity bookings and internet.

Franz Josef

Franz Josef owes its very existence and, of course its name, to the great block of ice that sits 5 km south of the village. Of the two principally tourist-based settlements (Franz and Fox), Franz is the larger and better serviced. As you might expect it is very much a seasonal destination, crowded in summer, quiet in winter.

Franz Josef – the glacier – was first sighted and officially documented by both Abel Tasman in 1642 and Cook in 1770, but first properly explored and named by geologist and explorer Julius von Haast in 1865. When he first explored its lower reaches it was almost 3 km nearer the coast than it is today. The official title of 'Francis Joseph Glacier' was given in honour of the Emperor Franz Josef of Austria. The spelling was later changed to Franz Josef in accordance with the internationally accepted version.

From the car park (along Glacier Access Rd) it is a 1½-hour return walk alongside the wide and rocky **Waiho River** bed to within 500 m of the glacier face. Unless properly equipped you cannot walk on the glacier itself; to do that you are strongly advised to join a guided **glacier walking trip**. The 280-m-high

Fox Glacier

Many people visiting the Glacier Region only visit one of the great monoliths, with Franz Josef being the most favoured. However, if you have time, Fox Glacier (25 km south of Franz and a further 8 km southeast) is no less dramatic. The Fox Glacier Valley and the chilly Fox River which surges from the glacier terminus, provide a significantly different atmosphere. The Fox Glacier was originally called the Victoria Glacier and was renamed in honour of former New Zealand Prime Minister, Sir William Fox, on a visit in 1872. The small village of Fox Glacier is the main service centre and sits on a site that was, as recently as 5000 years ago, covered by the present glacier.

Although less commercial, Fox, like its neighbour Franz, can be explored independently at its terminus, but you will need a guide to walk or climbed on it. Once again, however, the recommendation is to admire it from the air. There are a number of interesting walks within the valley, at the coast and around the reflective **Lake Matheson**, which lies 4 km west of the village – but at dawn and dusk don't expect solitude. Again the **DoC office** (Main Rd, T03-7510807) is the best source of unbiased information.

Around the region

Ship Creek.

South to Haast

From Fox Glacier you leave the great glaciers and towering peaks of the national parks behind and SH6 winds its scenic way ever southwards to Haast and to the most remote region of the west coast: South Westland. For many years Fox was as far south as any tourist ventured, the road from there becoming rough and eventually non-existent at Paringa. With the opening of the great Haast Pass Highway in 1965 the two roads were linked making the continuous journey possible. Given the terrain in South Westland, it is not hard to understand why such a link was so late in coming. Despite the intrusion, much of South Westland remains remote, unspoilt and remarkably beautiful.

The reflective waters of **Lake Moeraki** are a further 18 km south of Lake Paringa and from there SH6 rejoins the coast and climbs to **Knight Point** with its spectacular views of sea stacks and near inaccessible beaches. It was just south of Knight

Point that the Haast Highway was officially opened in 1965, thereby connecting Otago with south Westland and the west coast proper. A little further south is easy access to the beach at **Ship Creek**. Here you can choose from a number of excellent short walks to explore the beach, coastal forest and a small lake held captive by the dunes. From Ship Creek SH6 hugs the coast and passes some spectacular examples of coastal rimu, rata and kahikatea forest on its approach to Haast and the 750-m **Haast River Bridge**.

Haast

The Haast Region of South Westland contains some of the most unspoiled ecosystems in New Zealand. The stunning scenery, from mountaintop to coastal plain, includes pristine streams that flow into vast river mouths fringed with dense tracts of ancient coastal (Kahikatea) forests. Within the forest lie swamps and hidden lakes and all along their fringe are endless swathes of beach covered in sculpted driftwood. On the coastal plain the annual rainfall, at 5 m, is similar to that of much of the west coast. But above 1500 m, the average can be over three times that and, after a deluge, the great river can turn into a menacing torrent to which so many ravaged tree trunks attest.

Haast Junction (before Haast itself) is home to the DoC visitor centre, a petrol station and the World Heritage Hotel. A further 4 km south of Haast Junction, on the Jackson's Bay Road, is Haast Beach, another small conglomerate, including another petrol station, a motel, food store and some private homes. From there the road continues for 50 km before reaching a dead end and the remote village of **Jackson's Bay**. East of there an unsealed road accesses the **Arawata River** and the **Cascade Saddle**, in itself a memorable day trip.

Other than scenic drives and walks other activities in the area include the popular jet boating trips up the Haast and Waiatoto Rivers. And what a delightful name **Waiatoto** is. Now you know what to scream out in Maori the next time you stub your toe. It actually means 'red waters'.

Ellery River, Jackson River Valley.

For local information contact the **DoC Haast visitor centre** (Jnc. SH6 and Jackson Bay Road, Haast, T03-750 0809, doc.govt.nz).

Haast Pass

From Haast Township SH6 turns inland and follows the bank of the Haast River before being enveloped by mountains and surmounting what was, until 1960, insurmountable. The Haast Pass at 563 m is an ancient Maori greenstone trail known as Tiori-patea, which means 'the way ahead is clear'. Ironically, being the principal water catchment of the Haast River and plagued by frequent floods and landslips, the name is one of misplaced optimism as the modern-day road can testify. However, although sometimes treacherous and difficult to negotiate, the crossing captures the mood of the place, with names such as the **Valley of Darkness** and **Mount Awful**. Even beside the road there is suggestion of this, with other evocative titles like Solitary Creek No 2 and the first of three waterfalls, **Roaring Billy** 28 km inland from Haast. A further 25 km another waterfall – the competitively named **Thunder Creek Falls**– drop a vertical 28 m into the Haast River. They can be accessed from a short loop track beside the road.

The gorge, known as the **Gates of Haast**, is just a little further on and you can see the huge boulders and precipitous rock walls that proved such a barrier to road construction for so many years. Above the Gates the road and the river level off before the Haast Pass itself and the boundary of Westland and Otago. From here the scenery dramatically changes and you leave the mighty West Coast behind.

Best photo locations

❶ Christchurch
Page 216

Like any city, Christchurch has its obvious icons and the trams, the River Avon and (to an extent) its architecture are the main targets.

Good spots for trams include the main tram spot in Cathedral Square; Worcester Street Bridge looking east; the Arts Centre (western end of Worcester St) looking east; Armagh Street Bridge and New Regent Street.

Some of the best spots of the river are (from south to north): Antigua Boat Sheds (Rolleston Av); Cambridge Terrace (opposite 'The Strip' on Oxford Terr); around Worcester Street Bridge; the latter to Victoria Square.

Punting is of course a Christchurch classic and you can capture that on the standard return punt between the Worcester Street Bridge north to Colombo Street Bridge and back.

When it comes to architecture some the best locations are the modern Christchurch Art Gallery, The Arts Centre, Christ's College (especially around 1530 weekdays when the pupils spill out on to Rolleston Av) and of course, the Cathedral.

The botanical gardens are also a fine venue to capture that 'Garden City' aesthetic.

❷ Lake Pukaki & Mount Cook
Page 232

The view across the azure waters of Lake Pukaki to Mount Cook can be absolutely breathtaking, but photographic success here all hinges on the weather, or indeed the very lack of it. Time it right and it's the stuff of magazine covers, but on a cloudy day then it's, well, reading them!

This is one location that may require pre-planning and a visit when the forecast is good. The best time of day is dawn, early morning before convection clouds form. That said, high cloud and heavy shower clouds can create some added interest. The best location is right at the head of the lake just off the main highway.

The road to Mount Cook Village has numerous opportunities, but try to avoid the obvious (or you could say over-cooked) images that suggest you just stepped off a bus.

At Glentannerpark (see page 233) get down on to the braided riverbed and look for some reflections of the mountains, especially at dawn or dusk. From Mount Cook Village consider spending a night (dawn and dusk) up at the 1800m Mueller Hut (see page 233). The short walks to Kea Point and across the Hooker River (especially around the swing bridge) can also prove productive.

See key, page 61.

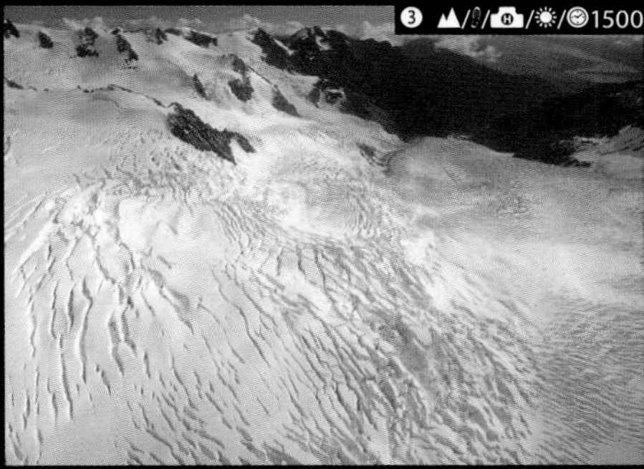

❸ West Coast, Franz Josef & Fox Glacier
Page 241
Three options here, the conventional shots from walkways (and by the way, stick to them); close-up ice shots on a guided walk; or the aerial option. All are productive, but if the weather is clear take the aerial option. If you do that and the rest will become a frenzy of image gathering – but don't forget your polarizer (and/or custom settings) to compensate for the snow's glare. Oh and if rain has stopped play – get out there and try to find an image that conveys the mood and the disappointment!

❹ Lake Matheson
Page 241
This location really draws in the crowds all trying to get that perfect photo. By all means try it, but you might find the final result ends up as a snapshot of the hordes trying to get the picture!

Sleeping

Hambledon $$$$
*103 Bealey Av, T03-379 0723,
hambledon.co.nz.*
Map: Christchurch, p218.
Old world charm in a large and
well-appointed 1856 mansion
with six lovely luxury suites (one
with a four-poster bed), one
self-contained apartment, a large
collection of antiques and a
peaceful garden.

Airport Christchurch Motel $$$
*55 Roydvale Av, Christchurch,
T03-9774970, T0800-800631,
airportchristchurch.co.nz.*
Map: Christchurch, p218.
Modern four-star handy to the
airport with self-contained
options. Bealey Avenue on the
way in from the airport has
dozens of other motel options.

Stonehurst $$$-$
*241 Gloucester St, Latimer Sq,
Christchurch, T03-3794620,
T0508-786633; stonehurst.co.nz.*
Map: Christchurch, p218.
Centrally located with a wide
range of options from
backpacker to apartment,
including powered sites
for campervans. Good
all-round option.

Hotel So $$
*165 Cashel St, Christchurch,
T03-9685050, T0508-165165,
hotelso.co.nz.*
Map: Christchurch, p218.
Funky, hip and cool are the
predominate adjectives in the
guestbook of this ultra modern
budget hotel located in the
centre of the city. Causing a bit of
a stir in the industry its interior
design and functionality makes
for an experience beyond the
norm. Think modern car then
equate to motel/hotel. Fresh
colours, sweeping curves and
clean lines throughout suggest
the futuristic has arrived. It has all
the facilities of a five star
including gym, sauna, guest
lounge and balcony, computer
facilities, laundry and café/bar,
yet at a fraction of the price.
Off-street parking is also
available at $15 per day.

Motor parks
Meadow Park Top Ten Holiday Park $$$-$
*39 Meadow St (off Papanui Rd at
the northwestern end of the city),
T03-3529176, meadowpark.co.nz.*
Map: Christchurch, p218.
Has a great range of options
from self-contained motels,
lodges and flats to chalets,
cottages and standard cabins,
powered/tent sites. That said,
you pay more for its location and
the facilities, which include a spa
pool, sauna and weight training
room. Look out for the sign off
Papanui Road as it's hard to spot.

Hanmer Springs
Heritage Hotel and Resort $$$$-$$$
*1 Conical Hill Rd, Hanmer
Springs, T03-315 0060,
heritagehotels.co.nz.*
Modern and located overlooking
the town centre. Rooms range
from the honeymoon suite to
standard, with self-contained
standalone villas also available. It
has all the usual facilities
including a good restaurant, bar
and a swimming pool. Two mins
from the hot pools.

Motor parks
Alpine Adventure Tourist Park $$-$
*200 Jacks Pass Rd, south of the
thermal resort, T03-3157112,
aatouristpark.co.nz.*
A good walk from the town
centre but nonetheless an
excellent choice with peaceful
and spacious sheltered sites,
excellent value cabins and good
facilities.

Kaikoura
Hapuku Lodge and Tree Houses $$$$
*Hapuku Rd (12 km north of
Kaikoura), T03-319 6559,
hapukulodge.com.*
A contemporary complex
offering seven elegant luxury en
suites and an apartment with
open fire and spa and the even
more popular luxury 'Tree
Houses' sleeping up to five. The

emphasis is very much on natural materials and a scattering of original New Zealand art. There is also a guest restaurant.

Lemon Tree Lodge $$$
31 Adelphi Terrace, T03-3197464, lemontree.co.nz.
A boutique B&B that caters especially for couples or single independent travellers. Renovated two-storey house with four tidy rooms, all with private deck or balcony and good attention to detail. Outdoor hot tub. Caring and well-travelled owners.

Motor parks
Kaikoura Top Ten Holiday Park $$$-$
34 Beach Rd, T03-319 5362, T0800-363638, kaikouratop10.co.nz.
The best motor park, only three minutes from the town centre and the beach. Modern facilities, motel units, en suite units, cabins and powered/tent sites.

McKenzie Country
Hermitage Hotel $$$$-$$$
Mount Cook Village, T03-435 1809, mount-cook.com.
Iconic with standard rooms or self-contained motel doubles, studios and chalets with basic facilities. Bear in mind that the price reflects the location but there is no faulting the hotel facilities, and the restaurants and bars are good.

Chalet Boutique Motel $$$
14 Pioneer Dr, Tekapo, T03-680 6774, thechalet.co.nz.
A fine lodge-style motel. By the lake (near the church) with six tidy apartments and plenty of activities on offer.

Motor parks
Lake Tekapo Motels and Motor Camp $$-$
Western end of the village close to Springs and Winter Park, Lakeside Drive, Tekapo, T03-680 6825, T0800-853853.
Spacious and peaceful in a fine lakeside spot. Self-contained motels, flats, cabins and sheltered powered/tent sites, camp kitchen.

Glentanner Park and Activity Centre $$$-$
SH80, 15 mins before Mt Cook, T03-435 1855, glentanner.co.nz.
Glentanner Park is the only motor park in the valley, and the base for several fixed-wing and helicopter scenic flight operators. Good facilities.

West Coast

Karamea
Rough and Tumble Bush Lodge $$$
Mokihinui River, 5 mins from Seddonville Pub (50 km north of Westport), T03-732 1337, roughandtumble.co.nz.
Classic and affordable bush lodge accommodation overlooking the Mokihinui River.

five cosy en suites with memorable views. Furnishings of native timber abound and an outdoor campfire, swimming hole and bush bath all add to the appeal. Excellent in-house cuisine. It is remote but well worth the effort.

Punakaiki & the Paparoa National Park
Hydrangea Cottages $$
North of the centre, Punakaiki T03-731 1839, pancake-rocks.co.nz.
Quality self-contained cottages. Very cute and reasonably priced.

Motor parks
Punakaiki Beach Camp $$-$
Owen St (off SH6), Punakaiki, T03-731 1894, holidayparks.co. nz/punakaiki.
Set next to the beach and only a short walk from the main village. It offers spacious grounds, cabins and powered/tent sites, camp kitchen.

Greymouth & around
Motor parks
Top Ten Greymouth Holiday Park $$$-$
2 Chesterfield St, Greymouth T03-768 6618, T0800-867104, top10greymouth.co.nz.
Spacious, alongside the beach, with full facilities.

Listings

Hokitika
Beachfront Hotel $$$
111 Revell St, Hokitika, T03-755 8344, beachfronthotel.com.
Modern, well facilitated with standard to luxury, most en suite and some with ocean views. A reputable restaurant/bar overlooking the beach.

Motor parks
Shining Star Log Chalets and Motor Camp $$-$
16 Richards Drive, Hokitika, T03-755 8921, shining@xtra.co.nz.
A fine motel/motor park with tidy self-contained lodges designed and built by the owners. It is close to the beach in a quiet location and also takes campervans and tents. Full facilities.

Okarito
Motor parks
Okarito YHA Hostel and DoC campsite $$-$
Palmerston St, Okarito, T0800-278299, yha.co.nz.
Something of novelty set in the former 1870s schoolhouse. Bookings can be made via the Franz Josef i-SITE or payment made at the warden's house close to the hostel. Coin-operated showers at the basic DoC campground opposite where fires are permitted. Beware of sandflies and take insect repellent.

The Glacier Region

Franz Josef
Franz Josef Glacier Country Retreat $$$$
Off SH6, 6 km north of Franz Josef, T03-752 0012, glacier-retreat.co.nz.
A replica of a traditional west-coast homestead in a peaceful farmland setting, owned by a fourth generation west coast family. 12 luxury en suite rooms with a historical edge. Four-poster beds and claw-foot or spa baths adds to the appeal.

Motor parks
Rainforest Retreat Holiday Park $$-$
Cron St, Franz Josef T0800-873346, T03-7520220, rainforestretreat.co.nz.
Affordable eco-based log cabins in a quiet setting, yet still close to the village. The various options include studios and family units. There are also campervan facilities and tent sites, with modern facilities including a camp kitchen. Spa and internet.

Fox Glaciar
Te Weheka Inn $$$$
Opposite the DoC/VIC, Main Rd, Fox Glacier, T03-7510730, teweheka.co.nz.
Pitched somewhere between a motel and a luxury boutique hotel. It has a striking design and offers modern suites. Tariff includes breakfast.

Motor parks
Fox Glacier Holiday Park $$-$
Cooks Flat Rd, Fox Glacier, T03-751 0821.
The main motor park in the village. Spacious, it has all the usual facilities including cabins, lodge rooms, flats, powered/tent sites and a backpacker dorm. Good facilities.

Haast
Heartland World Heritage Hotel $$$
Corner of SH6 and Jackson's Bay Rd, Haast Junction, T0800-502444, T03-750 0828, world-heritage-hotel.com.
Long-established and recently refurbished, it has 54 en suite units from standard to family, but is best known for its restaurant and bar. The open log fire is particularly attractive.

Motor parks
Haast Beach Holiday Park $$-$
Okuru (15 km south), Jackson's Bay Rd, T03-750 0860, accommodationhaastpark.co.nz.
Offers a number of basic motel units, self-contained and standard cabins, but is mainly noted for its location, friendliness and fine modern kitchen and lounge facilities

Eating & drinking

Christchurch has two popular drinking and eating conglomerates. The first is **The Strip** of lively restaurant/bars on Oxford Terrace. It is a good spot to be both in the evening and more especially during the day, when you can sup a bottle or glass of your favourite libation while watching the world (and the river) go by. Most pubs/bars stay open to at least 2300 with some on The Strip remaining open at weekends until 0230. Equally, if not more popular, is **Sol Square**, southeast of the city centre off Lichfield Street.

Charlotte Jane Hotel $$$
110 Papanui Rd, T03-3551028, charlotte-jane.co.nz.
Tue-Sun.
Map: Christchurch, p218.
Pacific Rim a la carte with seafood and lamb a speciality. Romantic atmosphere, al fresco seating and an open fire.

Tramway Restaurant $$$
T03-366 7511, tram.co.nz.
Map: Christchurch, p218.
An unusual and romantic dining option. In the evening you can join the popular dining tour that adds a very pleasant convivial edge to the usual sightseeing trip. Lamb, salmon, beef or single vegetarian main and one option for sweet the iconic Kiwi pavlova.

Dux de Lux $$
41 Hereford St, T03-366 6919.
Map: Christchurch, p218.
A bar-restaurant combo and something of a Christchurch institution. Perhaps the best thing is its position on the fringe of the Arts Centre complex. It is busiest at the weekend when the markets are in full swing, but remains popular well after dark. Attracting a mixed crowd, a lively atmosphere is guaranteed and there is a fine choice of seafood, vegetarian and Kiwi beers.

Annie's Wine Bar and Restaurant $$$-$$
Corner Rolleston Av and Hereford St, T03-365 0566.
Daily 1100-2300.
Map: Christchurch, p218.
Conveniently located in the heart of the Arts Centre and the former Arts College it retains a casual, lively atmosphere and is good brunch or lunch option. Also offers set dinner menus and an extensive wine list.

Fat Eddie's $$
Unit 10, SOL Square, 179 Tuam St, T03-943 2833.
Tue-Sun.
Map: Christchurch, p218.
One of a handful of fine drinking (and eating) venues in the city's latest hip precinct, Sol Square. Freddies is a cool jazz bar with live entertainment six nights a week, a pub-style menu, a good wine list and speciality cocktails. Try a Kiwi 'Wondering Eye'.

Hanmer Springs
Malabar $$$-$$
Alpine Pacific Centre, 5 Conical Hill Rd, Hanmer Springs, T03-315 7745.
Daily from 1800.
A fine mix of Indian and Malaysian in a casual setting. Takeaway service.

Alpine Village Inn $$
Jack's Pass Rd, T03-315 7005.
Mon-Fri 1100-2130, Sat-Sun 0900-2130.
Considered the local pub. Hearty, value pub food and relaxed friendly atmosphere.

Kaikoura
Donegal House $$
Schoolhouse Rd (6 km via SH1 north), T03-319 5083.
Daily 1100-1400 and 1800-2100.
A good all rounder in a lovely rural setting. Small, atmospheric Irish country hotel/pub/ restaurant with a mainly seafood menu including green-lipped mussels and local crayfish.

Pier Hotel Pub and Café $$
1 Avoca St, T03-319 5037.
Daily from 1700.
Combine a coastal walk to the wharf (1 km) with good pub-style grub, a fine atmosphere and views. Indoor and outdoor seating.

MacKenzie Country

Astro Café $$
*Mt John Observatory,
Tekapo (follow signs west end
of the village).*
Daily 0900-1700.
Set atop the 300-m Mount John.
Once you have taken in the
lakeside views this is another
excellent venue. Good coffee
and standard café fare.

**Clay Cliffs Vineyard and
Café $$**
*500 m south of Omarama on
SH8, T03-438 9654,
claycliffs.co.nz.*
Daily for lunch and dinner from
1100 (closed Jul).
Tuscan-styled restaurant with al
fresco dining in a lovely relaxing
setting. Try the local salmon.

**Old Mountaineers Café
Bar $$**
*Just below the DoC visitor centre,
Mount Cook Village,
T03-435 1890.*
Daily for lunch and dinner.
A fine alternative to the
Hermitage Hotel Restaurants,
offering a wholesome menu. It
has a congenial atmosphere with
open fire.

West Coast

Westport

Bay House Café $$
*Southern end of Tauranga Bay,
Cape Foulwind (near Westport),
T03-789 7133, thebayhouse.co.nz.*
The best local restaurant,
offering breakfast, lunch and an
à la carte menu for dinner and in
a superb setting overlooking the
bay and within walking distance
of the seal colony.

Greymouth

Jade Boulder Café $$
1 Guinness St, T03-768 0700.
Good daytime option attached
to the Jade Country shop – an
attraction in itself. Serves the
West Coast delicacy whitebait
year round.

Hokitika

Café de Paris $$$-$$
19 Tancred St, T03-755 8933.
Daily from 0830.
Award-winning restaurant with
imaginative French/Italian
influenced à la carte dinner and
changing blackboard menu for
breakfast and lunch.

Franz Josef

The Blue Ice Café & Pub $$
Main Rd, T03-752 0707.
Serves good pizza upstairs and à
la carte dining on the ground
level. All-out war on the free pool
table is its other speciality. .

Fox Glacier

The Plateau Cafe & Bar $$
*Corner Sullivan Rd and Main Rd,
T03-751 0058.*
Daily from 1100.
Modern decor with open fire and
a wide-ranging à la carte menu
including hot curries – perfect
after a day clambering over a
glacier or walking in the rain.

Haast

Cray Pot Café $
T03-750 0035, Jackson's Bay.
Daily 1030-1900.
Well, it's the end of the road
folks – a long way but worth it. A
quirky cross between a rail
carriage and a barge serving fish
and chips. You can eat in
(recommended) or take away,
but beware of the sandflies.

Entertainment

**Christchurch &
Banks Peninsula**

For performance and cinema
listings consult *The Press*
newspaper, stuff.co.nz/the-pres.
The free leaflet, *The Package*
available from the i-SITE is also
useful, thepackage.co.nz.

Bars & clubs

Christchurch Casino
*30 Victoria St, T03-365 9999,
chchcasino.co.nz.*
A well-established institution
and naturally a popular
entertainment venue.

Culture Club
*4 His Lordships Lane, Sol Sq,
Christchurch.*
Popular 1980s dance bar with
lots of Wham! Open from 2100
until very late Thu-Sat.

Shopping

Cinemas

Hoyts
392 Moorhouse Av (Old Train Station), T0508-446987.

Rialto
Corner Moorhouse Av and Durham St, T03-3749404.

Festivals & events

World Busker's Festival
(mid-Jan)
worldbuskersfestival.com.
A lively event attracting street performers and musicians from around the world.

Christchurch Arts Festival
(Jul/Aug)
artsfestival.co.nz.
Includes theatre, dance, classical and jazz concerts, cabaret and exhibitions of the visual arts.

West Coast

Festivals & events

Hokitika Wildfoods Festival
(Mar)
T03-755 8321, wildfoods.co.nz.
Hokitika enjoys such a human influx that it can jog the memories of the gold rush days at this mighty party dressed up as a 'wild' food scene. On offer is a vast array of culinary delights from possum pies to witchetty bugs. There's even the odd testicle – yum!

Christchurch & Banks Peninsula

Toffs Recycled Clothing
141 Gloucester St, just off Cathedral Sq.
An innocuous-looking place that gives no indication of the marvels inside. The perfect place for shopa-phobics with all manner of second-hand clothing and accessories, from snow chains to – if you're lucky – an Armani business shirt and silk tie. The challenge: try going in there for less than 20 minutes and coming out empty handed.

Activities & tours

Christchurch & Banks Peninsula

Adventure Canterbury
T0800-847455, adventurecanterbury.com.
One of the main activity operators in Christchurch, offering a wide array of trips and activities including jet boating, horse trekking, fishing, farm visits, winery tours and day trips to Hanmer and Akaroa.

Black Cat Group Lyttelton and Akaroa
T03-328 9078, blackcat.co.nz.
Offers an interesting array of catamaran cruises from Lyttelton and Hector's dolphin watching/ swimming cruises from Akaroa.

Mountain Bike Adventure Company
T03-339 4020, T0800-424534, cyclehire-tours.co.nz.
Offers a trip that goes up the Port Hills via the gondola to then descend by bike, from $50, plus tours from three to five days and hire from $35 per day.

Around Christchurch

Air Safaris
Main St, Lake Tekapo, T0800-806880, airsafaris.co.nz.
The 'Grand Traverse' is a 50-minute (200-km) trip that takes in Mt Cook and the glaciers. $280, child $195.

Alpine Horse Safaris
Hawarden, T03-314 4293, alpinehorse.co.nz.
Standard treks and some multi-day trips from $155.

Dolphin and Albatross Encounter
96 The Esplanade, Kaikoura, T03-319 6777, T0800-733365, dolphin.co.nz.
The main operator offering three-hour trips from West End at 0530, 0830 and 1230, from $150, child $140 (viewing-only $80, child $40). Albatross and seabird trips from $110, child $55.

Glacier Explorers
T03-435 1641, T0800-686 800, glacierexplorers.com.
Explore the terminal face of the Tasman Glacier by boat.

Glacier Sea-Kayaking
T03-4351890, mtcook.com
Explore the terminal face of the Tasman Glacier by kayak.

Glenstrae Farm 4 Wheeler Adventures
Kaikoura, T03-319 7021, T0800-004009, 4wheeladventures.co.nz.
4WD and quad-bike adventures. Based about 25 km south of the town it offers three-hour trips in the coastal hinterland, from $110. Courtesy pick-ups from Kaikoura.

Hanmer Springs Adventure Centre (HSAC)
20 Conical Hill Rd, T03-315 7233, hanmeradventure.co.nz.
Wide range of activities. Hire of mountain bikes, scooters, motorbikes (ATV adventures from $89), fishing tackle, rollerblades and ski equipment, also available.

Heli-bike Twizel
T03-435 0626, T0800-435424, helibike.com.
Wild rides range from 1½-3½ hours and cost $55-200.

Helicopter Line
T03-435 1801, helicopter.co.nz.
Its Mt Cook (East) operations are based at Glentanner park, 20-45 minutes, from $200-$400.

Mount Cook Ski Planes
Mt Cook Airport just 7 km south of Mt Cook Village, T03-430 8034, T0800-800702, skiplanes.co.nz.
This flight-seeing option offers snow-landings high up on the Tasman Glacier, from $340.

Seal Swim Kaikoura
T03-3196182, T0800-732579, sealswimkaikoura.co.nz.
Two-hour shore- and boat-based snorkeling tours from $70.

Whale Watch Kaikoura
T03-319 6767, T0800-655121, whalewatch.co.nz.
Based at the Whaleway Station (next to the Railway Station), accessed off Beach Rd (SH1) just beyond West End. It offers several two- to 3½-hour trips daily from $140, child $60.

Wings Over Whales
Peketa Airfield (6 km south of Kaikoura), T03-319 6580, T0800-226629, whales.co.nz.
Entertaining and personable flight-seeing trips 30-45 minutes from $145, child $75.

West Coast

Okarito Nature Tours
T03-753 4014, okarito.co.nz.
Kayak rental and guided trips to explore the scenery and natural history of the lagoon and its many channels, from $80.

Underworld Adventures
Charlestown, 27 km south of Westport, T0800-116686, caverafting.com.
Offers tours, caving and rafting trips to the Te Tahi and Metro limestone caves in Paparoa National Park, from $90.

White Heron Sanctuary Tours
Whataroa, T03-753 4120, T0800-523456, white herontours.co.nz.
Offers a 2½-hour tour by jet boat to access the hide that overlooks the colony, tours $110, child $45.

Glacier Region

Glacier walking
Fox Glacier Guiding
Alpine Guides Building, Main Rd, T03-751 0825, T0800-111600, foxguides.co.nz.
Offers two- to eight-hour excursions as well as heli- hike, ice climbing, mountaineering and alpine-hut trips, from $89.

Franz Josef Glacier Guides
Main Rd, T03-752 0763, T0800-484337, franzjosefglacier.com.
A highly experienced outfit offering four- to eight-hour glacier excursions as well as heli-hike and high-level alpine trips, from $97.

Ice climbing
Hukawai Glacier Centre and Ice Climbing Wall
Corner of Cowan and Cron streets, T03-752 0600, T0800-485292, hukawai.co.nz.
One of only seven such centres in the world and one of the largest. A 1½-hour tutored session will cost around $100.

Transport

River safaris
Haast River Safaris
The 'Red Barn' between Haast Junction and Haast Township, T0800-865382, haastriver.co.nz.
River safari up the Haast River Valley. The 1½-hour trips on its purpose-built jet boat depart daily at 0900, 1100 and 1400 and cost from $132, child $55.

Scenic flights
Flights start at around $95 for a 10-minute flight. A snow landing is recommended. There are several companies including:

Helicopter Line
Main Rd, T0800-807767, helicopter.co.nz.
Flights from 20-40 minutes and a three-hour heli-hike option.

Mountain Helicopters
T03-7510045, T0800-369423, mountainhelicopters.co.nz.
Flights from both Franz and Fox from 10 to 40 minutes. Good company with cheaper rates.

Mount Cook Ski Plane Adventures (Aoraki Mt Cook)
Main Rd, T03-752 074, mtcookskiplanes.com.
Offering the only fixed-wing glacier landings in New Zealand.

Sky diving
Skydive Glacier Country
T0800-7510080, skydivingnz.co.nz.
Offers tandems amidst some of the country's most stunning scenery, from $245-285.

For travel information and bookings contact the regional i-SITE visitor centres.

Christchurch is 336 km south of Picton (Kaikoura 183 km) via SH1; and 579 km north of Invercargill (Dunedin 362 km, Timaru 163 km) on SH1. Queenstown is 486 km southwest via SH1/SH8, and Greymouth, 258 km via Arthur's Pass and SH73.

Air
Christchurch International Airport is 12 km northwest of the city via Fendalton Rd and Memorial Av, T03-3585029, christchurch-airport.co.nz. **Metro buses**, T03-3668855, metro info. org.nz, offer a regular Red Bus City Flyer service to the CBD and Cathedral Square (hourly Mon-Fri 0600-2300, Sat/Sun 0800-2300, $7) (No 29, 20 mins). Various shuttles, including **Super Shuttle** (door to door), T03-3579950, T0800-SHUTTLE. A taxi from the airport costs around $40, Blue Star T03-3531200, T03-3799799, 24 hrs or First Direct, T03-3775555.

Bus
Regional and national **buses** arrive and depart from either Cathedral Square in Christchurch, or at the Christchurch Travel Centre, 123 Worcester Street, T03-377 0951. **Intercity** is the main bus company, T03-3651113, intercity.co.nz. Christchurch has an excellent local public bus system with a modern terminal,

the Bus Exchange, corner of Lichfield and Colombo streets. For all bus information contact T03-3668855, metroinfo.org.nz, or **Red Buses** T0800-733287, redbus. co.nz. The Free Yellow Shuttle takes in a north-south route from the casino, through Cathedral Square and down Colombo Street and back, every 10-15 minutes (Mon-Fri 0730-2230, Sat 0800-2230, Sun 1000-2000). It's worth jumping on to get your bearings. **Best Attractions Shuttle** T0800-484485, takes in the main city attractions including the Antarctic Centre and the Gondola, departing Cathedral Square, daily 0900-1800. Various fares including entry.

Train
Christchurch's train station is on Addington St, 3 km from the city centre at the southwestern tip of Hagley Park. **TranzScenic** operates the northbound 'TranzCoastal' service (departs 0730; to Kaikoura-Blenheim-Picton, from $40); and the deservingly popular 'TranzAlpine' (departs 0815; to Greymouth $149), T0800-872467, tranzscenic.co.nz.

Trains serve Blenheim and Kaikoura and the West Coast (Greymouth), but no points south of Christchurch, T0800-872467, tranzscenic.co.nz.

Contents

Winter at Milford Sound with the iconic Mitre Peak centre.

Otago & Southland

Introduction

I f you had time to visit only one region in New Zealand it would have to be Otago. Aesthetically it is both diverse and stunning with the (literally) 'Remarkable' mountain ranges in the west, through the barren and expansive landscapes of Central Otago to the green rolling hills and beaches of the Otago Peninsula combining to form the quintessential New Zealand landscape package. Dunedin, the capital, retains much of its Scottish heritage and a distinct grandeur borne of the gold booms of the 19th century. With the Otago Peninsula on its doorstep and the diverse and rare wildlife that thrives there, it is also known as the wildlife capital of the country. But without doubt the modern-day gold is lodged safely in the tourism bank and it belongs to Queenstown, which, with over 150 activities to get the pulse racing and the wallet fast emptying, is considered the adventure capital of the world.

Then, acting almost like an adrenalin overdose clinic, Otago's neighbour, Southland, provides a welcome sanctuary. It contains the most spectacular yet inaccessible landscapes in the country. Half of its coast is mountainous, remote and inhospitable – virtually unchanged since Cook first landed (briefly) in 1770. The other half is home to Southland's largest town, Invercargill, and the beautiful Catlin Coast. Amidst all that, knocking at its backdoor, is New Zealand's newest national park: Stewart Island, a place perhaps to fall gently back down to earth after all the scenic and activity overload.

... a long weekend
With only three days it has to be either Dunedin or Queenstown.
In Dunedin enjoy the sights of the city itself and spend a full day exploring the Otago Peninsula. If you can, include a day trip inland, either by car through the Maniototo to St Bathans, or on the Taieri Gorge Railway. In Queenstown, well, where do you start! Just be sure to include (if the weather allows) a fly-cruise package to Milford Sound.

... a week
With a week it is possible to combine Dunedin and Queenstown. From Queenstown spend half a day in Arrowtown, or a jet boating trip up the Dart River near Glenorchy. Wanaka provides an alternative venue. A trip by road to Milford Sound is a must, or a fly-cruise option followed by two days in the Catlins or on Stewart Island.

Queenstown is often dubbed adventure capital of the world.

Dunedin & Otago Peninsula

There is perhaps nowhere else in the world – and certainly nowhere so far from its roots – that boasts a Scottish heritage like Dunedin, the South Island's second largest city. A city born of Scottish immigrants who arrived in 1848 even the name means 'Edin on the Hill' after Edinburgh, the Scottish capital. The streets are also blatant in their similarity, sharing the names of Edinburgh's most famous, including Princes Street and George Street.

Immediately, you will also notice the echo of Scottish architecture – grand buildings of stone, built to last, which go far beyond the merely functional and, in true Scottish tradition, defy inclement weather. Most were built during the great Otago gold boom of the 1860s when the city enjoyed considerable prosperity and standing.

Modern-day Dunedin has many tourism assets, of which the Otago Peninsula is perhaps the best known. Dunedin's 'beautiful backyard' (as it is often called) is home to some rare wildlife including the only mainland breeding colony of albatross, the rare yellow-eyed penguins and Hooker's sea lions. There is also one other undeniable asset to Dunedin, and one that can perhaps be attributed to its Scots heritage: without doubt it has the friendliest people and offers the warmest welcome in New Zealand.

The Octagon

The Octagon forms the heart or central focus of the city and consists of a circular thoroughfare bisected by the city's main streets; George Street to the northeast of the Octagon and Princes Street to the southwest of it. These two streets form the hub of Dunedin's central business district. Presiding over the Octagon is a statue of **Robert Burns** the Scottish poet, whose nephew, the Reverend Thomas Burns, was a religious leader of the early settlers. There are many fine examples of the city's architecture, including the grand **Municipal Chambers** buildings, which now houses the i-SITE visitor centre. Next door to the Municipal Chambers is **St Paul's Cathedral**, just one of several noted for their robust architectural aesthetics. Others worth seeing are the **First Church of Otago** on Moray Place and **St Joseph's Cathedral** on the corner of Rattray and Smith Street.

The Octagon is also home to the **Dunedin Public Art Gallery** (T03-477 4000, dunedin.art. museum.co.nz, daily 1000-1700, free). It is the oldest art gallery in the country and of special note is its collection of New Zealand works that date from 1860 to the present day. There are also some works by the more familiar names like Turner, Gainsborough and Monet.

South & east of the Octagon

A five-minute walk east of the Octagon is Dunedin's iconic train station – a fine example of the typical Scottish desire to take architecture beyond the purely functional. Built in 1906, its grand towered exterior cannot fail to impress, but the interior too is rather splendid complete with stained-glass windows, Royal Doulton tiles, mosaics and brass fittings. For many years it served as a major hub of transportation south to Invercargill and north to Christchurch and beyond. With the steady decline of rail services in New Zealand it now is largely redundant but for the tourism-based **Taieri Gorge** rail journey (see page

Essentials

💲 **ATMs** Represented along Princes and George streets, with many accommodating currency exchange services. **Travelex**, 346 George St, T03-4771532.

⊕ **Hospital** **Dunedin Hospital**, 201 Great King St, T03-474 0999; Doctor, 95 Hanover St, T03-479 2900 (pharmacy next door).

✆ **Post office** 243 Princes St, T03-4773518, Mon-Fri 0830-1730 (Post Restante).

ℹ **Tourist information** **Octagon i-SITE visitor centre**, No 48, below the Municipal Chambers Building, T03-474 3300, dunedinnz.com, cityofdunedin.com, Mon-Fri 0800-1800, Sat-Sun 0845-1800. Also acts as a transport booking agent.

It's a fact (or a mystery)...

The trees in the Octagon are automatically and regularly watered from high up within their canopies and there is no protection afforded to pedestrians below. For the uninitiated, particularly on a cloudless day, it can be quite a spectacle as with no warning it starts to rain. Most say it is a council design blunder, while others reckon it is to remind city residents of their Scots heritage.

263) and the occasional 'steam-up' of working engines from around the country.

On the first floor of the station is the **New Zealand Sports Hall of Fame** (T03-477 7775, nzhalloffame.co.nz, daily 1000-1600, from $6, child $3) which celebrates the legacy of more than a century of New Zealand champions.

Just a few hundred metres from the train station, and boasting a couple of monstrous historic steam trains of its own, is the **Otago Settlers Museum** (31 Queens Gardens, T03-4742728, otago.settlers.museum.co.nz, daily 1000-1700, $6, children free; guided tours daily at 1100). First established in 1898 the emphasis here is on social history with many fine temporary and permanent displays. Recent additions include the Across the Ocean Waves exhibit, which focuses on the ocean crossings that many of the early settlers had to endure. The museum also serves as the base for Walk Dunedin, which offers two-hour city heritage walks departing daily at 1100, from $20.

Next door to the Settlers Museum is the new **Dunedin Chinese Garden** (T03-4773248, open daily 1000-1700 and Wed 1900-2100, $9, children free). Completed in 2008 using authentic Chinese materials crafted by a team of artisans/craftsmen for Dunedin's sister city of Shanghai it is a fine example and a great place to escape the buzz of the city.

North of the railway station is **Cadbury World** (280 Cumberland St, T03-4677967/T0800-223287, cadburyworld.co.nz; regular tours 0900-1515, $18, child $12), which recently opened its doors to the drooling public. Though they could never quite live up to the fantasy of Charlie and the Chocolate Factory the interactive tours offer an interesting and mouth-watering insight into the production of the irresistible stuff. Naturally, there is a shop that does very well.

Dunedin has its own **surf beach** fringing the suburb of **St Claire** (2.5 km) where it is not entirely unusual to see fur seals playing up with the surfers. **Tunnel Beach** is also a popular spot and a precursor to the splendid coastal scenery of the Otago Peninsula. A steep path through some bush

It's a fact...

120 million chocolate bars are sold in New Zealand annually, which equates to almost 40 bars per head of population or an estimated 4 kg per person every year.

First Church of Otago, Dunedin.

delivers you to some impressive weathered sandstone cliffs and arches. Beach access is south of the city centre near Blackhead, 1 km, one hour return; car park seaward end of Green Island Bush Road off Blackhead Road.

North & west of the Octagon

About 1 km north of the Octagon, is the 1906 'Edwardian time capsule' of **Olveston House** (42 Royal Terrace, T03-4773320, olveston.co.nz; guided 1-hr tours recommended, $15.50, child $7). Bequeathed to the city in 1966 by the last surviving member of the wealthy and much-travelled Theomin family, the 35-room mansion comes complete with an impressive 'collection of collections', containing many items from the Edwardian era. It gives an interesting insight into Dunedin of old and the lives of the more prosperous pioneer.

A few minutes' east of Olveston, the **Otago Museum** (419 Great King St, T03-474 7474, otagomuseum.govt.nz, daily 1000-1700, free; 'Discovery World' $9.50, child $4.50; guided tours daily at 1130), was established in 1868 and is one of the oldest in the country, with a staggering 1.7 million items. The museum's primary themes are culture, nature and science, all housed in newly renovated surroundings and displayed in the now almost obligatory state-of-the-art fashion. The Southern Land – Southern People exhibit is particularly good and is intended to reflect the unique beauty and diversity of Southern New Zealand. The latest edition to the permanent exhibits is **Discovery World Tropical Forest – Live Butterfly Experience**, featuring around 1000 imported tropical butterflies. The museum has a café on site.

A short stroll from the museum is the sprawling campus of the **University of Otago**. Founded in 1869, it was New Zealand's first university and is famous for its architecture as well as its contributions to medical science. The grand edifice of the original Administration building and clock tower (access from Leith St) is perhaps the most photographed icon in the city.

Another New Zealand 'first' in Dunedin are the **Botanical Gardens** north of the university campus, corner of Great King Street and Opoho Road, (T03-4774000, dawn to dusk). Nurtured since 1914 and arguably the best in New Zealand, the 28-ha site is split into upper and lower gardens that straddle Signal Hill. Combined they form an interesting topography and all the usual suspects, with a particular bent on rhododendrons (at their best in October), plants from the Americas, Asia and Australia, native species, winter and wetland gardens. If you tire of the flora there is also a modern aviary complex, housing many exotic and native birds including the 'cheeky' kea and kaka parrots. Also on site are information points, a café and a small shop, all in the Lower Garden. Access to the Lower Garden is from Cumberland Street while the Upper Garden is reached via Lovelock Lane. The **Centennial Lookout** (6 km, 1½ hours' walk) and Lookout Point offer grand views of the harbour and the city, and are accessed via Signal Hill Road (beyond Lovelock Av).

While in the north of the city, you might like to visit the famed **Baldwin Street**, which at a gradient of nearly one in three, is reputed to be the steepest street in the world. It's worth a look, if only to work out the building methodology and what happens when the residents are eating at a table or in the bath. Head north via Great King Street then veer right at the Botanical Gardens on to North Road; Baldwin is about 1 km (10th street) on the right.

Otago Peninsula

The beautiful Otago Peninsula, which stretches 33 km northeast from Dunedin out into the Pacific Ocean, is as synonymous with wildlife as Dunedin is with Scotland. If there were any place that could honour the title of being the **wildlife** capital of the country, this would be it. It is home to an array of particularly rare species including the enchanting yellow-eyed penguin and the soporific Hooker's sea lion, as well the more common New Zealand fur seals. But without doubt the peninsula's star attraction is the breeding colony of royal albatross

Sandfly Bay, Otago Peninsula.

on **Taiaroa Head**, at the very tip of the peninsula. The first egg was laid here in 1920 and the now thriving colony (the only mainland breeding albatross colony in the world) offers an extraordinary opportunity to observe these supremely beautiful masters of flight and long-haul travel. An organized day trip to see some or all of these wildlife delights is highly recommended and will leave a precious and lasting memory. Besides wildlife, the principal attractions on the Otago Peninsula are historic **Larnach Castle** and the stunning vista of **Sandfly Bay**, as well as activities such as sea kayaking, cruising and walking.

For wildlife and general activity operator listings and maps consult the i-SITE Visitor Centre and see page 289.

Royal Albatross Centre

Taiaroa Head, T03-478 0499, albatross.org.nz. Daily 0830-2100; seasonal; from $45, child $22. The observatory is closed 17 Sep-23 Nov each year, to allow the new season's birds to renew their pair bonds.

Even before you enter the centre, if the conditions are right, you can see the great birds wheeling in from the ocean on wings that span over 3 m (the largest of any bird) and with a grace that defies the effort. The albatross centre has some superb exhibits that include static and audio-visual displays and even a live close-circuit TV feed from the occupied nests in the breeding season.

There are a number of tours available. The 1½-hour Unique Taiaroa tour includes an introductory video, a viewing of the colony from the hilltop observatory, and a look at the remains of Fort Taiaroa. This is a series of underground tunnels,

Taieri Gorge Railway and the Otago Central Rail Trail

The Taieri Gorge Railway is considered a world-class train trip encompassing the scenic splendour and history of Otago's hinterland. The former goldfields supply line was completed in 1891 and, as one negotiates the Taieri Gorge with the aid of 12 viaducts and numerous tunnels, it very quickly becomes apparent why it took over 12 years to build. The four-hour trip gets off to a fine start amidst the splendour of Dunedin's grand train station before heading inland to the gorge and Pukerangi. An informative commentary is provided along the way and you are allowed to disembark at certain points of interest. Also, if you ask really nicely, you may also be able to ride alongside the locomotive engineer.

Details available at the train station or T03-477 4449, taieri.co.nz. Trips to Pukerangi/Middlemarch depart daily October-March at 1430 (additional trip on Sun at 0930), Pukerangi $72 return; extended trip to Middlemarch $80. Licensed snack bar on board.

If you wish, you can extend the rail journey by coach across the rugged Maniototo Plateau to Queenstown (6½ hrs), from $115.

Another popular alternative is to take a mountain bike (no extra charge) and disembark at Middlemarch (only selected trains, but one-way fares available). From there you can negotiate the 150-km Otago Central Rail Trail (the former goldfields railway from Middlemarch to Clyde). It is a wonderful bike ride that includes over 60 bridges, viaducts and tunnels and much of Central Otago's classic scenery. The i-SITE visitor centre can supply all the relevant details.

fortifications and a 'disappearing gun' that were originally built in 1885 in response to a perceived threat of invasion from Tsarist Russia.

Yellow-eyed Penguin Conservation Reserve

Just before the Albatross Colony at Harington Point; for bookings contact the reserve direct, T03-478 0286, penguinplace.co.nz.
Daily from 0800; May-Sep from 1515; $35, child $15.

This is the most commercial operation, set on a private reserve with an expanding colony of about 200 birds, which has been carefully created and managed as a workable mix of tourism, commercialism and conservation. Once provided with an introductory talk you are then delivered by 4WD truck to the beach where an amazing network of covered tunnels and hides allows you to view the birds discreetly. The breeding season and adult moult periods (mid-Oct to late Feb and early May) are the best times to see large numbers, but you are almost guaranteed to see at least half a dozen birds all year round especially around dusk.

Taieri Gorge Railway.

Northern & Central Otago

Northern and Central Otago are perhaps best described as 'in passing' destinations, worthy of a brief stop, but inevitably succumbing to the time-pressed angst to reach the main destinations of Dunedin or Queenstown.

The northern Otago town of Oamaru is often dubbed New Zealand's best-built town and offers a strange mix of grand colonial architecture and – believe it or not – wild penguins. A little further south the intrigue continues with the much-loved and wonderfully spherical Moeraki Boulders.

Central Otago is very often missed, and that alone is its appeal. The stark scenery of the Maniototo – which is the generic name for the flat high countryof the region – is very appealing, especially if some solitude is in order. In essence it can be the perfect antidote to the mayhem of Queenstown.

Typical landscape of the Maniototo, Central Otago.

Traction engines are a major feature of the annual Heritage Festival, Oamaru.

Oamaru

Oamaru is an unusual and appealing coastal town on the South Island's east coast, somehow befitting its position gracing the shores of Friendly Bay. Primarily functioning as a port and an agricultural service town, its modern-day tourist attractions lie in the strange combination of stone, architecture and penguins. Thanks to the prosperity of the 1860s-1890s, and the discovery of local limestone that could be easily carved and moulded, the early architects and stonemasons of Oamaru created a settlement rich in imposing, classic buildings, earning it the reputation of New Zealand's best-built town. Many old buildings remain, complete with Corinthian columns and gargantuan doorways, giving it a grand air. Add to that a small and congenial colony of yellow-eyed and blue penguins that waddle up to their burrows on the coast like dignified gents in 'tux and tails', and the town's appeal truly becomes apparent.

Most of the historic buildings and associated attractions are in the **Tyne-Harbour Street Historic Precinct** (begins at the southern end of Thames Street), which boasts the largest and best-preserved collection of historic commercial buildings in the country. There you will find a variety of tourist lures, from antique and craft outlets to second-hand bookstores, theatres and cafés.

But history aside, no visit to Oamaru would be complete without visiting its **penguin colonies**. The town has two very different species in residence – the enchanting little blue penguin (the smallest in the world) and the rare, larger, yellow-eyed penguin. There are two colonies and observation points, one at Bushy Beach (see below), where you can watch the yellow-eyed penguins from a hide for free, or the official harbourside **Oamaru Blue Penguin Colony** (T03-443 1195, penguins.co.nz, $20, child $10) that you must pay to access. The only time to view the penguins is from dusk (specific times are posted at the colony reception). There is a large covered stand from which you are given a brief talk before the penguins come ashore and waddle intently towards their burrows. The colony is accessed via Waterfront Road past the Historic Precinct.

The **Bushy Beach** yellow-eyed penguin colony and viewing hide is accessed on foot via the walkway at the end of Waterfront Road (30 minutes), or alternatively by car via Bushy Beach Road (end of Tyne Street from the Historic Precinct). The best time to view the birds is an hour or so before dawn and dusk when they come and go from their fishing expeditions.

For more information contact the **Oamaru i-SITE visitor centre**, corner of Itchen and Thames streets – T03-434 1656, tourismwaitaki.co.nz,

Moeraki boulder.

something near a layman's explanation at the **Moeraki Boulders Café Bar and Gift Shop**, T03-439 4827, which is signposted just off SH1. The path to the boulders (200 m) starts at the car park and you are requested to provide a donation of $2.

The small fishing village of **Moeraki**, 3 km from the boulders, can be reached along the beach by foot (3 hrs return) or by car via SH1. Once a whaling settlement, first settled as long ago as 1836, it is a very pleasant little enclave and a great place to stay on the way south. For a great short walk head for the historic **lighthouse** (6 km) and its adjunct reserve for yellow-eyed penguins, which are best viewed at dusk or dawn. In the village itself **Fleur's Place** (T03-439 4480, fleursplace.com) by the pier is a wonderful lunch or dinner venue.

Dunedin to Alexandra via the 'Pigroot'

From Palmerston, 55 km north of Dunedin (via SH1 and the coast), SH85 turns inland to follow the 'Pigroot' (the old coach road between the coast and the goldfields) to Ranfurly and Alexandra, with a small diversion to St Bathans. A diversion from the conventional route south or west and a distance of 150 km from Palmerston to Alexandra it is seldom taken by tourists, which is exactly why you should consider it!

Like the MacKenzie Country to the north it has an aesthetic and a mood all of its own. Five mountain ranges encompass the region and within their embrace lies the expansive **Maniototo Plain** that became the mainstay of the region's economy once the 1860s gold boom was over.

Highlights along the way include the art deco buildings of **Ranfurly** (the largest town in the region), curling in **Naseby** (see page 289) and the historic buildings and **Blue Lake** in St Bathans.

Mon-Fri 0900-1800 (1700 Easter-Nov), Sat-Sun 1000-1700 (1600 Easter-Nov). The centre has town maps and a wealth of information surrounding the historical buildings, local tours and things to see and do.

Moeraki & the boulders

On the coast about 40 km south of Oamaru are the **Moeraki Boulders**, a strange and much-photographed collection of spherical boulders that litter the beach. Although Maori legend has it that these boulders are tekaihinaki, or food baskets and sweet potatoes, science has determined that they are in fact 'septarian concretions', a rather classy name for 'rock gob-stoppers' left behind from the eroded coastal cliffs. To understand exactly how they are formed requires several PhDs in geology and physics, but you will find

Alexandra

At the junction of the Clutha and Manuherikia Rivers, Alexandra was one of the first gold mining towns to be established in Central Otago in 1862. Once the gold ran out at the end of the 1800s the orchardists moved in, making fruit growing Alexandra's modern-day industry. The town is at its best in autumn when the riverside willows and poplars, bathe the valley in another golden hue. Alexandra serves as the principal gateway to the **Otago Central Rail Trail**, which is becoming an increasingly popular multi-day mountain-biking adventure.

The main attraction in town is the **Central Stories Museum and Art Gallery** housed in the same building as the **i-SITE visitors centre**, 21 Centennial Av, Pioneer Park, Alexandra, T03-448 6230, centralstories.com.

Clyde

Just 10 km west of Alexandra is the pretty and historic village of Clyde. Backed by the concrete edifice of the Clyde Dam, which incarcerates **Lake Dunstan**. It offers a pleasant stop on the way to Queenstown or Wanaka. Originally called Dunstan and the hub of the rich Dunstan Goldfields, it assumed its present name in the late 1860s. Clyde in Scottish Gaelic is Clutha, which is the river that once flowed freely through the Cromwell Gorge and is the longest in the South Island. Amidst Clyde's very pleasant aesthetics are a number of historic old buildings including the Town Hall (1868), various pioneer cottages and a handful of its once 70 hotels. The Old Courthouse on Blyth Street is another fine example that was built in 1864.

Cromwell

At the head of Lake Dunstan, 23 km to the north of Clyde, is the tidy – and fruity – little town of Cromwell. Cromwell is faced with five very large dilemmas. The first four are a pear, an apple, a nectarine and a delightfully pert pink bottom (which we can only presume is an apricot) and the fifth is the town's proximity to Queenstown. It is the latter of course with which it struggles the most. Just how do you stop any tourist so intent on reaching perhaps the busiest tourist town in the country? Well, it seems some bright spark (there is always one) thought a sculpture of four man-eating pieces of fruit and celebrating the regions fruit-growing prowess (or indeed just a large and lovely pink bum) might be a great idea? Does it work? You decide.

Anyway, behemoth fruit aside, the former gold town, Cromwell, was originally called 'The Junction' due to its position at the confluence of the **Clutha** and **Kawarau rivers**. These important bodies of water form an integral part of the South Island's hydropower scheme. The museum attached to the i-SITE visitors' centre focuses on the early history and building of the Clyde Dam and is worth a look. The decision to build the dam in the 1980s, using Cromwell as the accommodation base, brought many changes to the town and gave rise to a mix of old-world charm and modern, tidy aesthetics. The main attraction in the town itself is the **Old Cromwell Town Precinct** at the end of Melmore Terrace and at the point where the two rivers merge. Several former buildings have been restored and now house local cafés and craft shops 1000-1630, free.

The **Goldfields Mining Centre** (SH6 west, 6 km towards Queenstown T03-4451038, goldfieldsmining.co.nz, daily 0900-1700, $20, child $10) provides the opportunity to join a guided tour of historic gold workings, a Chinese settlers' village, gold stamper batteries and a sluice gun. You can also pan for gold, go horse trekking or jet boating.

As well as its many orchards, the immediate area is also home to a number of **vineyards**, particularly around the pretty village of **Bannockburn** just to the south of Cromwell. It's a fine spot for lunch and the i-SITE visitor centre has full listings.

Queenstown & around

Oh dear…I know, I know. Your heart is in Queenstown, but your head is in your hands scanning the credit card bill a month later. Ladies and gentlemen, fasten your seat belts and welcome to Queenstown – Adrenalin Central, Thrillsville, New Zealand – the adventure capital of the world. You are perhaps studying this guide in your hotel or motor home with a pained expression trying to decide which of the 150-odd activities to try and, more importantly, how your wallet can possibly cope? But first things first: look out of the window. Where else in the world do you have such accessible scenery? And all that is free.

Queenstown has come a long way since gold secured its destiny in the 1860s. It is now the biggest tourist draw in New Zealand and considered one of the top (and almost certainly the most scenic) adventure venues in the world. It simply has so much to offer. Amidst the stunning setting of mountain and lake, over one million visitors a year partake in a staggering range of activities from a sedate steamboat cruise to the heart-stopping bungee jump. You can do almost anything here, from a gentle round of golf to paddling down a river in what looks like a blow-up carrot. Add to that a superb range of accommodation, services, restaurants and cafés and you simply won't know where to turn. And it goes on year-round, day and night. In winter the hiking boots are simply replaced by skis, the T-shirt with a jumper and, after sunset, the activity guide with the wine glass, knife and fork. It just goes on and on.

So, where to start? No doubt time is short, but regardless don't make your visit an exercise in indecision and stress. Queenstown is a graveyard for the indecisive and the impulsive. Once familiar with what is on offer (from the unbiased i-SITE visitor centre) do the deciding over a lunch, dinner or evening drinks. Meantime, there are a few sights on offer to get a better feel for the place.

Perhaps the best place to start is the **Skyline Gondola** (Brecon St, T03-4410101, skyline.co.nz, 0900-dusk, gondola $22, child $10) that delivers you to the Skyline Complex 450 m above the town on Bob's Peak. It boasts a world-class view and has a host of activities including The Ledge Bungy, The Luge, The Sky-Swing, paragliding and helicopter flight-seeing. The Kiwi Haka Maori performance is also based at Skyline with 30-minute shows nightly from $53 (includes gondola) and the option of an all-inclusive dinner (including show and gondola) from $104. Other on-site amenities include shops, a café (0930-2100) and a restaurant (see page 287). A good time to go up is just before sunset when the golden rays slowly creep up the **Remarkables range** and the town's lights come on.

Back down to earth and at the base of the gondola you might like to see the obligatory kiwi and friends in the **Kiwi Birdlife Park** (Brecon St, T03-4428059, kiwibird.co.nz, daily summer 0900-1800, winter 0900-1700, $35, child $15). Set in 8 ha of pine forest it displays all the usual suspects, including kiwi, owls, parakeets, tui and kea.

The waterfront is always a great buzz of activity. It hosts several lake-based activities including jet boating and fishing but the major draw is the iconic and delightful **TSS Earnslaw** (TSS stands for Two Screw Steamer). Named after the highest peak in the region, Mt Earnslaw (2819 m), she was launched at the most southerly end of **Lake Wakatipu**, Kingston, in 1912 and burns 1 ton of coal per hour. Despite her propensity to belch half of New Zealand's 'Kyoto-nasty smoke quota' into the air she is a lovely sight indeed and there are a number of cruising options available (see page 291).

Essentials

➲ **Getting there** See page 295 for transport details.
⑤ **ATMs** Represented along Camp St.
⊕ **Hospital** Douglas St, Frankton, T03-442 3053; Queenstown Medical Centre, 9 Isle St, Queenstown, T03-441 0500.
↻ **Post office** 13 Camp St, T03-442 7670, Mon-Fri 0830-1730, Sat/Sun 0900-1600.
❶ **Tourist information** Queenstown Travel and i-SITE visitor centre below the Clock Tower, corner of Shotover and Camp streets, T0800-668 888, T03-442 4100, queenstown-vacation.com and queenstown-nz.co.nz, open 0700-1900 (winter 1800).
    DoC 37 Shotover St, T03-4427935, doc.govt.nz is next to the **Information and Track Centre**, 37 Shotover St, T03-442 9708, infotrack.co.nz, daily 0830-1900, winter Mon-Fri 0900-1700, Sat-Sun 0930-1630 which provides up-to-date information on local walks and major tramps, and deals with transportation and hut bookings. It also offers gear hire and has the latest weather forecasts. For activity listings, see page 289.

Opposite the Steamer Wharf the **Queenstown Gardens** are well worth a visit and offer some respite from the crowds. There are oaks, some stunning sequoias and 1500 roses planted in 26 named rose beds.

Around the region

With time usually so short the vast majority of visitors to Queenstown settle for the almost omnipresent and stunning aesthetics on offer from the town itself or en route to the activities, but if you have a day or two to spare – and preferably your own transport – it is well worth exploring beyond its own much-hyped magnetism.

To the north, at the head of Lake Wakatipu, the small and far less developed settlement of Glenorchy (47 km) is the gateway to some of the country's most impressive scenery and several of its best tramping tracks, including the Routeburn, the Greenstone, Caples and Rees-Dart. But without even needing to don boots and gaiters you can explore the immediate area or partake in several activities including jet-boat trips, canoeing or horse trekking (see pages 291-293). The Dart River Basin reached almost legendary status when it was used as a set for the Lord of the Rings trilogy, but you don't need to know your Orcs from your Nazguls to appreciate its innate natural beauty, nor muse upon the small settlement of Paradise to agree that it was indeed aptly named.

Of a more historic bent is the small former gold rush settlement of Arrowtown, which sits tucked away in the corner of the Wakatipu Basin, 23 km south of Queenstown. It has a fascinating history that is now well presented in the village museum and complemented nicely with a main street that looks almost like a Hollywood film set. The origins of Arrowtown go back to 1862 when prospector William Fox made the first rich strike in the Arrow River Valley – a find that soon brought over 7000 other hopefuls to the area. The first few weeks of mining produced 90 kg alone. But history and aesthetics aside, behind the old doors and down the alley ways you will find a surprising number of fine shops, cafés, restaurants and pubs in which you can let the infectious and exhausting mania of Queenstown quietly subside.

Queenstown for free

The following are some great activities in and around Queenstown that won't cost more than a coffee and a few litres of petrol.

Even if the closest you want to come to bungee jumping is the elastic in your own underwear then you can still derive terrific entertainment from simply spectating. The best place to do that is at the original bungee site 23 km south of the town at the Kawarau Suspension Bridge run by the ubiquitous AJ Hackett Bungy Company. The multi-million dollar centre is testament to the commercial success of the concept in the last 20 years.

Feeling fit? You can walk (one hour one way) up to the Skyline Complex via the Ben Lomond Track, which starts on Lomond Crescent (via Brunswick Street off the Lake Esplanade). The summit (1748 m) ascent is a seven-hour return hike.

Take a drive to the Coronet Peak ski-field (18 km). The views are spectacular and you can watch the hangliders launch themselves in to the air. The short diversion to look down the barrel of the Shotover Valley (Skippers Road) is also worth it, but unless you have a 4WD vehicle don't go any further. On the way back, just beyond the Shotover Bridge, take a right and follow the road to the rivers edge. From there walk upstream to the waterfall and gorge lookout. The Shotover Jet comes up to the falls and they are also the last feature on many of the rafting runs. Don't stand too close to the river's edge – the jet boat drivers just love soaking unsuspecting spectators, especially with expensive camera gear.

Wanaka

Wanaka is almost unfeasibly pleasant and has to rank as one of the most desirable places in New Zealand. With the lake of the same name lapping rhythmically at its heels and its picture-postcard mountain backdrops – bordering as it does the Mount Aspiring National Park – it is easy to understand why Wanaka is such a superb place to visit, or indeed live. In recent years Wanaka has seen a boom in both real estate sales and tourism, but it is reassuring that its manic neighbour, Queenstown, will always keep growth in check. But for a while at least, Wanaka is just perfect: not too busy, not too quiet; developed but not spoilt, and a place for all

The Rob Roy glacier walk

If you haven't time or the energy for any of the major tramps, there is one day-walk in the Mount Aspiring National Park that is accessible from Wanaka and quite simply a 'must do'. From Wanaka drive (or arrange transportation) to the Raspberry Creek Car Park in the West Matukituki Valley (one hour). From there follow the river, west to the footbridge over the river and up in to the Rob Roy Valley. From here the track gradually climbs, following the chaotic Rob Roy River, through beautiful rainforest, revealing the odd view of the glacier above. After about 1½ hours you will reach the tree line and enter a superb hidden valley rimmed with solid rock walls of waterfall and ice. It is simply stunning and well deserving of the label 'The Jewel of the Park'. Keep your eyes, your ears open for kea, though they may find you before you find them. After some thorough investigation of the area, you can then retrace your steps back down the valley to the Matukituki River and the car park (five hours return). Alpine Coachlines can shuttle you to Raspberry Creek for a rather pricey $70 return, T03-443 7966, alpinecoachlines.co.nz. Departs 0915 and 1400 returning 1045 and 1530.

to enjoy. Although now you would never guess it, Wanaka's history goes back to the 1860s when it played an important role as a service centre for the region's itinerant gold miners. Today, its principal resources are activities and its miners are tourists. Year-round, there is a multitude of things to do from watersports and tramping in summer to skiing in winter. But it can also be the perfect place to relax and recharge your batteries beside the lake.

Wanaka town centre borders the very pretty **Lake Wanaka**. The aesthetics are awesome and the waters are also a prime attraction for boaties, water-skiers, kayakers and windsurfers. On the way into town you cannot fail to miss New Zealand's 'Leaning Tower of Wanaka', the centerpiece of **Stuart Landsborough's Puzzling World** (T03-443 7489, puzzlingworld.com, 0830-1730, $10, child $7, shop and café). This is a madcap and puzzling conglomerate of mazes, illusions and holograms that is worth a muse. The toilets and 'Hall of Following Faces' are particularly engaging.

Some 8 km east on SH6, surrounding Wanaka airfield, are a couple of interesting museums. The **New Zealand Fighter Pilots Museum** (T03-4437010, nzfpm.co.nz, daily 0900-1600, $10, child $5) honours the lives (and deaths) of New Zealand fighter pilots and provides an insight into general aviation history. Around the museum you might like to sit and watch terrified faces turn to ecstatic ones at the base of Skydive Wanaka (see page 294).

Wanaka i-SITE visitor centre is in the Log Cabin on the lakefront (100 Ardmore St, T03-443 1233, lakewanaka.co.nz, daily 0830-1830, winter 0930-1630).

Mount Aspiring National Park

Like most of New Zealand's majestic national parks, Mount Aspiring has an impressive list of vital statistics. First designated in 1964 the park has been extended to now cover 3500 sq km, making it New Zealand's third largest. It contains five peaks over 2600 m, including Aspiring itself – at 3027 m, the highest outside the Mount Cook range. It contains over 100 glaciers and enjoys an annual rainfall of between 1-6 m a year. It is home to some unique wildlife like the New Zealand falcon, the kea and the giant weta. It is part of a World Heritage Area of international significance – the list just goes on. But, it is not figures that best describe this park. It is without doubt the names, words and phrases associated with it. How about Mount Awful, Mount Dreadful, or Mount Dispute? Mount Chaos perhaps? Then there is the Valley of Darkness, Solitude Creek and the Siberia River. How about the Pope's Nose or the mind boggling Power Knob? This is a wilderness worthy of investigation and well beyond mere imagination; a park of stunning and remote beauty. Enough said. Get in there and enjoy, but go prepared.

The **DoC Mount Aspiring National Park visitor centre**, Upper Ardmore Street at the junction with McPherson Street, deals with all national park/ tramping hut bookings and local walks information. An up-to-date weather forecast is also available, T03-443 7660, doc.govt.nz, daily 0830-1630.

Southland

Fiordland, New Zealand's largest national park, has a moody magnificence, with its high mountains, forested hills and deep inlets such as Doubtful Sound and Milford Sound. The latter is the most accessible of the park's 14 fiords and one of the country's biggest visitor attractions. Further east, in contrast, is one of New Zealand's most prosperous dairy regions, which is also famous for its fishing.

Purakaunui Falls, Catlins Coast.

Tunnel vision

Begun in 1935 and completed in 1953, The Homer Tunnel is a remarkable feat of engineering and a monument to human endeavour. It provides the essential link between Milford Sound and the outside world. When you first encounter the entrance to the Homer at the base of what can only be described as a massive face of granite, the word 'drain' springs to mind. To travel through it fully clothed and in the comfort of a vehicle evokes enough horror but running through it in the dark? Naked?

Ol'Homey has become the venue for perhaps New Zealand's most unusual annual events – known in these parts (no pun intended) as the 'Great Annual Nude Tunnel Run'. The race was originally conceived in 2000 and now attracts over 50 participants (including yours truly). Competitors run completely naked from east to west (as distance of 1.2 km) carrying little except a torch.

The fastest male and female runners have their names engraved on the trophy, which for men is Ken doll and for women a Barbie (naked and in a running position, naturally)!

Te Anau

Te Anau sits on the shores of New Zealand's second largest lake (of the same name) and at the edge of the magnificent wilderness of the Fiordland National Park. Serving as the parks pretty little gatekeeper – and in particular the legendary State Highway 94 (SH94) to Milford Sound – poor Te Anau suffers a bit from seasonal 'affected' disorder. In summer it's utterly manic and it's not hard to understand why. With up to 70 coaches a day passing through en route to Milford Sound that's one mighty big toilet stop. But that's not all. Added to that are the plentiful perambulations of the species *Copious beardicus* – or 'trampers'. You see Te Anau is also considered by many as the walking (or tramping) capital of the world. Within a 100-km radius you have access to literally thousands of kilometres of world-class tramping tracks with such legendary names as The Kepler, Routeburn and the Milford (itself once declared by National Geographic as the best multi-day walk in the world).

But then, come autumn, for little Te Anau the proverbial golden leaf falls from the tourism tree. With the absence of a ski field to woo winter visitors the town is like an unused holiday house, with only its caretaker, waiting and wanting to turn the heating on again. It can be quite depressing and try getting a pint of milk at ten at night!

So whether you are wedged between a convoy of tour buses, are wondering if the lights are on but nobody's home, or indeed have a copious beard, give Te Anau a break literally. It can initially seem a rather dull little town, but once you acquaint yourself with its tidy centre, spacious open areas and beautiful lake views (and yes, its spiffy new supermarket) your desire to move on quite so hastily will fade.

For detailed regional information contact the **Fiordland i-SITE visitor centre** (Lakefront Drive, T03-2498900, fiordland.org.nz daily 0830-1800, winter 0830-1700). It deals with all local information and serves as the agents for domestic air and bus bookings. Real Journeys is the largest of the regional operators and they have an office downstairs from the i-SITE (open daily summer 0830-2100). It deals with its own considerable scope of transport, sights and activity bookings including local sightseeing trips on Lake Te Anau (including the Te Anau Caves) and to Milford and Doubtful Sounds.

Tip...

While you are in Te Anau do not miss the short 35-minute film *Ata Whenua* or *Shadowland*, a stunning visual exploration of the Fiordland National Park screened regularly at the contemporary Fiordland Cinema, The Lane, T03- 249 8812, fiordlandcinema. co.nz, daily 1300 and 1730, from $10.

Fields of lupins (considered a pest species) near Lake Te Anau.

It's a fact...

At 56 km long, 10 km across at its widest point, and covering an area of 352 sq km, Lake Te Anau is the largest of New Zealand's southern glacial lakes. Although a matter of contention it is thought the name Te Anau is a shortened form of Te Ana-au which means the cave of the swirling water current. (There are caves so named on the western shore).

The DoC Fiordland National Park visitor centre at the southern end of lakefront (T03-2498514, doc.govt.nz, daily 0830-1800, seasonal). is the principal source for information, track bookings office and up-to-date weather forecasts. There is also a small museum and audio-visual theatre ($3).

SH94 The Road to Milford

The 117-km trip into the heart of the Fiordland National Park and Milford Sound via SH94 from Te Anau is all part of the world-class Milford Sound experience. In essence it is a bit like walking down the aisle, past the interior walls of a great cathedral, to stand in awe at the chancel and the stunning stained-glass windows above. This may sound like an exaggeration but if nature is your religion, then the trip to Milford is really nothing short of divine. Of course much depends on the weather. Ideally it should be of either extreme – cloudless, or absolutely thumping it down. Under clear blue skies it is of course magnificent, but many say that the trip through the mountains is better during very heavy rain. It is an incredibly moody place, so don't be put off by foul weather.

From Te Anau you skirt the shores and enjoy the congenial scenery of **Lake Te Anau** before heading inland at **Te Anau Downs** (30 mins). This is principally a boat access point to the Milford Track. Another 30 minutes will see you through some low-lying alluvial flats and meadows as the Earl Mountains begin to loom large. In late December the valley is a flood of colourful lupins that may look spectacular but are non-native and considered a rapacious and troublesome weed within the park.

After penetrating some beech forest and entering the park proper you suddenly emerge into the expanse of the **Eglinton River Valley** with its stunning views towards the mountains. This is known as the 'Avenue of the Disappearing Mountain' and it speaks for itself.

At the northern end of the valley you then re-enter the shade of the beech forests and encounter **Mirror Lake** a small body of water overlooked by the **Earl Mountain Range**. The lookout point is a short walk from the road. On a clear day you can, as the name suggests, capture the mood and the scene twice in the same shot.

Several kilometres further on is **Knobs Flat** where there is a DoC shelter and information/display centre and toilet facilities. For much of the next 30 minutes you negotiate the dappled shadows on a near constant tunnel of beautiful beech forest before reaching **Lake Gunn**, which offers some fine fishing and a very pleasant 45-minutes nature walk through the forest. The copious growth of mosses and lichens here provide the rather unsubtle hint that the place can get very wet, very often!

From Lake Gunn you are really beginning to enter 'tiger country' as the road climbs to **The Divide,** one of the lowest passes along the length of the Southern Alps. Here a shelter and an assortment of discarded boots marks the start of the Routeburn and Greenstone/Caples Tracks. The car park also serves as the starting point to a classic, recommended (3-hrs return) walk to **Key Summit,** which looks over the Humboldt and Darran Ranges. Round the corner there is the Falls Creek (Pop's View) Lookout, which looks down the **Hollyford Valley**. Depending on the weather this will be a scene of fairly quiet serenity or one of near epic proportions as the swollen **Hollyford River** rips its way down to the valley fed by a million fingers of whitewater.

Following the river north is the Lower Hollyford Road and access to Lake Marian (1 km), a superb (3-hrs return) walk up through forest and past waterfalls into a glacial hanging valley that holds the lake captive. A further 7 km on is the charming

Fiordland National Park

Fiordland National Park is 1.25 million ha and the largest of New Zealand's 14 national parks. It is 10% of the country, twice the size of Singapore and plays host to 0.06% of the population. In 1986 it was declared a World Heritage Area on account of its outstanding natural features, exceptional beauty and its important demonstration of the world's evolutionary history. Four years later, in 1990, Fiordland National Park was further linked with three others –Mount Aspiring, Westland and Mount Cook (Aoraki) to form the World Heritage Area of South West New Zealand. It was given the Maori name Te Waipounamu (Te 'the'/ Wai 'waters'/ Pounamu 'greenstone' or 'jade'). Hopefully we can rest assured that with such official labels and protection it will remain the stunning wilderness it is.

Hollyford (Gun's) Camp, and the Hollyford Airfield, important access and accommodation points for the Hollyford Track, the trailhead for which is at the road terminus 6 km further on. The short 30-minute return walk to the **Humboldt Falls**, which again are spectacular after heavy rain, starts just before the car park.

Back on the main Milford Road the mountains begin to close in on both sides as you make the ascent up the Hollyford Valley to the 1200 m **Homer Tunnel**, an incredible feat of engineering, and a bizarre and exciting experience, like being swallowed by a giant drain.

At the entrance keep your eyes open for **kea** (native mountain parrots) that frequent the main stopping areas at either end of the tunnel. If they are not there, it is worth stopping a while to see if they turn up. Watching these incredibly intelligent avian delinquents go about their business of creating general mayhem in the name of food and sheer vandalism is highly entertaining. There will be plenty of photo opportunities and despite the obvious temptation DO NOT feed them. A parrot fed on white bread, crisps and chocolate is, obviously, a very sick parrot.

Once out of the tunnel you are now in the spectacular **Cleddau Canyon** and nearing Milford

Claddau Gorge, SH94 Milford Road, Fiordland National Park.

Sound. Instantly you will see the incredibly precipitous aspect of the mountains and bare valley walls. The rainfall is so high and rock and mudslides so frequent that the vegetation has little chance to establish itself. As a result the rainwater just cascades rapidly into the valleys. Note the creeks that cross under the road. There are so many they don't have names, but numbers. These all count up steadily to form the **Cleddau River**, which, at **The Chasm** (20-mins return), is really more waterfall than river, and has, over the millennia, sculpted round shapes and basins in the rock. From The Chasm it is five minutes before you see the tip of the altar of **Mitre Peak** (1692 m) and spire of **Mount Tutoko** (2746 m), Fiordland's highest peak. It's now only five minutes before your appointment with the Minister of Awe at the Chancel of **Milford Sound**.

Lake Manapouri

Driving into the small village of Manapouri 20 km south of Te Anau you are – depending on the weather – immediately met with stunning vistas across the eponymous lake. If it were anywhere else in the developed world, it would probably be an unsightly mass of exclusive real estate and tourist developments, but remarkably it isn't and instead seems quietly content to serve merely as an access point and see visitors off across the lake en-route to Doubtful Sound. There are 35 islands that disguise the boundaries of Lake Manapouri and at a forbidding 420 m it is mighty deep.

At the terminus of West Arm, and forming the main access point via Wilmot Pass to Doubtful Sound, is the **Manapouri Underground Power Station**. Started under a cloud of controversy in 1963 and completed eight years later it is the country's largest hydroelectric power station supplying 10% of the country's needs. A 2040 m (1:10) tunnel set in the hillside allows access to the main centre of operations – a large machine hall housing seven turbines and generators, fed by the water penstocks from 170 m above. What is most impressive is the 9.2-m diameter tailrace tunnel, which outputs the used water at the head of Doubtful Sound – an amazing 10 km from Lake Manapouri and 178 m below its surface. The power station can be visited as part of the Doubtful Sound package (see page 295).

Doubtful Sound

Doubt nothing, this fiord, like Milford Sound, is all it is cracked up to be – and more. Many who have made the trip to Milford feel it may be very similar and therefore not worthy of the time or expense to get there. But Doubtful Sound has a different atmosphere to Milford. With the mountain topography in Fiordland getting lower the further south you go, and the fiords becoming longer and more indented with coves, arms and islands, Doubtful Sound offers the sense of space and wilderness that Milford does not. Doubtful is, after Dusky, the second largest fiord and has 10 times the surface area of Milford and, at 40 km, is also more than twice as long. It is also the deepest of the fiords at 421 m. There are three arms and several waterfalls including the heady 619-m Browne Falls. Doubtful Sound hosts its own pod of about 60 bottlenose dolphins that are regularly seen by visitors as well as fur seals and fiordland crested penguins. It is also noted for its lack of activity. Captain Cook originally named it Doubtful Harbour during his voyage of 1770. He decided not to explore past the entrance, fearful that the prevailing winds would not allow him to get back out; hence the name. Doubtful Sound is accessed via Manapouri. For tour operators contact the i-SITE visitor centre and see page 295.

Tip...

Many say Doubtful Sound is the best sea kayaking venue in New Zealand with the added attraction of its resident pod of dolphin.

The Southern Scenic Route

The Southern Scenic Route is a tourist-designated route that roughly encompasses the journey from Te Ana south and east to Invercargill and then north via the Catlins Coast to Dunedin. Beyond Lake Manapouri and Doubtful Sound, the highlights of this trip are the undeveloped windswept villages of the south coast, the small seaside resort of Riverton, Southland's stoic and much-maligned capital Invercargill, a certain signpost in Bluff, Stewart Island and the scenic splendour and wildlife of the Catlins Coast.

Manapouri to Invercargill

Still reeling from the highs of Fiordland's stunning scenery, your journey south could include the main drag of Vegas and still seem boring, so just accept that fact and sit back and enjoy the peace and quiet of the road. SH99 has to be one of the quietest main roads in the country and between Manapouri and Riverton it's unusual to pass more than half a dozen cars even in summer. Generally speaking you will encounter very little with two legs. Instead what you will see is paddock upon paddock of sheep.

Tuatapere 80 km south of Manapouri is considered the gateway to the southeast corner of the Fiordland National Park (not that there are any roads) and in particular the 53-km Hump Ridge Track (31 Orawia Rd, T03-2266739, humpridgetrack. co.nz, daily 0900-1700, winter Mon-Fri 0900-1700), New Zealand's newest 'Great Walk'. On the first section of the Hump Ridge Track is the 36-m-high, 125-m-long Percy Burn Viaduct the largest wooden viaduct in the world. As well as that the former saw-milling and farming town and (mysteriously) self-proclaimed 'sausage capital' of the country has a few other notable local attractions, including some fine jet-boating operations up the Wairaurahiri River and Lake Hauroko, boasting the steepest lake-to-coast river fall in the country (W Jet, Clifden, T03-2255677, T0800-376174, wjet.co.nz).

A further 10 km south and SH99 reaches the coast at the evocatively named Te Waewae Bay then passes the windswept and tired looking

Around the region

Wind shorn trees along the coast, Southern Scenic Route.

village of **Orepuki**, before reaching Riverton.
Riverton – or Aparima, to use its former Maori name – is the oldest permanent European settlement in Southland and one of the oldest in the country. Located on the banks of the common estuary formed by the Aparima and Purakino rivers, it was formerly a safe haven for whalers and sealers and was first established as early as the 1830s. Now having gradually developed into a popular coastal holiday resort, Riverton is a fine place to stop for lunch, a short walk on the beach, or even to consider as a quieter alternative base to Invercargill, only 42 km to the east.

Invercargill

The Invercargill i-SITE visitors centre is housed in the Southland Museum and Gallery Building, Victoria Av, T03-214 6243, southlandnz.com.
Daily Oct-Apr 0900-1900, May-Sep 0900-1700.

When it comes to aesthetics a lot has been said about Invercargill over the years and sadly (and undeservingly) much of it has been negative. Invercargill is not pretty. Let's be honest. Stuck at the very rear end of New Zealand and sandblasted by the worst extremes of the southern weather, even its climate and geography are against it. This is nothing new or unusual, after all Scotland (to which Invercargill and the region as a whole is so closely linked) is an entire country that suffers the same affliction. But for Invercargill there is one added problem. For most tourists the city features late on the travel schedule and by the time they get here they are almost drunk on stunning world-class scenery. No remedy there of course, it's an inevitable 'coming back down to earth', but were it not for the geography and the climate one cannot help but wonder if the problem could all be addressed with one weekend of frenzied mass tree-planting.

However, that said, Invercargill has many good points, and although you will hear different, it is certainly not the underdog it is reputed to be. For a start, it is the capital of the richest agricultural region in the South Island and serves admirably as the commercial hub of the region. Its people are also very friendly, welcoming and are the first to admit they have ten times the sense of humour of any North Islander.

Invercargill is a fine base from which to explore the delights of Southland and the Southern Scenic Route. Within a two-hour radius are a wealth of internationally acclaimed experiences of which Stewart Island, the Catlins Coast and southern Fiordland are the most obvious and the most lauded. So, by all means linger for a while – you won't regret it – and before you leave (while no one is looking) plant a tree!

The main highlight in the town is the excellent **Southland Museum and Art Gallery** (edge of Queen's Park, Victoria Av, T03-2199069, southlandmuseum.co.nz, Mon-Fri 0830-1700 Sat-Sun 1000-1700, donation). It showcases all the usual fine Maori taonga and early settler exhibits and national and international art exhibitions, but is particularly noted for its Roaring Forties Antarctic and Sub-Antarctic Island display and audio-visual (25 mins, $2) shown several times daily. Also excellent is the museum's tuatara display and breeding programme. The **Tuatarium** is an utter delight and an opportunity to come face to face with a reptilian species older than the land on which you stand. **Henry**, the oldest resident at an estimated 110 years plus, usually sits only a foot or two away from the glass. You can try to stare the old fella out, but you will fail, because Henry has had plenty of practice.

There are some good walking options around the city including those around Bluff or the huge 30-km expanse of **Oreti Beach** 10 km west of the city (past the airport). It has the added attraction of allowing vehicles (with sensible drivers) on the sand and safe swimming.

Bluff

Some 27 km south of Invercargill, the small port of Bluff heralds the end of the road in the South Island. Most visitors to Bluff are either on their way or returning from Stewart Island, or come to stand and gawk at a wind-blasted signpost at the terminus of SH1, which tells them they are several thousand miles from anywhere: next stop Antarctica.

The town itself is as strange as it is intriguing. As a result of a dying oyster-fishing industry and protracted general social decline, there is a very palpable sense of decay in Bluff. While the vast majority of New Zealand's other towns progress and grow at a healthy pace, here, it is as if the clocks have stopped and no-one's home. However, human creations aside, on the southern side of the peninsula the coastal scenery is stunning. There is no shortage of wind down here and the entire

peninsula is sculpted accordingly. Bare boulder-clad hills shrouded in part with stunted wind-shorn bush and, on its leeward side, a surprisingly tall stand of native trees creates a fascinating mix of habitats. All well worth investigating along a network of fine **walking tracks**. The walks can be accessed from **Stirling Point** (road terminus) and you can climb to the top of **Bluff Hill** (Motupohue) at 270 m. From there you will be rewarded with fine panoramic views of the region and Stewart Island. The summit can also be reached by car from the centre of town (signposted).

It's a fact...

Bluff is not in fact the southernmost point on mainland New Zealand. That accolade goes to Slope Point in the Catlins, about 70 km east of the town.

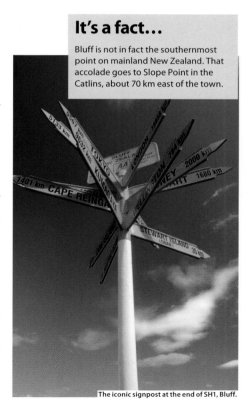

The iconic signpost at the end of SH1, Bluff.

Around the region

Stewart Island (Rakiura National Park)

Lying 20 km southwest off Bluff, across the antsy waters of Foveaux Strait, is the 'land of the glowing skies' (Rakiura) or Stewart Island. Often called New Zealand's third island (making up 10% of its total area), Stewart Island was described over a century ago by pioneer botanist Leo Cockayne, as 'having a superabundance of superlatives'. There is much truth in that. It can be considered one of the country's most unspoilt and ecologically important areas. Such are its treasures that only the country's national parks can compare, which is why it was only a matter of time before it entered the fold in 2001, with 85% of the island now enjoying the limelight as the newest of New Zealand's 14 national parks.

The island is home to many threatened plant and animal species, some of which are endemic or occur only on the island. Although fighting to survive the ravages of introduced vermin, its impressive bird breeding list alone includes two of the rarest in the world: a flightless parrot called a kakapo (of which only about 80 remain) and perhaps most famous of all the Stewart Island brown kiwi, the largest and only diurnal kiwi in New Zealand.

The pleasant little village of **Oban** on Halfmoon Bay is the island's main settlement. It is connected to several smaller settlements including Golden Bay, Horseshoe Bay, Leask Bay and Butterfield Bay, by about 28 km of mainly sealed road. The rest of the island is remote, largely uninhabited and only accessible by boat.

Other than to see kiwi (which are usually only seen in remote areas), tours of the nature reserve of **Ulva Island**, boat trips, kayaking and diving, people visit Stewart Island for two main reasons: either to bask in its tranquility and do very little in Oban; or attempt one of its challenging, very long and at times very wet tramping tracks.

Catlins Coast

If you like remote and scenic coastlines you are going to love the Catlins; the added bonus here is their location. Like the Wairarapa in the southwest of the North Island, the area is generally off the beaten track and certainly underrated. You can negotiate the Catlins from the north or the south via the publicized Southern Scenic Route, encompassing a 187-km network of minor now fully sealed roads. The journey between Invercargill and Dunedin (or in reverse) is often attempted in one day, which is definitely a mistake. A more thorough, comfortable and less frustrating investigation will take at least two days, preferably three. But, if you can really only afford one day, the highlights not to be missed are: from the north, **Nugget Point** (for sunrise); the opportunity to see **Hookers sea lions** at **Cannibals Bay** (morning); the

Purakaunui Falls and **Purakaunui Bay** (for lunch); then **McLean Falls**, **Curio Bay** and **Slope Point** in the afternoon.

The Catlins is noted for its rich wildlife and vegetation. Of particular note are the pinnipeds, or seals. The Catlins is the only mainland region where you can observe New Zealand fur seals, Hookers sea lions and Southern elephant seals in the same location. The region is also within the very limited breeding range of the rarest penguin on the planet – the **yellow-eyed penguin** (hoiho) – and the rare and tiny **Hector's dolphin**. Incredibly, with a little luck, all these species can be observed quite easily, independently and at relatively close range. The tracts of dense coastal forest that still remain are made up predominantly of podocarp and silver beech (but Curio Bay is home to a scattering of petrified fossil trees that are over 180 million years old) and are home to native birds like native pigeon (kereru) and morepork (a small owl). The forests also hide a number of attractive waterfalls.

From north to south the main centres for services and accommodation are Kaka Point, Owaka and Papatowai.

The i-SITE visitors centre in Invercargill and Gore can also supply information about the Catlins. The free The Catlins booklet and the websites catlins-nz.com and catlins.org.nz are both useful. **Owaka i-SITE visitor centre** and Museum (10 Campbell St, Owaka, T03-4158371, catlins-nz.com, open Mon-Fri 0930-1300 and 1400-1600, Sat/Sun 1000-1300 and 1400-1600).

Best photo locations

❶ Queenstown
Page 269

Good views are everywhere in and around Queenstown, but a few locations stand out in particular. The Skyline Gondola is an obvious draw, especially at dusk when the sun lights up the Remarkables range. Hang around after sunset too just as the lights of the town create their own impact.

Another beautiful and easily accessible spot is the view north across Lake Wakatipu to the Humboldt Range and Mount Earnslaw. The viewpoint is about 6 km after the Glenorchy road takes a dogleg turn north beside the lake. Dawn or dusk is best in calm conditions.

Far less accessible, with a steep rugged drive and a fair scramble (in summer) to get there, is the view of Lake Wakatipu and Queenstown from the Remarkables range. Before considering this trip make sure the weather is clear and settled, since you will be more than 2000 m above sea level. The ski field road is accessed off SH6 about 2 km south of Frankton. If the ski field is open you might consider taking a shuttle from Queenstown, T03-442 6534. From the Remarkables ski field buildings you are basically trying to reach the top of the Shadow Basin Chair Lift, the base of which is in the main car park. If the lift is open you have the option of using it, but in summer (or if you fancy the climb) then follow the path that zigzags up the slopes behind the main building to the Mid-Station. From the Mid-Station continue on the path in a rough line with the chairlift until you reach its terminus. The lookout is about 200 m directly behind and further up from this point. On a clear day surrounded by snow, you won't forget it!

Take a polarizer and you need another person for a sense of scale.

There are obviously many opportunities for 'action' shots in and around Queenstown. One of the best and most iconic is the bungee jumping at Kawarau Bridge (see page 270). Follow the footpath down to the rivers edge and from a low angle get the jumpers after their head dunking, preferably with the water spray (at high shutter speed) highlighted in the sun. Elsewhere, other possibilities include hang-gliding and summer mountain biking at the Coronet Peak ski field. Try slow shutter speeds and silhouettes against the sun.

❶ 📷/⏱/📷/☀/🔄1500

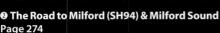

❷ The Road to Milford (SH94) & Milford Sound
Page 274

Quite simply one of the most beautiful and
photogenic places on the planet. The weather is
of course a major factor with the only certainty
being that there is lots of it! Winter is the best
season and dawn or dusk the best time of day,
with clear or – better still – clearing weather.
Reflections are best on a high tide, again at
dawn or dusk. The waterfront is the best hunting
ground, although anywhere along SH94 offers
numerous opportunities. Key Summit and Lake
Marian are also excellent. Be very careful at all
times, especially in winter. Do not go anywhere
far from a track or road alone.

❸ & ❹ Catlins Coast
Page 280

I have been trying to get an exceptional sunrise
at the Nuggets (Nugget Point) for 10 years, but
luck has been elusive. Dawn over-looking the
lighthouse and Nuggets is what you are after
and try to give yourself two or three days in the
area to have a chance. Other excellent locations
and subjects in the Catlins are the Hookers sea
lions at Cannibals Bay and the Purakaunui Falls
(slow exposure shots). Don't go closer than 6 m
from the sea lions and keep your angles low to
accentuate their size.

Sleeping

Corstorphine House $$$$
*23A Milburn St, Corstorphine,
T03-487 1000, corstorphine.co.nz.*
An 1863 Edwardian luxury
private hotel surrounded by 2.8
ha of private gardens and
commanding great views across
the city. The house is beautifully
appointed throughout offering
seven stylish themed suites from
the Scottish or Egyptian to the
art deco room and a restaurant.

Larnach Lodge $$$$-$$$
*145 Camp Rd, Otago Peninsula,
T03-476 1616, larnachcastle.co.nz.*
Accommodation at Larnach
Castle is some of the best in the
region. The lodge offers
beautifully appointed themed
rooms from the Scottish Room
with its tartan attire, to the
Goldrush Room which comes
complete with a king-size 'cart
bed' made out of an original old
cart found on the property. The
views across the harbour and
peninsula from every room are
simply superb. Breakfast is served
in the old stables; dinner is
optional in the salubrious interior
of the castle. Cheaper Stable Stay
rooms with shared bathrooms in
the former coach house are also
available. Book well in advance.

Nisbet Cottage $$$
*6A Eliffe Pl, Sheil Hill (east of the
city centre), T03-4545169,
natureguidesotago.co.nz.*

At the base of the Otago
Peninsula, a short drive to the city
centre. The congenial German
hosts operate Otago Nature
Guides (see Activities and tours,
page 289) and organize an
attractive accommodation/
nature tour package that includes
the peninsula penguin colonies
and albatross centre (two-night
Nature Package from $590 per
person). A choice of two tidy en
suites sleeping two to three, a
guest lounge with open fire.

Motor parks
Leith Valley Touring Park
$$-$
*103 Malvern St (towards the
northern end of town), T03-467
9936/T0800-555331,
leithvalleytouringpark.co.nz.*
An excellent little motor park in a
sheltered setting next to the
Leith Stream and about 2 km
from the city centre. It has
modern motel units, self-
contained cabins, powered/tent
sites, camp kitchen and a huge
cosy guest lounge.

Despite a healthy range of
accommodation and around
9000 beds in Queenstown, it is
essential to book two or three
days in advance in mid-summer
or during the height of the ski
season (especially during the
Winter Festival in mid-July).

Sofitel $$$$-$$$
*8 Duke St, T03-450 0045,
sofitelqueenstown.com.*
One of the most celebrated
hotels sitting in prime position
just above the town centre.
Luxury rooms, suites and
penthouses furnished in
European style and in warm
shades of beige and brown
marry well with the views. The
class extends to the facilities and
the in-house restaurant, but
perhaps, just perhaps, your
abiding memory will be of its
famous 'little' boy's room in the
lobby (go on girls – have a peek!).

Queenstown Lakeview Motor
Park $$$-$$
*Off Brecon St, T03-442 7252,
holiday park.net.nz.*
Although not a motel per say,
the modern units here are often
very good value, especially for
small groups. It is also centrally
located and has facilities on a par
with any standard mid-range
motel.

Queenstown Lodge and
Fernhill Apartments $$$-$$
*Sainsbury Rd (a little further out
at the west end of town), Fernhill,
T03-442 7107/T0800-756343,
queenstown lodge.co.nz.*
Reasonably priced ski lodge-
style property located at the
western fringe of town. It is quiet,
has off-street parking, a pizza
restaurant, spa, sauna and most
of the rooms offer excellent
views across Lake Wakatipu.

The lodge also administers a self-contained apartment complex offering good value one- to three-bedroom options and clients then have full use of lodge facilities.

Kinloch Lodge $$
T03-442 4900,
kinlochlodge.co.nz.
Historic lakeside budget lodge and the perfect base from which to explore the area before (and especially after) tramping the Routeburn or Greenstone tracks. Tidy doubles (the heritage doubles are very small), twins and shared dorms, all the usual facilities as well as a outdoor hot tub, a café/restaurant and a small shop. Road or water taxi transport is available from Glenorchy and local activities arranged. Really well managed and a memorable stay is just about guaranteed.

Queenstown Lakefront YHA $$
80 Lake Esplanade (at the western end of town), T03-4428413, yha.co.nz.
Deservedly popular and the larger of two YHAs in town. Alpine lodge style with a wide range of comfortable shared, twin and double rooms and modern facilities in a quiet location overlooking Lake Wakatipu. Limited off-street parking.

Motor parks
Queenstown Lakeview Motor Park $$$-$
Off Brecon St, T03-4427252, T0800-482735, holidaypark.net.nz.
After a revamp this park has increased in popularity and stature. The complex is the closest park to the town centre (2 mins) and includes tidy and good-value studio units, en suite cabins, luxury flats, as well as the standard powered/ tent sites. There is a spacious kitchen block with internet and lockable food cupboards.

Wanaka
Cardrona Hotel $$$
Crown Range (Cardrona) Rd, 26 km from Wanaka, T03-443 8153, cardronahotel.co.nz.
A little way out but well worth the journey, especially in winter when fires are lit in the gardens from dusk to welcome those coming off the ski field. The 16 comfortable en suite double rooms in the old stables are charming and front a beautiful enclosed garden and courtyard. There is a great rustic restaurant and bar attached and a spa. Bookings are essential.

Motor parks
Aspiring Campervan Park $$
Studholme Rd, T03-443 7766, campervanpark.co.nz.
An entirely different and new concept in motor camps. A Qualmark five-star, it charges well beyond the standard for a powered site, but has all mod cons including a spa (included in tariff) that looks out towards the mountains. Modern lodge, motel and tourist flats are also available.

Southland

Te Anau
Fiordland Lodge $$$$
472 Te Anau-Milford Highway (5 km north of Te Anau), T03-249 7832, fiordlandlodge.co.nz.
A purpose-built luxury lodge, built in the classic lodge style and commanding stunning views across the lake and mountains. Smart en suite guest rooms, two self-contained log cabins, quality restaurant and a large open fire. The high ceilings, full trunk pillars and huge windows add to the appeal. The owners also offer a wide range of guided excursions.

Te Anau Lake View Holiday Park $$$-$
1 Te Anau-Manapouri Highway (overlooking the lake on SH95), T03-249 7457, teanau.info, tracknet.net.
Spacious with a wide range of options from new motel units, to cabins, powered sites and tent sites. Internet café, sauna and spa, Sky TV. The added attraction here, other than the modern facilities is the organization of activities and ease of tramping track transportation in conjunction with the in-house 'Tracknet' company.

Motor parks

Te Anau Top Ten Holiday Park $$$-$

128 Te Anau Terrace, T03-2497462, teanautop10.co.nz.
A multi-award winner and one of the best holiday parks in the country. The facilities are excellent and well maintained. It lives up to its name as having a 'bed for every budget'.

Milford & Doubtful Sounds

Real Journeys $$$

T03-249 7416, T0800-656501, fiordlandtravel.co.nz.
Offers a range of overnight options on Milford and Doubtful Sounds. On Milford there are vessels varying in size and options from multi-share accommodation to cabins. All meals and activities (kayaking) included.

Milford Sound Lodge $$$-$

Just off the Milford Rd about 1 km east of the airfield, T03-249 8071, milfordlodge.com.
For the independent traveller this really is the only place to stay in Milford Sound.

Invercargill

Living Space $$

15 Tay St, T03-211 3800, T0508 454 846, livingspace.net.
Excellent value modern studio rooms and two- to three-bedroom apartments right in the heart of the town. Facilities include a comfy movie theatre, full kitchen facilities and off-street parking.

Motor parks

Invercargill Top 10 Holiday Park $$$-$

77 McIvor Rd (northern edge of Invercargill off SH6), T03-215 9032, T0800 486 873, invercargilltop10.co.nz.
By far the best option in Invercargill. Small, peaceful and friendly.

Stewart Island

Port of Call B&B and Bach $$$

Jensen Bay, T03-219 1394, portofcall.co.nz.
Set in an idyllic spot overlooking the entrance to Halfmoon Bay, cosy and friendly. It offers an en suite double and great breakfasts and views from the deck. There is also a self-contained bach (holiday house) offering plenty of privacy. In-house water taxi and eco-guiding operation, including kiwi-spotting.

South Sea Hotel $$$-$$

Corner of Elgin Terrace and Main Rd, Oban, T03-219 1059, stewart-island.co.nz.
A fine place to stay if you want to mix with the locals and experience Stewart Island life. A mix of traditional hotel rooms (some with sea views) and self-contained motel units on an adjacent property. Obviously there is an in-house bar where all the action (or lack of it) takes place and a restaurant where you can sample the local delicacy – muttonbird.

The Catlins Coast

Nugget Lodge Motels $$$

Only 2 km from Nugget Point and 6 km from Kaka Point, T03-412 8783, nuggetlodge.co.nz.
Two modern self-contained units sleeping three and two in a superb position beside the beach and overlooking the bay.

Papatowai Hilltop Backpackers $$

Papatowai, T03-415 8028, hilltop backpackers.co.nz.
An excellent place offering doubles with a great view (one en suite) and dorm beds. Log fire, modern facilities, hot tub, bikes, canoes, internet and much more.

Motor parks

Kaka Point Motor Park $$-$

On the edge of the town on Tarata St, T03-412 8801, kakapoint@hotmail.com.
Quiet place offering two cabins and sheltered powered/tent sites. Camp kitchen.

Mclean Falls Holiday Park and Motels $$$-$

T03-415 8338, catlinsnz.com.
Modern park at the southern end of the Catlins close to the Mclean Falls offering the full range of accommodation options from self-contained family chalets to rather pricey powered sites. Camp kitchen and restaurant/café on site.

Eating & drinking

Dunedin & Otago Peninsula

Bell Pepper Blues $$$
474 Princes St, T03-474 0973.
Lunch Wed-Fri, dinner Tue-Sat
from 1830.
Internationally recognized Chef
Michael Coughlin has built up
the reputation of this restaurant
as one of Otago's best for almost
two decades. Imaginative,
mainly Pacific Rim cuisine.

Speights Brewery $$$
*200 Rattray St, T03-477 7697,
speights.co.nz.*
Combine a tour of the iconic
Speights Brewery (Otago's most
popular beer) with a meal in the
brewery's own restaurant with
the NZ classics like seafood
chowder, blue cod, lamb shanks,
steak, venison and vegetarian
options, from $56.

Scotia Restaurant and Whiskey Bar $$
*Dunedin Railway Station,
T03-477 770,
scotiadunedin.co.nz.*
Mon-Fri 1100-late, Sat 1500-late.
Fine Scottish-themed restaurant
housed in the historic railway
station. Scots classics like haggis
and black pudding are of course
on offer, yet there are other
tastes to suit everyone, from
venison, smoked beef, steak,
salmon or salads and for sweet
bread and butter pudding. After
dinner sample one or two of the
300-odd whiskies proudly
showcased in the bar.

Queenstown & around

Gantley's $$$
*Arthur's Point Rd, T03-442 8999,
gantleys.co.nz.*
Daily from 1830.
A very romantic affair set in a
historic stone building 7 km out
of town towards Arrowtown.
Award winning, and its wine list,
like its cuisine, is superb.

Skyline Restaurant $$$
*Skyline Gondola Complex,
Brecon St, T03-441 0101,
skyline.co.nz.*
Daily lunch buffet 1200-1400,
dinner from 1800.
Offers a six-course 'Taste of New
Zealand' buffet, which includes
roast meats, seafood, local
produce and salads followed
by dessert and cheeseboard
from $47 (lunch), $72 (dinner).
The views are exceptional,
even at night.

Dux de Lux $$$-$$
14 Church St, T03-4429688.
Daily from 1130.
A nice mix of heritage and
atmosphere, it's another
award-winner with a good
selection of gourmet pizzas,
open fire outside, live bands at
the weekend and, of course,
some fine home-brewed ales.

Joe's Garage $$
*Searle Lane, T03-442 5282,
joes.co.nz.*
The secret hang out for locals
and noted for its great coffee
and light meals.

Minus 5C $$
Steamer Wharf, T03-442 6050.
Daily from 1030.
Sit back with a cocktail in this
beautifully sculpted ice cavern.
Entry costs $30 includes the first
drink and you are of course
kitted out with warm jackets and
gloves. Naturally this is more a
tourist attraction than a
conventional bar; so don't
expect to settle in for a session or
a game of darts.

Wanaka
White House Café and Bar $$$
*Corner of Dunmore and
Dungarvon streets, T03-443 9595.*
Daily from 1100.
Deservedly popular with an
imaginative Mediterranean/
Middle Eastern menu with
vegetarian options. Fine wine list.

Kai Whakapai $$
*Corner Helwick and Ardmore
streets, T03-443 7795.*
Good blackboard fare, coffee
and a great spot to watch the
world go by.

Entertainment

Te Anau
Redcliff Café and Bar $$$-$$
12 Mokonui St, T03-249 7431.
Daily 1800-late.
Small and intimate pub with open fire and restaurant (separate) offering some particularly good lamb and venison dishes.

Milford Sound
Blue Duck Pub and Café $$
Waterfront T03-249 7657.
Summer 0830-1700, bar 1100 till 'close' winter 0900-1630, bar 1630 till close.
This is your only option for eating with a full range of pub-style food from generous breakfasts to toasted sandwiches. There are also lunch options on cruises.

Invercargill
148 On Elles $$$
148 Elles St, T03-216 1000.
Closed Sun.
The city's most intimate fine dining option. An open fire adds to the atmosphere. Try the local seafood, venison or whitebait.

Zookeeper's Café $$
50 Tay St, T03-218 3373.
Daily from 1000-late.
Crowned by its corrugated elephant façade this is the best café in town, with a nice atmosphere, good coffee and good-value evening meals.

Cinemas
Hoyts Cinema
33 Octagon, Dunedin, T03-477 7019, hoyts.co.nz.

Cinemas
Embassy Cinema
11 The Mall, Queenstown, T03-442 9994.

Paradiso Cinema and Café
1 Ardmore St, Wanaka, T03-443 1505, paradiso.net.nz.
Famous for its one-of-a-kind movie offerings, complete with comfy chairs and homemade ice cream. The café is as laid back.

Festivals & events
Queenstown Winter Festival (Jul)
winterfestival.co.nz.
Queenstown's most famous and popular event (9 days), which of course has its focus on skiing, but also involves many other forms of entertainment.

Warbirds Over Wanaka (Mar)
T03-4438619, warbirdsoverwanaka.com.
New Zealand's premier air show is held biannually (next in 2010). The venue is the airfield, which hosts a wide variety of visiting 'birds', but also blows the dust off the New Zealand Fighter Pilots Museum's very own Spitfire.

Cinemas
Fiordland Cinema
The Lane, Te Anau, T03-249 8812, fiordlandcinema.co.nz.
Daily 1300 and 1730, from $10.

Reading Cinema
29 Dee St, Invercargill, T03-211 1555.

Shopping

Made in Glenorchy Fur Products
Corner Mull and Argyle St, Glenorchy, T03-442 7772, glenorchy-fur.co.nz.
Have you been wanting to get your dear mother or girlfriend that special homecoming present? Well, if so you have found 'ideal presents utopia'. Amid the obvious (and lovely) scarves, rugs and gloves are a fine range of possum fur nipple warmers. They are the genuine article and come in a marvelous array of colours.

Activities & tours

Naseby offers the best curling facilities in Australasia.

Maniototo Curling International

1057 Channel Rd, Naseby, T03-444 9878, curling.co.nz.
A state-of-the-art indoor curling rink that now serves as the hub for the ancient sport in New Zealand. It is great fun even for beginners and you can give it a go from $14 per hr.

Otago Central Rail Trail

The Otago Central Rail Trail has its own website, otagocentralrailtrail. co.nz, which is very useful. Various transport operators provide luggage and bike pick-up or drop-offs and bike hire (and/or guided tours) for both trails including: **Altitude Adventures**, T03-448 8917, altitude adventures. co.nz and **Trail Journeys** T03-449 2150 / T0800- 724587, trail journeys.co.nz.

Dunedin & Otago Peninsula

Elm Wildlife Tours

Elm Lodge, Dunedin, T03-454 4121/T0800-356563, elmwildlifetours.co.nz.
Provides a wide range of excellent award-winning eco-tours of the peninsula and the region. Its five- to six-hour peninsula tour is fun and informative, yet non-commercial, and gives you access to some of the most scenic private land on the peninsula. From $85 (albatross observatory and additional activities extra). Pick-ups available.

It's a fact...

The ancient Scottish game of curling has been a central feature of the Maniototo since the late 1870s, the first reported game was 6 July 1878.

Monarch Wildlife Cruises and Tours

Corner of Wharf and Fryatt streets, T03-4774276, wildlife. co.nz.
Award-winning outfit offering a variety of trips from one to seven hours taking in all the main harbour and peninsula sights.

Otago Nature Guides

See the yellow-eyed penguin colony at the beautiful Sandfly Bay. Tours in conjunction with its fine B&B accommodation in Nisbet Cottage (see Sleeping, page 284).

Queenstown & around

So, where do you start?
Well, there are over 150 activities to choose from, with everything from the tipples of a wine tour to the ripples of jet boating. And Queenstown is not just geared up for the young and the mad. There are activities to suit all ages, from infant to octogenarian and from the able to the less able. If a 91-year-old can do a bungee jump, surely the possibilities are endless? Of course it is the bungee that

Listings

made Queenstown famous. If you are prepared to make 'the jump' and have been saving your pennies to do so, then it is here that you must finally pluck up the courage. Heights vary from 40 m to 134 m, and if there is any advice to give (other than psychological and financial counselling) it is: do it in style and 'go high'.

The big four activities in Queenstown are considered to be the bungee, jet boating, rafting and flight-seeing. However, don't only consider what you are 'supposed' to do, but also what most others don't do – and also what you can do for free (see page 270).

The best advice is to head to the unbiased Queenstown Travel and Visitor Centre (see page 270), have a chat and avail yourself of the leaflets and information, then retire quietly to a coffee shop for a small nervous breakdown. Above all don't ruin it by rushing or being impulsive. Think before you jump! Oh, and one other thing, there are no refunds if you do end up holding on the bus driver like a koala does a tree.

The following provide an outline of the main activities and a sample of operators to wet the appetite. It is by no means comprehensive. Also note combo packages are available and are often good value.

Queenstown for kids

If you have kids and want to do the family thing, or conversely leave them in somebody else's capable hands, try one of the companies on this page. A fine resource for sourcing other activities for children of families is the *Kidz Go* magazine, available free from the (i-SITE or on-line kidzgo.co.nz.

Family Adventures, T03-442 8836, familyadventures.co.nz, offers full or half-day 'sedate' rafting trips for families from $155, child $110.

Ballooning

And no you can't jump out of it with a porcupine down your trousers and attached to a spring. **Sunrise Balloons** (T03-4420781, ballooningnz. com), offer the standard and sedate three-hour flight with champagne breakfast for $375, child $245.

Bungee jumping

A J Hackett

'The Station', corner of Shotover and Camp streets, T03-4424007/ T0800-286495, ajhackett.com.
A J Hackett and associates in 1988 created the first commercial bungee jump in the world at Kawarau Bridge about 12 km east of Queenstown. Although perhaps the most famous spot and certainly the most accessible, at 43 m it is now dwarfed by most of the others. Since 1988 Hackett has created several other sites in and around Queenstown from the **Ledge** at the Skyline Gondola Complex to the highest (ground based) 134-m **Nevis Highwire**. Jump prices range from $165 to a cool $240 for the Nevis. Given the

prices the best advice is to 'go high'– at the Nevis – it is simply rude not to.

It hasn't taken long for the Great Adrenalin Professors to realize that wetting your pants at high speed need not necessarily occur at vertical angles alone, so the fiendishly clever-and-rich chappies have now come up with various swing contraptions. The two options are:

Nevis Arc

A J Hackett, above.

Shotover Canyon Swing

Shotover Canyon Swing, T03-442 6990, T0800-279464, canyonswing.co.nz.
We won't get in to the technical details, suffice to say that the swing is 109 m high, with a 60-m freefall, 200-m arc using various jump styles from the Backwards and the Forwards, to the Downright Insane…
Prices start at around $170, spectators $30.

Cruising

It won't take you long to spot the delightful *TSS Earnslaw* plying the waters of Lake Wakatipu from the Steamer Wharf in Queenstown Bay. A standard 1½-hour cruise heads west across the lake to its southern edge to the Walter Peak Station. It departs from the Steamer Wharf, October to April every two hours from 1000-2000 (reduced winter schedule), from $48, child $20. A 3½-hour cruise, plus a farm tour of the **Walter Peak Station** which is designed to give an insight into typical Kiwi farming life (and to access lots of affectionate animals), costs $65, child $20. With a BBQ it's $22 extra. A four-hour evening dinner cruise costs $115, child $57.50. There are also 40-minute horse trekking and wagon rides available at Walter Peak from $105 (all inclusive). **Real Journeys** (Steamer Wharf, T0800-656503, realjourneys.co.nz).

Flight-seeing & aerobatics

There are numerous options available either by helicopter or fixed wing and you are advised to shop around. If you don't have time to reach Milford Sound by road then a scenic flight is highly recommended. Note that there are numerous fly-cruise-fly and bus-cruise-fly options on offer to Milford (ask at the i-SITE). Other flight-seeing options include Mt Cook and the glaciers, Mt Aspiring National Park and *Lord of the Rings* filming locations.

Prices range from a 30-minute local flight costing from about $200 to the full four-hour Milford Sound and Mt Cook experience, from about $400; shop around.

Fixed-wing operators offering flights to Milford Sound include: **Air Fiordland** (T03-4423404, airfiordland.com and Air Milford, T03-4422351, airmilford .co.nz). *A Lord of the Rings* Trilogy Trail is offered by the personable owners and staff of Glenorchy Air, Queenstown Airport, T03-442 2207, glenorchy.net.nz, trilogytrail.com, from $345, child $173.

If you fancy a flight with a difference try the Actionflite aerobatics Pitts Special, labelled as the 'Ferrari of the skies'. It reaches speeds of up to 300 kph with 3G turns. Guaranteed to get your angst waters flowing. Trips cost from $295 for 15 minutes. **Actionflite**, T03-4429708, T0800-478 8687, actionflite.co.nz. Helicopter operators include: **Glacier Southern Lakes** T03-442 3016/ T0800-801616, heli-flights.co.nz; **The Helicopter Line**, T03-442 3034, T0800-500575 helicopter.co.nz and **Over The Top Helicopters**, T0800-123359, T03-4422233, flynz.co.nz. The latter also offer heli-fishing and heli-skiing options.

Aspiring Air

Based at the Wanaka airfield, T03-443 7943, aspiringair.com. Offers a range of flights from a 20-minute local flight for $140 to its highly recommended four-hour 'Majestic Milford Sound' flight via the Mt Aspiring National Park, from $445.

Vintage Tigermoth Flights

Based at the airfield, T03-4434043, T0508-4359464, classicflights.co.nz. Offers something a little bit different, from $199.

Horse trekking

The best location for scenery is Glenorchy. **Dart Stables** based in Glenorchy offer several attractive options including two-hour trek ($100), five-hour 'Ride of the Rings' ($155). T03-442 5688, dartstables.com.

In summer the Queenstown ski fields are a popular venue for mountain biking.

Jet boating

Such is the marketing, somehow you seem familiar with the Shotover Jet before you even arrive in Queenstown. That indelible blurred image of a red boat full of smiley faces and Captain Cool in shades at the wheel. Jet boating is one of the 'Big 4' activities in Queenstown and, other than the thrills of the precipitous Shotover Gorge, there are also other independent operations on the Kawarau from Queenstown itself and the superb aesthetics of the Dart River. For thrills the Shotover is recommended; for scenery the Dart River.

Shotover Jet
The Station, Shotover St, T03-442 8570, T0800-SHOTOVER ,shot overjet.com (from $99); Kawarau Jet Marine Parade (lakeside), T03-442 6142, T0800-529272, kjet.co.nz, from $95; and Dart River Safaris, Glenorchy T03-442 9992 / T0800-327853, dartriver.co.nz, 3-6 hrs from $229, child $129 (includes transport from Queenstown).

Kingston Flyer
The famous vintage steam train puffs along for 1¼ hours on a 14-km track from Kingston, 47 km south of Queenstown from September to mid-May, daily 1000 and 1330, morning pick-ups available from Queenstown. Return ride $45, child $23,

one-way $35/$18 with transfer from $125, child $63. T03-248 8848, kingstonflyer.co.nz.

Mountain biking
There are many options, from the manic heli-bike to the low-level mundane. Independent hire and self-guided trail maps are also available. Operators include: **Fat Tyre Adventures,** T0800-328897, fat-tyre.co.nz and Vertigo **Mountain Biking,** 4 Brecon St, T03-442 8378, gravityaction.com.

Mountaineering & rock climbing
Mount Aspiring Guides
T03-443 9422, aspiringguides. com.
Offers a range of trips and packages all year round. Mt Aspiring $3750 2:1 client-guide ratio, with flights.

Wanaka Rock
T03-443 6411, wanakarock.co.nz.
Courses include introductory (1 day from $190), and abseil (half-day from $120).

Rafting
There is a glut of rafting operators, all trying to lure you with their ineluctable inflatables with most plying the rapids of the Shotover, Kawarau and Landsborough with such enchanting highlights as The Toilet and The Sharks Fin. A half-day adventure will cost around $150. Shop around for the best deal. **Challenge Rafting,** T03-442 7318/T0800-423836, raft.

co.nz; **Extreme Green Rafting,** T03-442 8517, nzraft.com and **Queenstown Rafting,** T03-442 9792, rafting.co.nz.

River sledging and surfing
River surfing is the cunningly simple concept of replacing a raft with your own personal body board. It is great fun and provides a far more intimate experience with the water. River sledging involves more drifting as opposed to surfing and provides more buoyancy. Costs from $135. Companies include: **Frogz Have More Fun,** T03-4412318 / T0800-437649, frogz.co.nz. **Mad Dog,** T03-4427797, river boarding.co.nz. **Serious Fun,** T03-442 5262/ T0800-737468 , riversurfing.co.nz.

Skiing
Wanaka has several great ski fields within 50 km of the town and encompassing standard ski and board slopes, cross-country and even a specialist snowboard freestyle park at the new Snow Park. **Cardrona, Snow Park** and **Snow Farm** are to the south, while **Treble Cone** is to the northwest. For general information and snow reports check out snow.co.nz; nzski.com; snow parknz.com; snowfarmnz. com or skilakewanaka.com.

Skydiving
Tandem Skydive Wanaka
*T03-443 7207, T0800-786877,
skydivenz.com.*
One of the best operators in the country and operates out of the airfield from heights of 12,000 ft ($295) and 15,000 ft ($395).

Tours
New Zealand Nomad Safaris
*T03-442 6699, T0800-688222
nomadsafaris.co.nz.*
Offers an excellent range of 4WD tours taking in some of the stunning scenery used in The *Lord of the Rings* film trilogy. Other tours concentrate on gold-mining remnants along the 'entertaining' Skippers Canyon Rd and quad bike tours from $220.

Queenstown Wine Trail Company
*T03-442 3799,
queenstownwinetrail.co.nz.*
Visits all the main Kawarau Valley vineyards, three to five hours from $114.

Tramping
Queenstown is a principal departure point for the Routeburn Greenstone-Caples and Rees-Dart Tracks. For detailed information, hut and transportation bookings visit the Information and Track Centre (see page 269). **Guided Walks New Zealand,** T03-4427126, nzwalks. com and **Ultimate Hikes**, The Station, T0800-659255, ultimatehikes.co.nz.

Southland

Cruises
The majority of day cruises (from around $60) explore the entire 15-km length of the sound to the Tasman Sea, taking in all the sights on the way, including the waterfalls, precipitous rock overhangs, seal colonies and an underwater observatory. On the overnight cruises (see **Real Journeys,** below) you take in all the usual sights, but can enjoy an extended trip, meals, accommodation and other activities including boat-based kayaking. The main cruise companies on Milford Sound are:

Milford Sound Red Boat Cruises
*T03-441 1137, T0800-264536,
redboats.co.nz.*
Another major operator, offering similar cruises and rates to Real Journeys (below), but they have no overnight cruises. They also own and operate Underwater Observatory, which can only be visited with their cruises.

Mitre Peak Cruises
T03-249 8110, mitrepeak.com.
One of the smaller cruise operators offering a low-passenger number (smaller boat), nature-orientated day cruises, from $64.

Real Journeys
*T03-249 7416, T0800-656501,
fiordlandtravel.co.nz.*

The largest operator with a veritable fleet for both day and overnight trips.

Real Journeys
*T03-249 7416, T0800-656501,
fiordlandtravel.co.nz.*
The main cruise company operating on Doubtful Sound. Day (8 hrs) trip begins with a cruise across Lake Manapouri, then a ride by coach over Wilmot Pass to Doubtful Sound, a three-hour cruise on the sound and a visit to The Manapouri Hydro-Electric Power Station on the return trip, from $275. Overnight trips are another option, from $288.

Kayaking
Fiordland Wilderness Experiences
*T03-249 7768, T0800-200434,
fiordlandseakayak.co.nz.*
A wide range of excursions on both Milford and Doubtful Sounds, from $155. The Milford trip is especially good, taking in the scenery of the Milford Road.

Roscos Milford Kayaks
T03-249 8500, kayakmilford.co.nz.
Offers a range of day safaris and the standard paddle on the sound from Te Anau. Operates year round.

Road tours
Kiwi Wilderness Walks
T021-359592, nzwalk.com.
A popular operator that provides a range of multi-day guided

eco-walks of Stewart Island with possibility of observing kiwi in daylight, an unforgettable experience. Recommended.

Trips and Tramps
T03-249 7081, T0800-305807, milfordtourswalks.co.nz.
Locally orientated, personable road day-trips to Milford Sound and many other venues (including cruise and walking options) from $165, child $100.

Catlins Wildlife Trackers Eco-tours
Papatowai, T03-415 8613, catlins-ecotours.co.nz.
Have been operating for more than 12 years and offers award-winning two- to seven-day eco-tours (from $600), which explore the region's forest, coast, natural features and wildlife.

Transport

Dunedin and Queenstown have **international airports** and serve all main domestic centres. Invercargill has a domestic airport and also serves Stewart Island.

All major bus companies ply the Dunedin, Queenstown, Te Anau and Invercargill routes. Several local bus companies and tour operators cover the Catlins Coast between Invercargill and Dunedin. Other than the tourist based Taieri Gorge Railway (ex Dunedin) there are no rail services. Bluff serves as the port for Stewart Island Ferry services.

Dunedin

Dunedin is 362 km south of Christchurch and 217 km north of Invercargill via SH1. Queenstown is 283 km south then west via SH8.

Dunedin International Airport is 27 km south of the city, T03-4862879, dnairport.co.nz. Several companies offer airport shuttles including **Super Shuttles** T0800-748885, supershuttle.co.nz Expect to pay from $20 for the shuttle and $60 for a taxi (one way). **City Taxis** T0800-771771; **Dunedin Taxis** T03-4777777. Most regional bus companies heading north or south stop at the airport.

Regional buses arrive and depart from **Ritchies/InterCity Travel**, 205 St Andrew St, T03-4717143, or from the Railway Station. There are no train services from/to Christchurch or Invercargill.

Queenstown

By road, Queenstown is 486 km from Christchurch, 283 km from Dunedin, 68 km from Wanaka and 170 km from Te Anau (Milford Sound 291 km).

Queenstown airport is 8 km east of the town in Frankton, T03-4423505, queenstown airport.co.nz. It receives direct daily flights from Auckland, Christchurch, Wellington and Dunedin. From the airport, **ConnectaBus** T03-4414471, costs $6 into town. **Kiwi Shuttle**, T03-4422107, serves the airport door to door. A taxi will set you back about $40, T03-4427788. **Regional buses** arrive and depart from The Station, corner of Camp and Shotover Streets. The i-SITE visitor centre.

Stewart Island

Stewart Island can be reached by air (20 mins) from Invercargill to Halfmoon Bay or the western bays (trampers) with **Stewart Island Flights**, T03-2189129, stewartisland flights.com, from $175 return ($95 one way). There are scheduled flights three times daily.

The principal ferry and island tourism operator is **Stewart Island Experience**, T03-2127660 / T0800-000511, stewartisland experience.co.nz, operates regular sailings from Bluff. The crossing by fast catamaran takes about one hour and costs $63 and $30 one-way. The company offers a regular daily shuttle service to and from Invercargill to coincide with the Stewart Island ferries ($16, child $8 one way). Contact direct for latest schedules, bookings advised, T0800-000511. Secure outdoor vehicle storage is available at Bluff.

Contents

Practicalities

Getting there

Being an island nation and 'last stop from anywhere', the majority of international visitors arrive by air and in to Auckland New Zealand's largest city and airport. Over recent years cruise ship visits have increased, but passengers are tied to a limited onshore itinerary.

Air

From Europe
The main route is usually via Heathrow or Frankfurt, either west with a stopover in the USA (Los Angeles), or east with stopovers in Southeast Asia or the Middle East. The Australasian airline market is currently very volatile and prices vary. The cheapest return flights, off-season (May-Aug), will be around £800 (€931), rising to at least £1100 (€1281) around Christmas. Mainstream carriers include **Air New Zealand**, airnewzealand.com, and **Qantas**, qantas.com (west via the USA); and **Singapore Airlines**, singapore air.com; **Thai Air**, thaiair.com; **Air Malaysia**, malaysiaairlines.com, and **Emirates**, emirates.com (all east via Asia, or the Middle East). As usual the best bargains are to be found online.

From the Americas
Competition is fierce with several operators including **Air New Zealand**, airnewzealand.com; **Qantas**, qantas.com; **Air Canada**, aircanada.com and **Lufthansa**, lufthansa.com all offering flights from Los Angeles (LAX) or San Francisco (SFO) to Auckland. One of the cheapest is the new Richard Branson venture **VAustralia**, vaustralia.com.au, that offers good deals via Sydney. **Air Canada**, aircanada.com, and **United**, united.com, connecting with Alliance partners at LAX fly from Vancouver, Toronto and Montreal. Prices range from CAN$1650-2700. There are also direct flights from Buenos Aires to Auckland with **Aerolíneas Argentinas**, aerolineas.com.ar, flying out of New York and Miami.

The cost of a standard return in the low season (May-August) from LAX starts from around US$1050, from New York from US$1500 and Chicago from US$1450. In the high season add about US$300 to the standard fare.

The flight time between LAX and Auckland is around 12½ hours.

From Australia
As you might expect there is a huge choice and much competition with trans-Tasman flights, in fact it is corporate warfare. Traditionally most flights used to go from Cairns, Brisbane, Sydney and Melbourne to Auckland but now many of the cheaper flights can actually be secured to Wellington, Christchurch, Dunedin and Queenstown.

Flights and especially ski package deals to Queenstown can also be cheaper and have been heavily promoted in recent years, but conditions usually apply, giving you limited flexibility. At any given time there are usually special deals on offer from the major players like **Qantas**, qantas.com.au; Qantas subsidiary **JetStar**, jetstar.com.au; **Air New Zealand**, airnewzealand.com.au, and **Pacific Blue**, pacificblue.com.au, so again shop around and online. Prices range from AUS$270-750 return. The flight time between Sydney and Auckland is three hours, Melbourne three hours 45 minutes.

Airport information
The two principal international airports in New Zealand are **Auckland** (T0800 247767, auckland-airport.co.nz) in the North Island and Christchurch (T64 3353 7774, christchurch-airport.co.nz) in the South. Auckland is by far the most utilized and better served of the two with direct flights worldwide, while Christchurch deals mainly with connecting flights via or to Australia. Additionally, Wellington, Dunedin and Queenstown also serve the East Coast of Australia.

Auckland airport is 21 km south of the city centre. **Shuttle bus** (airbus.co.nz) or taxis are the main transport services to the city and they depart regularly from outside the terminal building. The airbus will cost about $15 one-way $22 return, a taxi around $60. There is no rail link.

Tip...

Flights from Europe usually take from 25 to 30 hours including stops. A stopover of at least one night is recommended. Stopovers of a few nights do not usually increase the cost of the ticket substantially and it may be a fine opportunity to see cities like Hong Kong, Dubai or Los Angeles.

Getting around

Public transport in all its forms (except rail) is generally both good and efficient. All the main cities and provincial towns can be reached easily by air or by road. Although standard fares can be expensive there are a vast number of discount passes and special seasonal deals available, aimed particularly at the young independent traveller. Although it is entirely possible to negotiate the country by public transport, for sheer convenience you are advised to get your own set of wheels. Fuel prices compare favourably to most of Europe ($1.70 for unleaded, $1.10 for diesel).

Air

Domestic air travel
If you do not have your own hired or private vehicle then at least a few domestic flights are worth considering, especially between the islands. Currently **Air New Zealand** (T0800-737000, airnewzealand.co.nz); Qantas subsidiary **Jetstar** (T0800-800995, jetstar.com); and **Pacific Blue** (T0800-670000, pacificblue.co.nz) are the principal air carriers providing services between Auckland, Christchurch and Wellington and most regional centres. A one-way ticket from Auckland to Christchurch can be bought online for as little as $50.

Road

Bus
National bus travel in New Zealand is well organized and the networks and daily schedules are good. Numerous shuttle companies service the South Island and there are also many local operators and independent companies that provide shuttles to accommodation establishments, attractions and activities. These are listed in the Transport sections of the main travelling text.

The main bus companies are **Intercity**, intercitycoach.co.nz, and **Newmans** newmanscoach.co.nz. They often operate in

partnership. For information and reservations call the following regional centres: Auckland T09-583 5780; Wellington T04-385 0520 and Christchurch T03-365 1113. Intercity operates in both the North and South Islands, while Newmans operate throughout the North Island, except in Northland where **Northliner Express**, T09-307 5873, northliner. co.nz, co-operates with Intercity. Also popular are **Nakedbus.com**, which uses the same model of low overheads and internet-only booking service that the cheap airlines do. It has managed to undercut long-established companies.

All the major companies offer age, student and backpacker concessions as well as a wide variety of flexible national or regional travel passes with some in combination with the interisland ferry and rail.

Car

Other than a campervan this is by far the best way to see New Zealand. Most major international hire companies and many national companies are in evidence. You may also consider buying a vehicle for the trip and selling it again afterwards but research prices thoroughly and get the vehicle independently checked by the AA (aa.co.nz). There are specialist markets in both Auckland and Christchurch (www.backpackerscarmarket.co.nz)

A hire vehicle will give you the flexibility and freedom needed to reach the more remote and beautiful places. Outside the cities traffic congestion and parking is rarely a problem. In New Zealand you drive on the left (though most Aucklanders drive where they like). Make sure you familiarize yourself with the rules before setting out (NZ Road Code booklets are available from AA offices). The speed limit on the open road is 100 kph and in built-up areas it is 50 kph. Police patrol cars and speed cameras are omnipresent so if you speed you will almost certainly be caught. A valid driving license from your own country or an international license is required and certainly must be produced if you rent a vehicle. Parking in the cities can be very expensive. Do not risk parking in restricted areas or exceeding your time allotment on meters. Finally, never leave or hide valuables in your car and lock it at all times.

Motor homes or campervans?

What is the difference? Not a great deal really, except a motor home is generally larger and fully self-contained, while a campervan can be anything from a hired vehicle (van) to a decrepit private jalopy with 'Me Tarzan, you wanna ride?' emblazoned all over it. To stay out of trouble let's just refer to them as motor homes.

Motor homes

New Zealand is well geared up for campervan hire and travel and there's an accompanying glut of reputable international companies. Being a fairly compact country it is certainly a viable way to explore with complete independence. Although hire costs may seem excessive, once you subtract the inevitable costs of accommodation, provided you are not alone and can share those costs, it can work out cheaper in the long run. You will find that motor camps are available even in the more remote places and a powered site will cost $20-30 per night for two people. Note that lay-by parking is illegal and best avoided. Again, like car rental rates, campervan rates vary and are seasonal. Costs are rated on a sliding scale according to model, season and length of hire. The average daily charge for a basic two-berth/six-berth for hire over 28 days, including insurance is $195/295 in the high season and $75/120 in the low season. The average campervan works out at about 14-16 litres per 100 km in petrol costs. Diesel is cheaper than petrol but at present more harmful to the environment.

The most popular rental firms are **Jucy** (T0800-399736, T09-374 4360, jucy.co.nz); **Maui/Britz** T0800-651080, T00-800-20080801, maui.co.nz, britz.co.nz; **Kea Campers** T0800-520052, T09-4417833, keacampers.com and For more unconventional vehicles, **Spaceships**, T0800-SPACE SHIPS, T09-5262130, spaceships.tv, which offers Toyota People Movers or campervan hybrids complete with DVD and double bed.

Ferry

Other than a few small harbour-crossing vehicle ferries and the short trip to Stewart Island from Bluff in Southland, the main focus of ferry travel is of course the inter-island services across Cook Strait. The two ports are Wellington at the southern tip of the North Island and Picton in the beautiful Marlborough Sounds on the South Island.

There are two services: the **Interislander** (T0800-802802, T04-4983302, interislander.co.nz) and the smaller of the two companies **Bluebridge** (T0800-844844, T04-4716188, bluebridgeco.nz).

A standard vehicle with two passengers will cost about $265 one-way, a motor home with two passengers $365 and two passengers no vehicle $53 per person.

Train

For years the rail network in New Zealand has struggled to maintain anything other than a core network between its main population centres. However, that said, the trains in themselves are pretty comfortable, the service is good and the stunning scenery will soon take your mind off things. Within the North Island there is a daily service (Friday, Saturday and Sunday in winter) between Auckland and Wellington known as the Overlander. Within the South Island, the daily services between Picton and Christchurch (the TranzCoastal and Christchurch to Greymouth (the TranzAlpine) are both world-class journeys. For detail contact **TranzScenic**, T0800-872467, T04-4950775, tranzscenic.co.nz.

Also, designed specifically as a tourist attraction, the **Taieri Gorge Railway**, T03-477 4449, taieri.co.nz, runs from Dunedin to Middlemarch and back, with shuttle connections to Queenstown.

All fares are of a single class, but prices range greatly from 'standard' to 'super saver' so check carefully what you are entitled to and what deals you can secure.

Directory

Customs & immigration

All visitors must have a passport valid for three months beyond the date you intend to leave the country. Australian citizens or holders of an Australian returning resident visa can stay in New Zealand indefinitely. UK citizens do not need a visa and are automatically issued with a six-month visitor permit upon arrival. US, Canadian and other countries with a 'visa waiver' agreement with NZ also do not need a visa for stays of up to three months. Other visitors making an application for a visitor permit require: (a) a passport that is valid for at least three months after your departure from New Zealand; (b) an onward or return ticket to a country you have permission to enter; (c) sufficient money to support yourself during your stay (approximately NZ$1000 per month).

New Zealand Immigration Service (NZIS) T09-914 4100, T0508-558855, immigration.govt.nz.

Disabled travellers

Most public facilities are well geared up for wheelchairs, however older accommodation establishments and some public transport systems (especially rural buses) are not so well organized. It is a requirement by law to have disabled facilities in new buildings. Most airlines (both international and domestic) are generally well equipped. Disabled travellers usually receive discounts on travel fares and some admission charges. Parking concessions are also available for the disabled and temporary cards can be issued on production of a mobility card or medical certificate.

For more information within New Zealand contact: New Zealand Disability Resource Centre, 14 Erson Av, PO Box 24-042 Royal Oak, Auckland, T09- 625 8069, www.disabilityresource.org.nz.

Accessible Kiwi Tours Ltd, T07-362 7622, toursnz.com, is a specialist tour company acting specifically for the disabled, based in Rotorua in the Bay of Plenty.

Emergency

Compared to some countries the average Kiwi 'bobby' is amicable, personable and there to help, not intimidate. For police, fire or ambulance: T111. Make sure you obtain police/medical reports required for insurance claims.

Etiquette

New Zealanders are notoriously laid back, but reasonable manners are both expected and reciprocated. As a multicultural society there is a good general awareness and acceptance of religious and cultural differences.

For the basic Maori protocols refer to the culture section, page 31.

Families

Families and travellers with children will generally find New Zealand very child friendly and replete with all the usual concessions for travel and activities. With so many outdoor activities safety is a natural concern, but this is nothing common sense can't take care of.

There are a few hotels that will not accept children especially some of the higher end boutique B&Bs or lodges. Check in advance.

A good resource is *Kids Friendly New Zealand*, kidsfriendlynz.com. Also, in Queenstown and Wanaka look out for the independent magazine *Kidz Go*, kidz go.co.nz, available from the i-SITE visitor centres.

Health & safety

No vaccinations are required to enter the country but you are advised to make sure your tetanus booster is up to date.

The standards of public and private medical care are generally high, but it is important to note that these services are not free. Health insurance is

recommended. A standard trip to the doctor will cost around $60 with prescription charges on top of that. Dentists and hospital services are expensive. New Zealand's Accident Compensation Commission (acc.co.nz) provides limited treatment coverage for visitors but it is no substitute for travel/health insurance.

Other than the occasional crazed driver or banking CEO, there are few dangerous creatures in New Zealand with no snakes, crocodiles and so on. Although not poisonous, the dreaded sandfly is common particularly in the wetter and coastal areas of the South Island. These black, pinhead sized 'flying fangs' can annoy you beyond belief. There are numerous environmentally friendly repellents available at pharmacies.

Giardia is a water-borne bacterial parasite on the increase in New Zealand, which, if allowed to enter your system, will cause wall-to-wall vomiting, diarrhoea and rapid weight loss. Don't drink water from lakes, ponds or rivers without boiling it first.

The sun is dangerous and you should take extra care. Ozone depletion is heavy in the more southern latitudes and the incidence of melanomas and skin cancer is above average. Burn times, especially in summer, are greatly reduced so get yourself a silly hat and wear lots of sun block.

New Zealand's weather, especially at higher elevations, is changeable and can be deadly. If you are tramping, or going 'bush' make sure you are properly clothed, take maps, a first-aid kit and a compass. Above all inform somebody of your intentions.

Insurance

Although New Zealand honours its reputation as clean and green it has a dark side and crime rates are high, especially when it comes to theft – for which tourists are an obvious target. Full travel insurance is advised with extra premiums added for laptops and cameras. At the very least get medical insurance and coverage for expensive personal effects. **The New Zealand Accident Compensation Scheme** (acc.co.nz) covers visitors to New Zealand for personal injury by accident. Benefits include some emergency medical expenses, but do not include loss of earnings.

Whatever your policy read the small print and this applies to any hire car polices upon arrival. Many get caught out with excess and with expensive items not adequately covered for theft.

Internet

New Zealand had one of the highest per capita internet access rates in the developed world. Internet cafés and terminals are everywhere and if you are amongst the many who start losing it if you do not get your daily email fix you should be fine. As well as internet cafés, libraries and i-SITES are a good bet, they charge standard rates of $8-$12 per hour. Due to growing competition, rates are getting cheaper, sometimes as little as $3 per hour,

but shop around. The website internet-cafe-guide. com is useful for sourcing outlets.

Money

The New Zealand currency is the dollar ($), divided into 100 cents (c). Coins come in denominations of 5c, 10c, 20c, 50c, $1 and $2. Notes come in $5, $10, $20, $50 and $100 denominations.

Exchange rates (Oct 2009): US$1 = NZ$1.36; UK£1 = NZ$2.26; €1 = NZ$2.02; AUS $1 = NZ$1.25.

The safest way to carry money is in Traveller's Cheques (TCs). These are available for a small commission from all major banks. American Express (Amex), Visa and Thomas Cook cheques

Tip...

Wireless internet is available in New Zealand and coverage is generally good. Temporary and affordable (non contract) accounts with USB laptop data card ($245 extra) are available with Vodafone vodafone.co.nz.

are widely accepted. Most banks do not charge for changing TCs and usually offer the best exchange rates. Keep a record of your cheque numbers and keep the cheques you have cashed separate from the cheques themselves, so that you can get a full refund of all uncashed cheques. It is best to bring NZ$ cheques to avoid extra exchange costs.

All the major credit cards are widely accepted. Most hotels, shops and petrol stations use EFTPOS (Electronic Funds Transfer at Point of Sale), meaning you don't have to carry lots of cash. It is best suited to those who have a bank account in New Zealand, but credit cards can be used with the relevant pin number. If you intend to stay in New Zealand for a while you may be able to open an account with a major bank and secure an EFTPOS/ATM card and PIN. ATMs are readily available in almost all towns and though they accept non-host bankcards, it's best to stick to your own bank's ATMs so you do not incur hidden fees.

Credit cards can of course be used and some banks are linked to foreign savings accounts and cards by such networks as Cirrus and Plus.

Almost all towns and villages have at least one of the major bank branches. The main banks are the Bank of New Zealand (BNZ), the National Bank of New Zealand, the ASB Bank, Post Bank and Countrywide Bank with other trans-Tasman banks, like Westpac Trust and ANZ also in evidence. Bank opening hours are Monday-Friday 0900-1630 with some city branches opening on Saturday until 1230. If you need money quickly or in an emergency the best way is to have it wired to you via any major bank with **Western Union** (NZ) T1800- 3256000, westernunion.com; or via **Thomas Cook** and **Moneygram** (NZ) T0800-872893, thomascook.com.

Post

Post offices (most often called Post Shops) are generally open Monday-Friday 0900-1700, Sat 0900-1230. Within New Zealand standard (local) post costs 50c for medium letters and postcards (2-3 days); $1 for airmail (fast post) to domestic centres (1-2 days); $1.80 for airmail letters to Australia and $1.80 for postcards worldwide and $2.30 for standard overseas airmail letters to Europe, North America, East Asia, Australia and South Pacific. Domestic mail takes one to two days, perhaps longer in rural areas. When sending any cards or letters overseas be sure to use the free blue 'Air Economy' stickers. Books of stamps are readily available as are pre-paid envelopes and a range of purpose-built cardboard boxes. Average international delivery times vary depending on the day of the week posted, but a standard letter to the UK can take as few as four days (scheduled 6-12 days). North America is scheduled four-12 days and Australia and the South Pacific three-eight days. Post Restante services are available in most of the main centres. For details see www.nzpost.co.nz.

Smoking

It is illegal to smoke in bars, restaurants and the work place, except in the outdoor segregated sections, if provided. Smoking is not allowed on any public transport.

Telephone

The international code for New Zealand is 64. Within New Zealand there are five area codes: Auckland and Northland 09; Bay of Plenty, Coromandel, Taupo, Ruapehu and Waikato 07; Eastland, Hawkes Bay, Wanganui and Taranaki 06; Wellington 04; South Island 03. All telephone numbers in this book include the area code.

Telecom payphones are found throughout the country and are colour coded. Although there are both coin (blue) and credit card (yellow) booths available, the vast majority are phone-card only so you are advised to stock up. Cards come in $5, $10, $20 and $50 and are available from many retail outlets, visitor information offices and hostels. Unless you want to see just how fast digital numbers can disappear on screen, do not use these Telecom cards for anything other than domestic calls within New Zealand.

There is a wealth of cheap international calling cards and call centres available. One of the best is **E Phone** eph.co.nz, a calling card that accesses the net through an 0800 number. The cards vary in price from $10-$50 and can be bought from many retail outlets (look for the flag signs outside the shops). They can be used from any landline telephone. Voice instructions will tell you what to do and how much credit you have available before each call.

Local non-business calls are free from standard telephones in New Zealand, so it is not too offensive to ask to use a host's or friend's domestic (non-business) telephone. 0800 or occasionally 0508 precede toll-free calls. Try to avoid 0900 numbers as they are usually very expensive. The two major mobile service providers are **Telecom**, telecom.co.nz and **Vodafone**, vodafone.co.nz. Reciprocal arrangements are in place for the use of your own foreign mobile phone, but note these are designed not so much for your convenience as pay for the Telco CEOs latest marvellously facilitated ocean-going mega yacht.

Time difference

New Zealand Standard Time (NZST) is 12 hours ahead of GMT. From the first Sunday in October to the third Sunday in March the clock goes forward one hour.

Tipping

Tipping in New Zealand is at the customer's discretion. In a good restaurant you should leave a tip of 10-15% if you are satisfied with the service, but the bill may include a service charge. Tipping is appreciated in pubs and bars and taxi drivers also expect some sort of tip; on a longer journey 10% is fine. As in most other countries, hotel porters, bellboys, waiters and waitresses should all be tipped to supplement their meager wages.

Voltage

The New Zealand supply is 230/240 volts 50 hertz. Plugs are either two- or three-pronged with flat pins. North American appliances require both an adapter and a transformer; UK an adaptor only; Australian appliances are the same. Adaptors and transformers are widely available at hardware stores or the airport.

Tourist information

The official New Zealand Visitor Information Network is made up of around 100 accredited Visitor Information Centres (VICs) nationally known as i-SITES. Familiarize yourself with the green and black silver fern logo upon arrival.

National i-SITES are based in Auckland and Christchurch as well as the main tourist centres, like Rotorua and Queenstown. Open seven days a week, they provide a comprehensive information service including accommodation bookings and domestic airline, bus and train ticketing. Souvenir shops and occasionally other retail outlets, currency exchange and cafés are often attached.

Regional i-SITES are found throughout the country and there may be more than one in each region. They provide a general information booking service usually seven days a week and there is also a huge amount of free material.

Local i-SITES can be found almost anywhere, providing local information as well as assistance in accommodation and transport bookings. They are open at least five days a week, but are subject to varying seasonal and weekend hours. For detail refer newzealand.com/travel/i-sites.

Language

The Maori language is still spoken throughout New Zealand and generally encouraged and spoken with pride within the whanau and iwi (Maori family and tribes), but has never been given the respect it deserves in mixed (Pakeha/Maori) schools over the years, hence its general decline. To the layperson that cannot understand a word, it is an intriguing language to listen to, unusually repetitive in sound and hardly melodic. There is much accentuation and repetition of vowels and the 'w' and it is wise to be aware of a few basic rules before arriving in the country. Perhaps the most important feature is the pronunciation of 'wh' as the English 'f'. For example Whanau is pronounced 'Fha-now' and Whangarei is pronounced 'Fhongarei'. Likewise Whakapapa, or Whakarewarewa gets similar treatment and the 'a' is pronounced more like a 'u'.

Maori words and phrases

Aotearoa	New Zealand
Arikitribal	Leader
Atua	Spiritual being
Harakeke	Flax plant, leaves
Hawaiki	Ancestral Polynesian
Homeland	Hapusub-tribe/
	To be pregnant
He Aoa	Land or a world
He tangata	The people
Iwi	Tribe
Kaikaiawaro	A dolphin (Pelorus Jack)
	that cruised the Sounds
	and became a guardian
	for iwi
Kaitiaki	Protector, caretaker
Kapahaka	Group of Maori
	performers
Kiaora	Welcome
Kaumatua	Elders
Kawa	Protocols
Kete	Basket
Mana	Integrity, prestige, control
Manawhenua	People with tribal affiliations with the area
Maoritanga	'Maoriness'
Marae	Sacred courtyard or plaza
Mauri	Life essence
Moana	Large body of water, sea
Moko	Tattoo
Muka	Flax fibre
Ngati	People of Pa a fortified residential area
Paheka	White European
Poi	Ball attached to flax string
Pounamu	Sacred greenstone
Rangatira	Tribal leader
Taiaha	A fighting staff
Tangata	People/person
Tangihanga	Death ritual
Taonga	Treasure, prized object (often passed down by ancestors)
Tapu	Sacred, out of bounds
Te Ika-a-Maui	North Island
Tipuna	Ancestor
Tukutuku	Wall panels
Utu	Cost
Wahakatauki	Proverb or saying
Waiata	Song, flute music
Wairua	Soul
Waka	Canoe
Whakairo	Carvings
Whakapapa	Origins of genealogy
Whanau	Extended family/ to give birth
Whare	House
Whenua	Land

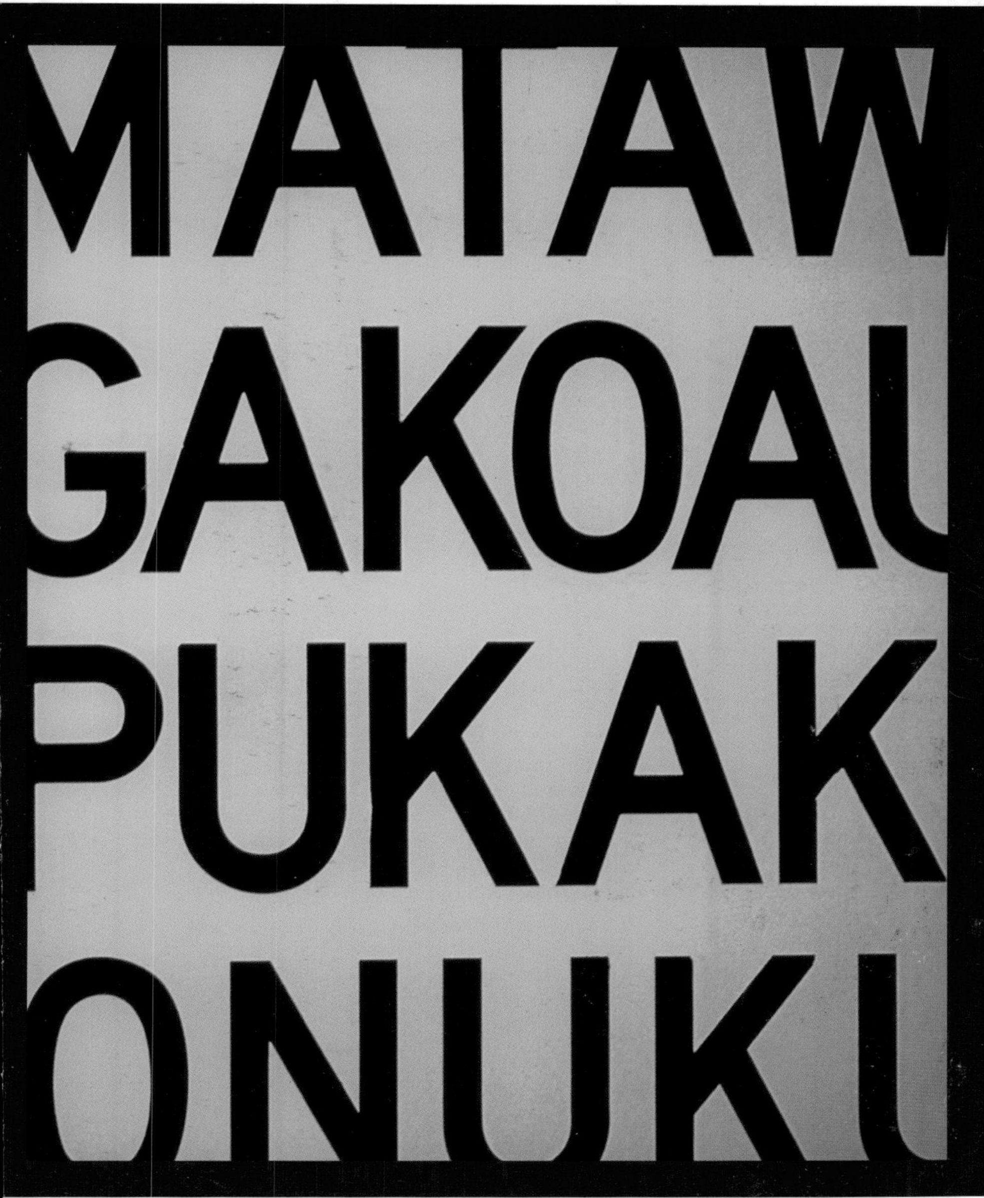
MATAW
GAKOAU
PUKAK
ONUKU

Index

Index

Index

Credits

Footprint credits

Project Editor: Felicity Laughton
Picture Editors: Kassia Gawronski,
Rob Lunn
Layout & production: Davina Rungasamy
Maps: Kevin Feeney
Proofreader: Ria Gane

Managing Director: Andy Riddle
Commercial Director: Patrick Dawson
Publisher: Alan Murphy
Publishing Managers: Felicity Laughton,
Jo Williams
Digital Editor: Alice Jell
Picture Research: Kassia Gawronski,
Rob Lunn
Design: Mytton Williams
Marketing: Liz Harper,
Hannah Bonnell
Sales: Jeremy Parr
Advertising: Renu Sibal
Finance & administration:
Elizabeth Taylor

Print
Manufactured in Italy by EuroGrafica
Pulp from sustainable forests

Footprint feedback
We try as hard as we can to make each
Footprint guide as up to date as possible
but, of course, things always change. If
you want to let us know about your
experiences – good, bad or ugly – then
don't delay, go to footprintbooks.com
and send in your comments.

Every effort has been made to ensure that
the facts in this guidebook are accurate.
However, travellers should still obtain
advice from consulates, airlines etc about
travel and visa requirements before
travelling. The authors and publishers
cannot accept responsibility for any loss,
injury or inconvenience however caused.

Publishing information

FootprintAustralasia New Zealand
1st edition
© Footprint Handbooks Ltd
January 2010

ISBN 978-1-906098-83-4
CIP DATA: A catalogue record for this
book is available from the British Library

® Footprint Handbooks and the Footprint
mark are a registered trademark of
Footprint Handbooks Ltd

Published by Footprint
6 Riverside Court
Lower Bristol Road
Bath BA2 3DZ, UK
T +44 (0)1225 469141
F +44 (0)1225 469461
www.footprintbooks.com

Distributed in North America by
Globe Pequot Press